Schadenfreude

When someone suffers a mishap, a setback or a downfall, we sometimes find ourselves experiencing schadenfreude – an emotion defined as deriving pleasure from another's misfortune. Schadenfreude is a common experience and an emotion which is seemingly inherent to social being. This book offers a comprehensive summary of current theoretical and empirical work on schadenfreude from psychological, philosophical, and other scientific perspectives. The chapters explore justice as an underlying motive for schadenfreude, and the role played by social comparison processes and envy in evoking pleasure at the misfortunes of others in interpersonal relations. Schadenfreude is also described as a common phenomenon in intergroup relations. This is a compelling volume on a fascinating subject matter that aims to increase our understanding of the nature of this emotion and the role it plays in social relations.

Wilco W. van Dijk is Associate Professor of Psychology at Leiden University.

Jaap W. Ouwerkerk is Associate Professor of Communication Science at the VU University Amsterdam.

Schadenfreude

Understanding Pleasure at the Misfortune of Others

Edited by

Wilco W. van Dijk

and

Jaap W. Ouwerkerk

CAMBRIDGE
UNIVERSITY PRESS

University Printing House, Cambridge CB2 8BS, United Kingdom

Cambridge University Press is part of the University of Cambridge.

It furthers the University's mission by disseminating knowledge in the pursuit of education, learning and research at the highest international levels of excellence.

www.cambridge.org
Information on this title: www.cambridge.org/9781107017504

First published 2014

Printed in the United Kingdom by Clays, St Ives plc

A catalogue record for this publication is available from the British Library

Library of Congress Cataloguing in Publication data
Schadenfreude : understanding pleasure at the misfortune of others / edited by Wilco W. van Dijk and Jaap W. Ouwerkerk.
page cm
Includes bibliographical references.
ISBN 978-1-107-01750-4
1. Envy. 2. Pleasure. 3. Humiliation. 4. Embarrassment. I. Dijk, Wilco W. van, 1968– II. Ouwerkerk, J. W. (Jaap W.)
BF575.E65S315 2014
152.4′8–dc23

2014001844

ISBN 978-1-107-01750-4 Hardback

Contents

Figures and tables

Figures

Tables

Contributors

AARON BEN-ZE′EV is Professor of Philosophy at the University of Haifa, Israel.

F. H. BUCKLEY is a Foundation Professor of Law at the George Mason University, USA.

MINA CIKARA is Assistant Professor of Social and Decisions Science at the Carnegie Mellon University, USA.

DAVID COMBS is an experimental psychologist at the Naval Research Laboratory of the US Navy, USA.

N. T. FEATHER is a Foundation Professor of Psychology at Flinders University, South Australia.

KURT FEYAERTS is Professor of Linguistics at the KU Leuven, Belgium.

AGNETA H. FISCHER is Professor of Emotion Theory and Research at the University of Amsterdam, the Netherlands.

SUSAN T. FISKE is Eugene Higgins Professor of Psychology at the Princeton University, USA.

CHARLES HOOGLAND is a graduate student at the Department of Psychology at the University of Kentucky, USA.

GISELINDE KUIPERS is Professor of Cultural Sociology at the University of Amsterdam, the Netherlands.

COLIN WAYNE LEACH is Professor of Psychology at the University of Connecticut, USA.

ANTONY S. R. MANSTEAD is Professor of Psychology at Cardiff University, Wales, UK.

BERT OBEN is a PhD candidate at the Department of Linguistics at the KU Leuven, Belgium.

DIEDERIK OOSTDIJK is Professor of English Literature at the VU University Amsterdam, the Netherlands.

JAAP W. OUWERKERK is Associate Professor of Communication Science at the VU University Amsterdam.

JOHN PORTMANN is Professor of Religious Studies at the University of Virginia, USA.

CAITLIN A. J. POWELL is Assistant Professor of Psychology at St. Mary's College of California, USA.

MARK ROTTEVEEL is an Assistant Professor of Psychology at the University of Amsterdam, the Netherlands.

D. RYAN SCHURTZ is Assistant Professor of Psychology at the Stevenson University, USA.

ELISE C. SEIP is a PhD candidate at the Social Psychology Program at the University of Amsterdam, the Netherlands.

RICHARD H. SMITH is Professor of Psychology at the University of Kentucky, USA.

RUSSELL SPEARS is Professor of Psychology at the University of Groningen, the Netherlands.

JILL M. SUNDIE is Assistant Professor of Marketing at the University of Texas at San Antonio, USA.

STEPHEN M. THIELKE is Assistant Professor of Psychiatry and Behavioral Sciences at the University of Washington, USA.

NIELS VAN DE VEN is Assistant Professor of Social Psychology at Tilburg University, the Netherlands.

WILCO W. VAN DIJK is Associate Professor of Psychology at Leiden University, the Netherlands.

LOTTE F. VAN DILLEN is Assistant Professor of Psychology at Leiden University, the Netherlands.

1 Introduction to schadenfreude

Wilco W. van Dijk and Jaap W. Ouwerkerk

This book is about that joyful feeling you may experience when someone else suffers a mishap, a setback, a downfall, a calamity, an adversity, or any other type of misfortune. The German language has coined the word *Schadenfreude* for this pleasure at the misfortunes of other people. The main aim of this edited volume is to offer a comprehensive summary of current theoretical and empirical work on schadenfreude from different perspectives and to inspire new research that will further our understanding of the nature of schadenfreude and the role it plays in social relations and society. In this first chapter we will set the stage by introducing the emotion of schadenfreude and its main underlying motives. The chapter will be concluded by a short overview of the book.

Schadenfreude

Schadenfreude is a compound word of the German words *Schaden*, meaning harm, and *Freude*, meaning joy, and is used nowadays as a loanword in the English language. In 1895 the *Oxford English Dictionary* (*OED*) included schadenfreude for the first time as an entry and defined it until recently as "malicious enjoyment of the misfortunes of others." The *OED* lists as the earliest citation for the word *Schadenfreude* in written English the book *On the Study of Words*, a collection of lectures of the philologist Richard Chenevix Trench addressed originally to the pupils at the Diocesan Training School in Winchester. In his second lecture (2nd edn, 1852) – *On the Morality in Words* – Trench, who later became Archbishop of Dublin, wrote:

> Thus what a fearful thing it is that any language should have a word expressive of the pleasure which men feel at the calamities of others; for the existence of the word bears testimony to the existence of the thing. And yet in more than one such a word is found. (Trench, 1852: 39–40)

In a footnote Trench mentions both the Greek word *επιχαιρεκακια* (*epichairekakia*) and the German word *Schadenfreude*. The inclusion of schadenfreude in the *OED* by the end of the nineteenth century indicates that by then the word was already used frequently in the English language.

Schadenfreude? Isn't that typically German?

The use of the loanword schadenfreude in the nineteenth century was not restricted to British English. On March 13, 1898, the *New York Times* used schadenfreude for the first time in its newspaper. In an article on foreign affairs Edward Beck wrote:

> Just now the Germans are rubbing their hands over the Anglo-French Sokoto imbroglio and indulging unctiously in that "schadenfreude" which is one of the less lovely characteristics of the Teutonic nation. (*New York Times*, March 13, 1898, p. 7)

Almost three decades later, on July 24, 1926, *The Spectator* published an article in which was written "There is no English word for *Schadenfreude*, because there is no such feeling here" (quoted from Kropf, 2006, p. 7). Is schadenfreude typically German, as both the *New York Times* and *The Spectator* suggest? Certainly not!

In his essay on the historical semantics of schadenfreude, Leo Spitzer (1942) discusses the possibility that the German word *Schadenfreude* might actually be calqued from the Greek word *epichairekakia*. He pointed out that the use of the German word *Schadenfreude* can be dated back to as early as the sixteenth century, but that equally old or even older references to the experience of schadenfreude can be found in other languages, for example, Greek (*epichairekakia*) and French (*joie maligne*). Some of the Greek references to pleasure at the misfortunes of others can be dated back to before the Common Era and can be found, for example, in the work of Aristotle (e.g., 350 BCE/1941). In present times, many languages have a specific word for pleasure at misfortunes. Most of these words are a compound of the words "harm" and "joy," for example, Danish (*skadefryd*), Dutch (*leedvermaak*), Estonian (*kahjurõõm*), Finnish (*vahingonilo*), Hebrew (*simcha la-ed*), Hungarian (*káröröm*), Mandarin Chinese (*xing-xai-le-huo*), Russian (*zloradiye*), and Slovenian (*škodoželjnost*). In our view, it is most likely that these words have been calqued from the Greek word *epichairekakia*, the German word *Schadenfreude*, or the French word(s) *joie maligne* for pleasure at the misfortunes of others.

Although many languages have a specific word for pleasure at the misfortunes of others, there are also many languages that do not (e.g., Italian, Japanese, and Spanish). Does this tell us anything significant about the prevalence of the experience of schadenfreude in different cultures? We don't think so, as several scholars have argued that the emotion lexicon of a language might not be informative about whether or not people are capable of experiencing a specific emotion. People from different cultures appear to be rather similar in their potential for the experience of emotions and, as a general rule, members of societies without a word for a particular emotional state readily understand the new term once its context is explained (e.g., Keltner, Haidt, and Shiota, 2006; Mesquita, Frijda, and Scherer, 1997). In his book *How the Mind Works*, Steven Pinker wrote:

> The common remark that a language does or doesn't have a word for an emotion means little ... Whether a language appears to have a word for an emotion depends on the skill of the translator and on quirks of the language's grammar and history. A language accumulates a large vocabulary, including words for emotions, when it has had influential wordsmiths, contact with other languages, rules for forming new words out of old ones, and widespread literacy, which allows new coinages to become epidemic. (Pinker, 1997, pp. 366–7)

Pinker continued by identifying the emotion schadenfreude as a case in point:

> When English-speakers hear the word *Schadenfreude* for the first time, their reaction is not, "Let me see ... Pleasure in another's misfortunes ... What could that possibly be? I cannot grasp the concept; my language and culture have not provided me with such a category." Their reaction is, "You mean there's a word for it? Cool!" (Pinker, 1997, p. 367)

Perhaps this was what went through the minds of those who introduced schadenfreude as a loanword into the English language more than a century ago (although one could doubt whether the word "cool" was included in these thoughts). Thus, although the word *Schadenfreude* is German, we cannot blame the Germans for the existence of pleasure at the misfortunes of others. This emotional experience has been coined with a specific term for at least two millennia and is surely not bound by the borders of the "Teutonic Nation." Deriving joy from the misfortunes of others seems to be of all times and all places. Or to quote Leo Spitzer:

> Schadenfreude is now seen as typical German, which it never was. People who experience schadenfreude are unfortunately everywhere, and critics who denounce them are also everywhere among civilised peoples. (Spitzer, 1942, p. 361, our translation)

Schadenfreude: diabolical or the ultimate pleasure?

As has already become apparent from the above quotes from the *New York Times* and *The Spectator*, people might regard the experience of schadenfreude with a degree of ambivalence. On the one hand, they might condemn it and many languages have proverbs, sayings, or adages that emphasize the negative moral connotation of schadenfreude. For example, the Spanish language, although lacking one specific word for schadenfreude, has such a saying – *Gozarse en el mal ajeno, no es de hombre buen* ("A man who rejoices in another's misfortune is not a good man"). Yet, people might admit, albeit reluctantly and uneasily, that there are some situations in which they "can't resist a little smile" if something bad happens to another person. In fact, many languages – for example, Dutch, Estonian, German, Hebrew, Hungarian, Norwegian, Slovakian, and Swedish – have sayings that can be summarized as "pleasure in the misfortunes of others is the ultimate pleasure" (although this saying might also be used in an ironic context). The Japanese language, which also lacks a specific word for schadenfreude, does have adages that stress the pleasure of this emotion (Masato Sawada, personal communication). One example of this is: *Hito-no-fukou-wa-mitsu no aji* ("The misfortunes of others taste like honey"), while another example (loosely) translates as "Next-door neighbours living poor is the taste of duck." This latter adage can be dated back to at least the beginning of the Edo period in Japan (1603–1868), in which duck was considered as a delicacy of the upper classes and as a rare and luxurious meal for the poor and working classes. Recently, in the Internet language of Japanese youth, the term *Meshi-Uma* is used to described schadenfreude, a term that derives from *Tanin-no-fukou-de-meshi-ga-umai* ("Food tastes good when served with the misfortunes of others").

Notwithstanding these positive notions about pleasure at the misfortunes of others, experiencing schadenfreude has mainly been condemned throughout history. That is, *schadenfroh* people have been accused of violating the obligation to cultivate the virtue of compassion, and schadenfreude has been regarded as a moral wrong and an emotion to be avoided. It has, for example, been described as a disguised expression of aggression (Aristotle, 350 BCE/1941); as fiendish, diabolical, and an "infallible sign of a thoroughly bad heart and profound moral worthlessness" (Schopenhauer, 1841/1965); as an "even more hideous cousin" of envy (Kierkegaard, 1847/1995); as a malicious and immoral feeling (Baudelaire, 1855/1955); and as harmful to social relations (Heider, 1958). Some scholars, however, have been less negative towards schadenfreude. To illustrate, in *Human, All Too Human*, Nietzsche answers the question "Is malicious joy devilish, as Schopenhauer says?" with the reply "All pleasure is, in itself, neither good nor bad" (Nietzsche, 1887/1908, p. 103). More recently, the contemporary philosopher John Portmann wrote in his book *When Bad Things Happen to Other People*: "Although *Schadenfreude* may include malice, it needn't presuppose malice" (2000, p. 4). Portmann argues that schadenfreude can be regarded as a corollary of justice and "To the extent that *Schadenfreude* signifies love of justice or repugnance to injustice, this emotion is a virtue" (2000, p. 9). Furthermore, Aaron Ben-Ze'ev (2000) argues that the moral evaluation of schadenfreude should be dependent upon the severity of the misfortune and the extent of the *schadenfroh* person's own involvement in causing the misfortune and their justification for the misfortune. He contends that although schadenfreude is not a virtue, it should (often) also not be considered a vice – or at least not a grave one.

In his book *Justice and Desert-Based Emotions: A Philosophical Exploration*, Kristján Kristjánsson (2006) criticizes both Portmann's (2000) and Ben-Ze'ev's (2000) claims that the notion of desert lies at the heart of schadenfreude and that therefore the experience of schadenfreude is often "morally acceptable." He states that this is a clear misrepresentation of the core of schadenfreude and inconsistent with "a long philosophical and pedagogical tradition" (2006, p. 98). He argues, for example, that *epichairekakia* as used by Aristotle refers to pleasure at others' *undeserved* bad fortune and not others' *deserved bad fortune* (this latter emotion was left unnamed by Aristotle). According to Kristjánsson, pleasure at others' *deserved* bad fortune should not be regarded as schadenfreude, but rather as *satisfied indignation*. Whereas satisfied indignation might be considered as "morally" acceptable, "real" schadenfreude has a different focus, that is, pleasure at another's misfortune without any moral concern. However, one problem with this distinction between "satisfied indignation" and "real" schadenfreude is that, even if a misfortune happening to an individual can objectively be regarded as being "undeserved," people have a tendency to belief in a just world (Lerner, 1980) and may therefore still assign personal responsibility to victims of objectively "undeserved" misfortunes (i.e., "bad things happen to bad people"), thereby leaving only a very limited number of situations that, according to Kristjánsson (2006), could be classified as "real" or pure schadenfreude.

So does experiencing schadenfreude make you a bad person or not? Concerning this moral verdict, it seems that the jury is still out. Playing devil's advocate, we argue that whether or not schadenfreude should be regarded as a vice depends on the reason why people enjoy another's misfortune. This is also the approach Martha Moers (1930) took in her "psychologisch-pädagogische" study of schadenfreude. She argued that the "moral worthlessness" (*sittlicher Unwert*) of schadenfreude could vary substantially depending on the reason why people experience this emotion:

> It [schadenfreude] can go through a whole gamut from minor moral worthlessness to the worst we know, such that it characterises the completely rotten core of a human personality. This variety of moral worthlessness, which may be embodied in schadenfreude, is essentially determined by the motives from which it originates,

and so, when we study these motives, we obtain a range of different types of schadenfreude. (Moers, 1930, p. 126, our translation)

Thus, Moers argued that the moral acceptability of schadenfreude depends upon the motive underlying the experience of schadenfreude. She discussed the different forms that schadenfreude may take, ranging from the mildly to the seriously morally negative joy. In her discussion she distinguished between *echten* or genuine schadenfreude – which should be considered reprehensible – and *unechten* schadenfreude – which should not be necessarily considered reprehensible. With *unechten* or *Pseudoschadenfreude*, Moers refers to situations in which the pleasure about an event coincidentally also entails a misfortune for another person, for example, when a situation is sensational or comical, or represents a just situation. In these cases the suffering of others is not necessary for the pleasure. However, with *echten* or genuine schadenfreude, Moers refers to situations in which another's misfortune is the core or the essence of the pleasure, for instance, when schadenfreude is evoked by hatred (*Haß*) or malicious envy (*Neid*). She wrote:

But if it shows a distinct lack of love or even hatred and envy towards other people, then we are dealing with the truly bad motives for schadenfreude, and hence genuine schadenfreude. (Moers, 1930, p. 132, our translation)

Although Moers made a clear distinction between *echten* or genuine schadenfreude and *unechten* schadenfreude and their moral evaluations, she also argued that in reality, different motives are often intertwined in schadenfreude and that actual experiences of this emotion are usually a combination of the two types of schadenfreude (for a related discussion of the work of Moers, see Kristjánsson, 2006).

Scholars still disagree about the moral evaluation of schadenfreude and also about which emotional experiences should be considered as genuine schadenfreude and which should not. This debate will probably continue for years to come. We adopt a broad view on the emotion of schadenfreude and it is not the aim of this book to resolve this debate. We define schadenfreude as pleasure at the misfortunes of others, independent of whether this emotion may (or should) be considered as morally acceptable or not. Disentangling the emotional experience of schadenfreude from its moral evaluation is also consistent with the current definition of schadenfreude in the *OED*. Earlier definitions in the *OED* explicitly associated schadenfreude with malice, "Malicious enjoyment of the misfortunes of others." In its most recent definition, the association with malice has disappeared, and currently schadenfreude is defined in the *Oxford Dictionaries Online* as: "Pleasure derived by someone from another person's misfortune." However, in line with the passive nature of schadenfreude (see Nietzsche, 1887/1908; Ortony, Clore, and Collins, 1988), we do restrict the term "schadenfreude" to the pleasure at misfortunes of others that are *not* directly caused by the *schadenfroh* person (otherwise we would consider this more akin to sadism) and are *not* the result of actively defeating others through direct competition (otherwise we would consider this more akin to victorious joy or gloating).

Why can we enjoy the misfortunes of others?

Schadenfreude can be categorized as a type of joy, but also as a specific and seemingly atypical type of joy. Whereas joy concerns being pleased about a desirable event, schadenfreude concerns being pleased about an event presumed to be undesirable for someone else (Ortony, Clore, and Collins, 1988). But schadenfreude might be less an atypical type of joy than first meets the eye. The essence of appraisal theories is the claim that it is not the objective properties of an event that produce an emotion, but rather the individual's subjective appraisal of the personal significance of the event (for an overview of appraisal theories, see Roseman and Smith, 2001). What makes appraisal theories of emotions especially powerful is that they can explain why the same event can evoke different emotions in different people (i.e., because they appraise the same situation differently) or why different events can evoke the same emotion in a person (i.e., because he or she appraises the different situations in the same way). For example, another's misfortune might evoke sympathy in some people and schadenfreude in others because they differ in how the misfortune is appraised. Since the appraisal of an event rather than an event per se elicits an emotion, it is impossible to list all the specific events that elicit a particular emotion, since any emotion – including schadenfreude – may be evoked by an infinite number of events, including events that have never before been experienced (Roseman and Smith, 2001). Thus, as it is the appraisal of another's misfortune rather than the misfortune itself that evokes schadenfreude, the various elicitors for schadenfreude do not need concrete common features. Objectively dissimilar events – such as an envied friend breaking a heel of her beautiful new shoes, an arrogant colleague being denied promotion, an untalented wannabe pop star being heavily criticized in a talent show, or a well-known (tel-)evangelist getting caught with his hand in the proverbial cookie jar – may all evoke schadenfreude if these misfortunes are appraised in the same way. But the question remains: *why* are we able to enjoy the misfortunes of others?

In his seminal article "The Laws of Emotion," Nico Frijda writes: "*Emotions arise in response to events that are important to the individual's goals, motives, or concerns*" (1988, p. 349, italics in original). In line with most appraisal theories, he argues that negative emotions are elicited by events that harm or threaten an individual's concerns, whereas positive emotions are evoked by events that satisfy these concerns. Thus, for an event to evoke schadenfreude, another's misfortune should be appraised by the *schadenfroh* person as satisfying some important personal concern. In other words, something about the other's misfortune should be beneficial for the person experiencing schadenfreude. Thus, the misfortunes of an envied friend, an arrogant colleague, an untalented wannabe pop star, or a well-known (tel-)evangelist can all evoke schadenfreude if these misfortunes provide the *schadenfroh* person with some psychological benefits. So what can people gain by the misfortunes of others in order to enjoy them? Or, to put it another way, what may be the concerns that underlie the emotion of schadenfreude? Below we will shortly address three major concerns that have received empirical support over the years: deservingness, envy, and self-enhancement.

The first important concern is *deservingness*. As most people care deeply about just and deserved outcomes, witnessing a situation that represents such an outcome typically evokes a positive emotion, even if it entails the misfortunes of others. Thus, if another's misfortune is appraised as just and deserved, it will evoke schadenfreude as it satisfies our concern for just and deserved outcomes. This is perhaps best captured by the words of John Portmann: "It is not the suffering of others that brings us joy, but rather the evidence of justice triumphing before our eyes" (2000, p. xiii). An appraisal of deservingness, for example, can explain why people can enjoy the misfortunes of those they dislike, resent, or consider hypocrites. Their suffering will often be regarded as just and deserved and therefore will appeal to our sense of justice.

A second concern that may underlie schadenfreude is *envy*. People experience envy when they lack another person's superior quality, achievement, or possession, and they either desire these or wish that the other lacked them. Envy is usually a very unpleasant emotion, which can include feelings of hostility, inferiority, and injustice (Smith and Kim, 2007). The misfortune of an envied other can evoke schadenfreude because it cuts away the very basis of envy; it renders the other less enviable and transforms a painful upward social comparison into a more favorable comparison (Smith et al., 1996; Van Dijk et al., 2006). Although some scholars have disputed the role of envy in evoking schadenfreude (e.g., Feather and Sherman, 2002; Hareli and Weiner, 2002; Leach and Spears, 2008), empirical support for a causal relation between envy (especially the malicious form) and schadenfreude is mounting.

A third concern that may underlie schadenfreude is *self-enhancement*. People have a strong concern for a positive self-evaluation and when this concern is threatened or harmed, they have a strong motivation to protect, restore, or enhance their self-evaluation (e.g., Taylor and Brown, 1988; Tesser, 1988). One possible route to a more positive self-view involves comparing one's own lot to that of less fortunate others (e.g., Collins, 1996; Wills, 1981; Wood, 1989). In other words, people can enjoy the misfortunes of others because it provides them with social comparison benefits and these satisfy their concern for a positive self-evaluation. A concern for a positive self-evaluation can explain why people who are momentarily threatened in their self-evaluation, or those who have low self-esteem, tend to experience more schadenfreude toward the misfortunes of others (Van Dijk et al., 2011a; Van Dijk et al., 2011; Van Dijk et al., 2012).

Thus, people can enjoy the misfortunes of others because these misfortunes satisfy some important personal concerns of the *schadenfroh*. Although scholars of schadenfreude have argued over which concern is the most (or only) important concern underlying schadenfreude, we agree with Martha Moers in arguing that the underlying concerns of schadenfreude are not mutually exclusive, and most often they are intertwined in actual experiences of schadenfreude. Which concern carries the most weight will depend upon the specific situation and the specific person experiencing schadenfreude. Schadenfreude is a multi-determined emotion, the list of underlying concerns is long, and the list of potential schadenfreude-evoking events seems to be endless. This is what makes schadenfreude such a fascinating and intriguing emotion, an emotion worthy of its own edited volume.

Overview of this volume

The main aim of this edited volume is to offer a comprehensive summary of current theoretical and empirical work on schadenfreude from philosophical, psychological, and other perspectives. The book is divided into five sections. Consistent with our analysis that justice-related concepts are considered an important factor underlying the evaluation and experience of schadenfreude, the three contributions in Part I (Schadenfreude as a justice-based emotion) focus on the relation of schadenfreude with *morality*, *deservingness*, and *hypocrisy*. In Chapter 2, contemporary philosopher John Portmann provides a moral analysis of schadenfreude and situations that evoke pleasure at the misfortunes of others based on theological and historical perspectives. Next, N. T. Feather gives an overview of his extensive psychological research program over the last twenty years in Chapter 3, focusing on how pleasure at another person's negative outcome is linked to judgments that the other deserves or does not deserve that negative outcome. The first section concludes with Chapter 4, in which Caitlin A. J. Powell presents psychological research on the various reasons why the misfortunes that are suffered by a hypocrite are often so enjoyable to others.

The five contributions in Part II (Schadenfreude as a comparison-based emotion) focus on how comparisons between one's own lot and that of others influence the experience of schadenfreude. In Chapter 5, contemporary philosopher Aaron Ben-Ze'ev argues that the role of a personal comparative concern in emotion is crucial for understanding pleasure in others' misfortunes. In line with our analysis that envy is considered an important concern underlying the experience of schadenfreude, the following two contributions focus on psychological research into the relationship between comparison-based envy and pleasure at the misfortune of others. In Chapter 6, Richard H. Smith, Stephen M. Thielke, and Caitlin A. J. Powell discuss how envy and schadenfreude relate to each other. Next, Niels van de Ven discusses in Chapter 7 recent research that shows how and when envy is an antecedent of schadenfreude. In Chapter 8, Jill M. Sundie presents research on the role of social comparison processes in evoking schadenfreude in a consumer context. The part is concluded with Chapter 9, in which Wilco W. van Dijk and Jaap W. Ouwerkerk examine the role of one's self-view in schadenfreude. They argue that striving for a positive self-evaluation constitutes an important underlying motive for the experience of schadenfreude.

Part III (Schadenfreude as an intergroup phenomenon) is comprised of four contributions that focus on the role of schadenfreude in relations between social groups. In Chapter 10, Mina Cikara and Susan T. Fiske demonstrate that specific stereotypes about a social group influence whether suffering of that group elicits schadenfreude. Next, based on a social identity perspective, D. Ryan Schurtz, David Combs, Charles Hoogland, and Richard H. Smith in Chapter 11 present research on group-based schadenfreude in a political and sports context. In Chapter 12, Jaap W. Ouwerkerk and Wilco W. van Dijk argue that intergroup relations may provide a special breeding ground for schadenfreude, and provide empirical evidence showing that schadenfreude is more readily evoked in intergroup relations that are characterized by rivalry and competition. The third section is concluded with Chapter 13, in which Colin Wayne Leach, Russell Spears, and Antony S. R. Manstead situate schadenfreude in social relations and describe studies on intergroup relations showing that the passive, opportunistic pleasure of schadenfreude can be distinguished from joy derived from outdoing a rival in direct competition, which they define as gloating.

As the title suggests, the three contributions in Part IV (Schadenfreude and related phenomena) focus on phenomena that are closely related to schadenfreude, namely *laughter*, *the desire for vengeance*, and *pouting*. In Chapter 14, F. H. Buckley discusses schadenfreude as an epitome of laughter. In Chapter 15, Elise C. Seip, Mark Rotteveel, Lotte F. van Dillen, and Wilco W. van Dijk compare schadenfreude with desire for vengeance. The fourth section is concluded with Chapter 16, in which John Portmann analyzes pouting in relation to schadenfreude and highlights the social and political aspects of both emotions.

In Part V (Schadenfreude in society, language, and literature), three contributions on schadenfreude are presented from the domain of sociology, linguistics, and literature, respectively. In Chapter 17, Giselinde Kuipers describes both how social life is shaped by schadenfreude and how schadenfreude shapes social life. Next, based on linguistic analysis of spontaneous conversations, Kurt Feyaerts and Bert Oben argue in Chapter 18 that the experience and expression of schadenfreude may serve to strengthen relations among peers. This last section is concluded with Chapter 19, in which Diederik Oostdijk presents a study of schadenfreude in nineteenth-century American literature.

The edited volume is concluded with Chapter 20, in which Agneta H. Fischer summarizes the main findings, identifies some gaps in our knowledge about schadenfreude, and reflects on potential future avenues for research and theorizing.

References

Aristotle (1941 [350 BCE]). In R. McKeon (ed.), *The Basic Works of Aristotle*. New York: Random House.

Baudelaire, C. (1955 [1855]). *On the Essence of Laughter* (translated by J. Mayne) New York: Phaidon Press.

Ben-Ze'ev, A. (2000). *The Subtlety of Emotions*. Cambridge, MA: MIT Press.

Collins, R. L. (1996). For better or worse: the impact of upward social comparison on self-evaluations. *Psychological Bulletin* 119: 51–69.

Feather, N. T. and Sherman, R. (2002). Envy, resentment, schadenfreude, and sympathy: reactions to deserved and undeserved achievement and subsequent failure. *Personality and Social Psychology Bulletin* 28: 953–61.

Frijda, N. (1988). The laws of emotion. *American Psychologist* 43: 349–58.

Hareli, S. and Weiner, B. (2002). Dislike and envy as antecedents of pleasure at another's misfortune. *Motivation and Emotion* 26: 257–77.

Heider, F. (1958). *The Psychology of Interpersonal Relations*. New York: Wiley.

Keltner, D., Haidt, J., and Shiota, L. (2006). Social functionalism and the evolution of emotions. In M. Schaller, D. Kenrick, and J. Simpson (eds.), *Evolution and Social Psychology*. New York: Psychology Press, pp. 115–42.

Kierkegaard, S. (1995 [1847]). *Works of Love* (edited and translated by H. V. Hong and E. H. Hong). Princeton University Press.

Kristjánsson, K. (2006). *Justice and Desert-Based Emotions: A Philosophical Exploration.* Aldershot: Ashgate.

Kropf, R. (2006). *Schadenfreude als Rezeptionsempfindung.* Munich: GRIN Verlag GmbH.

Leach, C. W. and Spears, R. (2008). "A vengefulness of the impotent": the pain of in-group inferiority and schadenfreude toward successful out-groups. *Journal of Personality and Social Psychology* 95: 1383–96.

Lerner, M. J. (1980). *The Belief in a Just World: A Fundamental Delusion.* New York: Plenum.

Mesquita, B., Frijda, N. H., and Scherer, K. R. (1997). Culture and emotion. In P. Dasen and T. S. Saraswathi (eds.), *Handbook of Cross-cultural Psychology. Basic Processes and Human Development*, Vol. 2. Boston, MA: Allyn & Bacon, pp. 255–97.

Moers, M. (1930). Schadenfreude. *Zeitschrift für pädagogische Psychologie und Jugendkunde* 3: 126–34.

Nietzsche, F. (1908 [1887]). *Human, All Too Human. A Book for Free Spirits* (translated by A. Harvey). Chicago: Charles H. Kerr & Company.

Ortony, A., Clore, G. L., and Collins, A. (1988). *The Cognitive Structure of Emotions.* Cambridge University Press.

Pinker, S. (1997). *How the Mind Works.* New York: Norton.

Portmann, J. (2000). *When Bad Things Happen to Other People.* New York: Routledge.

Roseman, I. J. and Smith, C. A. (2001). Appraisal theory: overview, assumptions, varieties, controversies. In K. S. Scherer, A. Schorr, and T. Johnstone (eds.), *Appraisal Processes in Emotion: Theory, Methods, Research.* Oxford University Press, pp. 3–19.

Schopenhauer, A. (1965 [1841]). *On the Basis of Morality* (translated by E. F. J. Payne). Indianapolis: Bobbs-Merrill.

Smith, R. H. and Kim, S. H. (2007). Comprehending envy. *Psychological Bulletin* 113: 46–64.

Smith, R. H., Turner, T. J., Garonzik, R., Leach, C. W., Urch-Druskat, V., and Weston, C. M. (1996). Envy and schadenfreude. *Personality and Social Psychology Bulletin* 22: 158–68.

Spitzer, L. (1942). Schadenfreude. *Monatshefte für Deutschen Unterricht* 34: 357–61.

Taylor, S. E. and Brown, J. D. (1988). Illusion and well-being: a social psychological perspective on mental health. *Psychological Bulletin* 103: 193–210.

Tesser, A. (1988). Toward a self-evaluation maintenance model of social hehavior. In L. Berkowitz (ed.), *Advances in Experimental Social Psychology*, Vol. 21. San Diego: Academic Press, pp. 181–227.

Trench, R. C. (1852). *On the Study of Words.* New York: Redfield.

Van Dijk, W. W., Ouwerkerk, J. W., Goslinga, S., Nieweg, M., and Gallucci, M. (2006). When people fall from grace: reconsidering the role of envy in *Schadenfreude. Emotion* 6: 156–60.

Van Dijk, W. W., Ouwerkerk, J. W., Van Koningsbruggen, G. M., and Wesseling, Y. M. (2012). "So you wanna be a pop star?" Schadenfreude following another's misfortune on TV. *Basic and Applied Social Psychology* 34: 168–74.

Van Dijk, W. W., Ouwerkerk, J. W., Wesseling, Y. M., and Van Koningsbruggen, G. M. (2011a). Towards understanding pleasure at the misfortunes of others: the impact of self-evaluation threat on schadenfreude. *Cognition & Emotion* 25: 360–8.

Van Dijk, W. W., Van Koningsbruggen, G. M., Ouwerkerk, J. W., and Wesseling, Y. M. (2011b). Self-esteem, self-affirmation, and schadenfreude. *Emotion* 11: 1445–9.

Wills, T. A. (1981). Downward comparison principles in social psychology. *Psychological Bulletin* 90: 245–71.

Wood, J. V. (1989). Theory and research concerning social comparisons of personal attributes. *Psychological Bulletin* 106: 231–48.

Part I

Schadenfreude as a justice-based emotion

2 Morality and schadenfreude

John Portmann

The German word *Schadenfreude* fills a void in the English language. We needed an approving word for passive delight in the misfortunes of other people in part because we regularly evaluate the character of others and in part because we often do so overconfidently, contrasting goodness and evil as if everyone naturally agreed with us. Can we morally approve of such joy? Embracing what might earlier have been considered a "negative" emotion (such as hatred or envy) hinges on the extent to which schadenfreude blossoms in the soil of justice. In the emotion's crucial tie to justice, a positive evaluation of schadenfreude emerges. Moral analysis of misfortune can exonerate some pleasure that has caused undue guilt and anxiety.

Condemnation of schadenfreude

Schopenhauer, an atheist, judged schadenfreude a mark of the devil. He urged communities to expel from their midst anyone caught enjoying the suffering of another human being.[1] Within a few decades of Schopenhauer's mid-nineteenth-century warning, an Anglican bishop, apparently the first person to publish the word *Schadenfreude* in the English language, also pronounced it evil.[2] This bishop even suggested that the word not be allowed into English (for analyses of these two condemnations, see Portmann, 2000). It is hardly surprising that twentieth-century German-to-English dictionaries defined schadenfreude as a *malicious* joy in the suffering of others, as opposed to simply "joy in the suffering of others."[3]

[1] Schopenhauer may have been influenced by ancient Jewish thought, according to which an intentional sin was punishable by expulsion from the community (as in Numbers 15:27–31).

[2] The English speaker in question was named R. C. Trench and lived in England.

[3] Philosophers and theologians might reasonably object to running together the separate concepts of pleasure and joy. For my purposes in this chapter, there is no need to distinguish the two. I thank Kevin Hart for this point.

Moral analysis of schadenfreude started off on a bad foot, at least in the English language.

Within Judaism and Christianity, moral opposition to schadenfreude almost certainly grew from successive endorsements of compassion, which unreflectively appears to be the opposite of schadenfreude. The Hebrew word for compassion bears an etymological resemblance to the Hebrew word for womb; in some Jewish thought, human compassion triggers the image of a loving mother and her child. In the book of Isaiah, for example, we read: "Can a woman forget her sucking child, that she should not have compassion on the son of her womb?" (Isaiah 49:15). The Jewish people consider themselves the "compassionate children of compassionate sires" and showing compassion is one of the main examples of the imitation of God (see Zwi Werblowsky and Wigoder, 1997, p. 169). However, misplaced compassion can unleash regret and unhappiness. Jewish theology certainly acknowledges the importance of the proper exercise of justice, with which compassion may sometimes seem to interfere. Justice often causes suffering (to a guilty person), and so suffering has at least one positive aspect. Here lies the beginning of a moral defense of schadenfreude.

Christian compassion is no less tricky. Christians, both Catholic and Protestant, generally interpret Jesus' exhortation to love thy neighbor as thyself to recommend far-reaching, inexhaustible compassion. Compassion may lead in different directions, though. Take abortion, for example. Some Christians defend abortion by arguing that it is wrong to allow unwanted children to be brought into the world and thus that compassionate concern for children justifies abortion. At the same time, other Christians argue that it is a failure of compassion to abort a child. Disagreement and even rancor may ensue. This disagreement also complicates the moral evaluation of schadenfreude.

A signal problem with the foundation of Christian ethics might seem to be lack of room for ambivalence. Jesus taught his disciples: "Anyone who is not for you is against you" (Luke 9:50, translations vary). Sometimes, perhaps often, our parents, spouses, and friends love *and* despise us. Love doesn't always happen in categorical, black-and-white ways. Schadenfreude challenges a rigid dichotomy of this sort, as it is possible to feel schadenfreude about someone you sincerely love.

Bernard Häring, the most influential Roman Catholic moral theologian of the twentieth century, exploited this ambivalence in his partisan condemnation of schadenfreude. Writing in German, Häring (1956) essentially argued that Catholics may not feel it toward other Catholics, only toward non-Catholics. According to him, God causes human suffering and Catholics may legitimately interpret the suffering of non-Catholics as a sign from God that non-Catholics should re-evaluate their lives.[4] Disagreement between how we interpret our experience and how others see us uncovers what we might call a "self-other asymmetry." This same asymmetry or dissonance will surface in an analysis of pouting (see Portmann, Chapter 16 in this volume); the asymmetry points to a fascinating inclination of others to construct our own emotional experiences for us. They take us to be lying (for example, "I don't think I'm biased") when we ourselves do not.

Häring is not the first to reason in us-versus-them terms, which psychologists sometimes refer to as a dichotomy between an "in-group" and an "out-group" (see Ouwerkerk and Van Dijk, Chapter 12 in this volume; Schurtz et al., Chapter 11 in this volume). For a very long time indeed, humans have treated preferentially members of their own tribe or group. It is surprising to find permission of this sort in Christianity, for Jesus tried to collapse the difference between "us" and "them." Christians were at times quite open about protecting their own kind, though Wade (2009, p. 236) noted: "Even the official church did not entirely forget its early renunciation of force. The Lateran Council of 1139 condemned a deadly new weapon – the crossbow – as immoral, and forbade its use, at least against Christians. It could, however, be used against Saracens [foreigners, probably Muslims]." The invention of a new and unusually powerful weapon worried the Church, so much so that it did not want Christians to use it against each other. Good Christians could defensibly use the weapon to harm a non-Christian, though.

Far from ridiculing Häring, I want to suggest that his stance illustrates the complexity of most condemnation – and even identification – of schadenfreude. We may be inclined to see justice where our rivals do not. Everyone likes to see justice done; our cheering for it may disarm someone who disagrees with our interpretation.

[4] In defense of Häring, we might think of the following quotation from Marilynne Robinson's Pulitzer Prize-winning novel *Gilead*. A dying Protestant minister writes the following advice to his young son: "This is an important thing, which I have told many people, and which my father told me, and which his father told him. When you encounter another person, when you have dealings with anyone at all, it is as if a question is being put to you. So you must think, What is the Lord asking of me in this moment, in this situation? If you confront insult or antagonism, your first impulse will be to respond in kind. But if you think, as it were, this is an emissary sent from the Lord, and some benefit is intended for me, first of all the occasion to demonstrate my faithfulness, the chance to show that I do in some small degree participate in the grace that saved me, you are free to act otherwise than as circumstances would seem to dictate. You are free to act by your own lights. You are freed at the same time of the impulse to hate or resent that person. He would probably laugh at the thought that the Lord sent him to you for your benefit (and his), but that is the perfection of the disguise, his own ignorance of it" (Robinson, 2006, p. 124).

Examples of schadenfreude

Because we cannot agree on what suffering is (its contours and its genuineness), it is hardly surprising that we cannot easily agree on a moral evaluation of schadenfreude.

Political correctness in the USA, for example, marshals compassion for racial and sexual minorities. We are all to respect underdog suffering now; indeed, we are given to believe that their suffering is vaster, deeper than ours. One consequence of political correctness is that it is not difficult to find people who guffaw at the idea that wealthy, heterosexual, Christian Caucasians can suffer terribly. The stories of miserable kings (for example, George VI of England [d. 1952], who stuttered and felt terror when called upon to speak in public) or queens (for example, Elizabeth [often referred to by her adoring fans as "Sissi": d. 1898], the Empress of Austria and Hungary, trapped in an unhappy marriage and devastated by her son's suicide) may elicit disdain and even anger from champions of the poor ("oh, poor little rich boy," someone might sneer).

A separate problem is faking it – pretending to feel pain or to suffer when one does not – or simply exaggerating one's suffering in order to gain the sympathy of others. Cynicism about whether others *really* suffer sets in (see Portmann, Chapter 16 in this volume on pouting).

I have argued elsewhere (see Portmann, 2000, pp. 52–7) that schadenfreude centers on trivial suffering as opposed to serious suffering (see also Ben-Ze'ev, Chapter 5 in this volume). I have also argued that the threshold between trivial and serious suffering resists quantification. A complete theory of schadenfreude would include a precise specification of this boundary, but I do not think it possible for more than even two persons to agree on its location. Note that even scientists sometimes run up against a similar threshold problem: puzzling over how to distinguish between the crucial categories of species and variety, Darwin (2003, p. 58) concluded in *The Origin of Species* that "the amount of difference required to give to any two forms the rank of species cannot be defined."

Against the background of this theoretical disagreement, let's consider a few examples. Schadenfreude can bloom in a wide variety of circumstances:

1) A powerful social institution stumbles, one long considered by many to be arrogant and aggressive (e.g., the Roman Catholic Church in twenty-first-century pedophile scandals).
2) A previously unknown recording artist achieves tremendous international success with his first CD; he trumpets his so-called genius but then fails to duplicate this success in subsequent efforts and disappears, forgotten by the public (e.g., the American Terence Trent D'Arby).

3) A young professor garners critical and public acclaim for her books, only to be humiliated by another philosopher in a well-known publication (e.g., Judith Butler, who was criticized for an obscure and clunky prose style by Martha Nussbaum in *The New Republic*, 1999).
4) A middle-class girl marries an English prince, divorces him, struggles financially after lavish spending, then is caught on film illegally selling access to her former husband (e.g., Sarah Ferguson, who divorced the Duke of York in 1996).

In each example, our emotional reaction begins in the knowledge that we ourselves have done nothing whatsoever to cause the contretemps of the person or group in question. Hence, our emotional reaction likely entails some element – perhaps small – of surprise. In the event that we feel pleasure, that sense of uplift rises from knowledge that it is gratuitous, free, something we have not paid for or earned. Our prior attitude toward the person or group beset by misfortune contributes to our emotional reaction. Although we can feel schadenfreude toward strangers (think of someone slipping on a banana peel), the richer form of schadenfreude stems from people we know or feel we know (for example, celebrities).

Moral evaluation of this emotion raises difficult questions about our own envy, the strength of our character, and our sense of what others deserve. An unknown singer who achieves sudden success and then boasts wildly may offend us; he does not invite us to share in his joy, but instead places himself on a pedestal high above us. When he fails, justice is done – or so it may seem. Perhaps we just envy successful people. The international media feasted on the fall from grace of the Duchess of York, who squandered her golden opportunity to enjoy a life of luxury and unusual privilege. She did not merit her good fortune, many concluded (see Feather, Chapter 3 in this volume) and she deserved to suffer exposure as a silly, shallow person. When an erudite young scholar basks in the praise of more established intellectuals, we may try to read his or her work and thereby gauge our own intelligence. Should we fail, we may puzzle over why. When another acclaimed scholar explains that the first writer deliberately attempted to prevent us from understanding by burying the message in muddy jargon, we may feel not only personally vindicated but also grateful to know that justice has been done. Schadenfreude readily blossoms in the soil of justice: front-page scandals of salacious Roman Catholic priests diminished the moral authority of an institution many believed to have fallen into corruption and hypocrisy. That fall pleased certain critics of the Catholic Church.

The set of examples of schadenfreude expands with the imagination: from happening to see a particularly expensive sports car being towed away (see Sundie, Chapter 8 in this volume) to seeing a bully get his due.

Other examples require a bit more reflection: an American who disliked the French, for example, might take pleasure in the number of French paintings (for example, those by Corot, Manet, and Monet) hanging in the National Gallery in Washington, DC. This American would reason that visiting French tourists would admire the paintings and secretly wish that the treasures hung in French galleries instead. To continue: an American tired of political correctness might rejoice that a person "in recovery" from alcohol or substance abuse or sex addiction is publicly confronted and blamed for his behavior, which a perhaps too-forgiving culture had been eager to blame on symptoms of a disorder beyond the poor soul's control (the poor soul in need of "empowerment" to escape his victimhood). Surely, schadenfreude flashes through many minds across the globe every day.

Fear of misfortune

No one wants to suffer, no one wants to be laughed at. We dread the very thought. In the early twentieth century, Sigmund Freud theorized the "pleasure principle," borrowing from Aristotle, who, in the *Nichomachean Ethics*, had posited that men seek to feel pleasure and to avoid pain. In the twenty-first century, legions of psychiatrists and therapists take such reasoning as a given. Why then would anyone deny himself the pleasure of another person's deserved misfortune? We have seen that Judaism and Christianity, to take just two examples, seem to exhort their members not to do so. In addition to the fear of not measuring up to our group's standards, we should add the fear of punishment, the fear that God will make us suffer for bad behavior. Beyond that, superstitiousness may provide a strong incentive to deny oneself pleasure in the misfortune of another.

Religious groups other than Jews and Christians also fear divine punishment for personal misdeeds. The anthropologist E. E. Evans-Pritchard (d. 1973) declared the Nuer in Africa "an unruly and quarrelsome people." What interested him was the fact that their religion makes them fearful of doing wrong and quick to apologize. Evans-Pritchard (as cited in Wade, 2009, p. 199) wrote:

> The Nuer have the idea that if a man keeps in the right – does not break divinely sanctioned interdictions, does not wrong others, and fulfils his obligations to spiritual beings and the ghosts and to his kith and kin – he will avoid, not all misfortunes, for some misfortunes come to one and all alike, but those extra special misfortunes which come from *dueri*, faults, and are to be regarded as castigations ... Any failure to conform to the accepted norms of behavior towards a member of one's family, kin, age-set, a guest, and so forth is a fault which may bring about evil

consequences . . . saying to him "*ca dwir* – I was at fault," and he may also offer a gift to wipe out the offence.

God rains on the party that is schadenfreude, and not just in Jewish and Christian thinking. God short-circuits the pleasure we feel in a nasty person's pain. The scientist Walter Burkert, interested in the worldwide similarity of religions, proposed three related ways in which ancient religions brought a sense of order and manageability to the world: first, by positing a supreme authority and hierarchical scheme of power; second, by understanding misfortune in terms of a causal pattern of crime, punishment, expiation, and salvation; and, third, by reinforcing a tendency to social reciprocity that is not only practically effective but also offers a sense of cosmic justice. Contemporary religions owe much to their ancient forebears, in Burkert's thought, which is to say that this sense of cosmic justice figures prominently in a variety of religious believers today. Westerners in particular may unthinkingly equate cosmic justice with God. Many believers instinctively ascribe responsibility for the suffering of others to God.

It makes sense to fear misfortune. This fear need not center on ourselves as individuals but may also manifest itself in patriotism or group pride. Before his famous imprisonment for promulgating the view that the earth revolves around the sun (instead of the converse), Galileo, a devout Roman Catholic, worried that Protestants would one day scorn the Vatican for not understanding the error of its thinking (thinking the Church had inherited from Aristotle and Ptolemy many centuries earlier). Sounding thoroughly altruistic, a true "team player," Galileo wrote in an impassioned letter (cited in Finocchiaro, 1989, pp. 112–13):

> The distressing thing is not so much that an erring man should be laughed at, but that our authors should be thought by outsiders to believe such things, and should be criticized and rejected as ignorant, to the great detriment of those whose salvation we care about.

Casting the issue in not only emotional but also strategic terms, Galileo foresaw the difficulty of winning back to the Catholic fold Protestants who worry that a Catholic error in science might belie other Catholic errors (in theology, for example). Along these lines, Galileo could imagine harm (which is reputational and emotional, not physical) done to sacred Scriptures, thus expanding his concern between dissident Christians to foreign peoples of different faiths. Christians who lean on the Bible to insist that the sun revolves around the earth fail to understand something important:

> They do not notice that the more scriptural passages they produce, and the more they persist in claiming that these are very clear and not susceptible to other

meanings besides what they advance, the greater the harm resulting to the dignity of Scripture if later the truth were known to be clearly contrary and were to cause confusion.

Galileo foresaw Catholic embarrassment over an official error that could be empirically proven. It is not reading too much into Galileo's letter to infer that he understood that this misfortune would give rise to schadenfreude from Protestants and perhaps Jews and Muslims as well. To this day, educated Westerners mock the Roman Catholic Church for having rebuked and punished Galileo, which is to say that the schadenfreude of the Church's critics goes on and on. And to this day, some consider Galileo a hero for his defiant pouting (according to legend, Galileo whispered in Latin immediately after publicly recanting: "And still it moves").

Fear of being scorned or fear of being found out for bad behavior may have positive effects. My point here has been simply to suggest that understanding schadenfreude requires sensitivity to the extent to which we will strive to avoid misfortune. We may ourselves enjoy schadenfreude, but we do not want to be the one who pays the bill for it. We do not want to be the one at whose misfortunes others cheer.

Complicity and passivity

A separate problem with defending schadenfreude arises from the culpability of complicity. The familiar Kitty Genovese story from 1964 continues to trouble many: a woman stabbed in public begged for help and was heard by at least twenty people living in the area, yet no one came to her aid or even called the police. Bystanders simply did not want to get involved and subsequently maintained their innocence.[5] Years before, a similar defense had circulated in Germany. Ordinary Germans protested that although the Nazis had perpetrated cruel injustices, vulnerable citizens themselves had no part in such crimes and were therefore morally innocent. Bystanders did not want to put themselves at risk.

Think of the examples of schadenfreude I have offered. Does the fact that we discover a misfortune – as opposed to cause it or observe it – exculpate us? On some level, I think it does. Remember that we can also respond to misfortune with sympathy or indifference. Even when we respond with joy, our role is still passive (see Ben-Ze'ev, Chapter 5 in this volume).

[5] Two scholars (Levitt and Dubner, 2009) have contested the accuracy of this now-familiar story, a building block in university psychology classes. Wilco van Dijk brought this to my attention.

According to the Roman Catholic theory of complicity, to take one relevant example, cooperation with evil can be either formal or material. "Formal" cooperation involves both intending to participate in the wrongdoing of another and actively doing so. "Material" cooperation, in contrast, occurs when a person contributes to the wrongdoing, even though he or she does not intend to do so. Such contribution may be carried out through an action which is morally neutral or even good. And so a moral defense of schadenfreude must reckon with the idea that those who laugh at a misfortune are guilty, even though they did nothing to bring about the misfortune. There is certainly something to this objection, although complicity in small-scale embarrassments probably deflates much of the objection.

There is something unnerving about a tradition capable of parsing immorality so finely but that at the same time permits what may strike many as immorality. Bernard Häring, condemning schadenfreude as a sin, defends it when those suffering happen to be the "awful enemies of God." If our enjoyment of another's suffering causally compels him or her to understand God better (and presumably accept Catholic teachings), then so much the better. It will not do simply to shrug our shoulders in the face of what appears to be the stupidity or religious fanaticism of our neighbors. What they think of us matters. Especially if one doesn't believe in God, one can see the threat that unfriendly neighbors pose. Some Christians in previous centuries believed in witches and viewed their neighbors as potential enemies. As Briggs (2001, p. 188) noted: "At its core lay the explanation of misfortune as the result of envy and ill-will, with the associated idea that thoughts can harm or kill." Although belief in witches has largely disappeared, securing the goodwill of others remains a matter of more than just theoretical importance.

The passivity of schadenfreude sets it apart from torture and sadism: the joy a torturer feels while torturing differs from the joy we feel when reading criticism of a professor with a turbid prose style, which explains why English needed a word for passive joy, joy for which we ourselves did not work. The important role of passivity has surfaced as a moral justification of sorts in various popular songs (for example, "Who's Sorry Now?", "Cry Me a River," and "Schadenfreude" from the Broadway musical *Avenue Q*). Such songs spring in part from folk wisdom, according to which "what goes around comes around."

Aggression

In contrast to passivity, we might consider the role of aggression in generating schadenfreude. Three Princeton University scientists studied the brains of baseball fans of opposing teams (the Yankees and the Red Sox). These social neuroscientists (Cikara, Botvinick, and Fiske, 2011) wanted to see which neurons lit up when loyalists and rivals experienced moments of victory or defeat. Specifically, they wanted to observe schadenfreude in the brain in order to see if this complex emotion is linked in the mind to heightened desire for aggression. They determined that it was (see Cikara and Fiske, Chapter 10 in this volume).

That aggression leads naturally to pleasure in seeing rivals or adversaries defeated should surprise no one. It would be a mistake to collapse schadenfreude into simple aggression, because we can feel schadenfreude toward people we genuinely like, as I have indicated, as well as toward people who are not rivals (for example, criminals and bullies). Although schadenfreude is more than just aggression, neuroscientists can revolutionize our understanding of human emotion (see also Portmann, Chapter 16 in this volume).

Envy

Schopenhauer believed that schadenfreude merely amounts to a form of envy. I think it is a mistake to run the two together, although I avow that envy – instead of justice – may explain a good deal of the private joy we feel when someone else suffers. We sometimes invoke justice to explain our joy to ourselves, even though we know on some level it is envy.

We find useful insights into envy in the thought of the ancient Greek philosopher Plutarch (c. 45–120 CE), particularly in the essay "On Envy and Hate." Remarkably good fortune often extinguishes envy, which is to say that after a certain point (again, one impossible to specify), most of us will cease to envy someone. We intuitively recognize when someone has pulled so far ahead of the pack that we will never be able to catch up with him or her. A second insight from Plutarch: extreme misfortune extinguishes envy. Although we may struggle to articulate when garden-variety misfortune becomes extreme, we will cease to feel schadenfreude toward a person who suffers terribly. If Plutarch is right, then we will stop envying a person once we learn that he or she is an alcoholic, say, or suffers from serious depression, or can no longer walk. Those known today as "passive-aggressive" will strain the applicability of Plutarch's insights but will not necessarily defeat them. All this is to affirm the relevance of envy (which hurts) to schadenfreude (which feels good), especially with regard to the shallow end of human excellence and suffering.

Another useful insight into envy comes from the American corporate mogul Jack Welch, CEO of General Electric from 1981 to 2001, who once declared: "A players hire A players, and B players hire B players." This line of thinking opens up a rarely discussed form of segregation: graduates of top universities need not apply for jobs at firms no one has ever heard of, because those working in non-prestigious firms will not hire people who have graduated from elite schools out of fear that the new hires will overshadow them. This mindset could engender envy and resentment, schadenfreude and pouting. Achieving excellence can antagonize others, and winners sometimes suffer because of their victories.

No one likes to be categorized as inferior. "B players" may have a natural incentive to search for justifications for their exclusion from the ranks of "A players" – reasons such as nepotism, elitist networking, or affirmative action. Those who believe in and yearn for a strict meritocracy may feel schadenfreude when someone falls from a height he or she did not climb on his or her own (think of Sarah Ferguson; see Feather, Chapter 3 in this volume and Portmann, Chapter 16 in this volume). Robert Solomon (2001, p. 102) has written: "The key to envy is that I do not have anything like a right or a claim to the possession or talent or honor in question."[6] This claim bears crucially on my argument. I am skeptical of Solomon's claim, although I may have fallen too completely under the spell of American optimism ("There's nothing I can't do!"). If Solomon were correct, then there should be much less schadenfreude in the world than I am persuaded there is. Solomon's claim needs some sort of appendage indicating that personal ability varies over time: an inferior person of some sort today may work very hard and emerge quite superior in the future. "B players" frequently deceive themselves about their excellence; sometimes, through determination, they do emerge as "A players." And so Solomon's claim is tricky.

Solomon's confidence raises the question of whether the envious person would agree that he or she is a "B player," an inferior person in a particular way. Here we see another self-other asymmetry, another example of how differently others may view or interpret some of our personal decisions.

Linguistic conventions can bias our moral classification of emotions as positive (that is, good) or negative (that is, bad). It is far from clear that Germans regard *Schadenfreude* to be patently immoral or that Dutch speakers automatically find moral fault in those they suspect of *leedvermaak* (the Dutch equivalent of schadenfreude). I have suggested that some Jewish and Christian sources have conditioned us into collapsing schadenfreude into related negative emotions (such as envy, malice, or aggression). Even in some scholarly vilifications of schadenfreude, we

[6] The kind of self-deception at work here also surfaces in pouting and *ressentiment*, a powerful and, I'm convinced, prevalent emotion. For an analysis of the relation between *ressentiment* and schadenfreude, see Portmann (2000).

can spot ambivalence, enough to give English speakers pause. As long as we take others seriously, we will have to allow the possibility that the pleasure they feel in the sufferings of others involves justice in a way that exonerates them of Schopenhauer's trumped-up charge. Virtuous people rejoice not so much that a culpable person suffers, but that justice has been done.

References

Briggs, B. (2001). Embattled faiths: religion and natural philosophy in the seventeenth century. In E. Cameron (ed.), *Early Modern Europe: An Oxford History*. New York: Oxford University Press.

Cikara, M., Botvinick, M. M., and Fiske, S. T. (2011). Us versus them: social identity shapes neural responses to intergroup competition and harm. *Psychological Science* 22: 306–13.

Darwin, C. (2003 [1859]). *On the Origin of Species*. New York: Signet Classics.

Finocchiaro, M. A. (1989). Letter to the Grand Duchess Christina (1615). In M. A. Finocchiaro (ed.), *The Galileo Affair: A Documentary History*. Berkeley: University of California Press.

Häring, B. (1956). *The Law of Christ*. Westminster: Newman Press.

Herrnstein Smith, B. (2009). *Natural Reflections: Human Cognition at the Nexus of Science and Religion*. New Haven: Yale University Press.

Levitt, S. D. and Dubner, S. J. (2009). *Superfreakonomics: A Rogue Economist Explores the Hidden Side of Everything*. New York: William Morrow.

Plutarch (1959). On envy and hate. In P. H. De Lacy and B. Einarson (eds.), *Plutarch's Moralia, Volume VII: Loeb Classical Library*. Cambridge, MA: Heinemann-Harvard University Press, pp. 91–107.

Portmann, J. (2000). *When Bad Things Happen to Other People*. New York: Routledge.

Robinson, M. (2006). *Gilead*. New York: Picador.

Solomon, R. (2001). *True to our Feelings: What our Emotions are Really Telling us*. New York: Oxford University Press.

Wade, N. (2009). *The Faith Instinct: How Religion Evolved and Why it Endures*. New York: Penguin.

Zwi Werblowsky, R. J. and Wigoder, G. (eds.) (1997). *The Oxford Dictionary of the Jewish Religion*. New York: Oxford University Press.

3 Deservingness and schadenfreude

N. T. Feather

When a person suffers a negative outcome and fails to achieve a desired goal, those who observe that outcome may experience a range of emotions. They may feel distressed and sympathetic, especially if the other person is a close acquaintance or a friend. They may feel angry and resentful about the fact that the negative event occurred if they believe that the other person was a victim and that the outcome violated moral values and social norms. They may also feel schadenfreude or happiness about the other person's misfortune, believing the negative outcome to be justified and deserved.

I propose that a key variable that influences all of these emotions is perceived deservingness. The way we react emotionally to the outcomes of others is associated with how deserved or undeserved we believe the outcomes are. Our beliefs about deservingness influence not only the way we feel about the negative outcomes that another person experiences, they also influence our feelings about the other's positive outcomes. Perceived deservingness is also an important variable that affects the way we feel about our own good of bad outcomes. These are strong claims, but they are justified by research findings and indeed by our own everyday experiences when we react to life events involving another person or self. Perceived deservingness has widespread effects on the emotions that we experience and these effects have only recently been investigated in systematic empirical research.

The focus of the present chapter is on perceived deservingness and schadenfreude, that is, on how pleasure about another person's misfortune or negative outcome is linked to judgments that the other deserves or does not deserve that negative outcome. I will be selective in my presentation, focusing mainly on my own theoretical approach and the studies that have been part of an extensive research program that spans the last twenty years or so.

The research reported in this chapter was supported by grants from the Australian Research Council.

Deservingness theory

The *Oxford English Dictionary* defines "deserve" as follows: "To acquire or earn a rightful claim, by virtue of actions or qualities ... to become entitled to or worthy of (reward or punishment, esteem or disesteem, position, designation, or any specified treatment)." Note that this definition relates deserving an outcome to both actions and qualities, and that it also refers to a person's entitlements.

I prefer to distinguish deservingness from entitlement on the basis that the sorts of deserved outcomes that I consider, whether they be positive or negative, are typically set within an instrumental behavior sequence; they are earned positive or negative outcomes that follow from a person's positive or negative actions. In contrast, entitlement usually refers to positive outcomes and to a framework of rights, norms, and legal and quasi-legal prescriptions.

Judgments of deservingness are often compatible with judgments of entitlement, but they can also be in conflict. For example, a football fan who behaves aggressively toward a supporter of the rival team may be perceived to deserve the retaliation that occurs, but at the same time may be entitled to protection under the law. A family member may be seen as entitled to some portion of an inheritance by virtue of kinship, but may not be seen to deserve it because of past negative actions toward the deceased.

I have discussed the distinction between deservingness and entitlement in more detail in my book *Values, Achievement, and Justice: Studies in the Psychology of Deservingness* (Feather, 1999b). I believe that it is more than a semantic distinction and that it can have psychological consequences. There is evidence to back this claim (e.g., Feather, 2002a, 2003, 2008b; Feather and Johnstone, 2001). Legal scholars and moral philosophers also make the distinction (e.g., Feinberg, 1970; Heath, 1976; Kristjánsonn, 2006; Miller, 1976; Sher, 1987; Von Hirsch, 1986). Others prefer to include deservingness as an example of a particular type of entitlement (Lerner, 1987).

How then can deservingness be analysed in the psychological sense? I have proposed that central to judgments of deservingness is the relation between how a person evaluates an outcome and the action that led to it. A positive or good outcome that follows from a positive or good action is normally perceived to be deserved. So is a negative or bad outcome that follows from a negative or bad action. In contrast, a positive or good outcome that follows from a negative or bad action is normally perceived to be undeserved. So is a negative or bad outcome that follows from a positive or good action. Perceived deservingness is therefore a product of a consistent or balanced set of relations between how a person evaluates both the outcome and the action that produced it. Inconsistency or lack of balance in the structure of action/outcome relations leads to negative perceptions of deservingness.

To give some examples, a student who studied hard for an exam (a positive action) and obtained a high grade (a positive outcome) would be perceived to deserve the high grade; a student who plagiarized another's work (a negative action) and obtained a high grade (positive outcome) would be perceived not to deserve the high grade. A person in an organization who profited following shady practices (negative action) would be perceived not to deserve the positive outcome (financial gain) he or she obtained. A student who put in a lot of effort in preparing for an exam (positive action) would be perceived not to deserve the low grade (negative outcome) he or she obtained on the final exam.

I have developed a structural model of perceived deservingness that includes the evaluative structure of actions and outcomes as a key component (Feather, 1999a, 1999b). Relations within the complete structure are from the point of view of the observer. In addition to the positive or negative evaluations of actions and outcomes, the model includes like/dislike relations that can apply either to the other person or to oneself. It also includes unit or ownership relations that allow for in-group or out-group membership. Other unit relations capture the idea that the other or the self is responsible for the action that is performed and that the outcome follows from or is contingent on the action. Differences in the strength of these variables are assumed to moderate the degree to which an outcome is perceived to be deserved or undeserved. Maximal perceived deservingness is assumed to occur when the structure of relations is completely balanced using Heider's (1958) principle. When the structure is out of balance, there would be some tension associated with the inconsistency and some pressure to change one or more of the relations in the model if that were possible.

As noted above, I assume that the key component in the structural model of deservingness is the relation between the evaluation of the outcome (positive or negative) and the evaluation of the action (positive or negative) that produced the outcome. What determines these evaluations? This is a complex question and more detailed discussion can be found in Feather, 1999a, 1999b, and 2006. I assume that these evaluations are influenced by a person's dominant needs and values, and also by prevailing social norms. For example, actions that help others would be evaluated more positively by those who hold strong benevolence or prosocial values; a successful outcome would be evaluated more positively by those holding strong achievement values or who have a strong need to achieve; an action would be evaluated positively or negatively if it was compatible/in conflict with existing social norms that prescribe what is appropriate/

inappropriate behavior; unethical practices would be evaluated more negatively by those for whom honesty is a core value.

Finally, I have described deservingness as a justice-related variable, although, consistent with most legal and philosophical analyses of desert, I do not consider it to encompass all aspects of justice. Justice is a broader concept and, as I noted previously, it also relates to external frameworks and social institutions that prescribe rights and entitlements. Beliefs about justice are also influenced by social comparison where the outcomes of others are considered (e.g., Hareli, 1999). For example, the low grade obtained by a student who worked hard preparing for an exam may be judged as undeserved but also fair, just, and legitimate in relation to the level of that student's performance in comparison to others. Here there is an issue of entitlement based on the relative quality of performance that involves social comparison.

Thus, concepts such as justice, fairness, and legitimacy are at a broader level than deservingness. An outcome may be perceived as just, fair, and legitimate because it is deserved but also because a person is entitled to it in terms of the rules, norms, or other legal or quasi-legal prescriptions that may involve social comparisons or other considerations, such as the presence of need. These distinctions have psychological implications and many are yet to be investigated. The present focus, however, is on perceived deservingness and its relation to schadenfreude. I now turn to selected findings from my research program that relate to this issue.

Tall poppy research: early studies

My interest in schadenfreude or pleasure in the misfortune of others developed from the study of how people react to "tall poppies" or people who hold high-status positions. Examples of tall poppies would be a student who consistently ranks at or near the head of the class, or politicians, entertainers, sportspeople, or high-profile celebrities who are well-known public figures on the national or international stage. It is commonly asserted that Australians like to cut tall poppies down to size by denigrating them or diminishing their high status in various ways.

I began a program of research in the late 1980s to investigate this assertion. Among the variables that I included in these studies were how much the tall poppy or high-status person deserved the fall from his or her high position and how pleased or happy people were when the tall poppy fell from that high position, i.e., how much schadenfreude they expressed.

The early studies have been described in previous reviews (Feather, 1994, 1996b). Two examples will suffice. In one study participants read about a high or average achiever who was discovered cheating on a major exam (Feather, 1989, 1994, 1999b). They answered a number of items about how they would react to the student who had cheated, which included how they would privately feel if the student was caught cheating by someone in authority, how pleased they would feel if the student was expelled from the university, and to what extent they thought the student deserved to be penalized. The results showed that participants reported feeling more pleased when the high achiever was caught cheating than when the average achiever was caught, and also more pleased when the high achiever was expelled when compared with the average achiever. The high achiever was also perceived to deserve to be penalized more than the average achiever, and pleasure or schadenfreude about being detected and expelled was positively related to perceived deservingness. So there was evidence supporting a positive link between higher status and reported schadenfreude, and between schadenfreude about the negative outcome and perceived deservingness of a penalty.

In another early study (Feather, Volkmer, and McKee, 1991) participants rated how they felt when a tall poppy who was either a nationally known high-profile politician, sportsperson, or entertainer suffered a hypothetical fall from high status. As was the case in the cheating study just described, participants reported more schadenfreude or pleasure about the fall when they perceived the tall poppy to be less deserving of their high status.

These two studies, along with other earlier studies that were focused on tall poppies, present similar and consistent findings about the relation between deservingness and schadenfreude. Participants did react differently to the fall of tall poppies compared with average achievers, but how pleased they reported feeling about the fall depended on how much the fall was perceived to be deserved. The more a misfortune or negative outcome was perceived to be deserved, the more pleasure or schadenfreude was reported. However, this relation applied generally and not only to tall poppies. Consistent with the structural model, perceived deservingness depended on how the action/outcome structure of relations was evaluated and it was also related to other variables, such as perceived responsibility and the degree to which the person who suffered the fall was liked and was seen as possessing integrity.

The complete set of studies sampled different cultures and domains, and they included measures of values, causal attributions, like/dislike and in-group/out-group relations, the personality and moral character of the tall poppy, and dispositional variables associated with favoring the reward of tall poppies or favoring the fall of tall poppies (for reviews, see Feather, 1994, 1996b, 1999b). But deservingness emerged as a central variable and its relation to schadenfreude stands as a strong and consistent finding.

Tall poppy research: later studies

This earlier research led to three studies that were designed to test the effects on schadenfreude and sympathy of perceived deservingness, envy, resentment, and a wish to cut down or denigrate the tall poppy or high achiever. Studies 1–3 in their order were Feather and Sherman, 2002; Feather and Nairn, 2005; and Feather, 2008a. All three studies first presented participants with hypothetical scenarios in which a person's usual performance on exams was described either as high or average (Study 1) or high (Studies 2 and 3). Deservingness was varied by describing the stimulus person as either working hard or putting in little effort in preparing for exams. I assumed that grades would be perceived as either deserved or undeserved depending on the effort that was expended.

In addition to rating how much the stimulus person was responsible for and deserved the performance outcome, participants rated how they would privately feel about the stimulus person on scales that varied across the three studies but that included feelings such as pleasure, anger, resentment, envy, and liking. They also rated how much they would denigrate the stimulus person by making negative remarks, by criticizing the stimulus person, and by wanting to see the person cut down to size. They also rated how much they thought the stimulus person's behavior (high or low effort) was positive and appropriate.

Each study concluded with an epilogue in which the stimulus person was described as suffering a failure in a final exam, finishing up with a mark of 45 percent for the topic overall. Participants again provided ratings of perceived responsibility and deservingness, in this case how much the stimulus person was responsible for the failure and deserved to fail. They also rated how pleased they were about the failure (schadenfreude), how sympathetic they felt toward the stimulus person, how friendly they felt toward the stimulus person after the failure, and how much they would be inclined to denigrate or criticize the stimulus person compared to previously (Studies 2 and 3).

There were some differences in the way in which the studies were designed. As already noted, in Study 1 (Feather and Sherman, 2002) the stimulus person was described as either a high or average achiever, while in the second and third studies (Feather and Nairn, 2005; Feather, 2008a) the stimulus person was a high achiever or tall poppy. Participants were also asked to role play in these latter two studies, taking the role of a low achiever in the second study (Feather and Nairn, 2005) or a low, average, or high achiever in the third study (Feather, 2008a) when making their judgments. The second and third studies also included a dispositional measure called "favor fall," designed to measure the degree to which participants held a negative attitude toward tall poppies in general, wishing to see them fall from their high positions (Feather, 1994, 1996b). Finally, each study provided a context for the subsequent exam failure that was designed to map into degree of personal responsibility for the negative outcome. The Feather and Sherman (2002) study used two contexts. In one context the stimulus person went to a party the night before one of the exams and did not revise some key topics; in the other context the student was presented with very difficult questions on one of the exams. In the second and third studies only the party context was used.

The results of the Feather and Sherman (2002) study showed that participants rated high effort as more positive and appropriate than low effort and that they were more resentful and less pleased about the high or average achiever when their achievement followed low effort rather than high effort. The high or average achiever who displayed low effort was also perceived as less responsible and less deserving of his or her achievement, and this achievement was seen as less justified. All of these differences were magnified when the stimulus person was described as a high achiever or tall poppy, a person who did well on just about every topic that he or she undertook. Participants were also more willing to see the low effort stimulus person "cut down to size" and they were more envious of the student who could obtain his or her grades without working hard. They also reported more envy toward the high achiever when compared with the average achiever. These results show how participants perceived the stimulus person initially.

How did these variables predict feelings of pleasure (schadenfreude) when the stimulus person subsequently failed the final end-of-year examinations? A path analysis (Figure 3.1) showed that deserving the high or average grades described in the initial scenarios had negative links to both resentment and to a wish to cut down or diminish the stimulus person (i.e., to less resentment and less wish to cut down). Resentment had

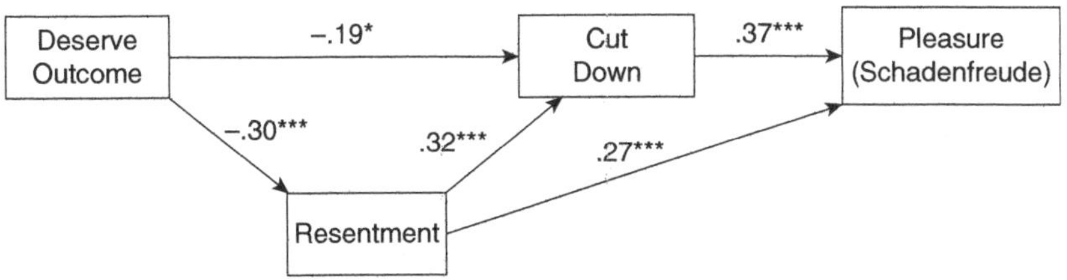

Figure 3.1 Path diagram linking variables assumed to lead to pleasure or schadenfreude concerning the stimulus person's failure in the epilogue (Feather and Sherman, 2002). *p < .05; ***p < .001

positive links to both a wish to cut down and to schadenfreude. A wish to cut down the stimulus person also had a positive link to schadenfreude. So resentment and a wish to cut down mediated relations between deservingness and schadenfreude, but envy did not predict schadenfreude (see Smith, Thielke, and Powell, Chapter 6 in this volume; Cikara and Fiske, Chapter 10 in this volume).

The results of the Feather and Sherman study also showed that schadenfreude was higher the more the stimulus person was perceived to deserve the failure that occurred in the subsequent final examination. It was also lower the more the stimulus person was liked.

The subsequent two studies (Feather and Nairn, 2005; Feather, 2008a) replicated the central findings from the Feather and Sherman (2002) study concerning deservingness, resentment, denigration, and schadenfreude, doing so for a stimulus person who was a high achiever. They also provided new information about how schadenfreude was related to an observer's own status and to a dispositional variable (favor fall) concerning a wish to see tall poppies fall.

As noted previously, in these subsequent studies participants were asked when making their judgments to adopt the role of a student whose performance status was low (Feather and Nairn, 2005) or low, average, or high (Feather, 2008a). They were also informed that this student was either a hard worker or put little effort into revision and preparing for exams. The results of the Feather and Nairn study showed that participants in the role of the low-performing student were more resentful of their low status if the low-performing student had worked hard. They perceived this low performance status as undeserved, and the resentment they reported about their own undeserved low status enhanced both resentment and envy toward the high achiever. Feather and Nairn noted that:

> This spill-over effect is relevant to many situations in everyday life. The resentment experienced by people who occupy low positions on the ladder of achievement and who perceive their low status to be undeserved may add to the feelings of resentment that are already experienced towards higher status persons whose positions of advantage are perceived to be undeserved. (Feather and Nairn (2005, p. 100)

The results of the Feather (2008a) study showed that both resentment toward the high achiever and pleasure or schadenfreude about the high achiever's failure in the final exams were higher for participants whose assigned role as a student was lower in performance status. Figure 3.2 illustrates the results from this third study. The paths from role-player status to both resentment and schadenfreude were negative. Participants with lower assigned status resented the high achiever more and they

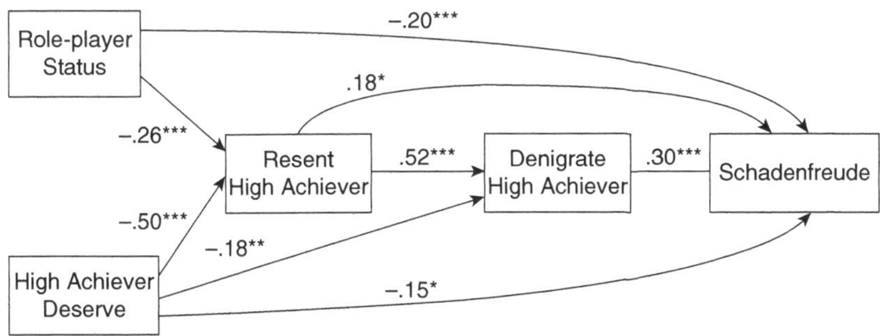

Figure 3.2 Path model predicting schadenfreude following the high achiever's failure in the epilogue (Feather, 2008a). Role-player status was coded 1 = low, 2 = average, 3 = high. *$p < .05$; **$p < .01$; ***$p < .001$

reported more pleasure or schadenfreude about the high achiever's subsequent failure. These findings relating to status may be compared with the results of other research on schadenfreude that refer either to the pain of inferiority (Leach and Spears, 2008) or to self-evaluation threat (Van Dijk et al., 2011; Van Dijk and Ouwerkerk, Chapter 9 in this volume). Both pain of inferiority and low self-evaluation may be assumed to reflect low perceived status with respect to some outcome or outcomes in general.

Figure 3.2 also shows that, as was the case in the Feather and Sherman (2002) study, the high achiever's deserved success was associated with less resentment and less denigration (negative path coefficients), resentment was associated with more denigration (positive path coefficient), and schadenfreude was associated with both more resentment and more denigration of the high achiever (positive path coefficients).

In both of the two subsequent studies, participants who scored higher on the favor fall scale (Feather, 1996b) reported more schadenfreude or pleasure about the high achiever's failure. I suggested (Feather, 2008a) that the dispositional measure of favor fall may reflect egalitarian values or a wish to achieve an equalization of lots (Heider, 1958), bringing people to the same level. It might also reflect the philosophical concept of *ressentiment* (Scheler, 1961) or global resentment about the unfairness of life (Parrott, 1991).

Taken as a whole, the results of these three later studies in the tall poppy research program again underline the importance of perceived deservingness as a variable that affects schadenfreude. They also bring to the fore the role of feelings of resentment about another person's positive outcome that coexist with beliefs that this positive performance outcome is undeserved because of low effort (a negative action). Resentment about the undeserved positive outcome then influences a wish to cut down or denigrate the undeserving other and these two variables together affect the experience of schadenfreude when the other person suffers failure. The studies also show that schadenfreude is greater the more the failure is perceived to be deserved and the lower the status of the outside observer.

Reactions to penalties

Concurrent with the research on tall poppies, I undertook a series of studies concerned with retribution and how outside observers reacted to penalties for offenses in terms of how pleased they were about the penalty and how sympathetic they were to the offender or perpetrator. The studies conducted in the 1990s were reviewed in *Values, Achievement, and Justice* (Feather, 1999b). Later studies added to the picture (Feather, 2002b, 2003; Feather, Boeckmann, and McKee, 2001a, 2001b; Feather and Dawson, 1998; Feather and Deverson, 2000; Feather and Johnstone, 2001; Feather and Souter, 2002).

These studies used hypothetical scenarios to investigate different types of offenses that included resisting police instructions at a protest meeting, use of excessive force by police officers, drug smuggling, shoplifting, plagiarism, driving at high speed and causing an accident, arson, child abuse, domestic violence, and releasing contaminated food to the public that caused poisoning. The perpetrators included public citizens, police officers, high-profile political figures, and marketing organizations.

In these studies the situations that were investigated involved a crime or offense (a negative action) that led to a penalty (a negative outcome). In terms of my structural analysis of deservingness, the conjunction of a negative action with a negative outcome would determine a judgment that the penalty was deserved. I expected that perceived deservingness would positively predict schadenfreude or feelings of pleasure about the penalty and would negatively predict sympathy for the perpetrators.

These studies assessed a range of variables in addition to deservingness, schadenfreude, and sympathy. Among these other variables were the perceived seriousness of the offense, the perpetrator's perceived responsibility for the offense, and the perceived harshness of the penalty. Because my model assumes that a person's values and prevailing social norms influence the way that person evaluates both actions and their outcomes, I also included measures of value priorities in these studies, focusing on the terminal and instrumental values assessed by the Schwartz Value Survey (SVS; Schwartz, 1992, 1996, 2006) and Right-Wing Authoritarianism (RWA) assessed by the RWA Scale (Altemeyer and Hunsberger, 1992).

There is not the space here to review these studies in detail. The results again showed the pervasive effects of perceived deservingness on how people react to outcomes. Again we found positive links between schadenfreude and how much a person was perceived to deserve a negative outcome, but in these studies this relation was found across a wide range of different situations. The results also shed light on how other social psychological concepts such as social context, social roles, social identity, social norms, attitude similarity, status, and entitlement might also be part of the picture.

A study of offenses committed either by a public citizen or police officers will serve as an example (Feather, 1998). The results showed that values and RWA influenced how participants rated the seriousness of the offense that was committed, a variable that I assumed would reflect the degree to which the perpetrator's action was negatively evaluated. The effects of values and RWA on perceived seriousness varied with social context, depending on whether the perpetrator was a public citizen or a police officer. Results of separate path analyses for the public citizen and police officer showed that deserving the penalty was linked to both responsibility and seriousness via positive paths. Schadenfreude, indexed by how pleased participants felt about the penalty, was linked to perceived deservingness via a positive path (see Feather, 1998 for details).

Thus, again there was evidence for a positive relation between schadenfreude or pleasure about a negative outcome and perceived deservingness. This study, along with a previous related one (Feather, 1996a), shows one way in which one can include values in the empirical enquiry about deservingness and its effects. It also demonstrates how values operate depending on the context that activates them (see also Feather, 1999b; Maio, 2010).

Deservingness and emotions

In recent years my research program has broadened out to investigate how discrete emotions such as pride, resentment, guilt, shame, regret, disappointment, and sympathy relate to judgments of deservingness either for the self or the other person (Feather, 2006; Feather and McKee, 2009; Feather, McKee, and Bekker, 2011). Schadenfreude is part of that analysis and it is assumed to occur when another person's negative outcome is perceived to be deserved. Table 3.1 presents the classification of these discrete emotions for oneself and the other when either a deserved or undeserved positive or negative outcome occurs. Deserved and undeserved judgments about outcomes in Table 3.1 are assumed to depend on the evaluative structure of the action/outcome relations. It can be seen

Table 3.1 *Discrete emotions relating to perceived deservingness/undeservingness and evaluated action/outcome relations for the other and the self*

	Positive outcome		Negative outcome	
	Positive action Positive outcome	Negative action Positive outcome	Negative action Negative outcome	Positive action Negative outcome
Focus of emotion	Deserved outcome	Undeserved outcome	Deserved outcome	Undeserved outcome
Other person	Pleasure Admiration	Anger Resentment Surprise	Schadenfreude (or pleasure)	Sadness Resentment Sympathy Surprise
Self	Pleasure Pride	Pleasure Guilt Regret Surprise	Sadness Guilt Regret	Sadness Disappointment Anger Resentment Surprise

Note. Intensity of emotions should vary depending on variables that moderate degree of deservingness or undeservingness and also on the strength of the positive or negative evaluations assigned to actions and their outcomes.

that schadenfreude is placed in the cell relating to another person whose deserved negative outcome follows a negative action. People feel pleased when a person who behaved badly gets his or her just deserts that are associated with a negative outcome such as a failure, a punishment, or some form of retribution.

My analysis allows for separate action and outcome effects (e.g., guilt when a negative action is performed by the self; surprise when an outcome is undeserved), for blended emotions such as guilt, shame, and regret, and for some slippage in the way in which the emotion labels are applied to the self and the other (e.g., one can feel reflected pride about a close other's high achievement following his or her positive action). It also allows for the moderating effects on deservingness of perceived responsibility for the action, perceived liking (like/dislike) and perceived social identity (in-group/out-group membership) in the case of the other person, and for perceived responsibility and self-evaluation (positive or negative) as a moderator of deservingness in the case of the self. The intensity of the emotions that are experienced is expected to vary depending on these moderating variables and also on the strength of the positive or negative evaluations assigned to actions and their outcomes (Feather, 2006; Feather and McKee, 2009; Feather, McKee, and Bekker, 2011). The major new contribution, however, is the focus on how discrete emotions relate to the appraisal of deservingness, depending on the evaluations of actions and their contingent outcomes and on whether deservingness applies to the outcomes of the self or the other.

Two recent studies test aspects of this analysis (Feather and McKee, 2014; Feather, McKee, and Bekker, 2011). The Feather and McKee study investigated the reactions of student participants to plagiarism committed either by the self or by a hypothetical classmate when writing a final essay. The study used scenarios that varied self versus other, like/dislike relations for the self or the other, and whether the plagiarism was detected or not detected, leading either to a negative outcome (a Fail grade) or a positive outcome (achieving a High Distinction for good work). In the self condition participants were asked to imagine that they were the student who committed the plagiarism. Participants in each condition rated a wide range of emotion items about how they would feel about the outcome. The emotion items were constructed to assess the discrete emotions in Table 3.1. Participants also rated items designed to assess the perceived deservingness of the outcome along with other variables. Of interest here are the results for the ratings of pleasure about the outcome that participants provided.

Although participants provided relatively low ratings of pleasure about either outcome (below the midpoint of the scale), the ratings were especially high when the disliked other in the scenario suffered a deserved negative outcome following the plagiarism when compared with the other three conditions. Thus, schadenfreude following the classmate's detection and punishment for plagiarism was higher when the classmate was disliked. This difference did not occur when the plagiarism was committed by the self. In this case reported pleasure about the negative outcome was very low regardless of positive or negative self-evaluation, but reported pleasure was stronger when the plagiarism was undetected and resulted in a positive outcome (a high mark for the essay).

The study by Feather, McKee, and Bekker (2011) presented student participants with hypothetical scenarios in which either the self or another person was applying for a job in the information technology (IT) area. In the self condition, participants were asked to imagine that they were the job applicant. The scenarios manipulated both the actions (positive or negative) taken by the self or the other in applying for the job as well as the final outcome (success or failure). In the positive action condition, self or other was described in a positive light (e.g., working hard on updating his or her CV, putting in a lot of care in writing the application, indicating a willingness to work hard, giving an accurate portrayal of his or her abilities, etc.). In the negative action condition, the self or the other was described more negatively (e.g., spending only a small amount of time on making some effort to update his or her CV, producing an application that was hastily written, saying little about how hard he or she would work, etc.). The outcome was either success in getting the job or failure to get the job. As in the preceding study, participants rated how they would feel about the outcome for a wide range of emotion items designed to assess the discrete emotions in Table 3.1 and they also rated perceived deservingness of the outcome as well as some other items.

Of main interest are the results concerning pleasure or schadenfreude about the other person's negative outcome. These results showed that there was a statistically significant interaction effect for ratings of pleasure involving focus (self versus other) and outcome (positive versus negative). Feelings of pleasure were highest when the other's negative outcome followed his or her negative action, that is, when the other person displayed little appropriate effort and failed to get the job. Thus, schadenfreude was again associated with a negative outcome by the other that was perceived to be deserved.

Related research and conceptual issues

Summary of findings

There are some clear conclusions about deservingness and schadenfreude that come from this review of studies from my research program. Over a wide range of contexts, perceived deservingness stands out as an important variable that influences reported pleasure about another's negative outcome or misfortune. The tall poppy research, the studies of reactions to penalties, and the more recent research on deservingness and emotions all provide evidence that is consistent with the conclusion that schadenfreude or pleasure about another person's negative outcome follows from the perception that the negative outcome is deserved.

There is also evidence about variables that moderate this relation. In achievement situations, for example, the degree of pleasure that is reported tends to be greater when the outside observer who reacts to a high achiever's negative outcome is of lower status along the same dimension of comparison (e.g., academic achievement). People are also more likely to report that another's negative outcome is deserved and also to feel more pleasure about that negative outcome when the other person is disliked rather than liked. In the case of status and achievement, schadenfreude is stronger among those who have a general disposition to favor the fall of tall poppies.

The results are also consistent with the assumption that the evaluation of actions and their outcomes is related to both the values that people hold and the social norms that are instantiated in particular situations. Actions and their outcomes are judged as positive and appropriate or as negative and inappropriate in relation to a person's dominant values and the prevailing norms that apply to a given social context. Finally, there is evidence that, in the case of achievement status, schadenfreude can be fueled by resentment when the higher status of the other person is perceived to be undeserved, leading to a wish to denigrate the other and to feelings of pleasure when the other person suffers a misfortune. In achievement situations, resentment about one's own perceived undeserved lower status can also feed into resentment about the higher status or success of the other person.

Deservingness and entitlement

How do these conclusions relate to other research on deservingness and schadenfreude? I exclude from this discussion the extensive research on belief in a just world that has followed from and added to Lerner's analysis (Lerner, 1980, 1987, 1998) because it is more directed toward how people react to victims and is not specifically directed toward schadenfreude as a possible reaction. Lerner's analysis of preconscious systems of belief about justice and more rational conscious systems that emerge later, and the earlier discussions of how children develop a personal contract and a social contract leading to a belief in a just world (Lerner, Miller, and Holmes, 1976) are important contributions to the psychology of justice, but are not specifically concerned with the analysis of schadenfreude.

My analysis of deservingness is more at the level of conscious judgment, but I do acknowledge (Feather, 1999b, 2006) that judgments of deservingness can be made quickly and relatively automatically when deservingness structures are completely balanced with all relations within the structures in harmony with each other. As noted previously, I also believe it is necessary to distinguish between deservingness and entitlement within the more general framework of justice and fairness (Feather, 1999b, pp. 24–6). Legal scholars and moral philosophers back this claim (e.g., Feinberg, 1970; Kristjánsonn, 2006; Sher, 1987). This is more than a semantic distinction. It also has implications for how people react to events in their lives. For example, in one study from my research program (Feather and Johnstone, 2001), nurses, when responding to the destructive behavior of a psychiatric patient (a schizophrenic or a personality disorder patient), clearly distinguished between whether the patient deserved to be punished or was entitled to prescribed care. In another study, participants distinguished between deservingness relating to the quality of performance and entitlement relating to an affirmative action policy when responding to a male or female job applicant's successful or unsuccessful pursuit of a job with an IT firm (Feather, 2008b).

I have focused on deservingness in this review, but there is also scope for studies on how emotions might relate to the violation of entitlements where the emphasis is on externally based rights, agreed-upon norms, or other legal or quasi-legal prescriptions, and where the entitlements usually refer to positive events and outcomes, such as caring for the patient or conforming to an affirmative action policy in the studies just mentioned. As noted previously, entitlement contrasts with deservingness where, in my analysis, the structure of a person's evaluated actions and their contingent evaluated outcomes are of key concern. But I would assert that both deservingness and entitlement are grounded in social and cultural norms, and values. Values and social norms influence the degree to which actions and their outcomes are evaluated as positive or negative in the case of deservingness. In the case of entitlement, they set the legal or quasi-legal constraints that influence whether or not a person is entitled to a positive outcome.

When entitlements relate to a person or group, a violation would normally lead to displeasure rather than pleasure, but to pleasure when the violation is corrected and justice is restored. The displeasure may often be blended with other emotions such as sadness, anger, and resentment, and feelings of dislike that can trigger protest or other forms of social action. This action may occur at either the individual or the collective level to correct the injustice associated with the violation (e.g., Feather, Woodyatt, and McKee, 2012; Thomas, McGarty, and Mavor, 2009; Van Zomeren, Postmes, and Spears, 2008).

Studies are also needed that investigate situations where deservingness and entitlement are in either a compatible or incompatible relation (see Feather, 2002a; Feather and Johnstone, 2001). For example, a person may be perceived to deserve an outcome and also to be entitled to it (a compatible relation) or to lack either deservingness or entitlement for an outcome (also a compatible relation). On the other hand, a person may be perceived to deserve an outcome without entitlement (an incompatible relation) or to be entitled to an outcome but not deserve it (also an incompatible relation). Consistent with my analysis, schadenfreude would be expected to be associated with a deserved negative outcome, but could be moderated and reduced in those situations where entitlements to positive outcomes are violated.

Assumption of personal causality

My analysis of deservingness puts it within the personal causality mode (Heider, 1958) where the self or the other person bears some personal responsibility for the action or event that led to the outcome. We do not usually judge a person as deserving an outcome that is produced by circumstances over which he or she has no personal control and for which there is no personal responsibility for the event and outcome (Feather, 1999b, p. 25). We do not say that a person deserved to win a lottery or deserved to lose a job because of a downturn in the economy. The results of my research show that deservingness is influenced by the level of perceived personal responsibility, but the relation is not a simple one-to-one relation (see below). In related research, Van Dijk et al. (2005) showed that deservingness mediates the relation between responsibility and schadenfreude, a result that is consistent with the assumption that deservingness implies a context of personal causation where there is a degree of perceived responsibility for an action and its outcome.

Weiner (1995, 2006) has consistently argued that judgments of responsibility predict emotions such as anger and sympathy, stigmatization, and how one reacts to the success or failure of others or of the self. However, in my analysis deservingness is further along the causal chain when one considers reactions to outcomes. It is usually a better predictor of these reactions than is perceived responsibility (e.g., Feather, 1992, 2006). People can either deserve or not deserve outcomes for which they remain responsible. Though related, the two variables of deservingness and responsibility do not always run in parallel, a point that I have consistently argued. For example, a hard-working student would be judged as responsible for the effort he or she put into studying for an exam and also as deserving a successful outcome; an athlete would be judged as responsible when he or she took drugs to enhance performance, but as not deserving winning a place in the finals.

Liking and moral character

As is the case in my research program, other research has also shown that the degree to which the other person is liked or disliked, as well as perceptions of the other's moral character (good versus bad), moderates the other's perceived deservingness for a misfortune and, as a consequence, schadenfreude or other emotions that are reported. Consistent with our findings from different studies, Hareli and Weiner (2002) reported results from a correlational study based on retrospective data that showed that schadenfreude was stronger the more the other person was disliked, the more the misfortune was deserved, and the less the other person was perceived to be of good character.

Using experimentally manipulated scenarios, Feather and Atchison (1998) also showed that the perceived deservingness of punishment for an offense (child abuse or arson) and anger about the offense were both negatively related to perceived moral character. In their study, less anger was reported about offenders who were judged to be more decent, reliable, worthy, and respectable. These offenders were also judged to be less responsible for the offense and to deserve the punishment less.

In a study of reactions to a driving offense that used scenarios in which moral worth was manipulated along with other variables, Feather and Deverson (2000) found the usual positive relation between positive affect or schadenfreude about the penalty that was imposed and the degree to which the offender was seen as responsible for the event and deserved the penalty. Schadenfreude was also negatively related to the perceived moral character of the driver. Liking the driver was positively related to perceived moral character; schadenfreude following the penalty was negatively related to how much the driver was liked (less liking predicted more positive affect about the penalty).

In a study that used 16 different vignettes or scenarios, Lupfer and Gingrich (1999) found that the congruence between moral character and outcome was a strong influence on perceived deservingness. Outcomes were more likely to be judged as deserved when there was congruence between the valences attached to the actors' character and the outcomes (+ + or − −) and undeserved when these valences were incongruent (+ − or − +). They also found that feeling pleased about the outcome in the vignettes was positively related to participants' ratings of deservingness.

I would expect perceived moral character to influence schadenfreude via deservingness. A person with stronger moral character would tend to be seen as less likely to initiate the negative event that leads to the negative outcome, and in that sense less responsible for the event and less deserving when compared with a person with weaker moral character, thereby attracting less schadenfreude or pleasure about the negative outcome. The actions of a person with stronger moral character would also be more likely to be tied to a strong moral base involving basic values such as honesty and concern for the welfare of others. Their actions would express these values. In contrast, the actions of a person with weaker moral character (such as a confidence trickster, a hypocrite whose actions belie his or her words, or a criminal offender) would be associated with different sorts of values that do not express moral virtue. This form of analysis would also have to acknowledge the power of the situation in influencing behavior in a particular direction, an influence that may override individual concerns and preferences.

We need more study into the effects of perceived moral character on reactions to others' outcomes. In my analysis, judgments of a person's moral character would depend on knowledge of that person's past behavior perceived in terms of goodness/badness, and also on information from other sources, such as acquaintances or the media in the case of public figures (Feather, 1999b, pp. 102–4). Perceived moral character clearly relates to social and cultural norms and values.

Benign and hostile envy

Where does envy fit into the picture? Envy is a complex emotion that has been the subject of a lot of conceptual analysis and much research (e.g., Heider, 1958; Salovey, 1991; Smith, 2008; Smith and Kim, 2007; Smith, Thielke, and Powell, Chapter 6 in this volume). I do not propose to add to this analysis in this chapter, except to say that I conceive of envy as an emotion that involves social comparison and reflects a person's wish to have the same sort of advantage or positive benefit that another person has in a domain of self-interest. A number of studies show that schadenfreude about another's misfortune is stronger the more the other person is envied (e.g., Brigham, et al., 1997; Smith et al., 1996; Smith et al., 2009; Van Dijk et al., 2006). However, the study by Feather and Sherman (2002) failed to find a relation between envy and schadenfreude. Nor did the research reported by Hareli and Weiner (2002).

My view is that envy may take different forms (e.g., Salovey, 1991; Smith, 2008; Smith, Thielke, and Powell, Chapter 6 in this volume; Van de Ven, Zeelenberg, and Pieters, 2009) and, in those cases where it is benign envy without negative feeling, it might be more appropriate to regard it as blending with admiration when another person secures a deserved advantage compared with the self (Feather, 2006). In other cases, however, envy may be accompanied by subjective feelings of injustice, especially when another person's advantage is perceived as either undeserved or a violation of entitlements and rights. These subjective feelings of injustice may then trigger resentment that blends with envy about the other person's advantage or good fortune. This resentment that relates to feelings of injustice may then be associated with enhanced schadenfreude or pleasure when the envied other who is perceived as undeserving of the advantage or who lacks entitlement to the advantage suffers a subsequent misfortune. Other feelings may also come into play, such as disliking the other person, anger that comes with frustration, and other forms of negative affect. But in many cases resentment that relates to perceived injustice is an important component of hostile envy in social comparison.

Status, pain of inferiority, and self-esteem

As described previously, results from a later study in the tall poppy program showed that the lower performance status of a role-playing student predicted schadenfreude when a high achiever suffered a subsequent failure in an examination (see Figure 3.2; Feather, 2008a). The role-playing student's lower status was also associated with resentment when he or she perceived this lower status to be undeserved, and this resentment enhanced resentment already expressed toward the undeserving high achiever, leading to stronger feelings of schadenfreude about the high achiever's failure (Feather, 2008a; Feather and Nairn, 2005). Thus, schadenfreude was associated with a direct effect involving the role-playing student's lower status and with an indirect effect via deservingness and resentment. As noted previously, these results relate to research by Leach and Spears on the pain of in-group inferiority where they conceptualize "intergroup schadenfreude as an unfolding emotional episode whereby unpleasant emotions about the self lead to a pleasant emotion about another party" (2008, p. 1383). They drew upon Nietzsche's (1887/1967) discussion of the "vengefulness of the impotent" and *ressentiment* that can be associated with externalized and displaced anger directed at the successful (see also Heider, 1958; Scheler, 1961). Their indirect pathway led to schadenfreude via the implied pain of inferiority and externalized anger that would become salient following the success of another group in a domain of interest.

In contrast, my emphasis is more on the resentment or feelings of injustice that are associated with undeserved outcomes both for the self and for the other person. In my view, the pain of inferiority that follows an invidious social comparison will often include feelings of injustice as an important component of the emotional mix, and this resentment should be distinguished from the displaced anger that may occur when a lower-status person is confronted with another group's or person's success or advantage.

As mentioned previously, the tall poppy research showed that schadenfreude was positively related to a general disposition to want to see tall poppies fall from their high positions. I have suggested a number of possible interpretations of this favor fall/schadenfreude relation (Feather, 2008a) that include a wish to achieve an equalization of lots, thereby reducing the comparative difference between the self and others (Heider, 1958), the operation of egalitarian values (Feather, 1994, 1996b; Feather and Adair, 1999), and reactions to the *ressentiment* and feelings of impotence that can be associated with low status and power (Nietzsche, 1887/1967; Scheler, 1961).

My research has also shown that favoring the fall of tall poppies tends to be stronger among those low in global self-esteem (Feather, 1994, 1996b; Feather and Adair, 1999). So those who tend to devalue themselves are also more likely to want to see tall poppies fall and presumably also to feel pleased when they do fall. Research by Van Dijk et al. (2011) is consistent with these findings. The authors argue that striving for a positive self-evaluation is an important motive for schadenfreude. The fall of a high achiever in a domain of interest may then attract more pleasure among those with low self-esteem and help them feel better about themselves (Van Dijk and Ouwerkerk, Chapter 9 in this volume).

However, once the tall poppy falls to a low position, those with low self-esteem may then feel some degree of sympathy and support for the fallen person. The results of an early study in my research program (Feather, 1991) showed that students in a South Australian high school with lower global self-esteem showed more support for Ben Johnson after he lost his gold medal at the Seoul Olympics because he had tested positive for having taken anabolic steroids. Johnson's fall brought him symbolically closer to those further down the ladder of achievement. Many of my later studies have included sympathy as a reaction to another person's negative outcome, in addition to schadenfreude. In my analysis of deservingness and emotions (Feather, 2006), sympathy is assumed to occur when the other's negative outcome is perceived to be undeserved (see Table 3.1). However, sympathy is not the mirror image of schadenfreude, but instead relates more to prosocial and empathic concerns for the other person (Brigham et al., 1997; Feather, 2008a; Feather and Nairn, 2005; Feather and Sherman, 2002; Weiner, 1986, 2006). Although relations between sympathy and other variables in my studies tend to be opposite in direction to those involving schadenfreude, this is not always the case.

Integrating multiple perspectives

In a recent study, Feather, Wenzel, and McKee (2013) provided an integration of the different perspectives on schadenfreude that I described in the previous sections by combining the variables that were their focus with perceived deservingness. We used realistic scenarios to manipulate in-group/out-group membership and perceived deservingness. The scenarios described a student in psychology from Flinders University (*in-group*) or from Adelaide University (*out-group*) who obtained grades that were consistently good. Deservingness was manipulated by describing the student as either hard-working or as putting in less effort, and also by varying his or her degree of responsibility for the award of a prestigious student internship at a university in America. High effort/more responsibility was assumed to determine more deservingness of the positive outcomes the student received; low effort/less responsibility was assumed to determine less deservingness. We call this variable *deserve success*.

In an epilogue to the scenario, each student applied to enter the Honours program in Psychology at Flinders University, but failed to be accepted. We assessed the degree of pleasure or schadenfreude about the student's failure reported by participants, all of whom were Flinders students in psychology.

We tested a structural model that linked schadenfreude with the deserve success manipulation and with global self-esteem, pain of inferiority, hostile and benign envy, resentment, perceived deservingness, and sympathy. These latter variables were assessed in the study using measures with high internal reliability.

The results of the study showed effects of in-group favoritism. Participants (Flinders students) reported more pleasure or schadenfreude when the Adelaide student failed and they reported more anger and sympathy for the Flinders student who failed. They also rated the Flinders student as less deserving of failure.

The final structural model that emerged from our analysis is presented in Figure 3.3. The model applied to both the in-group and out-group

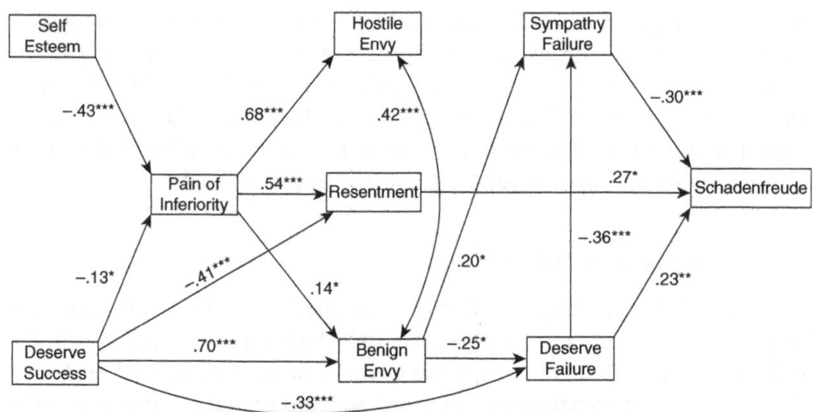

Figure 3.3 Path model linking global self-esteem and deserve success to schadenfreude via the mediating variables (Feather, Wenzel, and McKee, 2013). Deserve success was coded 1 = low, 2 = high. *$p < .05$; **$p < .01$; ***$p < .001$

conditions. It showed that the effects of self-esteem and the deserve success manipulation on schadenfreude were mediated through pain of inferiority, resentment, benign envy, deserve failure, and sympathy about the student's failure via direct and indirect paths. The significant paths in Figure 3.3 are consistent with what one would expect. Self-esteem had a negative link to pain of inferiority, which in turn had strong positive links to both resentment and hostile envy; deserve success had a negative link to resentment about the student's high grades, which in turn had a positive link to schadenfreude; deserve success also had a negative link to deserve failure and a positive link to benign envy; benign envy had a negative link to deserve failure and a positive link to sympathy; deserve failure had a positive link to schadenfreude; and sympathy had a negative link to schadenfreude.

These results show that deservingness had its effects in combination with variables that were the focus of the different theoretical perspectives that I described in the previous sections. These variables, together with deserve failure, were also part of the complex structure of relations linking to schadenfreude.

Schadenfreude and undeservingness

A final issue concerns the way schadenfreude is defined in relation to deservingness (see also Ben Ze'ev, Chapter 5 in this volume; Portmann, Chapter 2 in this volume; Powell, Chapter 4 in this volume). My analysis proposes that schadenfreude is likely to occur on the part of an observer when another person suffers a deserved misfortune and gets his or her just deserts. This emphasis on a deserved negative outcome is also present in philosophical analyses of schadenfreude by Ben-Ze'ev (2000) and Portmann (2000). The question should be raised, however, about whether schadenfreude can occur when another's negative outcome or misfortune is perceived to be undeserved. Kristjánsonn (2006) argues that the traditional view of schadenfreude is just that: pleasure following another's undeserved misfortune. He uses the term "satisfied indignation" to refer to the sort of pleasure that Ben Ze'ev and Portmann discuss and that has also been the focus of my analysis in this chapter. For Kristjánsonn, pleasure about another's deserved misfortune involves an emotion "whose focus is the alleviation of our previous indignation: the restoration of justice" (2006, p. 98). He sees dangers in conflating the two kinds of pleasure and prefers to keep them separate.

There are certainly situations where people may express transient pleasure at another's undeserved misfortune, for example, when someone slips on a banana skin or makes some accidental error. Such events may make the other person appear more human, and more so if they are of high status (e.g., Aronson, Willerman, and Floyd, 1966). However, these outcomes are outside of personal causality where intentions come into play and they may be attributed to external circumstances or to bad luck. In that sense they would be perceived as undeserved. As the misfortune becomes more serious (e.g., the person broke a leg after slipping on the banana skin), the emotion would change to sympathy relating to an undeserved negative outcome for other person (see Table 3.1).

We need more research on this sort of transient pleasure that may sometimes occur when we observe someone else's undeserved misfortune. When does it turn to sympathy and compassion? When is it malicious? How does it relate to envy? Does it blend with other emotions such as resentment? Are undeserved misfortunes sometimes perceived as unexpected, eliciting surprise and a degree of pleasure, especially when the negative event is a minor one? Studies directed at questions such as these should involve a range of different approaches and use not only vignettes or hypothetical scenarios that enable the controlled manipulation of variables, but also events and outcomes that are an important part of people's lives.

In addition, we need more research targeted at the direction of relations between deservingness and schadenfreude. My analysis proposes that the appraisal of deservingness is an important condition for the experience of schadenfreude. One could argue, however, that the cognitive judgment of deservingness follows schadenfreude as some sort of rationalization, justification, or cognitive interpretation of the affect that is experienced, i.e., that it is the immediate pleasure about the other's negative outcome that determines the judgment that the outcome is deserved, and that this cognitive judgment has subsequent implications for what follows in the behavioral episode.

I accept that causality can go in either direction, consistent with the argument that relations between cognition and emotion can be reciprocal or bidirectional, so that affect can also have an effect on deservingness judgments (Feather, 1999b, pp. 248–50; 2006, pp. 63–4). For example, in one study from my research program (Feather and Johnstone, 2001), nurses who were more angry about a psychiatric patient's negative behavior (damaging hospital property) also tended to judge the patient as more deserving of punishment, but entitled to proper care. However, the main focus in my research program has been on the effects of deservingness on subsequent affect, although I acknowledge that affect may also influence deservingness judgments in behavioral episodes. Both are intertwined and difficult to separate. Studies that investigate changes in cognition and affect over time and that include measures of brain imaging or other/physiological evidence together with verbal reports from the person experiencing the emotion may be necessary to resolve the issue (see Cikara and Fiske, Chapter 10 in this volume).

In the meantime, my review makes it clear that a person's belief about whether another person's misfortune is deserved is a key variable in determining how pleased the person is about that negative outcome. This is a sort of justified pleasure that in my analysis relates to a balanced set of relations that are assumed to underlie deservingness (Feather, 1999b) and, in the case of entitlement, to conformity with externally generated norms and legal or quasi-legal prescriptions. It is a pleasure that follows the restoration of justice and it may occur as an end product of episodes in which justice is seen to be violated and where resentment about this injustice plays a major role.

References

Altemeyer, B. and Hunsberger, B. (1992). Authoritarianism, religious fundamentalism, quest, and prejudice. *International Journal for the Psychology of Religion* 2: 113–33.

Aronson, E., Willerman, B., and Floyd, J. (1966). The effect of a pratfall on increasing interpersonal attractiveness. *Psychonomic Science* 4: 227–8.

Ben-Ze'ev, A. (2000). *The Subtlety of Emotions.* Cambridge, MA: MIT Press.

Brigham, N. L., Kelso, K. A., Jackson, M. A., and Smith, R. H. (1997). The roles of invidious comparisons and deservingness in sympathy and schadenfreude. *Basic and Applied Social Psychology* 19: 363–80.

Feather, N. T. (1989). Attitudes towards the high achiever: the fall of the tall poppy. *Australian Journal of Psychology* 41: 239–67.

(1991). Attitudes towards the high achiever: effects of perceiver's own level of competence. *Australian Journal of Psychology* 43: 121–4.

(1992). An attributional and value analysis of deservingness in success and failure situations. *British Journal of Social Psychology* 31: 125–45.

(1994). Attitudes toward high achievers and reactions to their fall. In M. P. Zanna (ed.), *Advances in Experimental Social Psychology*, Vol. 26. San Diego, CA: Academic Press, pp. 1–73.

(1996a). Reactions to penalties for an offense in relation to authoritarianism, values, perceived responsibility, perceived seriousness, and deservingness. *Journal of Personality and Social Psychology* 71: 571–87.

(1996b). Values, deservingness, and attitudes towards high achievers: research on tall poppies. In C. Seligman, J. M. Olson, and M. P. Zanna (eds.), *The Psychology of Values: The Ontario Symposium*, Vol. 8. Mahwah, NJ: Erlbaum, pp. 215–51.

(1998). Reactions to penalties for offenses committed by the police and public citizens: testing a social-cognitive process model of retributive justice. *Journal of Personality and Social Psychology* 75: 528–44.

(1999a). Judgments of deservingness: studies in the psychology of justice and achievement. *Personality and Social Psychology Review* 3: 86–107.

(1999b). *Values, Achievement, and Justice: Studies in the Psychology of Deservingness.* New York: Kluwer Academic/Plenum Press.

(2002a). Deservingness, entitlement, and reactions to outcomes. In M. Ross and D. T. Miller (eds.), *The Justice Motive in Everyday Life.* New York: Cambridge University Press, pp. 334–49.

(2002b). Reactions to supporters and opponents of uranium mining in relation to status, attitude similarity, and right-wing authoritarianism. *Journal of Applied Social Psychology* 32: 1464–87.

(2003). Distinguishing between deservingness and entitlement: earned outcomes versus lawful outcomes. *European Journal of Social Psychology* 33: 367–85.

(2006). Deservingness and emotions: applying the structural model of deservingness to the analysis of affective reactions to outcomes. *European Review of Social Psychology* 17: 38–73.

(2008a). Effects of observer's own status on reactions to a high achiever's failure: deservingness, resentment, schadenfreude, and sympathy. *Australian Journal of Psychology* 60: 31–43.

(2008b). Perceived legitimacy of a promotion decision in relation to deservingness, entitlement, and resentment in the context of affirmative action and performance. *Journal of Applied Social Psychology* 38: 1230–54.

Feather, N. T. and Adair, J. G. (1999). National identity, national favouritism, global self-esteem, tall poppy attitudes, and value priorities in Australian and Canadian samples. In J.-C. Lazry, J. G. Adair, and K. Dion (eds.), *Latest Contributions to Cross-cultural Psychology.* Lisse: Swets & Zeitlinger, pp. 42–61.

Feather, N. T. and Atchison, L. (1998). Reactions to an offence in relation to the status and perceived moral character of the offender. *Australian Journal of Psychology* 50: 119–27.

Feather, N. T., Boeckmann, R. J., and McKee, I. R. (2001a). Jail sentence, community service, or compensation: predicting reactions to a serious corporate offence. *Australian Journal of Psychology* 53: 92–102.

(2001b). Reactions to an offence in relation to authoritarianism, knowledge about risk, and freedom of action. *European Journal of Social Psychology* 31: 109–26.

Feather, N. T. and Dawson, S. (1998). Judging deservingness and affect in relation to another's employment or unemployment: a test of a justice model. *European Journal of Social Psychology* 28: 361–81.

Feather, N. T. and Deverson, N. H. (2000). Reactions to a motor-vehicle accident in relation to mitigating circumstances and the gender and moral worth of the driver. *Journal of Applied Social Psychology* 30: 77–95.

Feather, N. T. and Johnstone, C. (2001). Social norms, entitlement and deservingness: differential reactions to aggressive behavior of schizophrenic and personality disorder patients. *Personality and Social Psychology Bulletin* 27: 755–67.

Feather, N. T. and McKee, I. R. (2009). Differentiating emotions in relation to deserved or undeserved outcomes: a retrospective study of real-life events. *Cognition & Emotion* 23: 955–77.

(2014). Deservingness, liking relations, schadenfreude and discrete emotions in the context of the outcomes of plagiarism. *Australian Journal of Psychology* 66: 18–27.

Feather, N. T., McKee, I. R., and Bekker, N. (2011). Deservingness and emotions: testing a structural model that relates discrete emotions to the perceived deservingness of positive or negative outcomes. *Motivation and Emotion* 35: 1–13.

Feather, N. T. and Nairn, K. (2005). Resentment, envy, schadenfreude, and sympathy: effects of own and other's deserved or undeserved status. *Australian Journal of Psychology* 57: 87–102.

Feather, N. T. and Sherman, R. (2002). Envy, resentment, schadenfreude, and sympathy: reactions to deserved and undeserved achievement and subsequent failure. *Personality and Social Psychology Bulletin* 28: 953–61.

Feather, N. T. and Souter, J. (2002). Reactions to mandatory sentences in relation to ethnic identity and criminal history of the offender. *Law and Human Behavior* 26: 417–38.

Feather, N. T., Volkmer, R. E., and McKee, I. R. (1991). Attitudes towards high achievers in public life: attributions, deservingness, personality, and affect. *Australian Journal of Psychology* 43: 85–91.

Feather, N. T., Wenzel, M., and McKee, I. R. (2013). Integrating multiple perspectives on schadenfreude: the role of deservingness and emotions. *Motivation and Emotion* 37: 574–85.

Feather, N. T., Woodyatt, L. T., and McKee, I. R. (2012). Predicting support for social action: how values, justice-related variables, discrete emotions, and outcome expectations influence support for the Stolen Generations. *Motivation and Emotion* 36: 516–28.

Feinberg, J. (1970). *Doing and Deserving*. Princeton University Press.

Hareli, S. (1999). Justice and deservingness judgments – refuting the interchangeability assumption. *New Ideas in Psychology* 17: 183–93.

Hareli, S. and Weiner, B. (2002). Dislike and envy as antecedents of pleasure at another's misfortune. *Motivation and Emotion* 26: 257–77.

Heath, A. (1976). *Rational Choice and Social Exchange*. Cambridge University Press.

Heider, F. (1958). *The Psychology of Interpersonal Relations*. New York: John Wiley.

Kristjánsonn, K. (2006). *Justice and Desert-Based Emotions*. Aldershot: Ashgate.

Leach, C. W. and Spears, R. (2008). "A vengefulness of the impotent": the pain of in-group inferiority and schadenfreude toward successful out-groups. *Journal of Personality and Social Psychology* 95: 1383–96.

Lerner, M. J. (1980). *The Belief in the Just World: A Fundamental Delusion*. New York: Plenum.

(1987). Integrating social and psychological rules of entitlement: the basic task of each social actor and fundamental problem for the social sciences. *Social Justice Research* 1: 107–25.

(1998). The two forms of belief in a just world: some thoughts on why and how people care about justice. In L. Montada and M. J. Lerner (eds.), *Responses to Victimization and Belief in a Just World*. New York: Plenum. pp. 247–69.

Lerner, M. J., Miller, D. T., and Holmes, J. G. (1976). Deserving and the emergence of forms of justice. In L. Berkowitz and E. Walster (eds.), *Advances in Experimental Social Psychology*, Vol. 9. New York: Academic Press, pp. 133–62.

Lupfer, M. B. and Gingrich, B. E. (1999). When bad (good) things happen to good (bad) people: the impact of character appraisal and perceived controllability on judgments of deservingness. *Social Justice Research* 12: 165–88.

Maio, G. R. (2010). Mental representations of social values. In M. P. Zanna (ed.), *Advances in Experimental Social Psychology*, Vol. 42. Burlington: Academic Press, pp. 1–43.

Miller, D. (1976). *Social Justice*. Oxford: Clarendon Press.

Nietzsche, F. (1967 [1887]). *On the Genealogy of Morals* (translated by W. Kaufmann and R. Hollingdale) New York: Random House.

Parrott, W. G. (1991). The emotional experiences of envy and jealousy. In P. Salovey (ed.), *The Psychology of Envy and Jealousy*. New York: Guilford Press, pp. 3–30.

Portmann, J. (2000). *When Bad Things Happen to Other People*. New York: Routledge.

Salovey, P. (1991). *The Psychology of Envy and Jealousy*. New York: Guilford Press.

Scheler, M. (1961 [1915]). *Ressentiment* (translated by W. W. Holdhein). Glencoe, IL: Free Press.

Schwartz, S. H. (1992). Universals in the content and structure of values: theoretical advances and empirical tests in 20 countries. In M. P. Zanna (ed.), *Advances in Experimental Social Psychology*, Vol. 25. Orlando, FL: Academic Press, pp. 1–65.

(1996). Value priorities and priorities and behaviour: applying a theory of integrated value systems. In C. Seligman, J. M. Olson, and M. P. Zanna (eds.), *The Psychology of Values: The Ontario Symposium*, Vol. 8. Mahwah, NJ: Erlbaum, pp. 1–24.

(2006). Les valeurs de base de la personne: Théorie, mesures et applications. *Revue Française de Sociologie* 47: 249–88.

Sher, G. (1987). *Desert*. Princeton University Press.

Smith, R. H. (ed.) (2008). *Envy: Theory and Research*. Oxford University Press.

Smith, R. H. and Kim, S. H. (2007). Comprehending envy. *Psychology Bulletin* 133: 46–64.

Smith, R. H., Powell, C. A. J., Combs, D. J. Y., and Schurtz, D. R. (2009). Exploring the when and why of Schadenfreude. *Social and Personality Psychology Compass* 3: 530–46.

Smith, R. H., Turner, T. J., Garonzik, R., Leach, C. W., Urch-Druskat, V., and Weston, C. M. (1996). Envy and schadenfreude. *Personality and Social Psychology Bulletin* 25: 158–68.

Thomas, E. F., McGarty, C., and Mavor, K. I. (2009). Transforming “apathy into movement”: the role of prosocial emotions in motivating action for social change. *Personality and Social Psychology Review* 13: 310–33.

Van de Ven, N., Zeelenberg, M., and Pieters, R. (2009). Leveling up and down: the experience of benign and malicious envy. *Emotion* 9: 419–29.

Van Dijk, W. W., Ouwerkerk, J. W., Goslinga, S., and Nieweg, M. (2005). Deservingness and schadenfreude. *Cognition & Emotion* 19: 933–9.

Van Dijk, W. W., Ouwerkerk, J. W., Goslinga, S., Nieweg, M., and Galluci, M. (2006). When people fall from grace: reconsidering the role of envy in schadenfreude. *Emotion* 6: 156–60.

Van Dijk, W. W., Ouwerkerk, J. W., Wesseling, Y. M., and Van Koningsbruggen, G. M. (2011). Towards understanding pleasure at the misfortunes of others: the impact of self-evaluation threat on schadenfreude. *Cognition & Emotion* 25: 360–8.

Van Zomeren, M., Postmes, T., and Spears, R. (2008). Toward an integrative social identity model of collective action: a quantitative research synthesis of three social-psychological perspectives. *Psychological Bulletin* 134: 504–35.

Von Hirsch, A. (1986). *Doing Justice: The Choice of Punishments*. Boston, MA: Northeastern University Press.

Weiner, B. (1986). *An Attributional Theory of Motivation and Emotion*. New York: Springer-Verlag.

(1995). *Judgments of Responsibility: A Foundation for a Theory of Social Conduct*. New York: Guilford Press.

(2006). *Social Motivation, Justice, and the Moral Emotions: An Attributional Approach*. Mahwah, NJ: Erlbaum.

4 Hypocrisy and schadenfreude

Caitlin A. J. Powell

Whenever a public figure falls from grace due to immoral behaviour, the news media and public response is swift, especially with the advent of modern communication. The immoral individual is immediately disgraced and discredited, news story after news story gleefully outlining the precise detail of the mistake, and the public simultaneously condemning the wrongdoer while getting a little personal amusement out of his or her predicament. When a public figure has first taken a visible stance on a specific moral issue and then is caught violating that stated principle, however, the usual frenzy is magnified tenfold. People simply love watching hypocrites get caught in a web of their own making. As only Shakespeare could put it, 'For 'tis the sport to have the enginer/Hoist with his own petar' (*Hamlet*, Act III, Scene iv; Shakespeare, 1601/1980, p. 153).

Definition of hypocrisy

According to Newman, hypocrisy is conceived of as 'simulation or feigning to be what one is not; the acting of a false part; especially, the assuming of a false appearance of virtue or religion' (1986, p. 85). At a basic level, there is a fundamental inconsistency between what hypocrites claim to believe and how they behave (Stone et al., 1997; Barden, Rucker and Petty, 2005). In essence, hypocrisy can be defined as 'saying one thing, but doing another' or failing to 'practise what you preach' (Aronson, Fried and Stone, 1991).

There are other important qualifications that are needed in order for an individual to be considered hypocritical: in a study by Barden, Rucker and Petty (2005), individuals first making a statement about their personal values and then behaving in a way that violated those values were perceived to be more hypocritical than those whose behaviour preceded the values statement. According to these authors, this is because a spoken statement can often be seen as more of a dispositional change than a one-time behaviour; therefore, making moral statements after behaving immorally can denote a change in heart or an attempt to seek forgiveness for past actions, whereas behaving immorally after stating one's values tends to negate the values statement altogether and indicates weak character. The authors also mention that if the behaviour is exhibited privately rather than publicly, it also tends to suggest that the people behaving immorally appear to be making an active attempt to deceive others and, furthermore, this gives the impression that they know what they are doing is wrong. Therefore, private immoral behaviour after a public statement of values is seen as more hypocritical than if the immoral behaviour were public.

Another common aspect of hypocrisy is that hypocrites inject a moral component in the behaviour they proclaim to follow (Crisp and Cowton, 1994). According to Shelley (2006), inconsistent behaviour is considered to be hypocritical if it is an intended violation of a fundamental moral value and has significant moral 'gravity' or importance. Barden also states that a key component of hypocrisy is that when an individual 'says' one thing and 'does' another, a 'key component of the "saying" element is the personal communication of a personal standard' (Barden, Rucker and Petty, 2005, p. 1463). Many classic examples of hypocritical behaviour have a moral overlay where the hypocrites in question claim to act in moral ways, but secretly go against their stated beliefs (e.g., Batson et al., 1997; Batson et al., 1999; Batson, Thompson and Chen, 2002; Valdesolo and DeSteno, 2007). Newman's (1986) definition specifically provides examples of virtue or religion, which are steeped in moral structure.

Society tends to have a very poor view of those that behave in an inconsistent or deceptive manner (e.g., Asch, 1946; Tedeschi, Schlenker and Bonoma, 1971; Allgeier et al., 1979; Cialdini, 2000). One of Cialdini's (2000) basic principles of compliance (commitment/consistency) states that people have a basic need to remain consistent with their internal belief systems. He goes on to state that: 'The person whose beliefs, words, and deeds don't match is seen as confused, two-faced, even mentally ill' (2000, p. 54). Those who are inconsistent are perceived to be liars, and their deception is a violation of trust (Newman, 1986; Stone et al., 1997; Szabados and Soifer, 2004). By this standard, being inconsistent is almost worse than being consistently immoral.

If individuals are made aware of their own hypocrisy, this can lead to cognitive dissonance, which can then result in behaviour modification where the individuals attempt to alter their behaviour to better align with their stated values in order to resolve the aversive feelings created by inconsistency (i.e. Aronson et al., 1991; Barden et al., 2005). For example, in an early study on hypocrisy, Aronson et al. (1991) induced hypocrisy by having college students create a video of themselves giving a Public Service Announcement about condom use and then asking how many times in the past they had failed to use protection. Those in the induced hypocrisy condition were more likely to purchase condoms as they left the experiment.

Given that hypocrites risk facing harsh social sanctions, there would not appear to be much motivation for behaving in an inconsistent manner. However, some research suggests that hypocrisy can be rewarding as long as it is not revealed to others: for example, individuals often engage in minor deceptions of self-presentation to appear socially acceptable, even though their private behaviour may be outside the norm. Frank (1988) takes it one step beyond minor acts of deception: he suggests that individuals can be highly motivated to give the appearance of deep commitment to moral principles, as it often leads to an increase in others' trust and respect, which can then be taken advantage of. Research has shown that when given the opportunity, many individuals will choose options that allow them to appear moral while avoiding the costs of said morality (Batson et al., 1997, 2002). For instance, in a study by Batson et al. (1997), some of the participants flipped a coin to determine whether they would end up doing a boring task or whether their partner would. Of those who flipped the coin, 90 per cent of them told the experimenter that the results indicated their partner had been assigned the boring task. This gave all the appearance of fairness, while allowing the participant to actually take the better group assignment. Research also suggests that as power increases, so does the likelihood of engaging in hypocrisy. Specifically, powerful people have been shown to be more likely to condemn others for cheating, while at the same time being more likely to engage in cheating behaviour themselves (Lammers, Stapel and Galinsky, 2010).

Another reason why hypocritical behaviour may occur is due to moral self-licensing (Merritt, Effron and Monin, 2010) – sometimes, individuals' initial moral behaviour can paradoxically make them feel as though they are more free to engage in immoral behaviour later on. Therefore, individuals can go through extensive self-justification to excuse occasional immoral behaviour, e.g., 'I've been so good, just this once, I deserve a break'. Sometimes, the self-justification can reach the extreme limits of logic: when questioned about his affairs, Newt Gingrich claimed that when his infidelities took place, he was 'partially driven by how passionately I felt about this country, that I worked far too hard and things happened in my life that were not appropriate' (Associated Press, 2011).

Despite the possible rewards and justifications for behaving hypocritically, there is a distinct cost associated with the public becoming aware of said hypocrisy: hypocrites face severe social sanctions, a loss of reputation and trust, and often receive harsh punishments for their immoral acts. However, the important component of the uncomfortable feelings associated with hypocrisy may be that the inconsistent behaviour has been revealed to others. Indeed, it is very possible that through this self-justification, many hypocritical individuals are able to refrain from the uncomfortable feelings caused by cognitive dissonance until they are caught and exposed, revealing their behaviour in such a way that it becomes obvious to others. The participants in Batson et al.'s experiment believed their deceptions to be surreptitious; if their behaviours were made more obvious (like in the Aronson et al. study), it is very likely that dissonance, shame, embarrassment and behaviour modification would follow.

Deservingness

One reason why the punishment of hypocrites is so pleasing is the fact that their misfortune is perceived as deserved. In a study by Shelley (2006), participants rated scenarios to be more hypocritical if they were high in intentionality (where the actor had control over his or her behaviour), high in gravity (seriousness of violation) and low in sympathy. This would suggest that in order to be considered hypocritical, one must be perceived as having control over one's actions. According to Hamilton and Hagiwara (1992), perceived intentionality is directly related to higher sanctions: if it is perceived that individuals are responsible for their immoral behaviour, they are more likely to receive harsher punishment.

Individuals tend to have a general belief in a just world and, as such, often make the assumption that people tend to get what they deserve (Lerner, 1980, 1987; Callan, Ellard and Nicol, 2006; Feather, 2006) as that would be just or fair (Portmann, Chapter 2 in this volume). In his model of deservingness and emotions, Feather (2006) states that an individual's perceived responsibility for a negative outcome will lead others to see that individual as more deserving of said outcome (e.g., Heider, 1958; Shaver and Drown, 1986; Mikula, 2003). Research supports the idea that deserved misfortunes are more likely to create schadenfreude than undeserved ones (e.g., Feather and Sherman, 2002; Feather and Nairn, 2005; Feather, 2006; Ben-Ze'ev, Chapter 5 in this volume; Feather, Chapter 3 in this volume), and that when individuals feel that someone is responsible for their own misfortune, schadenfreude is more likely (Van Dijk et al., 2005). In order to be labelled as a hypocrite, one's actions must be perceived as intentional. Thus, when hypocrites engage in immoral behaviour, it is automatically presumed to be deserved. They have only themselves to blame, and onlookers have every reason to feel pleased due to the shift in relative fortune (Van Dijk and Ouwerkerk, Chapter 9 in this volume).

Moral typecasting

Yet another perspective that could further explain the connection between schadenfreude and hypocrisy can be found in the moral typecasting literature. According to Gray and Wegner (2009), individuals can often be sorted into moral agents (good and evil-doers) and moral patients (those that have good or evil done to them). Moral agents, both good and bad, tend to be imbued with certain qualities. First, they are seen as having more control over the situation, and therefore are more responsible for their actions. Second, they are perceived to be less vulnerable. Finally, people are more willing to inflict more pain on moral agents due to their presumed lack of sensitivity when compared to victims. Hypocrites fall into an interesting ambiguous area when it comes to this model, as they first appear to be heroes, but ultimately end up playing the role of the villain. Across both of these roles, however, the individual in question is a moral agent who is seen to be responsible for his or her actions, and therefore is also capable of withstanding harsher punishment. Furthermore, it is likely that observers would be even more harsh towards individuals who first appeared good and then violated expectations rather than towards people who were consistent evil-doers – to a certain extent, the act of deception might be perceived as worse than being obviously immoral the entire time, and any subsequent sanctions towards the hypocrites would be harsher as a result. In another study by Gray and Wegner (2011), if wrongdoing individuals initially framed themselves as heroes and emphasised their previous good deeds, participants assigned greater blame to them for their misdeeds. This was due to participants' perception of 'heroic' individuals' greater agency and ability to control the situation than when contrasted with those that framed themselves as victims. This would once again suggest that people tend to perceive the hypocrite as being responsible for his or her own downfall.

Initial research on the link between hypocrisy and schadenfreude would suggest that deservingness does play an important part in determining the reasons why the discovery of hypocrisy should prove so pleasing. A series of studies by Powell and Smith (2012) was undertaken to explore the nature of hypocrisy and why the punishment of hypocrisy leads to schadenfreude. In the first study, 131 undergraduates participated in a very straightforward manipulation of hypocrisy: first, they read an article that was an interview about a fellow student. In half of the interviews, the student spoke out strongly against plagiarism ('It really gets me mad when I see people cheating or plagiarising. That's just lazy') and the student in question was also a part of a student court that punished cheaters. The other half of participants read that the student was merely a member of the French club and that the student said nothing about his moral beliefs. Then, participants read a follow-up article where the same student from the earlier interview had been caught plagiarising and had been placed on academic suspension.

Participants rated the moralising student as being much more hypocritical and deserving of his misfortune than the student who did not moralise, and they also reported experiencing higher amounts of schadenfreude towards the moralising student. Hypocrisy and deservingness both significantly mediated the relationship between moralising and schadenfreude. There were no differences in initial dislike between the moraliser and the student who did not moralise, however. All participants read that the student in question had been caught plagiarising, which is an arguably deserved misfortune in and of itself, inherently full of intentionality, gravity and immorality. It is important to note, however, that participants rated the student who took a strong moral position against plagiarising as being even more deserving, and that those deservingness ratings, as well as ratings of perceived hypocrisy, help explain why participants were so pleased at the misfortune of the student who first spoke out against plagiarising (punishing others for doing so) and then got caught plagiarising himself.

Irony

According to Shelley (2006), hypocrisy can be thought of as a form of situational irony. This irony exists due to a person's actions bringing about an outcome that is in direct contradiction to their stated beliefs. In a series of studies by Shelley, participants read scenarios and provided both 'irony' and 'hypocrisy' ratings. These two ratings were consistently positively correlated. The presence of irony is one potential reason why the punishment and humiliation of hypocrites should prove so inherently amusing – the ironic juxtaposition of the formally moral being punished for immoral behaviour could be perceived as humorous.

Balance

Another way of looking at the connection between hypocrisy and schadenfreude involves the appealing symmetry or sense of balance provided by a hypocrite getting tripped up by precisely the thing that he or she told others not to do. Hypocrites knock themselves off of their own moral pedestals. One cannot help but be amused when the stalwart family-values politician turns out to be involved in a compromising affair or when the District Attorney known for her tough persecution of corruption gets caught taking money under the table. The combination of deservingness and situational irony created by a hypocrite getting himself or herself in trouble by breaking the very rules he or she created can lead to a pleasing sense of balance (Heider, 1958) or 'just deserts', as well as simply providing an amusing juxtaposition between a hypocrite's appearance of morality and hidden immoral tendencies. To further support this notion of balance as being an important component of the pleasing nature of hypocrisy, research would suggest that the punishment must fit the crime in order for individuals to be pleased by the outcome; if the punishment is too lax, observers feel unfulfilled, while if the punishment is too harsh, pity and moral outrage could turn the wrongdoer into a victim (Combs et al., 2010). In a study by Tripp, Bies and Aquino (2002) on workplace revenge, results indicated that said revenge was most pleasing when the act of revenge fitted the original offence. So, for instance, if a boss passed off a subordinate's report as if it were his own, employees found it much more satisfying if said boss were to be caught in his own lack of knowledge about the report, essentially getting caught in a trap of his own making, rather than being humiliated or embarrassed in some other way.

In addition, research would suggest that when a person's immoral behaviour is seen as being unrelated to his or her moral beliefs, others may be more likely to forgive the transgression. This is known as moral licensing. In a series of experiments, Effron and Monin (2010) demonstrated that when a person's transgressions were in a different domain from their initial moral deeds, participants were more likely to excuse their behaviour and were more forgiving, whereas those whose transgressions were in the same domain were seen as more hypocritical and were more likely to receive sanctions. Observers may give the person 'moral credit' for behaving morally in certain domains which balances out immoral behaviour in other areas – for instance, fighting discrimination in the workplace while being guilty of embezzlement was seen as being less morally wrong than appearing to fight discrimination and then demonstrating obviously racist hiring policies. To a certain extent, individuals that are moral in one domain but immoral in another are not perceived as being deceptive to the same degree or as betraying their ideals: yes, they are not behaving morally in every area of their lives, which indicates a certain amount of inconsistency, but their actions of morality have not been completely discredited or revealed to be false; rather, they can serve to balance the moral scales, making it so that others will be less likely to punish or condemn immoral behaviour in other areas. Therefore, in order to be considered a true hypocrite, it is necessary for a person's initial moral position and subsequent immoral actions to be in similar domains – and this similarity between initial moral word and subsequent immoral deed can lead to amusing situational irony, as well as a pleasing sense of balance.

Powell and Smith's second study (2012) explored whether similarity between initial moral position and subsequent immoral behaviour was an important component of the connection between hypocrisy and schadenfreude. In the study, 144 undergraduates first read an interview with a fellow student where the student either spoke out against plagiarising ('I think plagiarising is lazy') and was a member of a student court that punished plagiarisers, or read an interview where the student made no moral statement and was a member of the French club, as they did in Study 1. Next, participants read a follow-up article where that same student was either caught plagiarising or was caught stealing.

Results showed a two-way interaction for both perceptions of hypocrisy and schadenfreude: when the student said nothing at all about plagiarising beforehand, participants rated the plagiarising and stealing behaviours as equally hypocritical and equally schadenfreude-inducing. When the student made a statement against plagiarising first and then got caught plagiarising, however, the participants rated the student as being much more hypocritical and experienced significantly higher amounts of schadenfreude as a result of his misfortune (see Figures 4.1 and 4.2).

Interestingly, the student who first spoke out against plagiarising and then got caught stealing was not statistically different from the French

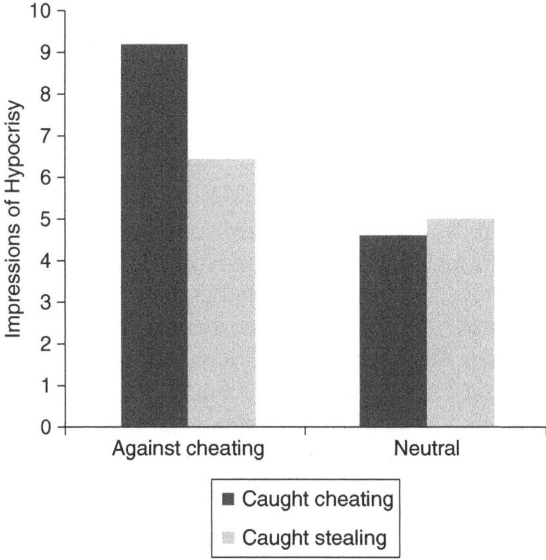

Figure 4.1 Impressions of hypocrisy towards those who are similar/dissimilar in the moral domain (Powell and Smith, 2012, Study 2)

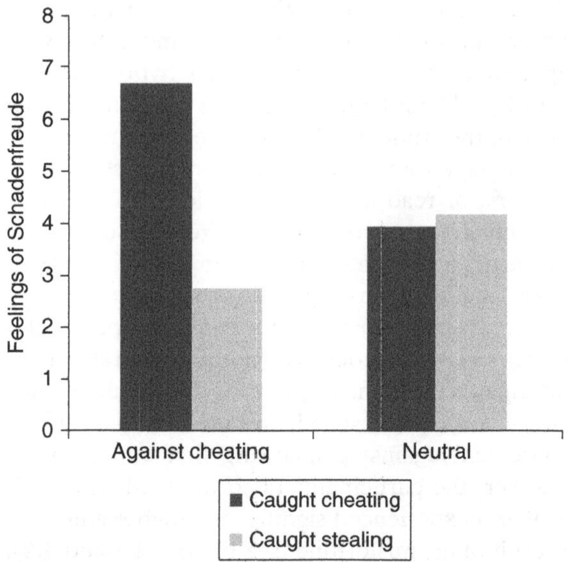

Figure 4.2 Feelings of schadenfreude towards those who are similar/dissimilar in the moral domain (Powell and Smith, 2012, Study 2)

club conditions mentioned above in terms of hypocrisy and schadenfreude, which would be predicted by Effron and Monin's (2010) work on moral licensing. In other words, making a general moral statement and then getting caught behaving immorally in another area did not lead to impressions of hypocrisy. Rather, only the student whose immoral behaviour matched his earlier moral statement was branded as a hypocrite, and his misfortune led to the highest amount of schadenfreude. Furthermore, in this study, all participants read about a person who got caught engaging in an immoral, intentional behaviour (plagiarising or stealing) where any punishment they received was undoubtedly deserved – all circumstances that are ripe for schadenfreude – and the behaviours were viewed as equally immoral when there was no additional moral overlay. But the most schadenfreude by far was expressed when the student first spoke out against plagiarising and then was caught engaging in that very same behaviour. Mediational analyses showed that the relationship between the morality/misfortune interaction and feelings of schadenfreude were significantly mediated by impressions of hypocrisy, but not by feelings of deservingness or dislike. Therefore, although deservingness can play a large part in terms of the reasons why the punishment of hypocrites is so fulfilling, it is not the only explanation.

Dislike

Hypocrites can often give an air of self-satisfied superiority while giving the appearance of being more moral than others, which can be off-putting (Shklar, 1984). In a series of studies by Monin, Sawyer and Marquez (2008), results indicated that individuals can feel threatened by someone who takes a moral stance, especially when this stance implies that they themselves are not moral. This can have a negative impact on individuals' self-image and, in turn, can lead to feelings of dislike towards the moral other. As Shelley so eloquently states, 'hypocrites are people whom we typically dislike. It would give us pleasure to expose and bring a hypocrite down a notch' (2006, p. 175). Research also would suggest that individuals are much more likely to experience schadenfreude towards a disliked other (Hareli and Weiner, 2002).

In addition, previous research suggests that when individuals are made to feel inferior, as they would if someone lorded his or her superior morality over them, they often respond with schadenfreude when the superior other suffers a downfall (Smith et al., 1996; Smith, 2000; Van Dijk et al., 2006; Smith and Kim, 2007; Leach, 2008; Smith, Theilke and Powell, Chapter 6 in this volume; Van Dijk and Ouwerkerk, Chapter 9 in this volume). Inferiority breeds resentment, hostility and envy, which are aversive, and this pleasing switch in fortunes can make the formally inferior immediately gain the moral upper hand without having to lift a finger.

Although Powell and Smith's two studies (2012) did not indicate that dislike was a significant mediator for feelings of schadenfreude, it is possible that as the participants' personal morality was not questioned or challenged, the students' initial moral stance was not off-putting enough.

Punishment of others

One possibility that was explored in an unpublished follow-up study by Powell and Smith was whether the hypocrite's active punishment of others could lead to more initial dislike towards them, which in turn could predict subsequent schadenfreude. Previous research did feature the student as a member of a student court that punished hypocrisy; however, Powell and Smith thought that by looking separately at the impact that just moralising had on impressions of hypocrisy and schadenfreude versus punishing others, it would be possible to determine the role that dislike potentially plays in the connection between hypocrisy and schadenfreude.

Although basic hypocrisy can be defined as 'saying one thing but doing another', one potential factor that could lead to especially high amounts of schadenfreude would be the extent to which the immoral individual persecuted and punished others for the same behaviour. In this particular case, hypocritical individuals have done much more than take a moral position about their own behaviour, giving the appearance of virtue; not only have they made themselves the moral standard, they have imposed this standard on others and enforced it through punishment and judgement. As a society, we tend to hold these types of hypocrites in the highest scorn – classic examples abound in politics and religion, where people made names for themselves by telling others how to behave and judging them for their sins, all the while engaging in the same sins behind closed doors. Mark Spitzer the former governor of New York who made his career busting prostitution rings only to get caught in the web of a high-priced call girl, comes to mind. Newt Gingrich was having an affair while at the same time leading a chorus of condemnation for Bill Clinton's dalliances, and the long shadow of that hypocritical act still dogs him almost twenty years later. Ted Haggard, the vocally anti-gay minister who was caught with his hand in the proverbial cookie jar, also fits the bill rather nicely, as do any prominent politicians or religious leaders who make a point of condemning all who violate specific values, but end up breaking the very rules they so loudly proclaim to enforce.

All too often, however, these enforcers of the moral standard can get caught up by their own rules. Authorities set the tone when it comes to the public's degree of moral disapproval and severity of sanctioning (Mulder, Verboon and De Cremer, 2009). This outward moralistic anger and penchant for punishment (O'Gorman, Wilson and Miller, 2005) can backfire, as others can adopt this same fervour when deciding how harshly they ought to be punished.

In the unpublished study by Powell and Smith mentioned earlier, 214 undergraduates either read about a fellow student who took a distinct moral position on plagiarising ('Well, I am a very moral person. I would never cheat or lie, particularly in regards to my academics. It really gets me mad when I see other people cheating or plagiarising. There's just something morally wrong with people who do that') or said nothing about morality. The student in question also either actively engaged in punishing others for immoral behaviour (i.e., was a member of a student court) or said nothing about the punishment of others. Participants then read the follow-up article where the student in question had been caught plagiarising. As in Powell and Smith (2012), initial dislike and impressions of morality were measured, as were subsequent deservingness, impressions of hypocrisy and schadenfreude.

There was a significant interaction for participants' ratings of the students' initial morality: results indicated that those who read about the student who moralised but did not punish others proscribed higher morality ratings to the student than those who read about the student who did not moralise and also did not punish, as expected. However, participants who read about the student who punished others rated the student as being more moral regardless of whether he mentioned having an internal belief system on the issue of plagiarism or not. This would suggest that the student's punishment of others inferred his moral stance, even if he wasn't overt about stating it – if one enforces a moral rule, one is automatically considered to have a higher sort of morality (Mulder, Verboon and De Cremer, 2009). The results also indicated that participants had significantly greater initial dislike for the student who punished others when compared to the non-punishment conditions, but that there were no effects on dislike when comparing moralisers and non-moralisers.

Perceptions of hypocrisy (see Figure 4.3) and deservingness had similar mean patterns to the earlier ratings of morality: the condition where the student did not moralise and also did not punish received low hypocrisy and deservingness ratings, and the other three conditions were equally high for both – and as with the morality ratings, the student who punished but did not moralise was perceived as being equally hypocritical and just as deserving as the student who punished and moralised. Finally, results indicated

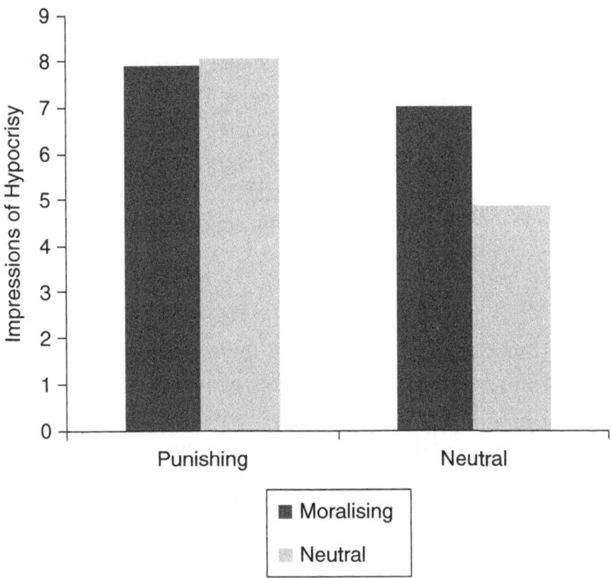

Figure 4.3 Impressions of hypocrisy towards those who punish others and those who moralise (Powell and Smith, unpublished data)

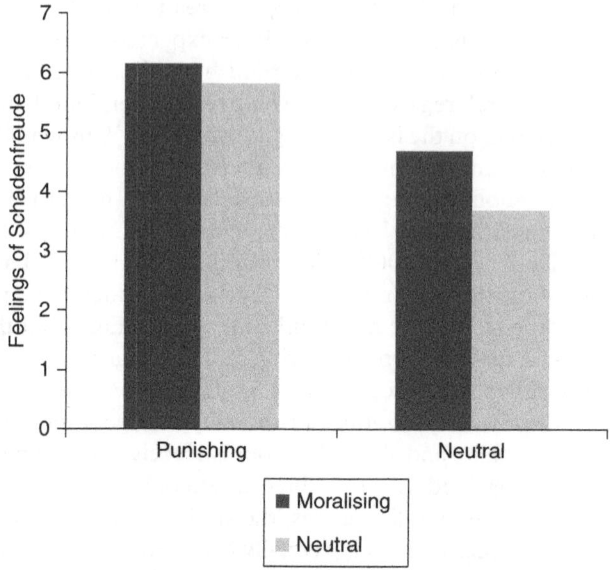

Figure 4.4 Feelings of schadenfreude towards those who punish others and those who moralise (Powell and Smith, unpublished data)

that the greatest amount of schadenfreude was experienced towards those who punished – there was no significant main effect for moralising, nor was there a significant interaction (see Figure 4.4). This would indicate that although participants perceived the student who moralised but did not punish others as both hypocritical and deserving of his misfortune – just as deserving as those who punished others – participants were happiest when the student who punished others was caught and punished himself.

Group membership

Other factors that can determine whether a person will be considered hypocritical or not include that person's group membership, as well as cultural differences in perceptions of inconsistent behaviour. Previous research has been established indicating that people tend to enjoy when misfortunes occur to disliked out-groups (Leach et al., 2003; Leach and Spears, 2004; Combs et al., 2009). Therefore, a hypocrite who is a member of an out-group is more likely to generate schadenfreude, as well as harsher sanctions. However, research on vicarious dissonance would suggest that in-group hypocrites are more likely to induce sympathy and forgiveness rather than sanctions and condemnation (Norton et al., 2003; Cooper and Hogg, 2007), and Valdesolo and DeSteno (2007) suggest that group members are often extended similar amounts of moral leniency that an individual within the group would apply to himself or herself – making allowances for others' immoral behaviour and engaging in self-justification just as if it were his or her own immoral behaviour in question. In the study by Valdesolo and DeSteno (2007), participants were more likely to rate out-group members' hypocritical behaviours as 'unfair' and were also more likely to give themselves and in-group members similarly high fairness ratings.

Conclusion

To conclude, there are numerous reasons as to why catching hypocrites in the act should lead to schadenfreude. One of the key components of hypocrisy involves perceived intentionality on the part of the hypocrite to behave immorally, which creates a sense that he or she deserved the misfortune of being caught. Initial research has established that deservingness does play a part in helping to explain why hypocrisy and schadenfreude are linked. Likewise, another component of hypocrisy involves a similarity between initial moral stance and subsequent immoral behaviour, which can create situational irony, a pleasing sense of balance and an amusing juxtaposition. Research on similarity has shown that if an individual's moral statement was in the same domain as his or her subsequent immoral actions, this led to increases in hypocrisy ratings, as well as increased schadenfreude. Finally, the tendency for hypocrites to establish their own moral superiority over others in a way that can be perceived as smug and off-putting, as well as their likelihood to punish others for immorality, can often lead to dislike, especially when the punishment of others is involved. All of these components set a well-lit stage for schadenfreude to make an appearance.

References

Allgeier, A. R., Byrne, D., Brooks, B. and Revnes, D. (1979). The waffle phenomenon: negative evaluations of those who shift attitudinally. *Journal of Applied Social Psychology* 92: 170–82.

Aronson, E., Fried, C. and Stone, J. (1991). Overcoming denial and increasing the intention to use condoms through the induction of hypocrisy. *American Journal of Public Health* 81: 1636–8.

Asch, S. E. (1946). Forming impressions of personality. *Journal of Abnormal and Social Psychology* 41: 258–90.

Associated Press (2011). Gingrich: love of country contributed to affair. *msnbc*, 9 March. Available at: www.msnbc.msn.com/id/41992152/ns/politicsdecision_2012/t/gingrich-love-country-contributed-affair.

Barden, J., Rucker, D. D. and Petty, R. E. (2005). "Saying one thing and doing another": examining the impact of event order on hypocrisy judgments of others. *Personality and Social Psychology Bulletin* 31: 1463–74.

Batson, C. D., Kobrynowicz, D., Dinnerstein, J. L., Kampf, H. C. and Wilson, A. D. (1997). In a very different voice: unmasking moral hypocrisy. *Journal of Personality and Social Psychology* 72: 1325–48.

Batson, C. D., Thompson, E. R. and Chen, H. (2002). Moral hypocrisy: addressing some alternatives. *Journal of Personality and Social Psychology* 83: 330–9.

Batson, C. D., Thompson, E. R., Seuferling, G., Whitney, H. and Strongman, J. (1999). Moral hypocrisy: appearing moral to oneself without being so. *Journal of Personality and Social Psychology* 77: 525–37.

Callan, M. J., Ellard, J. H. and Nicol, J. E. (2006). The belief in a just world and immanent value justice reasoning in adults. *Personality and Social Psychology Bulletin* 32: 1646–58.

Cialdini, R. B. (2000). *Influence: Science and Practice*, 4th edn. New York: Allyn & Bacon.

Combs, D. Y., Campbell, G., Jackson, M. and Smith, R. H. (2010). Exploring the consequences of humiliating a moral transgressor. *Basic and Applied Social Psychology* 32: 128–43.

Combs, D. Y., Powell, C. A. J., Schurtz, D. and Smith, R. H. (2009). Politics, schadenfreude, and ingroup identification: the sometimes happy thing about a poor economy and death. *Journal of Experimental Social Psychology* 45: 635–46.

Cooper, J. and Hogg, M. A. (2007). Feeling the anguish of others: a theory of vicarious dissonance. In M. P. Zanna (ed.), *Advances in Experimental Social Psychology*, Vol. XXXIX. San Diego, CA: Elsevier Academic Press, pp. 359–403.

Crisp, R. and Cowton, C. (1994). Hypocrisy and moral seriousness. *American Philosophical Quarterly* 31: 343–9.

Effron, D. A. and Monin, B. (2010). Letting people off the hook: when do good deeds excuse transgressions? *Personality and Social Psychology Bulletin* 36: 1618–34.

Feather, N. T. (2006). Deservingness and emotions: applying the structural model of deservingness to the analysis of affective reactions to outcomes. In M. Hewstone and W. Strobe (eds.), *European Review of Social Psychology*, Vol. XVII. New York: Psychology Press, pp. 38–73.

Feather, N. T. and Nairn, K. (2005). Resentment, envy, schadenfreude, and sympathy: effects of own and other's deserved or undeserved status. *Australian Journal of Psychology* 57: 87–102.

Feather, N. T. and Sherman, R. (2002). Envy, resentment, schadenfreude, and sympathy: reactions to deserved and undeserved achievement and subsequent failure. *Personality and Social Psychology Bulletin* 28: 953–61.

Frank, R. (1988). *Passions with Reason: The Strategic Role of Emotions*. New York: Norton Publishers.

Gray, K. and Wegner, D. M. (2009). Moral typecasting: divergent perceptions of moral agents and moral patients. *Journal of Personality and Social Psychology* 96: 505–20.

(2011). To escape blame, don't be a hero – be a victim. *Journal of Experimental Social Psychology* 47: 516–19.

Hamilton, V. and Hagiwara, S. (1992). Roles, responsibility, and accounts across cultures. *International Journal of Psychology* 27: 157–79.

Hareli, S. and Weiner, B. (2002). Dislike and envy as antecedents of pleasure at another's misfortune. *Motivation and Emotion* 26: 257–77.

Heider, F. (1958). *The Psychology of Interpersonal Relations*. New York: John Wiley & Sons, Inc.

Lammers, J., Stapel, D. A. and Galinsky, A. D. (2010). Power increases hypocrisy: moralising in reasoning, immorality in behavior. *Psychological Science* 21: 737–44.

Leach, C. W. (2008). Envy, inferiority, and injustice: three bases of anger about inequality. In R. H. Smith (ed.), *Envy: Theory and Research*. Oxford University Press, pp. 94–116.

Leach, C. W. and Spears, R. (2004). Intergroup schadenfreude: conditions and consequences. In C. Leach and L. Z. Tiedens (eds.), *The Social Life of Emotions*. Cambridge University Press, pp. 336–55.

Leach, C. W., Spears, R., Branscombe, N. R. and Doosje, B. (2003). Malicious pleasure: schadenfreude at the suffering of another group. *Journal of Personality and Social Psychology* 84: 932–943.

Lerner, M. J. (1980). *The Belief in the Just World: A Fundamental Delusion*. New York: Plenum.

(1987). Integrating societal and psychological rule of entitlement: the basic task of each social actor and fundamental problem for the social sciences. *Social Justice Research* 1: 107–25.

Merritt, A. C., Effron, D. A. and Monin, B. (2010). Moral self-licensing: when being good frees us to be bad. *Social and Personality Psychology Compass* 4: 344–57.

Mikula, G. (2003). Testing an attribution-of-blame model of judgments of injustice. *European Journal of Social Psychology* 33: 793–811.

Monin, B., Sawyer, P. J. and Marquez, M. J. (2008). The rejection of moral rebels: resenting those who do the right thing. *Journal of Personality and Social Psychology* 95: 76–93.

Mulder, L. B., Verboon, P. and De Cremer, D. (2009). Sanctions and moral judgments: the moderating effect of sanction severity and trust in authorities. *European Journal of Social Psychology* 39: 255–69.

Newman, J. (1986). *Fanatics and Hypocrites*. Buffalo, NY: Prometheus Books.

Norton, M. I., Monin, B., Cooper, J. and Hogg, M. A. (2003). Vicarious dissonance: attitude change from the inconsistency of others. *Journal of Personality and Social Psychology* 85: 47–62.

O'Gorman, R., Wilson, D. and Miller, R. R. (2005). Altruistic punishing and helping differ in sensitivity to relatedness, friendship, and future interactions. *Evolution and Human Behavior* 26: 375–87.

Powell, C. A. J. and Smith, R. H. (2012). Schadenfreude caused by the exposure of hypocrisy in others. *Self and Identity* 12(4): 413–31.

Shakespeare, W. (1980 [1601]). *Hamlet*. New York: Penguin Classics.

Shaver, K. G. and Drown, D. (1986). On causality, responsibility, and self-blame: a theoretical note. *Journal of Personality and Social Psychology* 50: 697–702.

Shelley, C. (2006). Hypocrisy as irony: toward a cognitive model of hypocrisy. *Metaphor and Symbol* 21: 169–90.

Shklar, J. (1984). *Ordinary Vices*. Cambridge, MA: Harvard University Press.

Smith, R. H. (2000). Assimilative and contrastive emotional reactions to upward and downward social comparisons. In L. Wheeler and J. Suls (eds.), *Handbook of Social Comparison: Theory and Research*. Norwell, MA: Kluwer Academic Publishers, pp. 173–200.

Smith, R. H. and Kim S. H. (2007). Comprehending envy. *Psychological Bulletin* 133: 46–64.

Smith, R. H., Turner, T. J., Garonzik, R., Leach, C. W., Urch-Druskat, V. and Weston, C. M. (1996). Envy and schadenfreude. *Personality and Social Psychology Bulletin* 25: 158–68.

Stone, J., Wiegand, A. W., Cooper, J. and Aronson, E. (1997). When exemplification fails: hypocrisy and the motive for self-integrity. *Journal of Personality and Social Psychology* 72: 54–65.

Szabados, B. and Soifer, E. (2004). *Hypocrisy: Ethical Investigations*. Orchard Park, NY: Broadview Press.

Tedeschi, J. T., Schlenker, B. R. and Bonoma, T. V. (1971). Cognitive dissonance: private ratiocination or public spectacle? *American Psychologist* 26: 685–95.

Tripp, T. M., Bies, R. J. and Aquino, K. (2002). Poetic justice or petty jealousy? The aesthetics of revenge. *Organizational Behavior and Human Decision Processes* 89: 966–84.

Valdesolo, P. and DeSteno, D. (2007). Moral hypocrisy: social groups and the flexibility of virtue. *Psychological Science* 18: 689–90.

Van Dijk, W. W., Ouwerkerk, J. W., Goslinga, S. and Nieweg, M. (2005). Deservingness and schadenfreude. *Cognition & Emotion* 19: 933–9.

Van Dijk, W. W., Ouwerkerk, J. W., Goslinga, S., Nieweg, M. and Gallucci, M. (2006). When people fall from grace: reconsidering the role of envy in schadenfreude. *Emotion* 6: 156–60.

Part II

Schadenfreude as a comparison-based emotion

5 The personal comparative concern in schadenfreude

Aaron Ben-Ze'ev

We all have enough strength to endure the misfortunes of others.
François de la Rochefoucauld

Schadenfreude is a perplexing emotion: on the one hand, it is pleasurable, some even argue one of the most pleasurable emotions, but on the other hand, it seems disgusting and inhumane, even sadistic, since we know we ought to be sad, rather than happy, about others' misfortunes. In order to understand such a dissonance, we should distinguish between the emotion of schadenfreude and sadistic behaviour. In both cases, someone gets pleasure from another's misfortune, but whereas schadenfreude is an *emotion* whose main concern, like that of other emotions, is a *personal comparative* concern, sadism is *behaviour* whose main concern is *deriving pleasure from deliberately inflicting pain on someone else*. Accordingly, schadenfreude is not as morally reprehensible as sadism and as the prevailing view considers it to be.

The personal comparative concern

Emotions are not theoretical detached attitudes; rather, they are interested experiences concerning the personal, and in particular the comparative, situation of the agent. Understanding something implies comparing it to different alternatives. This is true not only of intellectual reasoning, but of emotions as well. However, whereas intellectual comparisons typically express a detached and theoretical manner of comparison, emotional comparisons are made from a personal and interested perspective (see also Seip et al., Chapter 15 in this volume; Van Dijk and Ouwerkerk, Chapter 9 in this volume). An intellectual perspective sometimes attempts to overcome an emotional perspective.

The background framework against which emotional events are compared may be described as a personal baseline. The personal baseline determines the way in which we perceive our current, previous, ideal, and 'ought' states, as well as these states in other people. We can compare our current, novel situation to a different situation in which we have been or to that of significant others, such as parents, siblings, spouse, friends or important figures in our lives. This different state might be a previous actual state, an ideal state in which we desire to be or a state in which others think we ought to be. The different state of others can also be an actual state, an ideal state or a state in which we think they ought to be. Emotions are generated when a significant discrepancy between our current personal state and the compared state occurs.

The comparison of our current novel state to a previous actual state we have experienced can induce emotions such as sadness and happiness; the comparison to an ideal state is associated with disappointment, hope, fear, love, hate, sexual desire and disgust; the comparison with current states of others may generate emotions such as envy, jealousy, pity, compassion, happy-for (namely, happiness for others) and schadenfreude; and the comparison with normative states is connected to pride, shame, guilt and regret. Some emotions are related to several types of comparisons at the same time. For example, anger and gratitude often involve a comparison to a previous state and to an 'ought' state (namely, the situation in which we think we ought to be). From an emotional viewpoint, comparative evaluations often override evaluations concerning our absolute position.

The importance of the personal comparative concern in emotions comes clearly to the fore in cases where this concern is sufficiently powerful so as to make those who are objectively worse off feel happier than those in a better position. An illuminating example in this regard comes from a study that found that bronze medallists in the Olympic Games tend to be happier than silver medallists (Medvec, Madey and Gilovich, 1995). The suggested explanation for this surprising result is that the most compelling alternative for the silver medallists is winning gold, whereas for the bronze medallists, it is finishing without any medal at all. The silver medallists focused on having almost won gold because there is a qualitative difference between coming in first and any other outcome, and this exalted status seems to have been only one small step away. The silver medallists also finished only one step from winning bronze, but such a downward comparison does not involve much of a change in status. In contrast, bronze medallists are likely to focus their imagination downward, as there is a categorical difference between finishing third and finishing fourth. The situation of the silver medallists is similar to that of an individual who misses out on the jackpot, but wins a modest sum for coming close. The prize provides some enjoyment, but the knowledge of having just missed the jackpot is bound to come up from time to time and ruin otherwise joyful moments.

There is evidence that when people lose money, they still express joy and schadenfreude if the other person loses even more money than they do. Interestingly, when they actually win money, but the other person wins even more, they express less joy and more envy. Even a loss may seem like a gain when compared with another's greater loss, and a gain may seem like a loss when compared with another's greater gain (Dvash, 2011).

The personal comparative concern is not unique to humans and can be found even in capuchin monkeys (Brosnan and De Waal, 2003; Van Wolkenten, Brosnan and De Waal, 2007). Rudimentary comparative processes like this and a sense of fairness may even be found in dogs (Range et al., 2009; see also Dvash, 2011).

Schadenfreude

Although schadenfreude is a common emotion, many languages do not have a special term for this emotion. In fact, Maurice Blondel attacks the Germans for having this term, which he claims is 'without equivalent in any language' (Blondel, 1947, p. 7). I believe that such an attack is unjustified and the absence of an English equivalent for the German *Schadenfreude* is not an indication that this emotion is less common in English-speaking societies (see also Van Dijk and Ouwerkerk, Chapter 1 in this volume). The explanation for the scarcity of a special term for this emotion in many languages is probably the consequence of societies' desire to repress the presence of this emotion.

Many people consider schadenfreude to be the worst emotion. This extreme negative evaluation can lead to a collective attempt to repress this attitude. There are, of course, other attitudes, such as cruelty and sadism, that are morally worse than schadenfreude, but nevertheless have a special word denoting them. These attitudes, however, do not involve a moral predicament since their negative moral evaluation is not disputed and most people are able to avoid them. The case of schadenfreude is different as it is a very common emotion whose presence is not affected by its perceived negative character. Hence, there is a tendency to repress public acknowledgment of this attitude. Such collective repression cannot persist forever, since more and more people now acknowledge the prevalence of this emotion. Perhaps, too, there is a growing awareness that schadenfreude is not as morally reprehensible as it is usually considered (see Van Dijk and Ouwerkerk, Chapter 1 in this volume). This is what I would like to argue and I will do so by indicating the differences between the common emotion of schadenfreude and the cruelty in sadistic behaviour.

In describing schadenfreude, two features are obvious: our pleasure and the other's misfortune. These features express the personal comparative essence of schadenfreude: the fact that the other is in a worse situation makes our situation somewhat better (Van Dijk and Ouwerkerk, Chapter 9 in this volume). These features describe a significant conflict between our positive evaluation of the situation and the negative evaluation of the other person. A major reason for being pleased at the misfortune of another person is that this person's misfortune may somehow improve our comparative position. In calculating this position, the misfortune of others appears on the credit side. In this sense, schadenfreude is close to envy: in both, the comparison of our fortune with that of another person is crucial. However, contrary to envy, in schadenfreude we occupy the superior position. The personal comparative concern is significant in all emotions, but more so in those that, like envy and schadenfreude, are concerned with fortunes of others (Cikara and Fiske, Chapter 10 in this volume; Smith, Thielke and Powell, Chapter 6 in this volume; Van de Ven, Chapter 7 in this volume).

The role of the personal comparative concern in evoking schadenfreude is evident in many everyday cases (Ben-Ze'ev, 2000; Smith et al., 2009). For example, when driving north, if we see that the southbound traffic is jammed and is hardly moving, we are often pleased that others and not ourselves are travelling in that direction. Kant argues that 'in stormy weather, when comfortably seated in our warm, cozy parlor, we may enjoy speaking of those at sea, for it heightens our own feeling of comfort and happiness' (Kant, 1924, p. 218; see also Reid, 1788, p. 567). In both cases our situation is not actually improved and our gain is merely a psychological comparative one, indicating that there are people now who are in a worst situation than ours. There is indeed neurological evidence for the participation of the reward system in the experience of schadenfreude (Cikara and Fiske, Chapter 10 in this volume; Dvash, 2011).

Our personal gain while experiencing schadenfreude is mainly a psychological comparative gain and not necessarily an absolute or actual one. It is a kind of symbolic and sometimes even illusory gain, as it actually does not change the agent's situation. Consider, for example, the case in which someone has been elected to a position I desire and after a while it is clear that he is not fulfilling his duties successfully. His failure, however, does not imply that I will be given the position. If such an implication is present in my pleasure, then it is likely to be illusory. Similarly, if Tom divorces his wife and marries Rachel who then leaves him, Tom's first wife may be pleased about this, but this pleasure is no more than a psychological benefit since her own romantic life is unlikely to be improved.

Three additional characteristics

In order to take account of the full extent of the impact of the personal comparative concern in schadenfreude, it is not enough to characterise it as including our pleasure and the other's misfortune. I have suggested three additional typical characteristics: (a) the other person is perceived to *deserve* the misfortune; (b) the misfortune is relatively *minor*; and (c) we are *passive* in generating the other's misfortune (Ben-Ze'ev, 2000).

A central feature of schadenfreude is the belief that the other person *deserves* his misfortune (Feather, Chapter 3 in this volume; Portmann, Chapter 2 in this volume; Van Dijk and Ouwerkerk, Chapter 1 and Chapter 9 in this volume; Van Dijk et al., 2005). For example, when stuck in a traffic jam, should a driver pass us by driving on the hard shoulder, our anger will be replaced by pleasure when we see a policeman giving the driver a ticket. The belief that the other person deserves his misfortune expresses our assumption that justice has been done and enables us to be pleased in a situation where we are required to be sad. Moreover, this belief presents us as moral people who do not want to hurt other people. It should be clear that such deservingness judgments are done from the personal comparative perspective of the agent.

The more deserved the misfortune is, the more justified is the pleasure. A study of people's attitude towards the downfall of those in high positions shows that the fall was greeted with positive approval when the fall was seen to be deserved, but reactions were negative when the fall was seen to be undeserved. Deservingness was one of the key variables that affected reactions in these cases (Feather, 1996; Feather, Chapter 3 in this volume; Smith et al., 2009). Indeed, we often hear people who delight in others' misfortune saying that 'There is a God in Heaven' or that 'There is justice in the world'.

St Thomas Aquinas, who claims that one of the pleasures of the saints in Heaven will be to observe the torments of the damned in Hell, also emphasises the role of deservingness in the comparative concern underlying schadenfreude. He claims that 'everything is known the more for being compared with its contrary ... Therefore in order that the happiness of the saints may be more delightful to them and that they may render more copious thanks to God for it, they are allowed to see perfectly the suffering of the damned' (*The Summa Theologica*: supplement to Question XCIV: article 1; cited in Portmann, 2000). No doubt, Aquinas' argument gives us all a special incentive to achieve sainthood.

When we assume that a person's misfortune is deserved, we receive some kind of moral confirmation for this emotion, which at first seems morally unfounded. In the same vein, when we are happy about the failure of the 'bad guys' in a movie, we think that justice has been done. We identify with the 'good guys' so that the failure of the 'bad guys' becomes a success for our side. The assumption that justice has been done is also typical of comedies. The normal response of the audience to the happy ending typical of comedies is the normative judgment 'This is how it should be' (Frye, 1957, p. 167). In these situations, the assumption that the object deserves his misfortune is compatible with the belief that desire confers value on its object: the very fact of being pleased at someone's misfortune implies our belief that this misfortune is somehow deserved.

In light of the role of deservingness in schadenfreude, we may say that the gratification we feel when our beloved suffers and longs for us when we are away does not come from pleasure in another's misfortune, but from an awareness of the beloved's love for us even when we are not actually together.

Kant's description of schadenfreude is compatible with the view suggested here: 'Our pleasure in the misfortune of another is not direct. We may rejoice, for example, in a man's misfortunes, because he was haughty, rich and selfish; for man loves to preserve equality' (Kant, 1924, p. 220). Aristotle, who describes envy as 'pain felt at deserved good fortune', argues that the feeling – which has no name – of the person who rejoices at misfortunes involves 'rejoicing over undeserved ill fortune' (*Eudemian Ethics*: Aristotle, 1984, 1233b20). On this point, I differ from Aristotle. Unlike Aristotle, who characterises envy as involving a negative evaluation of the *other's deserved good fortune*, I believe that the focus of concern in envy is *our own undeserved misfortune*. And also unlike Aristotle, who describes schadenfreude as involving a positive evaluation of the other's *undeserved* misfortune, I consider it to involve a positive evaluation of the other's *deserved* misfortune.

It is not clear at what age schadenfreude actually emerges. One way of discovering this is to examine when a child begins to refer to the issue of deservingness while laughing at something. It seems to me that at quite an early age, children are able to say that they are pleased at the misfortunes suffered by the villain in a movie because he deserves his misfortune. The issue of deservingness is what distinguishes laughing at someone who slips on a banana peel from schadenfreude.

The second element in the overall characterisation of schadenfreude that needs clarification concerns the *minor* nature of the misfortune. This characteristic is closely associated with the personal comparative concern prevailing in schadenfreude. Comparison is possible when the two parties are not too far apart – when they are considered to belong to the same comparative framework. Accordingly, schadenfreude is concerned with small differences. This is compatible with my claim that the personal gain in schadenfreude is often symbolic and, in any case, not a considerable one.

In the event of a severe misfortune, the element of deservingness is missing. We do not usually perceive the people around us as deserving of severe misfortune. These people may deserve to be punished because they dare to be more successful than we are, but this does not justify severe misfortune befalling them or those near and dear to them.

When an event no longer constitutes a minor misfortune, but involves substantial suffering, schadenfreude gives way to pity. For example, should our noisy, inconsiderate and snobbish neighbour have his new car scratched, we may feel some pleasure; however, if his daughter becomes seriously ill, we are more likely to feel compassion or pity, not schadenfreude.

When the other person suffers a real disaster, the personal comparative concern is absent. When this person suffers a slight misfortune that is irrelevant to our own fortune, sympathy is likely to be generated. Sympathy does not necessarily presuppose a personal comparative concern. In saying that pity and sympathy do not necessarily involve personal comparative concern, I do not imply that no comparison is made while we experience these emotions. All types of meaning are relational and hence involve some kind of comparison. However, the personal comparative concern discussed here refers to a more profound comparison: that in which our self-esteem is affected by the comparison (Van Dijk and Ouwerkerk, Chapter 9 in this volume).

Envy, which also involves a personal comparative concern, is similar to schadenfreude in terms of small differences. When the other's superior situation is not comparable to our inferior situation, envy may turn into admiration. Admiration is close to pride and both are related to happy-for. When comparison is meaningless, schadenfreude or envy do not typically arise, or at least they are not intense. In great differences, where we cannot conceive of a way to bridge the gap, we accept the situation and hence the differences are of little emotional significance.

The third element is that schadenfreude is associated with the *passivity* of the agent who is enjoying the situation (see also Leach, Spears and Manstead, Chapter 13 in this volume; Portmann, Chapter 2 in this volume; Seip et al., Chapter 15 in this volume; Van Dijk and Ouwerkerk, Chapter 1 in this volume). In happy-for, we are ready to be personally involved in bringing about and sustaining the other's good fortune. Such readiness is typically absent in schadenfreude. An active personal involvement is contrary to the rules of fair competition; it would present us as deliberately harming the other, and hence as not being really superior. It may also be considered an offence; although the other person might deserve misfortune, or even punishment, we lack the authority to impose it. Typically, one of the greater contributions to the pleasure we take in others' misfortune is the feeling that the failure of our competitor is not due to our own wicked behaviour, but to inexorable fate. It is as if justice has been done in the spirit of the Talmudic saying: 'The tasks of the righteous get done by others.' This is a kind of unsolicited gift. Because of our passivity in schadenfreude, it is likely that this emotion is not very important in terms of the choices we make or the way in which we conduct our life, even though it is quite common. Elster claims that 'many who find a titillating pleasure in a friend's misfortune would be horrified at the thought of going out of their way to provoke it. Doing so by omission or abstention might be easier' (Elster, 1995, p. 256; see also Portmann, 2000).

Objections to the proposed description

The suggested importance of the personal comparative concern in schadenfreude could be questioned on two major grounds: (a) the other's misfortune is often substantial and hence the comparative concern is not at the heart of this emotion; and (b) the other's misfortune is often insignificant or irrelevant to our relationship with this person and hence the comparative concern is once again not central. The first objection states that the subject–object difference is too big for a comparison to take place, while the second assumes that because this difference is insignificant, it also precludes a comparison that can generate schadenfreude. When discussing these objections, we should bear in mind that in characterising typical cases, some exceptions are expected; it should, however, be determined whether the above objections refer to exceptions or to typical common cases.

Admittedly, in some circumstances the other's misfortune is grave, but it is still not significantly graver than that caused by this person to other people – especially to ourselves and those related to us. One may be pleased by the murder of a brutal dictator, but this murder is not too grave in comparison to what the dictator did to other people. Thus, many Romanians were pleased when Nicolae Ceauşescu was executed, because such a murder seemed well-deserved given what he did to his people.

Similarly, the infidelity of Kate's husband Richard might fill Inga with joy, since Kate used to be Inga's own husband's lover. Kate may suffer a great deal because of Richard's infidelity, and Inga might know it; nevertheless, in enjoying this event, Inga thinks that justice has been done and that Kate's suffering resembles her own, thus putting them on an equal footing. In such cases the other's misfortune may be substantial, but it is not much greater than what used to be, or might still be, our own misfortune. Here the punishment also fits, and in no way exceeds, the crime and we can continue to believe that justice has been done (Ortony, Clore and Collins, 1988, p. 104).

There are also cases in which the other's misfortune is severe in light of every plausible comparison and therefore it is preferable to classify these cases as pathological cases rather than typical cases of schadenfreude. The following are two such real examples. A mother whose son was killed in the army told me that before his death they had been regarded as a very happy family that had suffered no misfortune. When people came to visit them after her son's death, she felt that some of them were satisfied that finally her family had also experienced some misfortune. This is a pathological, rather than a typical, case of schadenfreude, since a child's death is the most severe misfortune that a parent can suffer. Another such example is of a man whose wife had an affair. As a result, they divorced, the wife married her lover and, shortly afterwards, gave birth to a son. A few years later when the child developed cancer, the man expressed pleasure that his ex-wife had been punished. This is also a pathological case, since not only is the wife's misfortune far too severe, but the misfortune is shared by an innocent child.

The second type of objection to the major role attributed to the comparative concern in schadenfreude refers to the insignificance or irrelevance of the other's misfortune. Examples of insignificant misfortunes are cases in which people slip on a banana peel without hurting themselves, spill tea over their companion or lose money but still have more than we have. Examples of irrelevant misfortunes are cases in which a corrupt leader of another country is arrested or when we see someone else getting a parking ticket. Both types of cases do not contain rivalry or an improvement in our comparative position. They have, however, symbolic importance in demonstrating some failure on the part of the other person and hence our satisfaction in occupying a better situation. Such insignificant and irrelevant failures might not justify elation, but there is no denying that some pleasure is felt in these situations. This is a pauper's joy. Joy over insignificant or irrelevant misfortune may also express humour rather than the emotion of schadenfreude.

As in other emotions, typical cases of schadenfreude consist of a subtle equilibrium of different characteristics. When the relative weight of one characteristic is changed, changes in the weight of other characteristics can be expected. If a cruel criminal suffers a substantive misfortune, one can still be pleased with this misfortune since the criminal deserves it, and in comparison with the crimes he committed, the misfortune is not too grave. In this case, the presence of a graver misfortune is made acceptable by the overriding weight of the issue of desert. This greater weight may also make the comparative concern less important. If a stranger pushes an old lady and then falls into a mud puddle, we may be pleased at his misfortune mainly because the issue of desert is so central. When it is less significant, other characteristics may be changed as well: for example, the misfortune would have to be less severe. When the misfortune is not severe, we might be actively involved in the other's misfortune and still be pleased by it. When the relative weight of one characteristic is too great, the nature of the emotion in question may be changed as well; as suggested, when the misfortune is too grave, schadenfreude may turn into pity or another type of joy.

Schadenfreude and sadism

Some people identify schadenfreude with sadism, arguing that the difference between them is negligible and that schadenfreude is a kind of sadism involving hate and cruelty (Stein, 1992; Whitman and Alexander, 1968). Although schadenfreude often has such a public image, this is true only of extreme and atypical cases that are different from the typical schadenfreude, which is based upon the personal comparative concern.

It is a common distorting inclination to take extreme cases as representing a whole category, whereas in fact they are quite rare. The unique characteristic of schadenfreude is the pleasure over someone's misfortune. An extreme manifestation of this pleasure is the sadistic enjoyment associated with cruel activities such as torture. It is obvious that this is not the typical case of schadenfreude. Many, if not all, people have experienced schadenfreude, but only a few have experienced sadistic pleasure associated with torture or the wish to torture someone. When we want to induce pleasure by watching movies, we choose to see comedies in which the other's misfortune is minor and not tragedies in which the other's misfortune is grave.

Common cases of schadenfreude are fundamentally different from sadism, hate or cruelty. Unlike schadenfreude, sadism is a type of behaviour and not an emotional state. The personal comparative concern, which is central to schadenfreude, has no place in sadism. The three additional typical characteristics of schadenfreude – namely, the dominant role of deservingness, the minor nature of the misfortune and our passivity – are absent from sadism.

In sadism, the issue of deservingness is not dominant at all: the other person is typically not perceived to deserve the misfortune and if such a perception is nevertheless present, it is not a dominant element. Personal egoistic pleasure, rather than deservingness, is central to sadism. The difference between schadenfreude and sadism is also evident in regard to the nature of the misfortune: in schadenfreude it is minor, while in sadism it is substantial. When the misfortune is severe, the personal comparative concern disappears and with it schadenfreude. Another difference concerns the subject's role: unlike typical schadenfreude, sadism involves the active role of the subject in generating the misfortune – in other words, the sadist is responsible for the suffering. The satisfaction in schadenfreude is different; it is mainly due to our momentary psychological superior position. This superiority does not require us to play an active role in bringing about the object's misfortune.

All these differences suggest that sadism is substantially different from schadenfreude. These differences are expressed in the fact that sadism alone involves cruelty. Cruelty is not an essential factor that makes us enjoy another person's misfortune; a sense of just deserts or competitive concern matter much more.

It may be argued that schadenfreude is related to hate and anger. Again, it seems that if such a relation is present, it is not central in typical cases. Hate usually requires a negative evaluation of another person's whole personality and anger involves the negative evaluation of another person's specific act. Schadenfreude seldom requires either. Its focus of concern is not the negation of another person's personality or activity, but confirmation of this person's bothersome situation. No doubt, if those we hate or with whom we are angry should fail, we will be glad – or at least not unhappy – but schadenfreude is not limited to these cases. On the contrary, it is often directed towards those with whom we are associated or whom we appreciate – hence, the comparative concern can be activated. In assuming that typical cases of schadenfreude involve minor rather than substantial misfortunes, I am not claiming that some people do not enjoy the great suffering of others. However, such feelings usually reflect hate or sadism rather than schadenfreude.

Moral value

The general prevailing view is that schadenfreude is morally evil (see also Van Dijk and Ouwerkerk, Chapter 1 in this volume). Thus, schadenfreude is often considered to be less acceptable than envy, which is regarded as a deadly sin. It would appear to be morally more perverse to be pleased with another person's misfortune than to be displeased with another person's good fortune. The sorrow implicit in envy is perceived to be directed at someone whose situation is generally good; hence, such a sorrow can scarcely hurt the other person. The joy implicit in schadenfreude is perceived to be directed at someone who is already in a bad situation; thus, the presence of schadenfreude serves only to worsen the situation. Accordingly, the presence of joy in schadenfreude is seen as morally worse than the presence of sorrow in envy. Indeed, Arthur Schopenhauer argues that to feel envy is human, but to enjoy other people's misfortunes is diabolical. For him, schadenfreude is the worst trait in human nature and he considers it to be closely related to cruelty (Schopenhauer, 1840/1965; see also Portmann, 2000).

Such severe moral criticism can be challenged. To begin with, I have indicated that we should distinguish between schadenfreude and cruelty as expressed, for example, in sadism or when the other person experiences great suffering. Accordingly, schadenfreude does not indicate a vicious character. In contrast to sadism, the delight in schadenfreude does not stem from the suffering of another person, but from our advantageous comparative position (Van Dijk and Ouwerkerk, Chapter 9 in this volume). Indeed, the most severe criticism of schadenfreude comes from those who fail to distinguish it from cruelty and sadism.

Portmann discusses various types of moral criticisms that are mounted of schadenfreude and indicates that despite such criticism, schadenfreude is a natural phenomenon that is not diabolic. The moral problem that schadenfreude poses is that taking pleasure in the suffering of another person appears to threaten the most basic ethical tenet of all: to do good and to avoid evil (Portmann, 2000).

The moral flaw in schadenfreude is bound up with the personal comparative concern and not with cruelty. Indeed, when this concern is not present, as when the other's misfortune is substantial, the emotion is absent as well. Since this concern is natural for humans, schadenfreude should also be considered as natural. Schadenfreude even seems to have some moral justification: it represents the right to be glad when our comparative position improves, although one might condemn the way in which we calculate the improvement in our position – that is to say, one might condemn the comparative concern. Moreover, owing to our passivity in schadenfreude, its negative aspects are less significant. This passivity reduces the danger of actually harming the object.

Schadenfreude is not a public mocking intended to humiliate someone; it is typically a private enjoyment lacking any element of severe mocking or humiliation. Moreover, it is not concerned with those in an inferior position to us, but rather with those who are basically similar to us. Accordingly, Rabbi Jonah of Gerona, the thirteenth-century moralist, argues that mocking the poor, which is overt blasphemy, is a more grievous sin than schadenfreude, which causes no injury by deed or speech (Harvey, 1992).

The important role that deservingness plays in schadenfreude implies that this emotion can be found only in people who are sensitive to moral considerations. People who are unable to distinguish deserved from undeserved situations cannot be pleased at deserved misfortune. Those who are pleased at the misfortune of others are not indifferent towards the person suffering the misfortune or towards misfortune in general; on the contrary, they are sensitive to misfortunes. They believe that this misfortune is deserved and in the long run may even reduce undeserved misfortunes, thus making the world a more just place in which to live.

The moral evaluation of schadenfreude should be determined in light of the following major factors: (a) the extent of the other's misfortune; (b) the extent of our involvement in bringing about this misfortune; and (c) the extent of the justification we attach to the other's misfortune. It has been suggested that in typical cases of schadenfreude the first two factors are marginal: the other's misfortune is minor and our involvement is minimal. Concerning the third factor, cases of schadenfreude involve our belief that justice has been done. All this implies that typical cases of schadenfreude are not strongly negative from a moral viewpoint; they are no worse than many other emotions. The greater the extent of the first two factors and the less justified the other's misfortune is, the more negative is the moral evaluation that should be attached to schadenfreude. Schadenfreude is not a virtue; however, it is also not a vice – at least not a grave one.

In light of the above considerations, doubts should be raised concerning the moral comparison of envy and schadenfreude. Although the conventional view suggests that schadenfreude is much worse than envy, it is doubtful whether this view adequately represents our moral codes and behaviour. It is indicative that envy, but not schadenfreude, is included in the traditional Christian list of the seven deadly sins (in addition to greed, sloth, wrath, lust, gluttony and pride); some even consider envy as the worst evil. Moreover, if schadenfreude addresses minor misfortunes, if we believe that justice has been done and if we are passive in eliciting the misfortune, then the moral justification of schadenfreude is no weaker than that associated with envy. It seems that the conventional view, which condemns schadenfreude more strongly than envy, stems from taking cruelty, sadism and hate as prototypical cases of this emotion. We have seen that this view is mistaken. Moreover, since schadenfreude is usually more transient than envy, its moral damage is often less evident.

References

Aristotle (1984). *The Complete Works of Aristotle: The Revised Oxford Translation* (edited by J. Barnes). Princeton University Press.

Ben-Ze'ev, A. (2000). *The Subtlety of Emotions.* Cambridge, MA: MIT Press.

Blondel, M. (1947). *Lutte pour la civilisation et philosophie de la paix*, 2nd edn. Paris: Flammarion.

Brosnan, S. F. and De Waal, F. B. (2003). Monkeys reject unequal pay. *Nature* 425: 297–9.

Dvash, J. (2011). The neural mechanism underlying competitive 'fortune of others' emotions: an fMRI study. Doctoral dissertation, University of Haifa.

Elster, J. (1995). *The Cement of Society: A Study of Social Order*. Cambridge University Press.

Feather, N. T. (1996). Values, deservingness, and attitudes toward high achievers: research on tall poppies. In C. Seligman, J. M. Olson and M. P. Zanna (eds.), *The Psychology of Values: The Ontario Symposium*. Hillsdale: Erlbaum.

Frye, N. (1957). *Anatomy of Criticism*. Princeton University Press.

Harvey, W. Z. (1992). A note on schadenfreude and Proverbs 17:5. *Iyyun* 41: 357–9.

Kant, I. (1924). *Lectures on Ethics*. New York: Harper.

Medvic, V. H., Madey, S. F. and Gilovich, T. (1995). When less is more: counterfactual thinking and satisfaction among Olympic medalists. *Journal of Personality and Social Psychology* 69: 603–10.

Ortony, A., Clore, G. L. and Collins, A. (1988). *The Cognitive Structure of Emotions*. Cambridge University Press.

Portmann, J. (2000). *When Bad Things Happen to Other People*. London: Routledge.

Range, F., Horn, L., Viranyi, Z. and Huber, L. (2009). The absence of reward induces inequity aversion in dogs. *Proceedings of the National Academy of Sciences* 106(1): 340–5.

Reid, T. (1967 [1788]). Essays on the active powers of man. In W. Hamilton (ed.), *Philosophical Works*. Hildesheim: Georg Olms.

Schopenhauer, A. (1965 [1840]). *On the Basis of Morality*. Indianapolis: Bobbs-Merrill.

Smith, R. H., Powell, C. A. J., Combs, D. J. Y. and Schurtz, D. R. (2009). Exploring the when and why of schadenfreude. *Social and Personality Psychology* 3: 530–46.

Stein, R. (1992). Schadenfreude: a reply to Ben-Ze'ev. *Iyyun* 41: 83–92.

Van Dijk, W. W., Ouwerkerk, J. W., Goslinga, S. and Nieweg, M. (2005). Deservingness and schadenfreude. *Cognition & Emotion* 19: 933–9.

Van Wolkenten, M., Brosnan, S. F. and De Waal, F. (2007). Inequity responses of monkeys modified by effort. *Proceedings of the National Academy of Sciences* 104: 18854–9.

Whitman, R. and Alexander, J. (1968). On gloating. In C. W. Socarides (ed.), *The World of Emotions*. New York: International University Press.

6 Empirical challenges to understanding the role of envy in schadenfreude

Richard H. Smith, Stephen M. Thielke, and Caitlin A. J. Powell

In this chapter we discuss how envy and schadenfreude relate to each other. While at first glance it may seem straightforward to document, characterize, and quantify their association, there are several key methodological challenges in exploring such questions and, in particular, defining, measuring, and operationalizing both phenomena. We first document the link between schadenfreude and envy in literary and philosophical traditions. Then we examine empirical research around them, pointing out the discrepancies between different approaches and sources of evidence. We highlight challenges in the definition and formulation of both terms. We find that in previous research the difference between benign and malicious envy has largely been overlooked and that malicious envy has been variably mischaracterized, leading to unjustified claims about the lack of association between envy and schadenfreude. After discussing further difficulties in successfully manipulating envy and in conceptualizing and measuring both emotions, we offer suggestions for future research.

Literary and philosophical traditions

If we think of literary and philosophical representations of the nature of envy, claims that envy can cause schadenfreude when the envied person suffers come as no surprise. Take Melville's character, Sergeant Claggart, who envies the handsome, happy, and innocent sailor, Billy Budd (Melville, 1924/1962). This is no garden-variety envy as it is laced with ill will, and its source seems to be a sickly, painful malady lodged at the center of Claggart's being. Although Billy has done nothing to deserve Claggart's ill will and is loved by most of Billy's fellow crew members, Claggart schemes to have Billy falsely accused of mutiny. Claggart is both engineer and witness to Billy's misfortune, and delights in it. As Melville outlines in uncommon subtle detail, Claggart's envy is the source of his malice, the goad for his efforts to sabotage Billy Budd, and the basis for his satisfaction when Billy suffers. Even though Claggart's envy is unconscious, it is integral to Melville's narrative. Claggart is not a sadist, insofar as he does not derive pleasure from inflicting pain on others generally (see Ben-Ze'ev, Chapter 5 in this volume, for a discussion on sadism), and we must appreciate envy's power to make sense of his malicious actions.

There are countless other examples from classic literature, such as Shakespeare's Iago and Cassius, both of whose envy lead them to bring about the destruction of the individuals they envy, and a satisfaction at the event (Shakespeare, 2008). They perform cruel or morally repugnant acts, but they are not sadists. A familiar contemporary example is the fictionalized character of Salieri in Peter Schaffer's play *Amadeus* (Shaffer, 2001). Schaffer used his creative license to imagine Salieri's envy-inspired orchestration Mozart's death. In this case and in the others, envy for the object of schadenfreude is the common theme, explicitly stated or easily inferred. Exactly because these literary creations are shown to feel envy, not only do we expect them to feel pleased if the object of their envy suffers, but we even expect them to be inclined to *cause* the suffering, usually in some secretive fashion (but see Ben-Ze'ev, 2000 and Chapter 5 in this volume for a discussion on the passive nature of most cases of schadenfreude). In any event, we would never expect the enviers to sympathize with the object of envy. These literary cases work as literature because they evoke core human sentiments: the motivations of the enviers are, while extreme, within the boundaries of normal human experience, not the perversions of sadistic sociopaths. When we realize that envy underlies their motives, we can make sense of these motives.

Philosophical traditions reinforce this rich and steady literary heritage and portray envy as a potent, natural reason for experiencing schadenfreude. Both Plato (2006) and Aristotle expressly linked envy with schadenfreude. Aristotle claimed that "the man who is delighted by others' misfortunes is identical with the man who envies others' prosperity. For anyone who is pained by the occurrence or existence of a given thing must be pleased by that thing's non-existence or destruction" (quoted in Griffin, 1931, p. 78). In other words, it follows logically and naturally that the pain of envy will be pleasantly relieved by diminishment of the envied object, even its *elimination*. Kant summed this up in the claim that envy "aims, at least in terms of one's wishes, at destroying others' good fortune" (Kant, 1797/1999, p. 459). Spinoza added another element to the equation by emphasizing the ill will inherent in envy and linking it with schadenfreude: "Envy is nothing but hate, insofar as it is considered so to dispose a man that he is glad at another's ill fortune and saddened by his good fortune" (1883, p. 24). Part of the philosophical tradition suggests, in fact, that one essential constituent of envy is the wish to undo the rival's advantage (D'Arms and Kerr, 2008). Envy-related experiences without this competitive desire or motivation are more akin to simple longing, as might be found in the desire for a high-status consumer good, without identifying any individual who possesses it (see Sundie, Chapter 8 in this volume). Although successfully bringing down a rival is not commensurate with enjoying another person's misfortune, these experiences are strongly connected in a competitive framework: simultaneously the rival is defeated, the envier triumphs, the rival suffers, and the envier feels pleasure. Therefore, schadenfreude naturally and almost by definition follows envy.

In sum, based on this legacy of literary imagination and philosophical thinking, we should expect that if someone envies another person, he or she would experience pleasure if that envied person suffers. Of course, this is not to claim that schadenfreude should *only* arise from envy (see Cikara and Fiske, Chapter 10 in this volume). For instance, the misfortunes of villains or norm violators who richly deserve their suffering because of their unacceptable actions should also produce schadenfreude, as countless tales from many literary and film traditions delineate. Furthermore, the fact of this cultural tradition linking envy with schadenfreude does not imply that the nature of this link lacks complexities. The best of these cultural examples exemplify these complexities. As we argue below, envy, as a compound, blended (and often disguised) emotion, usually contains ingredients that are closely related to deservingness and other predictors that fit common culturally recognized plot lines. In our view, this creates significant conceptual and methodological challenges that cannot be ignored if we are to make confident inferences from empirical work (for a discussion on some of these challenges, see Feather, Chapter 3 in this volume). We think it unwise to discredit prematurely the wisdom of the robust cultural tradition indicating that envy predictably generates schadenfreude if the envied person suffers. We believe that this tradition sets a high bar for empirical work that might counter it.

Empirical research on envy and schadenfreude

Does the social science research consistently confirm the cultural portrayals of how envy induces schadenfreude? Surprisingly, it does not. In contrast to research on other factors such as deservingness (for a review, see Feather, Chapter 3 this volume), the notion that envy precedes or is associated with schadenfreude has uneven empirical backing. Following an initial study by Smith and others (Smith et al., 1996) and a replication

(Brigham et al., 1997), of eleven subsequent published studies of which we are aware, five have found strong, direct support (Krizan and Johar, 2012; Sundie et al., 2009; Takahashi et al., 2009; Van Dijk et al., 2005; Van Dijk et al., 2006), two have found strong, indirect support (Cikara, Botvinick, and Fiske, 2011; Cikara and Fiske, 2012), while four have not (Feather and Nairn, 2005; Feather and Sherman, 2002; Hareli and Weiner, 2002; Leach and Spears, 2008). This inconsistency is puzzling: how could such a seemingly strong, intuitive link between envy and schadenfreude fail to enjoy highly reliable empirical support? We first address definitional challenges, then discuss issues of experimental manipulation.

Definitional challenges

Both envy and schadenfreude are concepts that at first glance seem intuitively obvious or even visceral, yet upon closer scrutiny prove challenging to define and measure. With regard to envy, several problems with definition affect how one should understand its relation to schadenfreude (e.g., Cohen-Charash, 2009; Leach, 2008; Miceli and Castelfranchi, 2007; Smith and Kim, 2007), notably the difference between benign and malicious envy (Van de Ven, Zeelenberg, and Pieters, 2009; see also Van de Ven, Chapter 7 in this volume). Regarding schadenfreude, it is challenging to distinguish the pleasure at another's real misfortune from the wish for another's misfortune and from efforts to create that misfortune. We will address each of these concepts separately.

Definitions of envy

In a recent review of research and thinking on envy, Smith and Kim offered this definition of envy: "An unpleasant, often painful emotion, characterized by feelings of inferiority, hostility and resentment caused by an awareness of a desired attribute enjoyed by another person or group of persons" (2007, p. 46). The features of this definition fit the traditional sense of envy and, blended together, they entail a powerful, painful affective state having ingredients that would explain why the envied person's misfortune would be pleasing – it would relieve the pain of inferiority and placate the ill will and resentment.

But this definition also suggests that other characterizations of envy might be less inclusive. Given that envy is not a "basic" emotion but rather a blended one (e.g., Campos et al., 1983), any definition that amounts to a blend of affects and construals allows alternative conceptions of what best constitutes its prototypical form.

Benign envy versus malicious envy Although envy, as a mostly private experience, can be hard to examine, close scrutiny suggests that there are two main types of envy (e.g., Belk, 2011; Foster, 1972; Silver and Sabini, 1978; Smith and Kim, 2007; Van de Ven, Zeelenberg, and Pieters, 2009; Van de Ven, Chapter 7 in this volume). In English people use envy to refer either to a benign, non-hostile form of the emotion or a malicious, hostile form. Benign envy, though it is an unpleasant state caused by the envying person noticing a desired advantage enjoyed by another, is largely free of painful inferiority and of hostile, resentful feelings (Van de Ven, Zeelenberg, and Pieters, 2009). In some languages the ambiguity of there being two types of envy is aided by having two words for the emotion, *both* in the general category of envy, but one representing benign and envy and the other malicious envy. For example, the Dutch have the word "*benijden*" for benign envy and "*afgunst*" for malicious envy (Van de Ven, Zeelenberg, and Pieters, 2009), while the Russians use "white envy" for benign envy and "black envy" for malicious envy.

Naturally, recognizing this distinction between benign and malicious envy influences both everyday thinking and research (see Feather, Chapter 3 in this volume; Powell, Smith, and Schurtz, 2008; Van de Ven, Zeelenberg, and Pieters, 2009; Van de Ven, Chapter 7 in this volume; Van de Ven et al., 2012; Van Dijk et al., 2006). First, manipulations of "envy" may succeed in producing either benign envy *or* malicious envy. Second, state measures of envy may correspond to one type of envy or the other. Depending on whether the methods allow for the distinction to be honored on both these levels, very little can be settled about how "envy proper" might relate to any number of associated phenomena, schadenfreude being just one.

Research by Leach and Spears (2008) is a case in point. In two studies the items used to measure envy were "would like to be like" and "want . . . to have [what the other has]." At times these items are referred to as being a measure of "coveting" rather than envy. But even traditional definitions of coveting have an edge that their items seem to lack (e.g., "to feel inordinate desire for what belongs to another" in *Webster's Online Dictionary*). These items are a mild expression of a person's reaction to another's advantage. They lack a face valid sense of invidious hostility or resentment and are clearly incompatible with malicious envy such as that exhibited by Claggart, Iago, Cassius, and Salieri. Thus, our view is that these studies indicate at best that only a benign form of coveting is unassociated with schadenfreude. The other studies that have failed to show a link between envy and schadenfreude have probably tapped benign envy rather than malicious envy as well (for a more detailed review of other studies, see Powell, Smith, and Schurtz, 2008).

Components of malicious envy

The three main features of malicious envy in Smith and Kim's definition – inferiority, hostility, and resentment – all have relevance for understanding why malicious envy, as a blend of these features, should predict schadenfreude. Prior studies showing a link between envy and schadenfreude have tended to use measures that entail or imply these features. Yet much of the research failing to find a link between envy and schadenfreude has assumed that one of more of these features are separate from envy. Leach and Spears (2008) emphasize inferiority, Hareli and Weiner (2002) focus on hostility, and Feather and colleagues (e.g., Feather and Nairn, 2005; Feather and Sherman, 2002; and see also Feather, Chapter 3 in this volume) feature resentment. In each case the constructs are presented as largely competing, mutually exclusive explanations that contrast with rather than complement envy. We will discuss each in turn.

Inferiority Leach and Spears' (2008) research focused on the role of inferiority in setting the stage for schadenfreude. They argued that inferiority and the painful emotions associated with such inferiority are a more potent cause of schadenfreude than other-focused emotions more directly associated with the other's success, such as envy, dislike, and resentment. Following Nietzsche (1967/1887), they suggest that the pain of inferiority leads to an externalization of this pain of inferiority in the form of anger at successful others, or *ressentiment*. In two studies they examined the relative contributions of inferiority, envy, and perceived illegitimacy of the advantage as causes of schadenfreude.

In one study (Study 2, noted above) participants were informed that their university had lost five of six matches in an unpublicized inter-university quiz bowl. This condition was intended to generate an initial sense of in-group inferiority (based on their university's poor record). The study assessed various feelings, including inferiority (e.g., "inferior," "frustrated," and "ashamed"), dislike of the out-group, anger ("angry," irritated," and "hostile"), and envy ("would like to be like" and "want . . . to have," as noted earlier). Participants then learned that the winning university in a second group of teams had lost to the winner of their own pool. Participants reported their happiness over this loss. A structural equation analysis suggested that pain about the in-group's inferiority explained schadenfreude at the failure of the successful out-group better than other variables, with envy toward this out-group showing essentially no predictive power.

Understanding the independent role of inferiority in schadenfreude and how it may interact with other factors such as envy are very important questions. Yet, the procedure did not directly manipulate either inferiority or envy. In our view, it was especially hard to know whether these conditions succeeded in generating a high degree of envy. Participants may not have considered performance on unpublicized quiz bowls (in which they were not participants) to be sufficiently important or self-relevant to create envy (Salovey and Rodin, 1986; Tesser, 1991). Furthermore, the items used to capture inferiority (e.g., "frustrated") were much more emotionally charged than the items used to measure envy ("would like to be like"). As one might expect, the envy measure was negatively correlated with disliking toward the out-group and uncorrelated with anger, suggesting that if envy was being measured, it was akin to benign envy.

One key point is that we view inferiority, in some form, to be part of envy. We argue that separating out inferiority entirely from envy is unjustified definitionally and, if removed wholly, biases its association with schadenfreude. How can the superiority of envied person be entirely separated from the inferiority one feels (Parrott and Smith, 1993; Smith et al., 1994; Smith et al., 1996; Smith et al., 1999; Van de Ven et al., 2009)? This is not to say that inferiority, perhaps chronic inferiority especially, cannot be conceived of as a separate construct. And, as a separate construct, it is very likely to explain instances of schadenfreude. For example, Van Dijk and his colleagues (see Van Dijk & Ouwerkerk, Chapter 9 in this volume) show clearly that people with either low state or low trait self-esteem (akin to inferiority) are primed to receive a pleasing self-esteem boost from misfortunes befalling others (Van Dijk et al., 2011a; Van Dijk et al., 2011b). Although these effects might be amplified by the presence of envy, they also occur separately from envy. Furthermore, some form of inferiority, conceived of a component of envy, could be examined as a component of envy having special explanatory power when it comes to explaining schadenfreude.

Hostility Hareli and Weiner's (2002) research was on "other-directed negative emotions" such as anger, hostility, and dislike. As with inferiority, we argue that disintegrating hostility from envy can misconstrue envy's role in some instances of schadenfreude. The blended emotion of envy, especially in its malicious form, includes ill will and hostility, and without this feature, it loses perhaps the main part of its malicious character. Other hostile emotions, caused by something other than an invidious comparison, create the conditions conducive to schadenfreude – as Hareli and Weiner's studies nicely show. Yet they construed any hostile feelings associated with envy as derived from envy rather than a defining feature of it: "Envy, therefore, is just one type of emotion that might arouse pleasure at another's misfortune, just as do other emotions, including hatred, anger, dislike, contempt, and disgust" (2002, p. 2). They expressly excluded items related to hostility in their measure of envy, as well as items clearly suggesting inferiority feelings. The resultant measure of envy focused on "desire to have something the other has" and "wishing to be like the other." This hostility-free envy clearly differs from any form of malicious envy. It was positively correlated with believing that the other person had good character and wanting to help this person.

Hareli and Weiner's measure of other-directed negative emotions included "anger," "hate," and "disgust," and these were associated with schadenfreude. In addition, they were negatively correlated with believing that the person had a good character, and positively correlated with believing that the misfortune was deserved, wishing something bad to happen, and wanting to hurt the other. We suggest that if this research had assumed that envy was a blended emotion, which included hostility (as well as some forms of inferiority and invidious resentment), then envy too (that is, malicious envy) would have revealed a similar pattern. A nuanced formulation of this relationship is found in the BIAS model (see Cikara and Fiske, Chapter 10 in this volume), which suggests that anger mediates the degree of passivity toward an envied target.

Resentment The main conceptual entry point for research on schadenfreude by Feather (for a review of this work, see Feather, Chapter 3 in this volume), who pioneered initial work on schadenfreude more generally (e.g., Feather, 1989), was on the role of the perceived deservingness of the misfortune, as opposed to envy felt toward the suffering person. Indeed, resentment is likely to produce open, guiltless pleasure, free of unseemly associations. This explanation for many instances of schadenfreude has great intuitive appeal and fits with many philosophical and psychological perspectives on human nature (e.g., Heider, 1958; see Portmann, 2000 and Chapter 2 in this volume), and, as we noted above, with untold literary and cinematic works. Feather and others (e.g., Feather, 2006; Feather and McKee, 2009; Feather, McKee, and Bekker, 2011; Van Dijk, Goslinga, and Ouwerkerk, 2008; Van Dijk, Ouwerkerk, and Goslinga, 2009; Van Dijk et al., 2005) have provided highly consistent evidence confirming this link, using a range of methods, and have made important distinctions between types of justice-related beliefs and feelings (for a review, see Feather, Chapter 3 in this volume).

Resentment and related justice-based feelings are clearly powerful explanations for many instances of schadenfreude. However, the relevant studies by Feather (Feather and Naim, 2005; Feather and Sherman,

2002) failed to support a role for envy in schadenfreude: "it was resentment rather than envy that fuelled schadenfreude" (Feather, 2008, p. 33). As with studies of inferiority and hostility, however, we argue that these results depended on measures of envy that lacked invidious resentment (as well as inferiority; for a more detailed assessment, see Powell, Smith, and Schurtz, 2008). Also, these studies used hypothetical scenarios that may have produced mild manipulations of envy and responses biased by self-presentational concerns (see also Powell, Smith, and Schurtz, 2008).

Smith (1991) reasoned that envy contains a sense of deservingness, but a highly subjective kind. People feeling envy, or at least malicious envy, begrudge the envied person's advantage and believe that the advantage is unfair (Van de Ven, Zeelenberg, and Pieters, 2012). Although these perceptions in part may be a function of attempts to cope with the painful disadvantage (a process akin to the notion of *ressentimente* posed by Nietzsche and invoked by Leach and Spears), Smith (1991) argued that these subjectively held beliefs (and resulting resentment) are an important part of the blend of emotions in envy, and malicious envy in particular. It may be that these subjective feelings of injustice are a key reason (among other reasons; see Hill and Buss, 2008) why people in the grip of malicious envy are willing to act aggressively toward the envied target: their actions seem not only to relieve envy but also to further justice (Smith et al., 1994). Measuring a construct such as subjective injustice is difficult, but to the extent that malicious envy contains resentment of this kind, a complete measure of malicious envy should tap this feature. By this logic (but see Leach, 2008; Miceli and Castelfranchi, 2007; and also Feather, Chapter 3 in this volume), research strategies that disaggregate any form of resentment from measures of malicious envy will create an incorrect sense of how malicious envy is associated with schadenfreude.

Carving up envy It is revealing to contemplate the implications of each of these lines of research for malicious envy. The research by Leach and Spears would remove inferiority feelings, the work by Hareli and Weiner would remove hostility, and that by Feather would remove invidious resentment. What would be left? Envy, even malicious envy, would amount to the "coveting" measure used by Leach and Spears ("wanting to have" and "would like to have"), which is clearly very different from malicious envy and from the portrayals of envy in literature and philosophy. As we noted above, even coveting has a sense of inappropriateness and excess to it that these items probably lack. As Sundie et al. (2009; and Sundie, Chapter 8 in this volume) illustrate, from the perspective of consumerism, envy requires recognition of social advantage and not just the wish for a high-status object – someone has to be driving the expensive car for one to feel envy. Using a measure only of "wanting the car" thus ignores the social core of the emotion. Again, this is not to claim in any way that the separate constructs of inferiority, hostility, and resentment are insignificant for schadenfreude. Each fit with cultural traditions and common-sense notions of what should explain many instances of schadenfreude. Rather, we argue that they are not fully separate from malicious envy in some related form. Furthermore, as Leach (2008) suggests, understanding how components of envy, however defined, may differentially relate to schadenfreude or other outcomes entails important questions.

Components of schadenfreude

Aside from the critical challenge of measuring any socially undesirable emotion, views on schadenfreude seem less fraught with measurement and conceptual questions than envy. But despite the immediacy of the emotional experience it entails, there are some important distinctions to make relative to envy. Consider, for instance, the difference between the following assertions:

1. I am happy that John suffered a misfortune ("experienced" schadenfreude).
2. I would be happy if John suffered a misfortune ("hypothetical" schadenfreude).
3. I have taken action to make John suffer a misfortune ("created" schadenfreude).

The subtle semantic differences between these statements conceal large cognitive and moral divisions, and consequences for how envy relates to schadenfreude. First, there is a stark material difference between wishing that the object of envy might suffer and taking pleasure at his or her actual suffering (only rarely does the object of envy suffer a misfortune – which may be one reason why it seems so subjectively justified when it happens). Second, while one might be happy at the envied person's real or hypothetical downfall "at the hands of fate," it is less likely that one would deliberately act to bring that downfall about (or report wishing it to happen) (Elster, 1998; see also Ben-Ze'ev, 2000 and Chapter 5 in this volume). In the literary examples we cited (Claggart, Iago, Cassius, and Salieri) the envious characters took action to undermine the objects of their envy; it would be hard for most of us to imagine taking such actions. Moral precepts strongly discourage one from actively plotting another person's downfall and thus creating schadenfreude, even if they would not preclude experiencing pleasure if the downfall happened on its own.

The typical view of schadenfreude is that it is a passive emotion (e.g., Ben-Ze'ev, 2000; see also Ben-Ze'ev, Chapter 5 in this volume; Portmann, 2000 and Chapter 2 in this volume; Van Dijk and Ouwerkerk, Chapter 1 in this volume), but considering distinctions between the passive feeling, the wishing and anticipation of suffering, and the taking of action to bring about suffering is likely to be necessary to understand fully how emotions such as envy relate to schadenfreude. For example, in certain forms of sympathetic magic like voodoo, the object of envy is symbolically tortured, allowing one safely to conflate wished and experienced schadenfreude. Generally, envious motives might predispose the engineering of an envied person's suffering, but only if it can be achieved in private or if the envious person can disguise the motive even from himself or herself. By contrast, if someone clearly deserves to suffer by an objective standard of justice, then feelings of "righteous indignation" may cause open actions to bring about the person's downfall – producing suffering and, arguably, a degree of schadenfreude. Envy has been identified as a motivator for genocide (see Cikara and Fiske, Chapter 10 in this volume), and in certain circumstances groups may be all too willing to take action to eliminate or show aggression to targets of envy – and to find doing so pleasing.

Each of these three manifestations of schadenfreude thus might have different measurable associations with envy (either benign or malicious) that help elucidate the nature of envy and of schadenfreude. For instance, while a person might smile at the mishap suffered by a benignly envied object, this does not mean that he or she would take steps to cause that downfall, or even to wish it. Mild forms of malicious envy toward someone, however, might make one decidedly glad at her or his suffering, yet without any conscious intentions to take action bring about that suffering. Intense malicious envy might lead to the pleasing engineering of the envied person's downfall – though an action taken in private and often rationalized as warranted.

The nature of the real or hypothetical suffering experienced by the envied person may also determine the association with envy. Even if one experiences pleasure if a competitor loses out on a promotion, would one delight if that same person were tortured and murdered (Ben-Ze'ev, 2000; Hareli and Weiner, 2002)? Traditionally, for schadenfreude to arise, the suffering is associated with and commensurate with the envy, with the result that, as Kant noted, the other's good fortune (for which one feels envy) is destroyed – but not more (again, for a discussion of similar issues, see Ben-Ze'ev, Chapter 5 in this volume).

All of these factors just noted create problems for quantifying the association between envy and schadenfreude, but also suggest important directions for future research. In the next section we will outline some additional challenges with manipulating envy and schadenfreude in experimental conditions.

Additional empirical challenges

The scientific understanding of the association between envy and schadenfreude grows out of studies involving voluntary research participants in controlled settings. This approach obviously differs markedly from the observation, introspection, and intuition that undergird literary and philosophical accounts. Under scrutiny, research manipulations of envy and schadenfreude have many potential limitations, of which we consider four of the most important: the difficulty of generating intense envy in laboratory situations; generalizing from hypothetical pleasure and pain; interpreting self-reports of socially undesirable emotions; and the inaccessibility of important unconscious reactions.

Generating intense envy

It is likely that none of the existing research on envy and schadenfreude has generated intense, or even particularly strong, instances of malicious envy. For example, the studies by Leach and Spears (2008) attempted to provoke intergroup comparisons through an unpublicized university quiz bowl contest in which the participants themselves did not directly participate. Most participants may have cared little about the sport of quiz bowls or the success of the in-group or the out-group, and any envy that developed may have been hypothetical or benign. We do not mean to single out this research. Even the studies that have found effects for envy on schadenfreude have probably not succeeded in creating the deeply personal malicious envy that "hits people where they live," at least for the majority of participants. In a practical sense, research manipulations may be unable uniformly to create conditions that broadly engender malicious envy in participants. This is not to claim that one must create virtual Claggarts in the lab, but only that regardless of how envy might be measured, either weak or artificial manipulations may fail to reveal correspondingly robust effects on schadenfreude. It may be, for instance, that malicious envy must be in a domain that is especially self-relevant (e.g., Salovey and Rodin, 1986) or must reach a threshold level of intensity before the balance is tipped in the direction of fully *reported* schadenfreude.

Hypothetical pleasure and pain

Some research paradigms ask participants to consider how they would feel "if" someone were to suffer. While participants seem able to understand

and evaluate these conditions to a certain degree, this is a far cry from the way they might feel if they in fact experienced the pain of envy, the pleasure of schadenfreude, or both (see Powell, Smith, and Schurtz, 2008; Van Dijk et al., 2006). Research using manipulations of actual envy and using actual misfortunes (with the purpose of the research disguised) appears to recapitulate more accurately the associated emotions and valuations. By analogy, asking participants to consider their degree of schadenfreude and envy is akin to asking the question: "Imagine that you have a 500-pound weight crushing your left toe, and rate how much it would hurt. Now imagine that the weight is removed, and rate how good you feel." Evincing and evaluating painful experience in this way seems a very doubtful approach, yet it is a common basis for quantifying the association between envy and schadenfreude. In sum, it is probably difficult to reproduce realistic envy-inducing stimuli or to simulate experienced schadenfreude, at least when considering examples found in literary accounts.

Misrepresented self-reports

As we and others have noted (e.g., Van Dijk et al., 2006; see also Powell, Smith, and Schurtz, 2008), an acute problem with studying emotions such as envy and schadenfreude is social desirability. Participants may not report what they are actually feeling, choosing instead to describe the feelings they expect others to approve of or to have (Parkinson and Manstead, 1993). Even though participants in all the studies we have considered were relatively sure of their anonymity, it still may be hard for them to endorse envy and associated feelings. This is especially true when the item labels for emotions have negative connotations. Most of the studies failing to show an effect for envy on schadenfreude have been transparent in this respect. To some participants, this research may seem to be seeking out sadistic thoughts or desires of the type that most people would not want to endorse.

Unconscious reactions

Related to the issue of self-reporting is the fact that people may be unaware of their envy to varying degrees. The experience of envy is likely to be quickly suppressed or transmuted into a more palatable emotion (Elster, 1998; Parrott, 1991; Smith, 2004), for example. Envy may be less a simple or primary emotional state than an evolving experience, which generates other emotions. Again, it can be hard to acknowledge negative emotions even in a private sense, especially those that are socially repugnant, and acknowledging their causes should prove even harder. In none of the literary examples we considered did the envious characters recognize or confront envy, even though the narrative showed it (and the readers understood it) as a key motivation for their feelings and actions.

The use of neuroscience methods may lend some insights. In a study by Takahashi et al. (2009), brain activation associated with pleasure and reward was more likely in reactions to negative events happening to enviable targets than average targets, although these were hypothetical, not actual events. Cikara and Fiske (2011 and Chapter 10 in this volume) examined participants' reactions to the suffering of high-status, competitive (and thus enviable) targets or to the suffering of other targets less likely to be envied. Because of social desirability, Cikara and Fiske did not expect open reports of schadenfreude when the enviable target suffered compared to the other targets. Rather, for example, they expected participants to feel "less bad" about such negative events – which is what happened. But they supplemented self-report measures with physiological measures of smiling. When the envied target was paired with a negative as compared with a positive event, smiling was more likely. This was not true for the non-envied targets. Cikara and Fiske had expected social desirability to affect participants' self-reports and, indeed, participants' self-reported responses were not correlated with smiling.

It is worth noting that even psychotherapy, which is often structured so that people can safely examine their motivations and feelings, offers only fleeting glimpses into the unconscious – unlike literature. It re-creates affective states in real time and gives the patient the opportunity to establish the origins of emotional experiences. This process likely happens only with a highly structured supportive structure, an insightful patient, and an adept facilitator. While it is impossible to prove the existence of or the natural reactions to hidden affective states, we propose that in most circumstances, people who feel inferiority, invidious resentment, and hostility toward another advantaged person will not consciously recognize that envy is the origin. Nor would they necessarily acknowledge that their wish for the other person to suffer might originate from their experience of envy. They might develop other explanations for their wish that the other would be "cut down to size," as through cosmic or civil justice. For the purposes of research, the fact that these defenses are generated on an unconscious or subconscious plane clearly makes it hard to measure envy and schadenfreude through self-reported behaviors or appraisals. No wonder that some scholars such as Elster (1998) doubt the usefulness of laboratory paradigms for examining many human emotions and direct a focus instead on literary works.

A transmutational approach to studying envy and schadenfreude

The practical and theoretical challenges of studying envy and schadenfreude notwithstanding, we suggest that attempts to measure their association should try to account for these challenges. One way to formulate envy, which may help to address these challenges, is to consider envy as having a broader "episodic" nature (Parrott, 1991). The full experience of envy in this sense involves both an instant reaction – the "pang" of envy – as well as the immediate process of coping with the reaction that goes in typical, transmuting directions (e.g., Elster, 1998; Smith, 2004; Smith & Kim, 2007). As we have emphasized, along with many scholars, because envy entails both shameful inferiority and hostility, few people should want to admit to feeling it, either to others or to themselves. Defensive processes are likely to operate straight away to transmute the feeling into something having a more palatable label, through a route that is unlikely to reach full awareness. Thus, envy might often be "felt" as defence against the noxious initiating experience rather than as a primary affective response. Schadenfreude, when linked to envy, may often be mediated by these defensive reactions as much as by just the "pang" of envy (Powell, Smith, and Schurtz, 2008).

Recent research by Sundie et al. (2010; also see chapter 8 in this volume) suggests the value of taking a transmutational approach to understanding envy and schadenfreude (Elster, 1998; Smith, 2004; Smith and Kim, 2007). Participants were told that the study concerned consumers' snap judgments about other consumers. They read a profile about an ostensibly real person together with a quote about the person's experiences with an automobile and a photo of the automobile, including the make of automobile (either a Mercedes or a Ford Focus). They then gave their reactions to this profile, including measures of envy and hostility. Next, they gave their "gut" reactions to an apparent Internet posting by a friend of the automobile's owner that included a photo of it with its hood up, along with a description of how its engine had broken down. Structural equation analysis indicated that the manipulation of envy created envy and that this envy was associated with schadenfreude. However, this association was mediated by hostility. The authors interpreted this pattern as indicating that envy leads to hostility as a defensive coping process and that this invidious hostility in turn creates schadenfreude.

By considering transmutational processes rather than just the narrow unit of envy-producing event, this research suggests an integration of different perspectives on how envy, and malicious envy in particular, relates to schadenfreude. It also used a number of the methodological strategies that are well suited for examining envy and schadenfreude, such as an effective cover story, generally self-relevant domains, and pilot-testing stimuli that would create reasonably strong forms of envy. However, some of the choices made by the authors recapitulate one of the problematic methods we described above. The descriptors "envious" and "jealous" were used as a measure of envy. "Injustice," "resentment," and "anger" were used as a *separate* measure of hostility (notice that this latter measure fused resentment with hostility – yet another example of how challenging these constructs are to tease apart). It is likely that the measure of envy was ambiguous about its benign or malicious nature. Also, it is possible that some of the hostile feelings that may have been captured in the measure of envy were siphoned off by the measure of hostility with which it was correlated. Another feature absent in their measure of envy at the item level was inferiority (as the authors also note). In our view, of course, in order to measure malicious envy, one would need to include inferiority, invidious resentment, and hostility as constituents of envy in some form rather than disaggregating them entirely.

Concluding remarks

We began our chapter by evoking literary and philosophical views that strongly link envy and schadenfreude. It goes without saying that literary and philosophical approaches to understanding human emotions have their own set of limitations. However, the consistency of themes linking envy and schadenfreude emerging from these approaches contrasted sharply with the inconsistency in the empirical literature. We have argued that this inconsistency likely arises from how successfully research addresses a number of methodological challenges, in particular: (1) the distinction between benign and malicious envy; (2) the complex blending of inferiority, hostility, and invidious resentment in the experience of envy; (3) the conceptualization of schadenfreude and the nature of the real or desired suffering; (4) the strength of how envy is manipulated; (5) the social repugnance of the various emotions and thoughts induced by envy and schadenfreude; and (6) the accounting for unconscious, defensive processes by which the brain experiences, recognizes, connects, and separates the two experiences. All the research cited in this chapter has contributed in important ways to our understanding of how envy and schadenfreude may be linked, and we hope that future research will take these issues into account.

References

Belk, R. (2011). Benign envy. *Academy of Marketing Science Review* 1: 117–34.
Ben-Ze'ev, A. (2000). *The Subtlety of Emotions*. Cambridge, MA: MIT Press.

Brigham, N. L., Kelso, K. A., Jackson, M. A., and Smith, R. H. (1997). The roles of invidious comparisons and deservingness in sympathy and schadenfreude. *Basic and Applied Social Psychology* 19: 363–80.

Campos, J. J., Barrett, K. C., Lamb, M. E., Goldsmith, H. H., and Stenberg, C. (1983). Socioemotional development. In P. H. Mussen (ed.), *Handbook of Child Psychology*, Vol. 2. New York: Wiley, pp. 783–915.

Cikara, M., Botvinick, M. M., and Fiske, S. T. (2011). Us versus them: social identity shapes neural responses to intergroup competition and harm. *Psychological Science* 22: 306–13.

Cikara, M. and Fiske, S. T. (2012). Stereotypes and schadenfreude: behavioral and physiological markers of pleasure at others' misfortunes. *Social Psychological and Personality Science* 3: 63–71.

Cohen-Charash, Y. (2009). Episodic envy. *Journal of Social Psychology* 39: 2128–73.

D'Arms, J. and Kerr, A.D. (2008). Envy and the philosophical tradition. In R. H. Smith (ed.), *Envy: Theory and Research*. Oxford University Press, pp. 39–59.

Elster, J. (1998). *Alchemies of the Mind: Rationality and the Emotions*. Cambridge University Press, pp. 165–9.

Feather, N. T. (1989). Attitudes towards the high achiever: the fall of the tall poppy. *Australian Journal of Psychology* 41: 239–67.

(2006). Deservingness and emotions: applying the structural model of deservingness to the analysis of affective reactions to outcomes. *European Review of Social Psychology* 17: 38–73.

(2008). Effects of observer's own status on reactions to a high achiever's failure: deservingness, resentment, schadenfreude, and sympathy. *Australian Journal of Psychology* 60(1): 30–41.

Feather, N. T. and McKee, I. R. (2009). Differentiating emotions in relation to deserved or undeserved outcomes: a retrospective study of real-life events. *Cognition & Emotion* 23: 955–77.

Feather, N. T., McKee, I. R., and Bekker, N. (2011). Deservingness and emotions: testing a structural model that relates discrete emotions to the perceived deservingness of positive or negative outcomes. *Motivation and Emotion* 35: 1–13.

Feather, N. T. and Nairn, K. (2005). Resentment, envy, schadenfreude, and sympathy: effects of own and other's deserved or undeserved status. *Australian Journal of Psychology* 57: 87–102.

Feather, N. T. and Sherman, R. (2002). Envy, resentment, schadenfreude, and sympathy: reactions to deserved and undeserved achievement and subsequent failure. *Personality and Social Psychology Bulletin* 28: 953–61.

Foster, G. (1972). The anatomy of envy. *Current Anthropology* 13: 165–202.

Griffin, A. K. (1931). *Aristotle's Psychology of Conduct*. London: Williams & Norgate.

Hareli, S. and Weiner, B. (2002). Dislike and envy as antecedents of pleasure at another's misfortune. *Motivation and Emotion* 26: 257–77.

Heider, F. (1958). *The Psychology of Interpersonal Relations*. New York: John Wiley & Sons, Inc.

Hill, S. E. and Buss, D. M. (2008). The evolutionary psychology of envy. In R. H. Smith (ed.) *Envy: Theory and Research*. Oxford University Press, pp. 60–70.

Kant, I. (1999 [1797]). *The Cambridge Edition of the Works of Immanuel Kant: Practical Philosophy* (translated and edited by M. Gregor). New York: Cambridge University Press.

Krizan, Z. and Johar, O. (2012). Envy divides the two faces of narcissism. *Journal of Personality* 80: 1415–51.

Leach, C. W. (2008). Envy, inferiority, and injustice: three bases of anger about inequality. In R. H. Smith (ed.), *Envy: Theory and Research*. Oxford University Press, pp. 94–116.

Leach, C. W. and Spears, R. (2008). "A vengefulness of the impotent": the pain of in-group inferiority and schadenfreude toward successful out-groups. *Journal of Personality and Social Psychology* 95: 1383–96.

Melville, H. (1962 [1924]). *Billy Budd: An Inside Narrative*. University of Chicago Press.

Miceli, M. and Castelfranchi, C. (2007). The envious mind. *Cognition & Emotion* 21: 449– 79.

Nietzsche, F. (1967 [1887]). *On the Genealogy of Morals* (translated by W. Kaufmann and R. J. Hollingdale). New York: Random House.

Parkinson, B. and Manstead, A. (1993). Making sense of emotion in stories and social life. *Cognition & Emotion* 7: 295–323.

Parrott, W. G. (1991). The emotional experiences of envy and jealousy. In P. Salovey (ed.), *The Psychology of Jealousy and Envy*. New York: Guilford Press, pp. 3–30.

Parrott, W. G. and Smith, R. H. (1993). Distinguishing the experiences of envy and jealousy. *Journal of Personality and Social Psychology* 64: 906–20.

Plato (2006). *Philebus* (translated by B. Jowett). Available at ReadHowYou Want.com.

Portmann, J. (2000). *When Bad Things Happen to Other People*. New York: Routledge.

Powell, C. A. J., Smith, R. H., and Schurtz, D. R. (2008). Pleasure in an envied person's pain. In R. H. Smith (ed.), *Envy: Theory and Research*. Oxford University Press, pp. 148–64.

Salovey, P. and Rodin, J. (1986). The differentiation of social-comparison jealousy and romantic jealousy. *Journal of Personality and Social Psychology* 50: 1100–12.

Shaffer, P. (2001). *Amadeus*. New York: Harper Perennial.

Shakespeare, W. (2008). *The Complete Works of Shakespeare*, 6th edn (edited by D. Bevington). New York: Longman.

Silver, M. and Sabini, J. (1978). The perception of envy. *Social Psychology Quarterly* 41: 105–17.

(1991). Envy and the sense of injustice. In P. Salovey (ed.), *Psychological Perspectives on Jealousy and Envy*. New York: Guilford Press, pp. 79–99.

Smith, R. H. (2004). Envy and its transmutations. In L. Z. Tiedens and C. W. Leach (eds.), *The Social Life of Emotions*. Cambridge University Press, pp. 43–63.

Smith, R. H. and Kim, S. H. (2007). Comprehending envy. *Psychological Bulletin* 133(1): 46–64.

Smith, R. H., Parrott, W. G., Ozer, D., and Moniz, A. (1994). Subjective injustice and inferiority as predictors of hostile and depressive feelings in envy. *Personality and Social Psychology Bulletin* 20: 705–11.

Smith, R. H., Parrott, W. G, Diener, E., Hoyle, R. H., and Kim, S. H. (1999). Dispositional envy. *Personality and Social Psychology Bulletin* 25: 1007–20.

Smith, R. H., Turner, T. J., Garonzik, R., Leach, C. W., Urch-Druskat, V., and Weston, C. M. (1996). Envy and schadenfreude. *Personality and Social Psychology Bulletin* 25: 158–68.

Spinoza, B. (1883). *Ethics*. New York: Macmillan & Co.

Sundie, J. M., Ward, J., Beal, D. J., Chin, W. W., and Oneto, S. (2009). Schadenfreude as a consumption-related emotion: feeling happiness about the downfall of another's product. *Journal of Consumer Psychology* 19: 356–73.

Takahashi, H., Kato, M., Matsuura, M., Mobbs, D., Suhara, T., and Okubo, Y. (2009). When your gain is my pain and your pain is my gain: neural correlates of envy and schadenfreude. *Science* 323: 937–9.

Tesser, A. (1991). Emotion in social comparison and reflection processes. In J. Suls and T. A. Wills (eds.), *Social Comparison: Contemporary Theory and Research*. Hillsdale, NJ: Erlbaum, pp. 115–45.

Van de Ven, N., Hoogland, C., Smith, R.H., Van Dijk, W. W., Breugelmans, S.M., and Zeelenberg, M. (2012). When envy leads to schadenfreude. Manuscript submitted for publication.

Van de Ven, N., Zeelenberg, M., and Pieters, R. (2009). Leveling up and down: the experiences of benign and malicious envy. *Emotion* 9: 419–29.

(2012). The appraisal patterns of envy and related emotions. *Motivation and Emotion* 36: 195–204.

Van Dijk, W. W., Goslinga, S., and Ouwerkerk, J. W. (2008). The impact of responsibility for a misfortune on schadenfreude and sympathy: further evidence. *Journal of Social Psychology* 148: 631–6.

Van Dijk, W. W., Ouwerkerk, J. W., and Goslinga, S. (2009). The impact of deservingness on schadenfreude and sympathy: further evidence. *The Journal of Social Psychology* 149: 290–2.

Van Dijk, W. W., Ouwerkerk, J. W., Goslinga, S., and Nieweg, M. (2005). Deservingness and schadenfreude. *Cognition & Emotion* 19: 933–9.

Van Dijk, W. W., Ouwerkerk, J. W., Goslinga, S., Nieweg, M., and Gallucci, M. (2006). When people fall from grace: reconsidering the role of envy in schadenfreude. *Emotion* 6: 156–60.

Van Dijk, W. W., Ouwerkerk, J. W., Wesseling, Y. M., and Van Koningsbruggen, G. M. (2011a). Towards understanding pleasure at the misfortunes of others: the impact of self-evaluation threat on schadenfreude. *Cognition and Emotion* 25: 360–8.

Van Dijk, W. W., Van Koningsbruggen, G. M., Ouwerkerk, J. W., and Wesseling, Y. M. (2011b). Self-esteem, self-affirmation, and schadenfreude. *Emotion* 11: 1445–9.

7 Malicious envy and schadenfreude

Niels van de Ven

Envy is a close relative of schadenfreude. Where envy is the unhappy feeling that arises when another person has something desirable, schadenfreude is the happy feeling that arises when another person suffers a misfortune. Both envy and schadenfreude are emotions of which we are aware that we should not experience them. After all, we know that we should feel happy for someone else's success and feel bad when they suffer a misfortune. Envy has often been thought to be an important cause of schadenfreude. But as Smith, Thielke, and Powell describe in Chapter 6 in this volume, the research on this came to mixed conclusions. In this chapter I will discuss recent research that seems to solve these discrepancies and shows how and when envy is an antecedent to schadenfreude.

Smith, Thielke, and Powell (Chapter 6 in this volume) already described the mixed results found in the scientific literature on the relationship between envy and schadenfreude (see also Van Dijk and Ouwerkerk, Chapter 1 in this volume). Where some research found a relationship between envy and schadenfreude (Brigham et al., 1997; Smith et al., 1996; Van Dijk et al., 2005; Van Dijk et al., 2006), other research found that this relationship seemed to actually be caused by other factors such as feelings of inferiority (Leach and Spears, 2008), resentment (Feather and Sherman, 2002), perceptions of deservingness (Feather and Nairn, 2005), or disliking the other (Hareli and Weiner, 2002). In their chapter, Smith, Thielke, and Powell give an excellent overview of the empirical and conceptual challenges that arise when studying the relationship between schadenfreude and envy, and give a number of reasons why this relationship has often been questioned. In this chapter I will focus on one of those issues, namely the importance of distinguishing between two types of envy as a potential cause of schadenfreude. I will first discuss the distinction between benign and malicious envy before turning to research that tested how these types of envy relate to schadenfreude.

Envy

Envy can be defined as the emotion that "arises when a person lacks another's superior quality, achievement, or possession and either desires it or wishes that the other lacked it" (Parrott and Smith, 1993, p. 906). It is a frustrating, negative feeling that arises because someone else is better off than oneself (Kant, 1780/1997). This upward social comparison to the other person is the key to envy: it is this comparison that triggers feelings of inferiority, and realizing that one misses out on something important makes it such a frustrating experience. A person who feels envy focuses on the gap between oneself and the other, thinking both about one's own lacking and the other's success (Smith and Kim, 2007).

Emotions evolved because they have a function that helps the organism deal with the environment (Cosmides and Tooby, 2000; Keltner and Gross, 1999). Negative emotions in particular trigger a feeling that an important goal is not being met. For example, we feel anger when someone (or something) is perceived to deliberately block our goals and regret when a wrong decision was made. In turn, the emotion triggers action tendencies that help us deal with this threat to our important goals: anger motivates us to agitate against that which blocks our goal, while regret motivates behavior to prevent a similar mistake in the future. For envy, the goal that is being threatened is that of having a good status within one's group. The action tendencies that envy elicits are aimed at making sure that someone else is not better off, to resolve the threat to one's own status.

The two types of envy

Envy comes in two forms: a benign and a malicious one (Foster, 1972; Parrott, 1991; Silver and Sabini, 1978; Smith and Kim, 2007). Envy in general contains feelings of frustration because someone else is better off than you are, and it activates behavior aimed at solving this problem. This can be done in two ways: either by moving up oneself to the level of the superior other or by pulling down the envied other to one's level. The benign form of envy motivates behavior that reduces the gap with the other by a motivation aimed at moving oneself up, while the malicious form of envy motivates behavior aimed at pulling down the other person. As I explain later, it is this form of envy that has a clear connection to schadenfreude (see also Feather, Chapter 3 in this volume).

When people think about envy, the prototypical form that comes to mind is usually malicious envy. It has long been seen in a negative light, and is even one of the seven deadly sins in the Catholic tradition. Indeed, various classic stories are based on the destructive nature of envy, sometimes even ending with murder: Cain killing Abel, and Iago plotting against Othello. Indeed, research confirms the negative behavior that envy can lead to: people gossip more about those whom they envy (Wert and Salovey, 2004), they are willing to pay money if by doing so they can destroy even more money from the person whom they envy (Zizzo and Oswald, 2001), and groups in which someone is envious of another person are less effective and perform worse (Duffy and Shaw, 2000).

Most research on envy also focused on this destructive, malicious form of envy. Various scholars speculated that there could also be a more benign form of envy, with, for example, more motivation following the frustration that is part of envy (Foster, 1972; Parrott, 1991; Silver and Sabini, 1978; Smith and Kim, 2007). Consistent with this is that research on social comparison found that some frustration is necessary for an upward social comparison to motivate people to do better themselves (Johnson, 2012). Indeed, envy researchers at times also find a relationship between envy and motivation next to more destructive action tendencies (Cohen-Charash, 2009; Schaubroeck and Lam, 2004).

Recently, the value of separating a benign form of envy from the malicious form has been articulated clearly (Belk, 2011; Feather, Chapter 3 in this volume; Smith, Thielke, and Powell, Chapter 6 in this volume; Tai, Narayanan, and McAllister, 2012; Van de Ven, Zeelenberg, and Pieters, 2009). Van de Ven, Zeelenberg, and Pieters find that these types of envy differ in terms of how they feel and the action tendencies that they trigger. Even more importantly, a series of studies showed how these types of envy lead to different behavior. First, when confronted with a superior fellow student, students who were (or were made to be) benignly envious had a higher motivation and even actual better performance on a subsequent intelligence test, while those who were maliciously envious did not improve motivation and performance (Van de Ven, Zeelenberg, and Pieters, 2011b). Second, consumers who were made to be benignly envious of someone who owned a new iPhone wanted to pay more for an iPhone, while consumers who were made to be maliciously envious were willing to pay more for a BlackBerry (a related but different product that allowed for differentiation; Van de Ven, Zeelenberg, and Pieters, 2011a). Finally, the distinction between benign and malicious envy also mattered in relation to the fear of being envied by others. The fear of being envied is a pervasive fear in many cultures (Foster, 1972; Schoeck, 1969). However, a closer examination of this shows that people only seem to fear being maliciously envied, not being benignly envied (Van de Ven, Zeelenberg, and Pieters, 2010). The different effects of the envy types on motivation make it likely that this distinction also matters for envy's relationship with schadenfreude.

Envy and schadenfreude

The distinction between benign and malicious envy is important to understand how envy relates to schadenfreude. As discussed before, some research found a relationship, but other research questioned this and stated that it was actually caused by other factors. In recent research (Van de Ven et al., 2012), we tried to resolve this unclarity. I will discuss these findings here and will show that malicious envy is an antecedent of schadenfreude, whereas benign envy is not. After that, I will explain how malicious envy influences schadenfreude in relation to some other known influences on schadenfreude.

In the first study, we had some participants recall an instance in which they were benignly envious of someone, while another group recalled an instance in which they were maliciously envious. Next, we asked them to imagine that the person whom they envied suffered a minor misfortune (that they sat down in gum on a park bench). We found that those who were maliciously envious of someone indicated that they would experience a lot more schadenfreude when that person suffered a misfortune than those who were benignly envious.

In a second study, we conceptually replicated the first study, with a different manipulation of the envy types. Earlier research found that malicious envy typically arises when the perceived advantage of the envied person is undeserved, while benign envy arises if the advantage is more deserved (Smith et al., 1994; Van de Ven, Zeelenberg, and Pieters, 2010; Van de Ven et al., 2012; for more on the importance of perceptions of deservingness as antecedents to emotions, see Feather, Chapter 3 in this volume; and Feather, McKee, and Bekker, 2011). Participants read a scenario about another student who possessed expensive clothing, was very popular, and performed very well at university. This was either rather undeserved (as the advantage was held because of a rich father and cheating on tests) or deserved (via hard work), eliciting malicious or benign envy, respectively. The participants were asked to imagine that this other student then suffered a misfortune by spilling red wine on new shiny white trousers at an important party, after which they were asked how much schadenfreude they would experience if that happened. As expected, participants who read about the student with the undeserved advantage of the envied person experienced more malicious envy and more schadenfreude than those in the deserved advantage condition.

The first two studies were run in the Netherlands, where two different words exist for the types of envy. We of course think a relationship between malicious envy and schadenfreude also exists in countries where only one word exists for both types (such as the English language). A third study therefore tested the relationship between the two emotions in the USA. All participants recalled an instance in which they were envious of someone. We measured how intense their envy was and how deserved they felt that it was that the other held the advantage over them. Then we asked them to imagine that the person whom they envied suffered a misfortune (sat in gum on a park bench). As expected, in general it was the case that more intense envy did not lead to more schadenfreude, because this combined the benign and malicious types. Closer examination shows that when the advantage was undeserved, and the envy was thus likely to be malicious, envy was related to schadenfreude. This was not the case if the advantage was deserved. In three studies we thus found that malicious envy is an antecedent for schadenfreude, while benign envy is not.

In a final study, we tested whether malicious envy predicts schadenfreude if we simultaneously take effects of feelings of inferiority, perceptions of deservingness, and dislike of the other into account. In a large study, participants read an interview with a superior, enviable student. In a seemingly unrelated newspaper article, they read that the student lost a wallet at a party and had to expend great effort to cancel credit cards, etc. We measured how maliciously envious participants were of the superior student, how inferior they felt to this person, how deserved they felt that the misfortune was, and how much they disliked the person. The results were clear; malicious envy was the strongest antecedent of schadenfreude of all these factors. Seeing the misfortune as deserved and dislike of the other also led to more schadenfreude, but feelings of inferiority did not. Normally, these three other constructs are part of the experience of malicious envy (Smith and Kim, 2007; Smith, Thielke, and Powell, Chapter 6 in this volume; Van de Ven, Zeelenberg, and Pieters, 2009). In the typical experience of malicious envy, these other feelings are present, so for practical purposes it is good to realize that in situations that elicit malicious envy, a number of antecedents to schadenfreude join to create a strong effect.

These studies solve a part of the empirical challenges and discrepancies pointed out by Smith, Thielke, and Powell (Chapter 6 in this volume) on the relationship between envy and schadenfreude. Only malicious envy leads to more schadenfreude, while benign envy does not. Researchers who want to test for the possible effects of envy on schadenfreude (or any other variables) should thus be aware that whether envy is operationalized in a benign or malicious form can strongly influence the results one obtains.

Furthermore, when studying envy, one has to realize that envy is such a widely condemned emotion that we often hide the experience not only from others, but also even from ourselves. Foster (1972) found that when people were asked how often they experienced envy, 50 percent said that they virtually never experienced this emotion. This is tricky for those of us who try to study envy. In our research on envy, we quickly found out that if we ask people whether they are envious of someone (especially for the malicious type), we typically find a floor effect with little variation around a very low score. Changing the question slightly to whether they are *somewhat* envious of someone helps (Van de Ven, Zeelenberg, and Pieters, 2011b). The same holds for recall studies in which we ask people to recall an instance in which they were envious of someone, in which some people will indicate to never experience envy. However, if we add the sentence "envy is an emotion that all people typically experience once in a while," we typically find that all people can remember instances in which they were envious, quite a few of them with rather intense experiences (Van de Ven, Zeelenberg, and Pieters, 2009).

Conclusion

This chapter started with the notion that envy and schadenfreude seem to be close: where envy is the unhappy feeling that arises when another person has something nice, schadenfreude is the happy feeling that arises when another person suffers a misfortune. I presented research we recently conducted that demonstrates that malicious envy is indeed an important antecedent to schadenfreude. By understanding the causes of schadenfreude, we also hope to get a better insight into the function of this emotion.

All emotions have a function (Cosmides and Tooby, 2000; Keltner and Gross, 1999). In general, negative emotions arise when there is a threat to one's goals (anger signals that someone blocks your goal progress, regret that a mistake is made, and envy that someone else is better off than you are). Positive emotions arise when things are going well and goals are being met (Fredrickson, 1998; see also Van Dijk and Ouwerkerk, Chapter 1 in this volume). Schadenfreude is a positive emotion: even though it is condemned and generally frowned upon, it is a pleasant feeling. So what is the function of schadenfreude? It could be that it serves as a signal that someone who was better off than oneself (and had elicited envy) no longer holds as strong an advantage after the misfortune. This means that envy is no longer necessary. Envy is an emotion that uses resources: it uses both cognitive resources by focusing attention on the situation (Hill, DelPriore, and Vaughan, 2011) and physical resources by activating a motivation to work harder (Van de Ven, Zeelenberg, and Pieters, 2011b). In particular, the malicious type of envy is potentially costly: first, people generally frown upon those who experience malicious envy, so acting upon that emotion risks social punishment; and, second, it can be so intense that people are willing to pay some money if doing so hurts the envied person even more (Zizzo and Oswald, 2001). Given these costs, schadenfreude might serve as an important signal that what had previously caused envy is no longer relevant. Schadenfreude thus signals that the resources put into the envious motivation can be held back and that no negative behavior toward the envied person is needed (avoiding the potential social risks).

References

Belk, R. (2011). Benign envy. *Academy of Marketing Science Review* 1: 117–34.

Brigham, N. L., Kelso, K. A., Jackson, M. A., and Smith, R. H. (1997). The roles of invidious comparisons and deservingness in sympathy and schadenfreude. *Basic and Applied Social Psychology* 19: 363–80.

Cohen-Charash, Y. (2009). Episodic envy. *Journal of Applied Social Psychology* 39: 2128–73.

Cosmides, L. and Tooby, J. (2000). Evolutionary psychology and the emotions. In M. Lewis and J. M. Haviland-Jones (eds.), *Handbook of Emotions*. New York: Guilford Press, pp. 91–115.

Duffy, M. K. and Shaw, J. D. (2000). The Salieri syndrome: consequences of envy in groups. *Small Group Research* 31: 3–23.

Feather, N. T., McKee, I. R., and Bekker, N. (2011). Deservingness and emotions: testing a structural model that relates discrete emotions to the perceived deservingness of positive or negative outcomes. *Motivation & Emotion* 35: 1–13.

Feather, N. T. and Nairn, K. (2005). Resentment, envy, schadenfreude, and sympathy: effects of own and other's deserved or undeserved status. *Australian Journal of Psychology* 57: 87–102.

Feather, N. T. and Sherman, R. (2002). Envy, resentment, schadenfreude, and sympathy: reactions to deserved and undeserved achievement and subsequent failure. *Personality and Social Psychology Bulletin* 28: 953–61.

Foster, G. (1972). The anatomy of envy. *Current Anthropology* 13: 165–202.

Fredrickson, B. L. (1998). What good are positive emotions? *Review of General Psychology* 2: 300–19.

Hareli, S. and Weiner, B. (2002). Dislike and envy as antecedents of pleasure at another's misfortune. *Motivation and Emotion* 26: 257–77.

Hill, S. E., DelPriore, D., and Vaughan, P. (2011). The cognitive consequences of envy: attention, memory, and self-regulatory depletion. *Journal of Personality and Social Psychology* 101: 653–66.

Johnson, C. (2012). Behavioral responses to social comparisons: from dastardly deeds to rising above. *Social Psychology Compass* 6: 515–24.

Kant, I. (1997 [1780]). *Lectures on Ethics*. Cambridge University Press.

Keltner, D. and Gross, J. J. (1999). Functional accounts of emotions. *Cognition & Emotion* 13: 467–80.

Leach, C. W. and Spears, R. (2008). "A vengefulness of the impotent": the pain of in-group inferiority and schadenfreude toward successful out-groups. *Journal of Personality and Social Psychology* 95: 1383–96.

Parrott, W. G. (1991). The emotional experiences of envy and jealousy. In P. Salovey (ed.), *The Psychology of Jealousy and Envy*. New York: Guilford Press, pp. 3–30.

Parrott, W. G. and Smith, R. H. (1993). Distinguishing the experiences of envy and jealousy. *Journal of Personality and Social Psychology* 64: 906–20.

Schaubroeck, J. and Lam, S. S. K. (2004). Comparing lots before and after: promotion rejectees' invidious reactions to promotees. *Organizational Behavior and Human Decision Processes* 94: 33–47.

Schoeck, H. (1969). *Envy: A Theory of Social Behavior*. New York: Harcourt, Brace and World.

Silver, M. and Sabini, J. (1978). The perception of envy. *Social Psychology Quarterly* 41: 105–17.

Smith, R. H. and Kim, S. H. (2007). Comprehending envy. *Psychological Bulletin* 133: 46–64.

Smith, R. H., Parrott, W. G., Ozer, D., and Moniz, A. (1994). Subjective injustice and inferiority as predictors of hostile and depressive feelings in envy. *Personality and Social Psychology Bulletin* 20: 705–11.

Smith, R. H., Turner, T. J., Garonzik, R., Leach, C. W., Urch-Druskat, V., and Weston, C. M. (1996). Envy and schadenfreude. *Personality and Social Psychology Bulletin* 22: 158–68.

Tai, K., Narayanan, J., and McAllister, D. (2012). Envy as pain: rethinking the nature of envy and its implications for employees and organizations. *Academy of Management Review* 37: 107–29.

Wert, S. R. and Salovey, P. (2004). A social comparison account of gossip. *Review of General Psychology* 8: 122–37.

Van de Ven, N., Hoogland, C. E., Smith, R. H., Van Dijk, W. W., Breugelmans, S. M., and Zeelenberg, M. (2012). Envy and schadenfreude. Unpublished manuscript.

Van de Ven, N., Zeelenberg, M., and Pieters, R. (2009). Leveling up and down: the experiences of benign and malicious envy. *Emotion* 9: 419–29.

(2010). Warding off the evil eye: when the fear of being envied increases prosocial behavior. *Psychological Science* 21: 1671–7.

(2011a). The envy premium: how envy increases product value. *Journal of Consumer Research* 37: 984–98.

(2011b). Why envy outperforms admiration. *Personality and Social Psychology Bulletin* 37: 784–95.

(2012). The appraisal patterns of envy and related emotions. *Motivation and Emotion* 36: 195–204.

Van Dijk, W. W., Ouwerkerk, J. W., Goslinga, S., and Nieweg, M. (2005). Deservingness and schadenfreude. *Cognition and Emotion* 19: 933–9.

Van Dijk, W. W., Ouwerkerk, J. W., Goslinga, S., Nieweg, M., and Gallucci, M. (2006). When people fall from grace: reconsidering the role of envy in schadenfreude. *Emotion* 6: 156–60.

Wert, S. R. and Salovey, P. (2004). A social comparison account of gossip. *Review of General Psychology* 8: 122–37.

Zizzo, D. J. and Oswald, A. (2001). Are people willing to pay to reduce others' income? *Annales d'Economie et de Statistique* 63/64: 39–65.

8 Schadenfreude and consumer behavior

Jill M. Sundie

Schadenfreude, feeling happy about the downfall of another, often stems from an unfavorable social comparison with a "superior" or "high achieving" other (e.g., Smith et al., 1996). As such, it may not be immediately obvious what schadenfreude has to do with consumer psychology or marketing. But as social advantages go, the display of prestige products is a quick, common, and highly visible way of broadcasting one's wealth and success – a form of social superiority over others. Thus, consumption practices may routinely create conditions ripe for schadenfreude, and a recent anecdotal experience of mine lends some credence to this idea.

My colleagues and I recently published a paper linking conspicuous consumption to mating motives, showing that men who are open to short-term sexual relationships preferred to spend money more extravagantly when romantic opportunities were salient (Sundie et al., 2011). Thanks to a crafty university press release, the paper drew some mass-media attention, but one relatively minor finding was the key focus of nearly all of the media stories covering the research – that a man with a Porsche was no more desirable to women as a marriage partner than if he instead drove an inexpensive, compact car. The idea that a prestige sports-car owner might "lose out" in the long-term mating game seemed newsworthy to most reporters covering our research. In short, people seemed to love the idea that a man flaunting a flashy sports car might experience some sort of romantic downfall or, at least, fail to excel over his more frugal competitors.

Schadenfreude seems to reside naturally within the zero-sum game of status competition. As Thorstein Veblen pointed out over a century ago in his classic *Theory of the Leisure Class* (1899), the flaunting of luxury possessions to convey one's "advantage" or high status has occurred across societies and epochs (Veblen, 1899, pp. 1–5). Egyptian pharaohs displayed their wealth with golden thrones, elaborate artworks, and giant pyramids; Incan potentates lived in immense palaces surrounded by gold; and Indian maharajahs built extravagant and ostentatious palaces and kept collections of rare, exotic animals on their grounds. Such showy displays of wealth have been documented in diverse cultures: in feudal Europe, Japan, among Polynesian Islanders, Icelandic communities, Amazonian foraging tribes, and the Melanesian people of Australia (Bird and Smith, 2005; Godoy et al., 2007; Veblen, 1899). Schadenfreude captures joy prompted by seeing the mighty – and, arguably, the material symbols of their status and advantage – fall (see Smith, Thielke, and Powell, Chapter 6 in this volume; Van de Ven, Chapter 7 in this volume; see also Cikara and Fiske, Chapter 10 in this volume, for a similar argument relevant to the intergroup context).

The broad appeal of schadenfreude in a status competition context has been leveraged to market products, such as in bargain airliner JetBlue's clever post-recession advertising campaign "targeted" to downtrodden CFOs and hedge fund managers, which featured the copy:

> JetBlue's fares start at very low prices. Let's just say, they're way, way, way less than the $5,300 an hour you used to pay for your private jet. Now, in exchange for these shareholder-friendly prices, you'll have to share the plane with strangers. Just think of it as jetpooling, only we find the other people for you. (Garfield, 2009)

Schadenfreude is even the name of a new women's fashion accessory company marketing costume jewellery versions of oversized gemstone rings (http://schadenfreude-inc.com).

Schadenfreude through the consumer's lens

Is the consumer realm just another social context in which we can observe schadenfreude? Or are there unique aspects of the consumption experience that can help illuminate antecedents and consequences of schadenfreude not easily observed in other relevant domains of social behavior? I will argue that consumer behavior is both an interesting and uniquely fruitful realm in which to consider what fuels the experience of schadenfreude, and what the consequences of that emotional experience might be. In this chapter I review the work of a variety of researchers who have begun to explore what happens at the intersection of schadenfreude and consumer psychological research, and suggest some future research directions for those interested in exploring schadenfreude through the lens of the consumer.

One objective of this chapter is to outline the documented consumer-relevant conditions that give rise to the experience of schadenfreude. In doing so, I will consider some dimensions of social comparison that involve consumption, and the social advantages that stem from an entity's material wealth or possessions. I will consider how consumption practices can give rise to some unique forms of in-group identification (and out-group derogation), as well as consumption-relevant emotions that have been shown to set the stage for schadenfreude, such as envy, anger, and feelings of injustice. Consumer research that has helped contribute to our understanding of how dark emotions, such as envy, encourage schadenfreude in response to a target's downfall will be reviewed. This work suggests that downfall-elicited schadenfreude can be prompted by the failure of a person, group, or other socially meaningful entity and the material symbols of that entity's economic success.

In addition to these precursors to schadenfreude, we can also examine consumer-relevant consequences of feeling happy about another's downfall. How do consumers evaluate a failed product or brand after experiencing feelings of schadenfreude? Does thinking about another person's failure make one feel more vulnerable to experiencing negative outcomes, leading to self-protective behavior involving more conservative (less risky) consumption choices? Such consequences of schadenfreude that have relevance for consumer behavior will be reviewed and discussed.

Antecedents and consequences of schadenfreude in the consumer context

What might lead a consumer to experience schadenfreude? Some scholars have pointed to roots in prior hostile feelings toward the target experiencing the downfall (Hareli and Weiner, 2002; Smith and Kim, 2007). In the consumption context, we can think of the target of schadenfreude as being a person, a product, a brand, a group of consumers (e.g., iPhone owners; Ouwerkerk and Van Dijk, Chapter 12 in this volume), or even a firm. Prior aggressive, hostile feelings toward such targets could originate from multiple sources. For example, the downfall could be viewed as a deserved punishment for a normative violation, with schadenfreude reflecting the satisfaction of knowing that the violator has been punished. For example, if a person feels ill will towards Walmart because of its alleged mass discrimination against female employees in promotion decisions (Lichtenstein, 2011), he may feel delighted to learn that a grassroots effort by a town's citizens to ban Walmart from building a new store has succeeded. Alternatively, it could be that hostile feelings come from the perception that someone has an unjust advantage, with schadenfreude following from an event that reverses that person's fortune. In a status consumption context, this latter example is a likely precursor to feeling schadenfreude, with the hostile feelings often rooted in envy of another person's advantage via his or her prestigious possessions.

Prior empirical work has examined a number of antecedents to schadenfreude, including individual achievement, with particular focus on academic and social success (Brigham et al., 1997; Feather and

Sherman, 2002; Hareli and Weiner, 2002; Smith et al., 1996; Van Dijk et al., 2006). Some evidence indicates that this enhancing effect of target person advantage on schadenfreude may be partially mediated by feelings of envy (Brigham et al., 1997; Smith et al., 1996; Van Dijk et al., 2006). This role of envy, however, has not been consistently observed in research examining the link between social advantage and schadenfreude experienced post-downfall (Feather and Sherman, 2002; Hareli and Weiner, 2002; Smith, Thielke, and Powell, Chapter 6 in this volume). Other studies have highlighted the antecedent role of other hostile negative feelings, such as dislike and resentment, suggesting that envy is not closely related to the experience of schadenfreude. So, although envy may play a role in setting the stage for schadenfreude, other emotions appear to be involved as well.

Sundie et al. (2009) examined the possibility that envy evoked from advantage in a consumer context transmutes into hostile feelings that ultimately can give rise to schadenfreude (Smith and Kim, 2007; Smith, Thielke, and Powell, Chapter 6 in this volume). This work helped to enhance our understanding of how envy, through its connection to other hostile feelings such as resentment, can lead to schadenfreude. In one experiment, participants read a scenario about a hypothetical individual of their same age and life stage (a fellow student) who possessed a product that conferred either higher or lower social status (an expensive sports sedan versus an economy car). Participants then rated their emotional reactions to the story, completing both positive (e.g., admiring) and negative (e.g., envious) emotion measures. The participants next learned about the failure not of the target person, but of the target person's product (i.e., the student's car breaks down in a public setting). Then, emotional reactions to the failure were assessed to uncover the extent to which schadenfreude was experienced. Participants completed both positive (e.g., happy) and negative (e.g., sympathetic) emotion measures, with the positive emotional reactions to the failure constituting schadenfreude. Social advantage involving the ownership of a prestige product led people to feel more envy, but, consistent with the transmutational character of envy, hostility (i.e., resentment, anger, feeling of injustice) mediated the envy–schadenfreude relationship.

In a replication and extension of the study just described, Sundie et al. (2009) examined whether flaunting behavior (in this case, flaunting a high-status car in a public setting) would enhance the experience of schadenfreude when the car later failed, compared to a scenario where the car owner instead behaved modestly. We also examined whether a desire for the automobile itself, versus envy of the social attention such a product might afford, played a role in driving the schadenfreude response.

We tested whether hostile feelings mediated any envy–schadenfreude relationship in an attempt to replicate the meditational relation found in our initial study (described above). To enhance a feeling of similarity with the target in this study, participants were asked to imagine the person in the scenario they were about to read was a casual social acquaintance (*not* a close friend) and fellow student. If randomly assigned to the flaunting condition, participants read about a Porsche owner who boasted about his car and behaved in a way designed to capture the attention of observers at an outdoor eatery he drove to for dinner with a group of friends. If randomly assigned to the modesty condition, participants instead read about a car owner who appeared to be uncomfortable with, and attempted to quell, any attention he received because of the car. Next, the very public product failure was described and participants' emotional reactions to the failure were assessed. The results of this study provided additional evidence that hostile feelings are key in linking envy to schadenfreude; hostility again mediated the envy–schadenfreude relationship. When separating the experience of envy into coveting of the product versus the social attention the product affords, we found that *only* envy of social attention the car afforded (not an envious desire for the car itself) predicted experiencing the hostility that encouraged schadenfreude. Lastly, when the target in this study engaged in flaunting behavior, this further enhanced schadenfreude, via enhanced envy of social attention and heightened hostility.

In the studies reported in Sundie et al. (2009), we focused exclusively on the appraisals and resultant emotions that accompany an upward social comparison involving a status product. An upward comparison occurs when a person perceives that a relevant target has outperformed him or her on a self-relevant dimension. When such motivationally relevant comparisons occur, people engage in a general appraisal process in an attempt to understand the meaning and personal implications of the situation (Lazarus, 1991; Smith and Lazarus, 1993; Weiner, 1985). Based on the appraisals involved in upward social comparisons (e.g., the discrepancy is self-relevant, negative), envy is a likely emotional response (Salovey and Rodin, 1984; Tesser and Collins, 1988; Van Dijk and Ouwerkerk, Chapter 9 in this volume). This logic presumes that the public failure of a status product conveys more than just a faulty product design or poor product quality, but is also a blow to the status afforded to the owner of the product. As such, the product failure can serve to take the owner "down a notch" in the eyes of observers, reducing the upward nature of the preceding social comparison, or perhaps even eliminating it. As an example of the latter result, if the observer of a prestige car's mechanical failure herself owns a brand that conveys less status, but runs very reliably, the observer may feel equal or even superior in status to the failed product owner on that dimension. In either case, the downfall of the threatening comparison person's possession can be gratifying and can encourage the schadenfreude response.

Other scholars have investigated antecedents to schadenfreude using product-focused manipulations of social advantage. Pancer and Ashworth (2009) examined whether perceptions of deservingness of a person's status product ownership would dampen the schadenfreude response; rather, they predicted that if a status product is perceived to be undeserved, conditions would be ripe for schadenfreude to occur. To manipulate deservingness in their study, Pancer and Ashworth varied whether the car owner (a fellow college student) received the car as a gift from his or her parents (low deservingness) or had personally paid for the car (high deservingness). The car the student owned conveyed either high status (a new BMW) or lower status (a used Ford). After participants learned that the car had been damaged in an accident, schadenfreude responses were assessed. Schadenfreude was indeed more intense when the car purchased by the student's parents was destroyed (in the low deservingness condition). As in Sundie et al. (2009), schadenfreude was more pronounced when it was a luxury vehicle that sustained the damage compared to a lower status car. This work parallels other findings on deservingness and schadenfreude in the social psychological literature (e.g., Feather, Chapter 3 in this volume; Van Dijk, Ouwerkerk, and Goslinga, 2009).

Antecedents to schadenfreude have also been examined within socially meaningful groups of consumers. Hickman and Ward (2007) took their interest in schadenfreude to the unique context of the brand community. Brand communities are groups united by their shared interest in a particular product or brand, and they can possess many of the same features as other interdependent social groups: a shared consciousness, rituals, and traditions. Loyal brand community members often experience feelings of moral obligation to the brand and to their fellow community members (Muniz Jr. and Schau, 2001). In some product categories, rival brand communities coexist (think Mac vs. PC in the computing realm). In their work, Hickman and Ward found that community members who were particularly biased in favor of their brand (relative to the rival brand) were more likely to report engaging in within-group "trash talk" about the rival brand and publicly derogating the rival brand, and experienced more schadenfreude when the rival brand suffered from a public downfall, such as an ethics violation or a mechanical failure. This "dark side" of brand community identification echoes other psychological research on group-based schadenfreude (e.g., Cikara and Fiske, 2012; Chapter 10 in this volume; Leach and Spears, 2008, 2009; Ouwerkerk and Van Dijk, Chapter 12 in this volume).

Building upon the idea that people can form and maintain strong connections with their favored brands, my colleagues and I examined whether self-brand connections would influence emotional responses to product failure (Sundie et al., 2014). The higher a person's self-brand connection, the more central the brand is to that person's identity (Escalas and Bettman, 2003). One need not possess a brand to feel a strong connection to it; consider a teenage boy with a poster featuring an expensive, powerful Ferrari on his bedroom wall – he may feel very connected to that brand, but only aspire to actually own it. This aspirational type of brand connection is likely to be quite common when the brand is particularly prestigious and expensive to purchase (i.e., a high-status brand), as many people will be unable to afford it. How might a person with a strong self-connection to a status brand respond when confronted with an otherwise similar other who owns their favored brand? At least two responses are possible. One possible response is to feel envy (e.g., he has it and I don't!) that will quickly transmute into hostile emotions such as anger; a response found to predict schadenfreude in previous research (Smith, Thielke, and Powell, Chapter 6 in this volume; Sundie et al., 2009; Van de Ven, Chapter 7 in this volume). Another possibility is that observing another with a coveted product will promote more positive responses such as happiness for the other and admiration (e.g., I want to be that guy!), a response we would expect to be more weakly connected to feeling schadenfreude and perhaps more strongly connected to feeling sadness, or empathy, post-failure.

In an initial study, we manipulated self-brand connection by presenting participants with a variety of high-status vehicles (all with retail prices of around $80,000) and asking them to choose either: (a) their favorite brand; or (b) their least favorite brand, based on random assignment. Next, participants read a scenario involving a similar other (in age, life stage) who possessed either the favored (in the high self-brand connection condition) or least favored (in the low self-brand connection condition) vehicle and were asked to rate their emotional responses to the scenario. Emotions measures were drawn from Sundie et al. (2009, Study 2) and assessed a balance of positive and negative reactions. Subsequently, participants learned that the vehicle had broken down and were asked about their emotions again, but in relation to the product failure scenario (both positive and negative feelings; the positive emotions connoted schadenfreude).

Our first question involved whether different types of people existed in terms of the emotional reactions they experienced after reading about the initial (pre-failure) scenario involving the high-status vehicle owner. To examine this, we analyzed the emotional responses using latent class modeling. Four classes emerged: (1) high envy and high hostility (e.g., anger); (2) low envy and high positive emotions (e.g., happiness); (3) high envy and high positive emotions (e.g., admiration); and (4) low envy but higher feelings of injustice and unfairness.

Second, we were interested in how self-brand connection influenced the emotional responses. To examine this, we computed the proportion of people in each class coming from the high versus low self-brand connection conditions. We found that people with a high self-brand connection predominated in the first class (hostile envy) and the third class (non-hostile envy) above. The emotional responses of people in these two classes are conceptually connected to two distinct forms of envy discussed in previous research: envy proper and benign envy (Feather, Chapter 3 in this volume; Smith and Kim, 2007; Smith, Thielke, and Powell, Chapter 6 in this volume; Van de Ven, Chapter 7 in this volume), respectively. In contrast, people in the low self-brand connection condition predominated in the classes experiencing lower levels of envy (groups 2 and 4) above.

We then computed the average level of schadenfreude experienced by participants in each class. Consistent with what we would expect based on previous research (Sundie et al., 2009), people experiencing hostile envy (class 1) reported the highest level of schadenfreude post-failure (and it should be recalled that a majority of these people were in the high self-brand connection condition). The next highest level of schadenfreude was reported by people who experienced feelings of injustice (class 4), but little envy (it should be recalled that a majority of people in this class were in the low self-brand connection condition). The emotional responses of this class may result from an appraisal that the target did not deserve his social advantage (Feather, Chapter 3 in this volume). Quite a bit lower in schadenfreude were the participants reporting non-hostile envy (class 3 – the majority of whom were also in the high self-brand connection condition). The lowest level of schadenfreude was reported by those who responded positively to the similar other with the high-status vehicle, experiencing positive emotions such as happiness for that target person, and little envy (class 2). This research suggests that examining the diversity of emotional responses that people have when confronted with a similar advantaged other may help further illuminate the precursors to schadenfreude.

In addition to these explorations into the causes of schadenfreude in the consumer context, consumer researchers have investigated some consequences of feeling joy at another's downfall. Two groups of scholars examined consumption-relevant consequences of schadenfreude, showing that there are indeed some effects of feeling these emotions that are relevant for marketers to consider (Kramer, Yucel-Aybat, and Lau-Gesk, 2011; Sundie et al., 2009). In the two experiments described above, my colleagues and I explored how observing a product failure might evoke actions that could harm a brand (Sundie et al., 2009). Specifically, we examined how feeling schadenfreude might prompt people to spread negative word-of-mouth (potentially damaging brand-related gossip) about the failed product or brand. Ordinarily, negative word-of-mouth is associated with one's own bad product, brand, or service experiences. For instance, if a person receives horrible service at a restaurant, she may tell her friends, co-workers, and family about that experience and thereby discourage them from eating at that establishment. We demonstrated in our studies that just observing another person's product failure may evoke negative word-of-mouth by way of relating the story of the failure to others. Feeling schadenfreude encourages such behavior and, in effect, allows the enjoyable schadenfreude experience to be transferred to others not present for the failure event through the re-telling of the story. Stories evoking schadenfreude make for juicy gossip, and brand managers of unreliable products should beware.

In addition, feeling schadenfreude after a product failure led our participants to report more negative affect toward the failed brand and lower overall attitudes toward the brand (Sundie et al., 2009). So, even though consumers may have an envious desire for a high-status product and the social benefits it affords, feeling schadenfreude when the product fails seems to elicit *negative* feelings toward that brand. While it is unclear how long these effects will last for consumers, it is clear that marketing campaigns designed to encourage consumer envy involving a status brand may have an unanticipated downside.

In another stream of research, Kramer and his colleagues examined whether the experience of schadenfreude would heighten people's expectations of negative outcomes for themselves, and therefore influence subsequent product evaluations and choices (Kramer, Yucel-Aybat, and Lau-Gesk, 2011). The authors hypothesized that feeling schadenfreude would make the possibility of experiencing bad outcomes seem more probable to people and that experiencing such feelings would change the way they evaluated consumption alternatives that varied in risk. Kramer and his colleagues predicted that feeling schadenfreude would make people more risk averse and demonstrated that people who experienced schadenfreude subsequently evaluated "safe" middle-of-the-road products more favorably than products with more extreme features or characteristics. In another study, Kramer and his colleagues used a choice task to illustrate that schadenfreude led to risk aversion – after experiencing schadenfreude, significantly more people preferred to receive a guaranteed payout of $25, versus a gamble involving a 20 percent chance of winning $250 and an 80 percent of winning nothing (two outcomes with an equivalent expected value). Kramer's team of researchers provided evidence that such effects were indeed mediated by people's heightened expectations of negative outcomes after recalling an experience that elicited schadenfreude.

New directions in schadenfreude-linked consumer behavior

Kapoor (2007) found that people could easily generate instances of consumption motivated by spite, and dark desires such as revenge. In fact, consumption of a particular product was sometimes motivated by a singular desire – to see another person experience a downfall. In Kapoor's study, a female participant reported buying the same expensive dress for a school dance that her friend had already purchased (even though she didn't really want that dress) so that her friend would feel angry and humiliated enough not to attend the event. Another participant reported buying a new cell phone to show off his wealth to his ex-girlfriend and her new boyfriend, with the explicit goal of making her new beau look inferior. This work suggests that the *anticipation* of experiencing schadenfreude when attaining desired vengeance may motivate some instances of consumption. Indeed, hostile emotions seem to be key in generating a feeling of joy upon observing another's failure (Sundie et al., 2009, 2014). Future consumer research could examine the role that the anticipation of schadenfreude plays in motivating status consumption, where the promise of being able to "purchase" social superiority may encourage people to spend extravagantly in order to bring about another's downfall.

The desire to gain and maintain status is a central and universal human motive (Kenrick et al., 2010). The consumption and display of products and brands is a highly visible and easy method by which to quickly project and assess a person's status. This form of advantage is also easy to manipulate, as it only requires a simple survey within a population of interest to determine what products or brands are of high versus low status. Researchers attempting to elicit social comparisons with emotional consequences for diverse individuals may find it quite fruitful to look to the consumer context for effective operationalizations of social advantage.

Researchers interested in studying intergroup schadenfreude may find brand communities both easily accessible and cooperative, particularly with the role that the Internet plays in creating and maintaining the bonds between these people. Just as in sports, rival brand communities exist (the rival brand's group of followers being akin to the "rival team"). These groups often flourish with the encouragement of the companies who promote the brands, with firms sometimes subsidizing and maintaining places (virtual and/or physical) and opportunities for community members to interact (think about the Apple store, for example). These brand communities are still a mostly untapped resource for people interested in conducting group-based research.

Sundie et al. (2014) suggest that social comparisons involving a status-linked product can elicit diverse emotional responses from similar others. Even when the status product does not elicit envy, social justice concerns may drive the schadenfreude response post-failure. While envy can transmute into hostile emotions, including a feeling of injustice, envy does not seem to be required to evoke the injustice response. Future research focusing on the people who feel low envy but intense injustice in response to upward comparisons may help illuminate the roles of envy versus deservingness in promoting schadenfreude. Investigating individual differences that predict membership in the classes of emotional responses found in Sundie et al. (2014) may further enhance our understanding of the antecedents and consequences of the schadenfreude response.

Research on schadenfreude in the consumer context has helped to illuminate the antecedents to this dark, yet often delicious emotional experience, and has generated knowledge about some unique consequences of feeling joy in another's downfall. Beyond just an interesting context in which to study schadenfreude, consumer behavior is a potentially fruitful and still mostly unexplored realm in which schadenfreude quite naturally resides. As with other kinds of social behavior, consumption can be motivated by desires for revenge, envy, anger, a feeling of social injustice, and many other affectively laden experiences. Some of these promote schadenfreude when witnessing an entity's downfall. By expanding our definition of a socially meaningful target to include products, brands, and firms, it becomes clear that schadenfreude's reach is perhaps even further and wider than previously thought, and an integral part of the social experience – after all, every human is a consumer.

References

Bird, R. B. and Smith, E. A. (2005). Signaling theory, strategic interaction, and symbolic capital. *Current Anthropology* 46: 221–48.

Brigham, N. L., Kelso, K. A., Jackson, M. A., and Smith, R. H. (1997). The roles of invidious comparisons and deservingness in sympathy and schadenfreude. *Basic and Applied Social Psychology* 19: 363–80.

Cikara, M. and Fiske, S. T. (2012). Stereotypes and schadenfreude: affective and physiological markers of pleasure at out-group misfortunes. *Social Psychological and Personality Science* 3: 63–71.

Escalas, J. E. and Bettman, J. R. (2003). You are what you eat: the influence of reference groups on consumers' connections to brands. *Journal of Consumer Psychology* 13: 339–48.

Feather, N. T. and Sherman, R. (2002). Envy, resentment, schadenfreude, and sympathy: reactions to deserved and undeserved achievement and subsequent failure. *Personality and Social Psychology Bulletin* 28: 953–61.

Garfield, B. (2009). A little clever schadenfreude may fill up some airline seats. *Advertising Age* 80(7), February 23. Available at: www.adage.com/article/ad-review/jetblue-s-advertising-campaign-fill-airline-seats/134782.

Godoy, R., Reyes-García, V., Huanca, T., Leonard, W. R., McDade, T., Tanner, S., Vadez, V., and Seyfried, C. (2007). Signaling by consumption in a native Amazonian society. *Evolution and Human Behavior* 28: 124–34.

Hareli, S. and Weiner, B. (2002). Dislike and envy as antecedents of pleasure at another's misfortune. *Motivation and Emotion* 26: 257–77.

Hickman, T. and Ward, J. (2007). The dark side of brand community: inter-group stereotyping, trash talk, and schadenfreude. *Advances in Consumer Research* 34: 314–19.

Kapoor, H. (2007). An exploratory examination of negative emotions as motivators of consumption. Atlantic Schools of Business Conference, Wolfville, NS, September 28–30.

Kenrick, D. T., Griskevicius, V., Neuberg, S. L., and Schaller, M. (2010). Renovating the pyramid of needs: contemporary extensions built upon ancient foundations. *Perspectives on Psychological Science* 5: 292–314.

Kramer, T., Yucel-Aybat, O., and Lau-Gesk, L. (2011). The effect of schadenfreude on choice of conventional versus unconventional options. *Organizational Behavior and Human Decision Processes* 116: 140–7.

Lazarus, R. S. (1991). *Emotion and Adaptation*. New York: Oxford University Press.

Leach, C. W. and Spears, R. (2008). "A vengefulness of the impotent": the pain of in-group inferiority and schadenfreude toward successful out-groups. *Journal of Personality and Social Psychology* 95: 1383–96.

(2009). Dejection at in-group defeat and schadenfreude toward second- and third-party out-groups. *Emotion* 9: 659–65.

Lichtenstein, N. (2011). Wal-Mart's authoritarian culture. *New York Times*, June 21. Available at: www.nytimes.com/2011/06/22/opinion/22Lichtenstein.html?r=1andscp=4andsq=walmartandst=cse.

Muniz Jr., A. M. and Schau, H. J. (2005). Religiosity in the abandoned Apple Newton brand community. *Journal of Consumer Research* 31: 737–47.

Pancer, E. and Ashworth, L. (2009). Getting what they don't necessarily deserve: the role of fairness in the experience of schadenfreude. In S. Samu, R. Vaidyanathan, and D. Chakravarti (eds.), *Asia-Pacific Advances in Consumer Research: Vol. 8*. Duluth, MN: Association for Consumer Research, pp. 2–3.

Salovey, P. and Rodin, J. (1984). Some antecedents and consequences of social comparison jealousy. *Journal of Personality and Social Psychology* 47: 780–92.

Smith, C. A., and Lazarus, R. S. (1993). Appraisal components, core relational themes, and the emotions. *Cognition and Emotion* 7: 233–69.

Smith, R. H. and Kim, S. H. (2007). Comprehending envy. *Psychological Bulletin* 133: 46–64.

Smith, R. H., Turner, T. J., Garonzik, R., Leach, C. W., Urch-Druskat, V., and Weston, C. M. (1996). Envy and schadenfreude. *Personality and Social Psychology Bulletin* 22: 158–68.

Sundie, J. M., Beal, D. J., Perkins, A., and Roche, S. (2014). Self-brand connection, envy and schadenfreude. Manuscript in preparation.

Sundie, J. M., Kenrick, D. T., Griskevicius, V., Tybur, J. M.,Vohs, K. D., and Beal, D. J. (2011). Peacocks, Porsches, and Thorstein Veblen: conspicuous consumption as a sexual signaling system. *Journal of Personality and Social Psychology* 100: 664–80.

Sundie, J. M., Ward, J., Beal, D. J., Chin, W. W., and Oneto, S. (2009). Schadenfreude as a consumption-related emotion: feeling happiness about the downfall of another's product. *Journal of Consumer Psychology* 19: 356–73.

Tesser, A. and Collins, J. E. (1988). Emotion in social reflection and comparison situations: intuitive, systematic, and exploratory approaches. *Journal of Personality and Social Psychology* 55: 695–709.

Van Dijk, W. W., Ouwerkerk, J. W., and Goslinga, S. (2009). The impact of deservingness on schadenfreude and sympathy: further evidence. *The Journal of Social Psychology* 149: 290–2.

Van Dijk, W. W., Ouwerkerk, J. W., Goslinga, S., Nieweg, M., and Gallucci, M. (2006). When people fall from grace: reconsidering the role of envy in schadenfreude. *Emotion* 6: 156–60.

Veblen, T. (1899). *The Theory of the Leisure Class*. New York: Macmillan.

Weiner, B. (1985). "Spontaneous" causal thinking. *Psychological Bulletin* 97: 74–84.

9 Striving for positive self-evaluation as a motive for schadenfreude

Wilco W. van Dijk and Jaap W. Ouwerkerk

Le malheur des uns fait le bonheur des autres. (French proverb)

When someone else suffers a mishap, a setback, a downfall, or another type of misfortune, people often experience sympathy and have feelings of concern and sorrow for the other. However, these events can also elicit schadenfreude – pleasure at the misfortunes of others. Whereas our moral tradition exalts and praises sympathetic people because they show concordance and sympathetic identification, *schadenfroh* people, by showing discordance and antagonism, seem to violate the obligation to cultivate the virtue of compassion (Heider, 1958; Portmann, 2000). Indeed, throughout history, schadenfreude has predominantly been condemned and regarded as a vice (Portmann, Chapter 2 in this volume; Van Dijk and Ouwerkerk, Chapter 1 in this volume). To illustrate, schadenfreude has been viewed as a malicious and immoral feeling (Baudelaire, 1855/1955), as a disguised expression of aggression (Aristotle, 350 BCE/1941), as harmful to social relations (Heider, 1958), as an "even more hideous cousin" of envy (Kierkegaard, 1847/1995), and as fiendish, diabolical, and "an infallible sign of a thoroughly bad heart and profound moral worthlessness" (Schopenhauer, 1841/1965). Although schadenfreude typically carries a negative connotation, people sometimes "cannot resist a little smile" when another person suffers a misfortune. Given the many displays of schadenfreude in television shows, blogs, magazines, and interpersonal communication (e.g., in gossip), it appears inherent to our human nature.

Why do people enjoy the misfortunes of others? The purpose of our present chapter is to examine the role of one's self-view in schadenfreude. We will argue that striving for a positive self-evaluation constitutes an important underlying motive for the experience of schadenfreude. In the following discussion we provide a theoretical framework in which we combine insights from appraisal theories on emotions and research on self-evaluation, social comparison processes, and self-affirmation, and present the main findings of our research program on the relation between self-evaluation and schadenfreude.

Schadenfreude and the appraisal of the misfortunes of others

A central tenet of appraisal theories is the claim that emotions are elicited by cognitive evaluations (appraisals) of events and specific emotions are elicited by a distinctive pattern of appraisals (for an overview of appraisal theories, see Roseman and Smith, 2001). Appraisal theories state that different individuals who appraise the same event or situation in different ways will feel different emotions. For example, an individual who evaluates the end of a relationship as an undesired event will experience emotions such as sadness, whereas an individual who evaluates this same event as desirable will experience emotions such as relief. Furthermore, a given individual who appraises the same event in different ways at different times will feel different emotions at these different times. For example, an individual who blames himself or herself for the problems in a relationship tends to experience emotions akin to guilt, whereas when this appraisal changes from self-blame to other-blame, the experienced emotion is likely to change from guilt to anger. Moreover, different events that are appraised in similar ways tend to produce the same emotions. For example, when a partner is blamed for the problems in a relationship or blamed for other negative events, all these events typically elicit anger. Thus, it is not the event itself that evokes an emotion, but rather a person's subjective appraisal of the personal significance of this event. Moreover, all events that evoke the same emotion tend to share a pattern of appraisals or, in other words, are evaluated in similar ways. This implies that events that evoke schadenfreude should to some extent be evaluated in the same way (Van Dijk and Ouwerkerk, Chapter 1 in this volume).

In his seminal article "The laws of emotions," Frijda argues that emotions point to the presence of some concern: "*Emotions arise in response to events that are important to the individual's goals, motives, or concerns*" (1988, p. 349, italics in original). In essence, every emotion hides a concern. Events that satisfy one's concerns (or promise to do so) yield positive emotions; conversely, negative emotions are elicited by events that harm or threaten one's concerns. Thus, for an event to elicit schadenfreude, another's misfortune should be appraised by the *schadenfroh* person as an event that satisfies some important personal concern. The common pattern of appraisal in events that evoke schadenfreude should reflect that something in another's misfortune is beneficial for the person experiencing schadenfreude. But which concerns give the misfortunes of others its positive emotional meaning? Which concerns does schadenfreude hide? These concerns may be different from one occurrence of schadenfreude to another and from one person to the other. There may be many reasons to enjoy the misfortunes of others, but they should have in common that they all point to the presence of an important concern. In other words, schadenfreude-eliciting events refer to events that are appraised by the *schadenfroh* person as beneficial for his or her concerns. Below we will first discuss this issue in relation to earlier research on schadenfreude and will follow this with a more elaborate discussion of the role of self-evaluation in the experience of schadenfreude.

Schadenfreude and deservingness

Different scholars argue that schadenfreude derives from the evaluation of the misfortune as deserved (Ben-Ze'ev, 2000 and Chapter 5 in this volume; Feather, 2006 and Chapter 3 in this volume; Portmann, 2000 and Chapter 2 in this volume). This viewpoint is perhaps best captured by the words of the contemporary philosopher John Portmann: "It is not the suffering of others that brings us joy, but rather the evidence of justice triumphing before our eyes" (2000, p. xiii). The notion that schadenfreude is predictably evoked when someone gets his or her come-uppance has received ample empirical support (see, e.g., Feather, 1994, 2006 and Chapter 3 in this volume; Powell, Chapter 4 in this volume; Van Dijk et al., 2005). To illustrate, in one of our own studies (Van Dijk et al., 2005) participants responded to (allegedly real) interviews in which information was provided about a (male or female) fellow student who suffered a misfortune. We experimentally varied in these interviews whether the student was either responsible or not responsible for the misfortune. Results showed that participants experienced more schadenfreude when the student was responsible for his or her misfortune rather than when he or she was not, and that this effect was mediated by the perceived deservingness of the misfortune. In other words, the more a student was seen as responsible for his or her own misfortune, the more this misfortune was seen as deserved, which in turn evoked more schadenfreude. Moreover, in other studies we replicated this relationship between deservingness and schadenfreude using different manipulations of deservingness (Van Dijk, Goslinga, and Ouwerkerk, 2008; Van Dijk, Ouwerkerk, and Goslinga, 2009). As most people care about just and deserved outcomes, they can enjoy deserved misfortunes (Feather, 1994 and Chapter 3 in this volume). An appraisal of deservingness might also explain (at least partly) why people enjoy the misfortunes of those they dislike (Hareli and Weiner, 2002; Van Dijk et al., 2006; Zillmann and Bryant, 1980; Zillmann and Knobloch, 2001), resent (Feather and Sherman, 2002), or consider as hypocrites (Powell, Chapter 4 in this volume). To the extent that people appraise the misfortunes of those they dislike, resent, or consider hypocrites as just and deserved, these misfortunes satisfy an important concern and therefore these misfortunes can be pleasing.

Schadenfreude and envy

In addition to the link between deservingness and schadenfreude, many scholars have advocated the relationship between envy and schadenfreude (Cikara and Fiske, Chapter 10 in this volume; Heider, 1958; Plato, 1925; Smith, Thielke, and Powell, Chapter 6 in this volume; Spinoza, 1677/2002; Van de Ven, Chapter 7 in this volume; Van Dijk and Ouwerkerk, Chapter 1 in this volume). Envy is typically a very unpleasant emotion and entails feelings of inferiority, hostility, and injustice (Smith and Kim, 2007). A misfortune befalling an envied person can be pleasing because it is usually appraised as beneficial for the envious person, that is, it renders the advantaged other less enviable and thereby cuts away the very basis of envy. In other words, it transforms an invidious social comparison into a more favorable one, thereby providing a social comparison benefit relative to the earlier comparison with the initially envied other (Smith, Thielke, and Powell, Chapter 6 in this volume; Van de Ven, Chapter 7 in this volume; Van Dijk and Ouwerkerk, Chapter 1 in this volume). Although several scholars have questioned the role of envy in schadenfreude (e.g., Feather and Sherman, 2002; Hareli and Weiner, 2002; Leach and Spears, 2008), ample studies have provided empirical support for the link between envy and schadenfreude (Cikara and Fiske, Chapter 10 in this volume; Feather, Chapter 3 in this volume; Smith, Thielke, and Powell, Chapter 6 in this volume; Smith et al., 1996; Takahashi et al., 2009; Van de Ven, Chapter 7 in this volume; Van Dijk et al., 2006).

Schadenfreude, self-evaluation, and social comparison

In addition to concerns related to deservingness and envy, we propose that striving for a positive self-evaluation is another important motive underlying the experience of schadenfreude. We argue that people can be pleased by another's misfortune because this misfortune improves their position relative to the other person and the self-enhancing aspect of a more favorable comparison enables them to derive pleasure from it (for a related argument, see Buckley, Chapter 14 in this volume). More specifically, we argue that the misfortunes of others can be pleasing because these provide people with opportunities to protect, maintain, or enhance a positive self-view.

In line with Allport's suggestion that a person's "most coveted experience is the enhancement of his self-esteem" (1937, p. 169), many psychologists regard the protection, maintenance, or enhancement of (a positive) self-evaluation as a primary motive of human behavior (see, e.g., Baumeister, 1991, 1994; Brown and Dutton, 1995; Sedikides and Strube, 1997; Taylor and Brown, 1988; Tesser, 1988). According to Baumeister: "The desire for a favorable view of the self is well established. Its many forms ... suggested the conclusion that a need for some sense of self-worth is one of the pillars of finding a meaningful life" (1994, p. 72). One possible route to a positive self-evaluation involves downward social comparisons, comparing one's own lot to those of less fortunate others (Wills, 1981). We argue that (at least part of) the pleasure in schadenfreude stems from the social comparison benefits provided by the misfortunes of others.

Social comparisons will elicit strong emotions when they are directly relevant to a person's goals, motives, or concerns (Smith, 2000). In terms of social comparison theories, comparison processes occur more easily and have more impact when people are confronted with another person's performance or outcomes in a domain that is important and relevant to the self, particularly when this other is psychologically close (Tesser, 1991). High self-relevance and psychological closeness enhance both the likelihood of comparisons being made and the resulting impact of the comparison on the self (Lockwood and Kunda, 1997; Smith, 2000). Psychological closeness is defined here in a unit-relation sense, referring to the connection that exists between people who are "perceived as belonging together in a specifically close way" (Heider, 1958, p. 201). People are perceived as belonging together if they can be subsumed by some social construct. Examples of social constructs that might serve as a meaningful basis for closeness are gender, nationality, religion, social status, or family membership. However, research has shown that only a minimal degree of similarity between people (e.g., sharing birthdays) is sufficient to create a sense of "belonging together" (Miller, Downs, and Prentice, 1998). Applying these insights to the context of schadenfreude, and connecting them to our contention that the misfortunes of others can be pleasing because they provide people with opportunities to protect, maintain, or enhance their self-evaluation, leads to the prediction that schadenfreude should be most intense when a misfortune happens to a close other in a self-relevant domain.

In a recent study we examined the impact of the closeness of the comparison other and the relevance of the comparison domain on schadenfreude by experimentally varying both these aspects of social comparison information (Van Dijk, Smith, and Ouwerkerk, 2012). Informed by research on gender differences in social comparison processes, we manipulated the closeness of the comparison other by varying the gender of the person who suffered a misfortune. Earlier research has shown that gender is a social construct that can serve as a basis for similarity and that people have a preference for same-gender comparisons (Major, Testa, and Bylsma, 1991). Therefore, in our study we confronted (male and female) participants with either a male or female comparison other. For our female participants, another woman should be a more close and relevant social comparison target, whereas for our male participants, another man should be. Furthermore, we manipulated the relevance of the comparison domain by varying the type of misfortune the other person suffered. Research has shown that Korean, Dutch, and American men reported greater distress than women from these countries when a rival surpassed them in relation to financial prospects, job prospects, and physical strength. Korean, Dutch, and American women reported greater distress when a rival surpassed them on facial and bodily attractiveness (Buss et al., 2000). In our study we therefore confronted our participants with the misfortune of a (male or female) comparison other who failed either in the domain of status and achievements or in the domain of physical attractiveness. We hypothesized that male participants would experience the most schadenfreude when a male target (a close comparison other for male participants) suffers a misfortune in the domain of status and achievements (a highly self-relevant domain for male participants). By contrast, female participants should experience the most schadenfreude when a female target (a close comparison other for female participants) suffers a misfortune in the domain of physical appearance (a highly self-relevant domain for female participants).

Participants were asked to read a scenario in which they attended a reunion from their high school where the most popular student from their days in high school delivered a speech. During this speech, it became apparent that this former classmate had suffered several setbacks. Both the gender of the target and the specific misfortune were experimentally varied. For some participants the target was a male student, whereas for the others the target was female. Furthermore, some participants were informed that the speech contained bad jokes and that one could notice that he or she had not been very successful after leaving school. Other participants were informed that during the speech, it became apparent that he or she gained weight considerably, dressed out of fashion, and did not look that attractive anymore. After reading this scenario, participants were asked questions pertaining to their feelings toward the setbacks that had befallen their former classmate. Results supported our hypothesis. Male participants experienced the most schadenfreude when a former male classmate turned out to be unsuccessful, whereas female participants experienced the most schadenfreude when a former female classmate lost her looks.

These findings corroborate our notion that schadenfreude is increased when a close other suffers a misfortune in a domain that is important for the *schadenfroh* person. Arguably, these misfortunes provide the best opportunities to enhance one's self-evaluation and therefore elicit strong positive feelings. These findings underscore the importance of the relevance of both the social comparison other and the social comparison domain in the experience of schadenfreude. Moreover, these findings are in line with our notion that schadenfreude is more intense when social comparison benefits are larger. More specifically, a misfortune happening to a close other in a self-relevant domain should be especially pleasing when this misfortune highlights one's own advantages rather than disadvantages and thereby provides an opportunity to enhance one's self-evaluation.

Schadenfreude, self-esteem, and self-threat

The theory of downward comparison (Wills, 1981) posits that people can enhance their own self-evaluation by comparing themselves with a less fortunate other, and that these downward comparison processes can be evoked by a threat to one's psychological well-being. Downward comparisons can occur on an active basis by derogating another person – thereby increasing the psychological distance between the self and the other – or harming the other person – thereby creating the opportunity for comparison with a less fortunate other. However, downward comparison can also occur on a more passive basis, for example, by taking advantage of available opportunities for downward comparison when witnessing another person suffering a misfortune. Downward comparison theory posits that downward comparisons are motivated by self-enhancement and that this motivation is increased by a threat to one's self-evaluation. Wills' influential paper, "Downward comparison principles in social psychology," initiated much research on downward comparison processes and the findings of many studies are consistent with this view (e.g., Aspinwall and Taylor, 1993; Gibbons et al., 2002). Because the basic process of downward comparison is motivated by self-enhancement, it follows that individuals who are temporarily or chronically threatened in their self-evaluation will have a greater motivation for self-enhancement, and hence will more often engage in downward social comparison processes (Wills, 1981). Consistent with this notion, research has shown that self-evaluations of individuals with low self-esteem become more favorable after exposure to downward comparison information compared to those with high self-esteem (Affleck et al., 1987; Aspinwall and Taylor, 1993; Gibbons and Gerrard, 1989; Morse and Gergen, 1970; Reis, Gerrard, and Gibbons, 1993), and that this effect is more pronounced when low self-esteem individuals experienced an acute self-evaluation threat (Gibbons and McCoy, 1991).

By combining our contention that the protection, maintenance, or self-enhancement of a positive self-evaluation is an important motive for people to enjoy the misfortunes of others with the above assumptions of downward social comparison theory, we hypothesized that schadenfreude following another's misfortune will be more intense when people's motivation to self-enhance becomes greater. In other words, people should experience more schadenfreude when they are chronically low in self-evaluation and/or when they experience an acute self-evaluation threat. We tested these predictions in a series of studies. A first study addressed the relationship between self-esteem and schadenfreude (Van Dijk et al., 2011a), whereas a second and third study addressed the relationship between an acute self-evaluation threat and schadenfreude (Van Dijk et al., 2011b). Finally, in a fourth study we examined the impact of a "double whammy" – a combination of both a chronic (i.e., low self-esteem) and an acute self-threat – on schadenfreude (Van Dijk et al., 2012).

In our first study of this series we hypothesized that low self-esteem people will experience more schadenfreude following the misfortune of a high achiever than high self-esteem people. This expectation is consistent with downward comparison theory. For example, it has been argued that low self-esteem people have a strong motivation for self-protection and often engage in downward comparison processes (Aspinwall and Taylor, 1993; Wills, 1981). Moreover, low self-esteem people may feel more threatened by relevant social comparisons to others who perform well in important domains (Gibbons, 1986; Tesser, 1988). Therefore, we expected that, as compared with high self-esteem people, low self-esteem people feel more threatened in their self-views by a relevant high achiever, and this increased self-threat intensifies their schadenfreude if this high achiever suffers a misfortune.

To test this notion we conducted a study in which we assessed both participants' self-esteem and their schadenfreude following another's misfortune (Van Dijk et al., 2011a, Study 1). In this study we first assessed participants' self-esteem by means of the State Self-Esteem Scale (Heatherton and Polivy, 1991), a well-validated measure of self-esteem. Next, participants were presented with two interviews that introduced a high-achieving student who subsequently suffered a misfortune. In the first interview, the student was described in terms of high academic achievements and high likelihood to get a good job. Before participants read the second interview, they completed measures that assessed their feelings of self-threat evoked by the high-achieving student. Next, participants read an interview with the student's supervisor that was allegedly conducted three months after the interview with the student. From this interview, participants learned that the student had recently suffered a setback, as the supervisor stated that the student had given a very poor presentation of his or her thesis and had to rewrite major parts of it. Consequently, the student would suffer a serious delay in his or her studies. We then assessed participants' schadenfreude toward this misfortune. As expected, participants with lower self-esteem experienced more schadenfreude toward the misfortune of the high-achieving student than those with high self-esteem. Moreover, this relationship was mediated by the self-threat evoked by the high achiever. In other words, low self-esteem individuals felt more threatened by the high-achieving student and, consequently, experienced more schadenfreude. Again, these findings support our notion that the misfortunes of others can elicit schadenfreude because they may provide an opportunity to protect a threatened self-view.

In two subsequent studies we examined the impact of a direct self-evaluation threat on schadenfreude (Van Dijk et al., 2011b). The first study allegedly consisted of two unrelated parts. In the first part, a self-evaluation threat was manipulated by providing participants with either negative or positive feedback on a self-relevant task. It was explained that they had to complete a task that assessed their "Inconsistent Rules Processing Ability." To increase the relevance of this task, participants were led to believe that performance on the task had been shown to correlate strongly with the capacity for analytic thinking and intellectual abilities in general. After completing this task, participants received either negative or positive feedback on their performance. In the negative feedback condition they were led to believe they had scored among the worst 10 percent of the student population, whereas in the positive feedback condition they were led to believe they had scored among the best 10 percent of the student population (a check indicated that this procedure successfully manipulated how threatened participants felt in their self-evaluation). Subsequently, in the alleged second part of the study, participants were presented with two written interviews as in the study described earlier. In the first interview, a fellow student was again described as having a high potential in terms of achievement and likelihood to get a good job. In the second interview with the student's supervisor, participants were told that the student had recently suffered a setback. Following this second interview, participants' experience of schadenfreude was assessed. The results showed that participants who had received negative feedback on the earlier self-relevant task experienced more schadenfreude toward their fellow student's misfortune than those who had received positive feedback. A second experiment – in which we contrasted a negative feedback condition with a no feedback condition and used a different misfortune – replicated our finding that negative feedback intensifies schadenfreude.

In the three studies described above we showed that individuals who have low self-esteem or experience a more direct self-evaluation threat, and therefore have a greater need to restore their self-worth, feel more schadenfreude following another's misfortune than those who have high self-esteem or do not experience a self-evaluation threat, respectively. In a fourth study of this series we wanted to gain further empirical support for our notion that schadenfreude reflects an appraisal of a situation as satisfying one's concern for protecting, maintaining, or enhancing feelings of self-worth by examining the interplay between people's self-esteem (i.e., their chronic self-evaluation threat) and an acute self-threat (Van Dijk et al., 2012). Wills' (1981) influential paper initiated many studies on downward comparison processes. Several of these studies have demonstrated that, following an acute self-threat, individuals with low self-esteem show the most favorable reactions to downward comparisons by virtue of the "double whammy" of low self-esteem and an acute self-threat (Aspinwall and Taylor, 1993; Gibbons, 1986). In such a situation, people will be especially motivated to restore their self-worth and, consequently, another's misfortune should be the most pleasing. Thus, we argue that the impact of an acute self-threat on schadenfreude following another's misfortune will be stronger for individuals with low self-esteem than for those with high self-esteem.

To test this idea we conducted a study in which we assessed participants' self-esteem and subsequently confronted them with either a direct self-esteem threat or self-esteem boost by providing them with negative feedback or positive feedback on a self-relevant task (cf. Van Dijk et al., 2011b). Following this experimental manipulation, participants watched a very unfavorable performance of a contestant in the Dutch version of the TV show *American Idol* and we assessed their schadenfreude. Results showed that participants with low self-esteem experienced more schadenfreude following the unflattering TV performance after they had just received negative feedback on the self-relevant task, as compared with those who had just received positive feedback. Thus, consistent with our hypothesis, these participants were especially motivated to restore their threatened self-worth. Moreover, participants with high self-esteem did not differ in their experience of schadenfreude as a function of feedback, indicating that their high self-esteem provided them with a sufficient buffer against a self-threat posed by negative feedback on the self-relevant task.

Together, these studies lend strong support for our contention that striving for a positive self-evaluation is an important underlying motive for the experience of schadenfreude. First, we showed that people experience more schadenfreude toward the misfortunes of relevant social comparison others, especially when these misfortunes happen in a domain that is important for the *schadenfroh* person. Second, we demonstrated that people experience more schadenfreude when their concern for enhancing their self-evaluation was stronger, due to a chronic self-evaluation threat (i.e., low self-esteem), an acute self-evaluation threat (i.e., negative feedback on a self-relevant task), or a combination of these threats. Thus, people can indeed be pleased by another's misfortune because this misfortune helps to satisfy an important concern of people, that is, the protection, maintenance, or enhancement of their (positive) self-evaluation.

Schadenfreude, self-enhancement, and self-affirmation

Our notion that the misfortunes of others can provide people with self-enhancement opportunities implies that people should feel more self-enhanced after they experienced schadenfreude. Moreover, if schadenfreude increases when people's concern for a positive self-evaluation becomes stronger, it implies that schadenfreude should decrease when this concern weakens, for example, when alternative means for self-enhancement are available. We tested these implications in two studies.

In a first study we aimed to demonstrate that, after a misfortune occurs, the intensity of schadenfreude is positively related to enhanced feelings about the self. Support for this hypothesis would provide further evidence for the important role of self-evaluation in evoking schadenfreude. In this study we used an autobiographical narrative approach to test our hypothesis. Autobiographical narratives provide subjective accounts of what happened from one person's (i.e., the narrator's) point of view and indicate the aspects of an incident a person regards as important and meaningful enough to be included in the story (Gergen and Gergen, 1988). Although the autobiographical method has less internal validity than controlled laboratory experiments, its high external validity is a major advantage. As such, they provide a valuable complement to controlled experimental methods conducted in laboratory settings (Baumeister, Stillwell, and Heatherton, 1995; Baumeister, Stillwell, and Wotman,

1990; Zechmeister and Romero, 2002). Hence, in this study – which was part of a larger study on the phenomenology of schadenfreude – we asked participants to describe a schadenfreude experience, to report the intensity of their schadenfreude, and to indicate their subsequent feelings about the self. Results of this study showed that, after the misfortune occurred, schadenfreude is indeed related to enhanced feelings about the self. These findings again suggest that the misfortunes of others may satisfy people's striving for a positive self-evaluation. Interestingly, in several of the participants' autobiographical narratives, the relationship between schadenfreude and self-enhancement was explicitly mentioned. For example, one participant described part of a schadenfreude situation as "a feeling of triumph, that feels good. And yes, it is true, your self-view also becomes better of it." Another participant described the following schadenfreude situation: "the fact that a fellow student did not pass her exams. You feel sorry for the other, but you are also happy. Because it makes you extra good if you do pass the exams. Thus, you feel better and stronger through the misfortunes of others." Of course, these are only a few individual observations, but they correspond with the positive correlation we obtained between schadenfreude and enhanced feelings about the self, and are in line with our reasoning that striving for a positive self-evaluation constitutes an important motive for the experience of schadenfreude.

In our second study of this series, we hypothesized that schadenfreude should increase when people's motivation to self-enhance becomes greater, whereas it should decrease when this motivation diminishes. We examined this hypothesis by investigating the relationships between self-esteem, self-affirmation, and schadenfreude. First, we expected that people with low self-esteem would experience more schadenfreude at the misfortune of a high achiever than people with low self-esteem. This expectation is consistent with the findings of our studies described earlier. Second, we expected that providing low self-esteem people with an opportunity for self-affirmation would attenuate their schadenfreude at the misfortune of a high achiever. This expectation is based on self-affirmation theory (Steele, 1988). According to this theory, an opportunity to affirm self-integrity will decrease defensive reactions to threatening information. Typically, self-affirmation procedures involve asking people to identify an important value or aspect of life and subsequently giving them the opportunity to reflect upon this self-relevant aspect (McQueen and Klein, 2006). Indeed, self-affirmation procedures like this have been shown to reduce defensiveness in, for instance, dissonance reduction (Steele and Liu, 1983), rumination (Koole et al., 1999), and health information processing (Van Koningsbruggen, Das, and Roskos-Ewoldsen,

2009). Moreover, self-affirmation has been found to reduce the use of defensive strategies in threatening social comparison situations (Tesser and Cornell, 1991).

Since self-affirmation procedures bolster feelings of self-integrity, Steele (1988) suggested that it should reduce the motivation for self-protection or self-enhancement through other means (e.g., the misfortunes of others). Accordingly, we hypothesize that an opportunity to self-affirm will attenuate schadenfreude for low self-esteem people. In other words, offering people low in self-esteem an opportunity for self-affirmation to restore their global sense of self-integrity should reduce their need to use the misfortunes of others to achieve this goal. In our final study we tested this idea (Van Dijk et al., 2011a, Study 2). We first assessed participants' self-esteem and then presented them with two interviews that introduced a high-achieving student who subsequently suffered a misfortune. In the first interview, a student was again described in terms of high academic achievements and high likelihood to get a good job (cf. Van Dijk et al., 2011a, Study 1). Before participants read the second interview, they completed measures that assessed their feelings of self-threat evoked by the high-achieving student and some participants were given the opportunity to self-affirm, whereas others were not given such an opportunity. Finally, all participants read an interview with the student's supervisor from which they learned that the student had recently suffered a setback and we subsequently assessed their schadenfreude. The results show that the earlier reported indirect relationship between self-esteem and schadenfreude (Van Dijk et al., 2011, Study 1) is contingent on an opportunity of self-affirmation. In other words, when no opportunity for self-affirmation is available, low self-esteem participants experience a stronger self-threat when confronted with a high-achiever, and this self-threat in turn increases their schadenfreude. This response, however, is attenuated when they are given an opportunity to self-affirm. In other words, self-threat mediated the relationship of self-esteem with schadenfreude for non-affirmed participants, whereas for self-affirmed participants, the relationship between self-esteem and schadenfreude was not mediated by self-threat.

The results of our last two studies provide further support for our notion that the misfortunes of others can evoke schadenfreude because they provide people with an opportunity to enhance their self-views. First, we showed that people feel more self-enhanced when they experienced schadenfreude. Second, we demonstrated that providing people with an alternative means for self-enhancement, through the opportunity to self-affirm in an unrelated context, attenuated the experience of schadenfreude. Sherman and Cohen argue in their review paper on self-affirmation theory: "Much research within the self-affirmation framework examines whether an affirmation of self-integrity, unrelated to a specific provoking threat, can attenuate or eliminate people's normal response to that threat. If it does, then one can infer that the response was motivated by a desire to protect self-integrity" (2006, p. 187). Thus, as self-affirmation manipulations represent an accepted method for testing whether a response is motivated by self-evaluative concerns, these findings again provide strong support for the notion that schadenfreude can be motivated by a concern for positive self-evaluation.

Conclusions

The findings of the six reported studies yielded a coherent pattern of results supporting the contention that striving for a positive self-evaluation is an important underlying motive for schadenfreude. Our present analysis is by no means restricted to people's *individual* self-worth. According to social identity theory (Tajfel, 1978; Tajfel and Turner, 1979), part of people's self-concept stems from the knowledge that they belong to certain groups, referred to as their *collective* self or social identity. Furthermore, based on a self-enhancement perspective, Tajfel and Turner (1979) have suggested that people strive for a positive evaluation of the collective self (i.e., a positive social identity) and hence want groups to which they belong to be distinguished favorably from other groups. Social identity research has also suggested that threats to a positive evaluation of the collective self will increase malicious responses to out-groups that pose such a threat (for a review, see Branscombe et al., 1999).

Indeed, this line of reasoning is supported by several studies on intergroup schadenfreude. For example, research shows that schadenfreude is more intense when the domain of an out-group's misfortune is more important to in-group members (Leach et al., 2003). In addition, studies demonstrate that people experience more schadenfreude toward an out-group when they identify more strongly with their in-group (Schurtz et al., Chapter 11 in this volume). Moreover, our own studies show that domain interest and affective in-group identification interactively predict schadenfreude in intergroup relations (Ouwerkerk and Van Dijk, Chapter 12 in this volume), indicating that intergroup schadenfreude is most intense when the social comparison context is more relevant to one's collective self. This corroborates our contention that striving for positive self-evaluation is an important underlying motive for schadenfreude.

References

Affleck, G., Tennen, H., Pfeiffer, C., Fifield, J., and Rowe, J. (1987). Downward comparison and coping with serious medical problems. *American Journal of Orthopsychiatry* 57: 570–8.

Allport, G. W. (1937). *Personality: A Psychological Interpretation*. New York: Holt.

Aristotle (1941 [350 BCE]). In R. McKeon (ed.), *The Basic Works of Aristotle*. New York: Random House.

Aspinwall, L. G. and Taylor, S. E. (1993). The effects of social comparison direction, threat, and self-esteem on affect, self-evaluation, and expected success. *Journal of Personality and Social Psychology* 64: 708–22.

Baudelaire, C. (1955 [1855]). *On the Essence of Laughter* (translated by J. Mayne). New York: Phaidon Press.

Baumeister, R. F. (1991). *The Meaning of Life*. New York: Guilford Press.

(1994). Self, and identity: a social psychology perspective. In A. Tesser (ed.), *Advanced Social Psychology*. Boston, MA: McGraw-Hill, pp. 51–98.

Baumeister, R. F., Stillwell, A. M., and Heatherton, T. F. (1995). Personal narratives about guilt: role in action control and interpersonal relationships. *Basic and Applied Social Psychology* 17: 173–98.

Baumeister, R. F., Stillwell, A. M., and Wotman, S. R. (1990). Victim and perpetrator accounts of interpersonal conflict: autobiographical narratives about anger. *Journal of Personality and Social Psychology* 59: 994–1005.

Ben-Ze'ev, A. (2000). *The Subtlety of Emotions*. Cambridge, MA: MIT Press.

Branscombe, N. R., Ellemers, N., Spears, R., and Doosje, B. (1999). The context and content of social identity threat. In N. Ellemers, R. Spears, and B. Doosje (eds.), *Social Identity: Context, Commitment, Content*. Oxford: Blackwell, pp. 35–58.

Brown, J. D. and Dutton, K. A. (1995). The thrill of victory, the complexity of defeat: self-esteem and people's emotional reactions to success and failure. *Journal of Personality and Social Psychology* 68: 712–22.

Buss, D. M., Shackelford, T. D., Choe, J., Buunk, B. P., and Dijkstra, P. (2000). Distress about mating rivals. *Personal Relationships* 7: 235–43.

Feather, N. T. (1994). Attitudes towards high achievers and reactions to their fall: theory and research concerning tall poppies. In M. P. Zanna (ed.), *Advances in Experimental Social Psychology*, Vol. 26. New York: Academic Press, pp. 1–73.

(2006). Deservingness and emotions: applying the structural model of deservingness to the analysis of affective reactions to outcomes. *European Review of Social Psychology* 17: 38–73.

Feather, N. T. and Sherman, R. (2002). Envy, resentment, schadenfreude, and sympathy: reactions to deserved and undeserved achievement and subsequent failure. *Personality and Social Psychology Bulletin* 28: 953–61.

Frijda, N. H. (1988). The laws of emotion. *American Psychologist* 43: 349–58.

Gergen, K. J. and Gergen, M. M. (1988). Narrative and the self as relationship. In L. Berkowitz (ed.), *Advances in Experimental Social Psychology*, Vol. 21. New York: Academic Press, pp. 17–56.

Gibbons, F. X. (1986). Social comparison and depression: company's effect on misery. *Journal of Personality and Social Psychology* 51: 140–8.

Gibbons, F. X. and Gerrard, M. (1989). Effects of upward and downward social comparison on mood states. *Journal of Clinical and Social Psychology* 8: 14–31.

Gibbons, F. X., Lane, D. J., Gerrard, M., Reis-Bergan, M., Lautrup, C. L., Pexa, N. A., and Blanton, H. (2002). Comparison-level preferences after performance: is downward comparison theory still useful? *Journal of Personality and Social Psychology* 83: 865–80.

Gibbons, F. X. and McCoy, S. B. (1991). Self-esteem, similarity, and reactions to active versus passive downward comparison. *Journal of Personality and Social Psychology* 60: 414–24.

Hareli, S. and Weiner, B. (2002). Dislike and envy as antecedents of pleasure at another's misfortune. *Motivation and Emotion* 26: 257–77.

Heatherton, T. F. and Polivy, J. (1991). Development and validation of a scale for measuring state self-esteem. *Journal of Personality and Social Psychology* 60: 895–910.

Heider, F. (1958). *The Psychology of Interpersonal Relations*. New York: Wiley.

Kierkegaard, S. (1995 [1847]). *Works of Love* (edited and translated by H. V. Hong and E. H. Hong). Princeton University Press.

Koole, S. L., Smeets, K., Van Knippenberg, A., and Dijksterhuis, A. (1999). The cessation of rumination through self-affirmation. *Journal of Personality and Social Psychology* 77: 111–25.

Leach, C. W. and Spears, R. (2008). "A vengefulness of the impotent": the pain of in-group inferiority and schadenfreude toward successful out-groups. *Journal of Personality and Social Psychology* 95: 1383–96.

Leach, C. W., Spears, R., Branscombe, N. R., and Doosje, B. (2003). Malicious pleasure: *schadenfreude* at the suffering of another group. *Journal of Personality and Social Psychology* 84: 932–43.

Lockwood, P. and Kunda, Z. (1997). Superstars and me: predicting the impact of role models on the self. *Journal of Personality and Social Psychology* 73: 91–103.

Major, B., Testa, M., and Bylsma, W. H. (1991). Responses to upward and downward social comparisons: the impact of esteem-relevance and perceived control. In J. Suls and T. A. Wills (eds.), *Social Comparison: Contemporary Theory and Research*. Hillsdale, NJ: Erlbaum, pp. 237–60.

McQueen, A. and Klein, W. M. P. (2006). Experimental manipulations of self-affirmation: a systematic review. *Self and Identity* 5: 289–354.

Miller, D. T., Downs, J. S., and Prentice, D. A. (1998). Minimal conditions for the creation of a unit relationship: the social bond between birthdaymates. *European Journal of Social Psychology* 28: 475–81.

Morse, S. and Gergen, K. J. (1970). Social comparison, self-consistency, and the concept of self. *Journal of Personality and Social Psychology* 40: 624–34.

Plato (1925). *Plato* (translated by H. N. Fowler and W. R. M. Lamb). New York: Putnam.

Portmann, J. (2000). *When Bad Things Happen to Other People*. New York: Routledge.

Reis, T. J., Gerrard, M., and Gibbons, F. X. (1993). Social comparison and the pill: reactions to upward and downward comparison on contraceptive behavior. *Personality and Social Psychology Bulletin* 19: 13–20.

Roseman, I. J. and Smith, C. A. (2001). Appraisal theory, overview, assumptions, varieties, controversies. In K. S. Scherer, A. Schorr, and T. Johnstone (eds.), *Appraisal Processes in Emotion: Theory, Methods, Research*. Oxford University Press, pp. 3–19.

Schopenhauer, A. (1965 [1841]). *On the Basis of Morality* (translated by E. F. J. Payne) Indianapolis: Bobbs-Merrill.

Sedikides, C. and Strube, M. J. (1997). Self-evaluation: to thine own self be good, to thine own self be sure, to thine own self be true, and to thine own self be better. In M. P. Zanna (ed.), *Advances in Experimental Social Psychology*, Vol. 29,. New York: Academic Press, pp. 209–69.

Sherman, D. K. and Cohen, G. L. (2006). The psychology of self-defence; self-affirmation theory. In M. P. Zanna (ed.), *Advances in Experimental Social Psychology*, Vol. 38. New York: Academic Press, pp. 183–242.

Smith, R. H. (2000). Assimilative and contrastive emotional reactions to upward and downward social comparisons. In J. Suls and L. Wheeler (eds.), *Handbook of Social Comparison: Theory and Research*. New York: Kluwer Academic/Plenum Publishers, pp. 173–200.

Smith, R. H. and Kim, S. H. (2007). Comprehending envy. *Psychological Bulletin* 133: 46–64.

Smith, R. H., Turner, T. J., Garonzik, R., Leach, C. W., Urch-Druskat, V., and Weston, C. M. (1996). Envy and *schadenfreude*. *Personality and Social Psychology Bulletin* 22: 158–68.

Spinoza, B. (2002 [1677]). *Ethica* (translated by H. Krop). Amsterdam: Prometheus/Bert Bakker.

Steele, C. M. (1988). The psychology of self-affirmation: sustaining the integrity of the self. In L. Berkowitz (ed.), *Advances in Experimental Social Psychology*, Vol. 21. San Diego, CA: Academic Press, pp. 216–302.

Steele, C. M. and Liu, T. J. (1983). Dissonance processes as self-affirmation. *Journal of Personality and Social Psychology* 45: 5–19.

Tajfel, H (ed.). (1978). Social categorization, social identity and social comparison. In H. Tajfel (ed.), *Differentiation between Social Groups: Studies in the Social Psychology of Intergroup Relations*. London: Academic Press, pp. 61–76.

Tajfel, H. and Turner, J. C. (1979). An integrative theory of intergroup conflict. In W. G. Austin and S. Worchel (eds.), *The Social Psychology of Intergroup Relations*. Monterey, CA: Brooks/Cole, pp. 94–109.

Takahashi, H., Kato, M., Matsuura, M., Mobbs, D., Suhara, T., and Okubo, Y. (2009). When your gain is my pain and your pain is my gain: neural correlates of envy and schadenfreude. *Science* 323: 937–9.

Taylor, S. E. and Brown, J. D. (1988). Illusion and well-being: a social psychological perspective on mental health. *Psychological Bulletin* 103: 193–210.

Tesser, A. (1988). Toward a self-evaluation maintenance model of social behavior. In L. Berkowitz (ed.), *Advances in Experimental Social Psychology*, Vol. 21. San Diego, CA: Academic Press, pp. 181–227.

(1991). Emotion in social comparison, and reflection processes. In J. Suls and T. A. Wills (eds.), *Social Comparison: Contemporary Theory and Research*. Hillsdale, NJ: Erlbaum, pp. 115–45.

Tesser, A. and Cornell, D. P. (1991). On the confluence of self-processes. *Journal of Experimental Social Psychology* 27: 501–26.

Van Dijk, W. W., Goslinga, S., and Ouwerkerk, J. W. (2008). Responsibility, schadenfreude, and sympathy: further evidence. *Journal of Social Psychology* 148: 631–6.

Van Dijk, W. W., Ouwerkerk, J. W., and Goslinga, S. (2009). The impact of deservingness on schadenfreude and sympathy: further evidence. *Journal of Social Psychology* 149: 290–2.

Van Dijk, W. W., Ouwerkerk, J. W., Goslinga, S., and Nieweg, M. (2005). Deservingness and *schadenfreude*. *Cognition and Emotion* 19: 933–9.

Van Dijk, W. W., Ouwerkerk, J. W., Goslinga, S., Nieweg, M., and M. Gallucci (2006). When people fall from grace: reconsidering the role of envy in *schadenfreude*. *Emotion* 6: 156–60.

Van Dijk, W. W., Ouwerkerk, J. W., Van Koningsbruggen, G. M., and Wesseling, Y. M. (2012). "So you wanna be a pop star?": schadenfreude following another's misfortune on TV. *Basic and Applied Social Psychology* 34: 168–74.

Van Dijk, W. W., Ouwerkerk, J. W., Wesseling, Y. M., and Van Koningsbruggen, G. M. (2011b). Towards understanding pleasure at the misfortunes of others: the impact of self-evaluation threat on schadenfreude. *Cognition and Emotion* 25: 360–8.

Van Dijk, W. W., Van Koningsbruggen, G. M., Ouwerkerk, J. W., and Wesseling, Y. M. (2011a). Self-esteem, self-affirmation, and schadenfreude. *Emotion* 11: 1445–9.

Van Koningsbruggen, G. M., Das, E., and Roskos-Ewoldsen, D. R. (2009). How self-affirmation reduces defensive processing of threatening health information: evidence at the implicit level. *Health Psychology* 28: 563–8.

Wills, T. A. (1981). Downward comparison principles in social psychology. *Psychological Bulletin* 90: 245–71.

Zechmeister, J. S. and Romero, C. (2002). Victim and offender accounts of interpersonal conflict: autobiographical narratives of forgiveness and unforgiveness. *Journal of Personality and Social Psychology* 82: 675–86.

Zillmann, D. and Bryant, J. (1980). Misattribution theory of tendentious humor. *Journal of Experimental and Social Psychology* 16: 146–60.

Zillmann, D. and Knobloch, S. (2001). Emotional reactions to narratives about the fortunes of personae in the news theater. *Poetics* 29: 189–206.

Part III

Schadenfreude as an intergroup phenomenon

10 Stereotypes and schadenfreude

Mina Cikara and Susan T. Fiske

> *But it is Schadenfreude, a mischievous delight in the misfortunes of others, which remains the worst trait in human nature ... In general, it may be said that it takes the place which pity ought to take – pity which is its opposite, and the true source of all real justice and charity ... Envy, although it is a reprehensible feeling, still admits of some excuse, and is, in general, a very human quality; whereas the delight in mischief [Schadenfreude] is diabolical, and its taunts are the laughter of hell.*
>
> (Schopenhauer, *Parerga and Paralipomena*, volume II, Chapter VIII (*On Ethics*), section 114)

People perceive others' misfortunes everyday; yet how people respond to another person's pain is strongly affected by their pre-existing prejudices about the individual experiencing the outcome. In many cases people experience pity or empathy when they see other people suffering, but this responses is not universal (Cikara, Bruneau, and Saxe, 2011). Schadenfreude is the dark side of people's response to another's troubles, referring to the perceiver's experience of pleasure at another's misfortune (Heider, 1958). At least three conditions commonly predict schadenfreude (Smith et al., 2009): when observers gain from the misfortune (Smith et al., 2006; Van Dijk and Ouwerkerk, Chapter 1 in this volume); when another's misfortune seems deserved (Ben-Ze'ev, Chapter 5 in this volume; Feather, 1999, 2006, and Chapter 3 in this volume; Feather and Nairn, 2005; Portmann, Chapter 2 in this volume; Van Dijk et al., 2005); and when a misfortune befalls an envied person (Smith, Thielke, and Powell, Chapter 6, this volume; Smith et al., 1996; Takahashi et al., 2009).

Envy – and perhaps by extension schadenfreude – is not reserved only for individual targets (Fiske, Cuddy, and Glick, 2007; Smith and Kim, 2007). Given that emotions just as easily operate at the intergroup level as at the interpersonal level (see Smith, 1993; Tiedens and Leach, 2004), merely encountering a successful out-group may *imply* one's comparative inferiority, engendering group-based envy (Smith, 1991; Tajfel and Turner, 1979) – and potentially schadenfreude – when the out-group or one of its members suffers a misfortune (Ouwerkerk and Van Dijk, Chapter 12 in this volume; Schurtz et al., Chapter 11 in this volume). Indeed, Leach et al. (2003) have demonstrated that *objective* in-group inferiority (i.e., losing in a competition) and subjective feelings of inferiority (Leach and Spears, 2008, 2009) lead to schadenfreude toward third-party groups that suffer subsequent losses. Previous studies examining intergroup schadenfreude, however, have employed well-defined, categorical, overtly competitive groups (e.g., rival universities, political parties, soccer teams – for example, Combs et al., 2009). In this chapter we examine whether mere stereotype content is sufficient to elicit schadenfreude. In other words, can high-status, competitive groups, merely by who they are and not by what they have done, evoke malicious joy at their misfortunes?

The Stereotype Content Model

Recent research in social cognition has firmly established that people differentiate each other not simply along an in-group/out-group boundary, but rather by the extent to which they (dis)like and (dis)respect a target or group. The Stereotype Content Model (SCM: Cuddy, Fiske, and Glick, 2007; Fiske et al., 2002; Fiske et al., 2007) organizes beliefs about social and cultural groups along two fundamental dimensions: warmth and competence.

Warmth and competence are systematically ascribed to different groups. Experimental and survey research using the SCM demonstrates that the content of a stereotype and type of prejudice reserved for a social group follow from two social structural variables: 1) a group's status in society; and 2) a group's perceived cooperation. First, out-groups are perceived as more competent to the extent that they are perceived as having high status. Across a sample of 19 nations, the status–competence correlation averages 94 across groups (Fiske et al., 2007). The reason for this association is unclear: it may be that people believe social position reflects a group's inherent traits (Gilbert and Malone, 1995) or it might reflect the lay theory that people get what they deserve (Lerner and Miller, 1978). In either case, this status–competence association reinforces existing status hierarchies (Ridgeway and Berger, 1986).

The second part of the social structure hypothesis holds that out-groups are seen as relatively warm to the extent that they are not competitive. In contrast, out-groups that compete for valued resources are perceived as having negative intent ("if you're not with me, you're against me"). Warmth and competition are negatively related, with an average correlation of -.52 across groups (Fiske et al., 2007; with improved measures, the correlation approaches -.80 – Kervyn, Fiske, and Yzerbyt, under review). Negative affect toward out-groups arises when their goals seem incompatible with

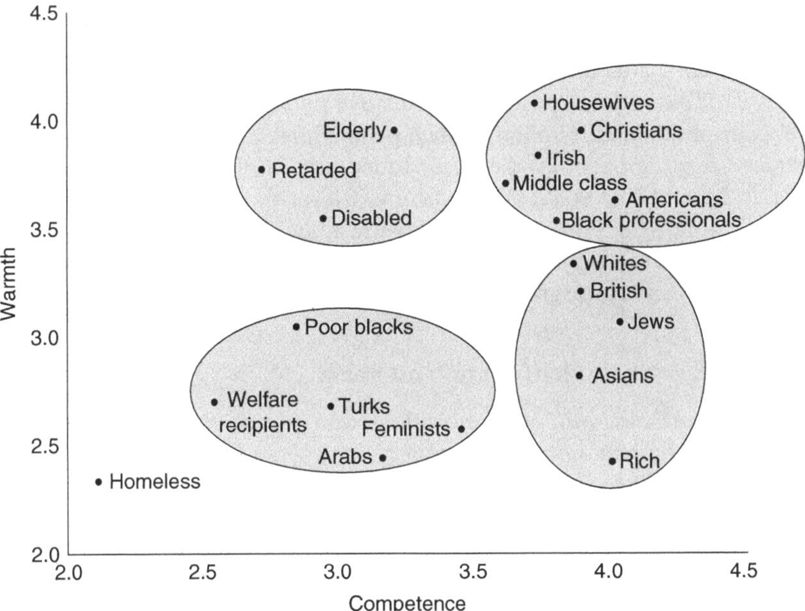

Figure 10.1 Stereotype Content Model, warmth by competence space (Fiske et al., 2007)

in-group goals (Fiske and Ruscher, 1993). If out-groups are successful, they receive grudging respect, but are denied warmth.

Thus, whether a social group does or does not have high status will determine if they have *capability* to harm the in-group, which will guide people's perceptions of the social group's *competence*. Likewise, whether a social group seems cooperative or competitive determines if they allegedly have *intent* to harm the culturally dominant group (or in-group), which will guide people's perceptions of that social group's *warmth*. This 2 (low/high warmth) x 2 (low/high competence) mapping describes four broad stereotype categories and the emotional responses that these categories elicit (see Figure 10.1). Groups high on both warmth and competence (e.g., the middle class) elicit emotions such as pride, whereas groups low on both warmth and competence (e.g., welfare recipients, drug addicts) elicit emotions such as disgust. Groups falling in the mixed quadrants elicit ambivalent emotions; pity is elicited by people perceived as low in competence and high in warmth (e.g., elderly), whereas envy is reserved for people perceived as high in competence but low in warmth (e.g., the rich, Asians, Jews, and businesswomen). It is this last group on which this chapter focuses.

Here, we define envious prejudice as the negative affective response people experience as the result of a contrastive comparison with targets who are seen as high-status (therefore competent) and competitive (therefore cold). This is different from positive, assimilative upward comparison emotions (e.g., inspiration, admiration), which people might feel toward cooperative targets (e.g., groups in the pride quadrant of the SCM: Algoe and Haidt, 2009; Fiske et al., 2002; Ortony, Clore, and Collins, 1988; Smith, 2000). Note, again, that envy and pleasure at the suffering of another group can take place at both the individual level (e.g., Smith et al., 1994; Tangney et al., 1992) and at the group level (Scheff, 1994; Walker and Smith, 2002).

Envy, schadenfreude, and harm

Social comparison with other individuals and groups is a central phenomenon within human societies (Festinger, 1954; Fiske, 2011; Olson, Herman, and Zanna, 1986; Suls and Wheeler, 2000). People possess a drive to evaluate their opinions and abilities, so when objective means are unavailable, people evaluate themselves in comparison to other people (Festinger, 1954); that is, people engage in social comparison to gain information (Gibbons and Gerrard, 1991). Social comparisons have both cognitive and affective consequences, depending on whether they are relevant/irrelevant or favorable/unfavorable (e.g., Brickman and Bulman, 1977; Morse and Gergen, 1970; Salovey and Rodin, 1984; Taylor and Lobel, 1989; Tesser, 1991; Tesser, Millar, and Moore, 1988). Indeed, although people compare downward to feel better (Wills, 1981), people compare upward to otherwise-similar others in order to feel inspired (see Fiske, 2011, for context); if the target is competitive, the affective consequence of upward social comparison may be envy.

Envy

Envy occurs when people perceive another person's or group's relative advantage (Heider, 1958; Parrott and Smith, 1993; Smith, 2000; Smith and Kim, 2007; Smith, Thielke, and Powell, Chapter 6 in this volume), though certain factors may influence the intensity with which one feels envy. For instance, envy is at its most intense between two socio-economically comparable individuals or groups that compete in similar domains (Salovey and Rodin, 1984; Silver and Sabini, 1978; Tesser, 1991). Festinger (1954) suggested that self-evaluations often derive from social comparisons with people who are self-relevant (i.e., sharing similar attributes, characteristics, and interests). This may initially seem to contradict the SCM's predictions; however, evidence demonstrates that average participants perceive targets who fall in the SCM's *envy* quadrant as being familiar, similar to themselves, and preferred targets for social interaction (Harris, Cikara, and Fiske, 2008). Whether or not participants *actually* are similar to envied targets is irrelevant so long as they perceive that they are similar.

Envy appears to be a universal emotion that manifests in cultures around the world (Foster, 1972; Schoeck, 1969). Capuchin monkeys (Brosnan and De Waal, 2003) and dogs (Range et al., 2009) reject rewards if other animals receive relatively greater rewards; six-month-old babies cry when their mothers pay attention to lifelike dolls (Hart and Carrington, 2002). Envy is a particularly potent emotion in terms of its impact on interpersonal behavior, from the perspectives of both the envying and the envied (Ben-Ze'ev, Chapter 5 in this volume; Van Dijk and Ouwerkerk, Chapter 9 in this volume). Envy generates a desire to punish others who are better off than oneself (Fehr and Fischbacher, 2005; Kirchsteiger, 1994). For example, contrary to what classical economic theory might seem to predict, people will pay to reduce others' earnings (Beckman et al., 2002; Zizzo, 2003; Zizzo and Oswald, 2001). They also prefer to walk away from negotiation empty-handed rather than accept an unfair deal (Guth and Tietz, 1986) and will work less hard if they feel their compensation is lower than their colleagues' (Frank, 1985). Thus, from the perspective of those *feeling* envy, envy can promote self-defeating behaviors in service of avoiding situations that lead to another's relative advantage.

Envy also engenders aggression, both overt and subtle, when envied groups challenge the status quo (Cuddy, Fiske, and Glick, 2007; Wert and Salovey, 2004). Historically, envied targets have often been subject to genocide and mass violence (e.g., European Jews in the nineteenth and twentieth centuries: Epstein, 2003; Staub, 1989). While envied targets are not the *only* targets of genocide, they may be particularly vulnerable because the attacks seem contradictory: people also cooperate with them in times of social stability (Cuddy, Fiske, and Glick, 2007). On a more subtle scale, women who occupy high-power positions in the workplace are respected, but are often seen as cold and are frequently targets of backlash as a result (e.g., hiring discrimination, harsher appraisals, and sabotage: Rudman and Fairchild, 2004). In general, targets that are seen as competitive are also perceived as being capable of defending themselves, so it seems more acceptable to attack them relative to other targets (Glick, 2002).[1]

[1] It is important to distinguish envy from resentment at this point, as they may seem synonymous on the surface and are frequently conflated. Upward contrastive social comparisons are likely to elicit envy *and* resentment along with subjective feelings of inferiority (E. R. Smith, 1993; R. H. Smith, 1991, 2000). However, resentment could also be directed downward toward groups that elicit disgust (e.g., welfare recipients). Therefore, resentment may target all groups that are perceived as exploitative, irrespective of their status/competence. Envy, in contrast, should be reserved specifically for *competent and cold* targets.

Schadenfreude

Schadenfreude replaces pity when the misfortune has befallen an envied target (Brigham et al., 1997; Smith et al., 1996). Note that other factors, in addition to envy, predict schadenfreude: anger and hate toward the target (Hareli and Weiner, 2002), perceived deservingness of the target (see Ben-Ze'ev, Chapter 5 in this volume; Feather, Chapter 3 in this volume; Portmann, Chapter 2 in this volume), and resentment (Feather and Nairn, 2005; Feather and Sherman, 2002; see also Cuddy, Fiske, and Glick, 2007). Recent research demonstrates that self-evaluation threat increases schadenfreude in response to other's misfortunes, above and beyond self-reports of envy and dislike for the target (Van Dijk et al., 2011; see also Van Dijk and Ouwerkerk, Chapter 9 in this volume). Subjective experience of in-group defeat also increases negative feelings toward victorious out-groups (for reviews, see Ellemers, Spears, and Doosje, 1999; Smith and Kessler, 2004; Tajfel and Turner, 1979). Prejudice may be more prevalent among those who have experienced a loss in status or resources (e.g., "poor white racism," frustration-aggression hypothesis; see also Leach and Spears, 2008; Leach et al., 2003). For example, Dutch soccer fans' schadenfreude in response to a German team's loss increased with an interest in soccer, but also with an increased threat of Dutch inferiority (Leach et al., 2003).

Hostile components of envy subsume all of the identified factors to some degree, and context or previous experience with the envied target may alter which predictors are most potent. Thus, rather than exploring the many emotions that may be mediators of the relationship between envy and schadenfreude, the current framework uses systematic principles to predict which *targets* are most likely to be targets of envy and whether they are also targets of schadenfreude when they suffer misfortunes.

Are stereotypes sufficient?

Smith et al. (1996) suggested that others' success may immediately imply our own inferiority, giving rise to envy, and then schadenfreude when the superior person suffers a misfortune; however, experiments separating the effects of in-group pain from emotions targeting the out-group (e.g., envy, anger) were lacking. Most recently, Leach and Spears (2008) have demonstrated that in-group inferiority (e.g., losing in a competition) is separate from envy and that the former (but not the latter) leads to schadenfreude toward third parties when those groups suffer subsequent losses mainly because of the *subjective* experience of painful emotions associated with the psychological threat of in-group inferiority.

One open question is how much information is necessary or sufficient to evoke a painful upward comparison? Social comparisons are comparable to contrast effects: they often occur quickly, require few cognitive resources, and are outside of subjects' control (Gilbert, Giesler, and Morris, 1995; Pelham and Wachsmuth, 1995; Wedell, 1994). When people evaluate others, they almost cannot help but do so in comparison to the self (Dunning and Hayes, 1996; Holyoak and Gordon, 1983; Karylowski, 1990; Mussweiler and Bodenhausen, 2002; Sherif and Hovland, 1961; Srull and Gaelick, 1983). If a person identifies along some dimension with the target of comparison, assimilation is more likely than contrast (Brewer and Weber, 1994). In contrast, comparisons with out-group members make salient information that distinguishes oneself from the target, leading to contrast effects (Mussweiler and Bodenhausen, 2002).

Our prediction is that knowledge of a group's stereotype will automatically activate envious prejudice and related emotions (i.e., pain of in-group inferiority and anger at the out-group) when the stereotype comprises high status and competitiveness. In other words, exposure to competitive, high-status groups may be sufficient to engender envy as well as pain and anger, all of which drive pleasure at others' pain. If stereotypes are sufficient to activate this response, it may occur even if the envied group is not in direct competition with the in-group. This is particularly important as it suggests that groups need not have a long history of interaction or direct competition to elicit these malevolent reactions. Indeed, SCM research demonstrates that awareness of the content of a group's stereotype is sufficient to elicit envy (Fiske et al., 2002; Cuddy, Fiske, and Glick, 2007).

Harm

People perceive others' empathy toward them as a sign of "fellow feeling" (Bavelas et al., 1986). Demonstrating pleasure instead of empathy in response to someone's misfortune may be a clear sign that one's interests are not aligned with a victim's interests (Leach and Spears, 2009). Building on the emotion-related predictions of the SCM, the behaviors from intergroup affect and stereotypes (BIAS) map framework predicts that group stereotypes also elicit specific constellations of behavior as a function of their perceived warmth and competence (Cuddy, Fiske, and Glick, 2007). According to the BIAS map, envied persons and groups are frequently targets of passive help (e.g., associating), but also active harm (e.g., attack, sabotage), perhaps under conditions of social unrest (see Figure 10.2).

The BIAS map research has demonstrated that the relationship between envy and active harm is fully mediated by anger (Cuddy, Fiske, and Glick, 2007). Therefore, the prediction is that envied targets elicit not

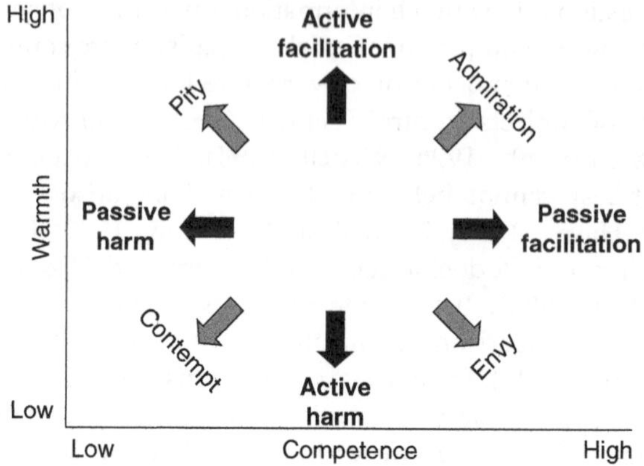

Figure 10.2 BIAS map (Cuddy, Fiske, and Glick, 2007)

only emotions like pain and anger (when they have good fortune), and pleasure (when they suffer a misfortune), but also harmful behaviors when the opportunity is available.

Finally, maybe schadenfreude reinforces discrimination and harm against people and groups who are perceived as competing for limited resources. If in fact watching a competitive group's misfortune is accompanied by the experience of pleasure, it suggests a dangerous learning cycle whereby pleasure reinforces the likelihood of subsequent harm, even if the perceiver was not personally responsible for the initial misfortune. If this is correct, people who experience more schadenfreude in response to targets' suffering should also be more willing to harm those targets.

Empirical evidence

We predict that group stereotypes comprising status (associated with competence) and competitiveness (associated with coldness: Fiske et al., 2002) will spontaneously activate envious prejudice. Envy requires an upward comparison, so the status prediction is self-evident; however, we posit that competitiveness is also crucial; people typically experience positive, upward, emotional responses (e.g., inspiration) in response to *cooperative*, high-status groups (Smith, 2000). If stereotypes are indeed sufficient to activate envious prejudice, schadenfreude may occur even if the envied group is not presented in an explicitly competitive context (e.g., a member of a competitive group). Again, this is particularly important as it suggests that groups need not have a long history of interaction to elicit these malevolent affective reactions. Finally, examining the effects of status and competitiveness, rather than specific social groups, allows us to generalize our results to any group based solely on stereotype content.

We conducted a series of studies to address these hypotheses. In the first study, participants responded to positive, negative, and neutral events happening to a variety of targets from the SCM (Cikara and Fiske, 2012). We hypothesized that participants would experience more schadenfreude in response to negative events that befell high-status, competitive (i.e., envied) targets as compared to targets from the other three SCM quadrants. We anticipated that participants, perhaps due to social desirability concerns, might not explicitly report schadenfreude. Even when a target's superior status is made explicit (e.g., superior academic achievement, victory in a sporting event), self-reported schadenfreude means do not exceed the midpoint of the scale (Leach and Spears, 2008; Leach et al., 2003; Smith et al., 1996; Van Dijk et al., 2006). As a result, we also collected physiological measures of positive and negative affect (i.e., facial electromyography or EMG). To the extent that participants experienced schadenfreude (*not just neutral affect*) in response to high-status, competitive targets' misfortunes, we predicted that participants would smile more as compared to when other targets experienced misfortunes.

In order to allow for ambivalent responding, we asked participants "if you saw this happening in real life, how good would it make you feel?" and "how bad would it make you feel?" Asking participants both questions – as opposed to using a bipolar 'good to bad' scale – allowed them to say, for instance, that they felt bad, but also slightly good in response to targets' misfortunes. As we hypothesized, participants reported that they felt *least bad* about *negative* events and *least good* about *positive* events when they happened to envy targets as compared to when they felt disgust, pity, and pride in relation to targets. Participants did not, however, report feeling significantly better when negative events befell envied targets as compared to all the other targets.

The implicit measure of positive affect assessed facial muscle responses, focusing on the ZM (zygomaticus major; cheek muscle) because it correlates reliably with positive affect (e.g., Brown and Schwartz, 1980). For pride, pity, and disgust targets, participants exhibited a greater ZM response when the target was paired with a positive as compared to a negative event; only envy targets elicited greater ZM response when the target was paired with a negative as compared to a positive event. Though participants did not want to explicitly report feeling pleasure when envy targets experienced a misfortune, these facial EMG findings provide preliminary evidence for the *presence of positive affect* (i.e., smiling) – not just the absence of negative affect – in response to envied targets' misfortunes.

Participants' self-reported responses were not correlated with their facial EMG responses. These null results are predicted, however, if we account for the possibility that social desirability changes people's self-reported affective responses to the target–event pairs. Any sort of reporting bias increases error in self-report measurement, rendering it less valid and less likely to covary with other measures. These findings also suggest that if we remove social desirability constraints, we should observe the predicted relationships among self-report and physiological assessments of schadenfreude. We return to this claim in the fourth study.

In a second study, we sought to replicate the first study and to assess participants' endorsement of harm against different SCM targets (Cikara and Fiske, 2011). Again, participants felt worst about positive events and best about negative events when they happened to "envy" targets as compared to all other targets from the SCM.

We contacted participants one to two weeks after the lab portion of the study with a web-survey. Participants were presented with the following scenario: "You are participating in a Fear Factor-type game show and have just won a challenge. This exempts you from the 'punishment' the rest of the players face: they are all going to receive mild electric shocks, which are painful, but not lethal. The game show host gives YOU the choice to decide whether all five of the players are going to get shocks or if one person should get a stronger shock (which again is painful, but not lethal) while you spare the other four." Afterwards, participants were presented with each target from the scan and were asked, one at a time, to imagine that each target was the *one* person they could shock to keep the other players from receiving their punishments. For each target, participants reported how willing they would be to volunteer the person to receive a shock so that the others could avoid the punishment (rated likelihood was 1= *not at all*, 7 = *extremely*).

We framed the harm question as a trade-off scenario, because forced-choice measures may reveal spontaneous biases, which are otherwise difficult for experimenters to detect and for participants to report (Cikara et al., 2010). First, the demand characteristics are loosened because participants believe that their responses reflect *both* their willingness to spare the other contestants and their willingness to harm the target. However, we hold the unspecified "contestants to be spared" constant; therefore, response variation can only reflect differences in willingness to harm individual targets (i.e., participants may rely on stereotype content to guide their willingness to harm different individuals). The game-show scenario also creates a situation in which target stereotypes constitute the only information available for participants' consideration.

As predicted, participants reported that they would be more willing to volunteer an envy target than pity, disgust, and pride targets (though this last comparison was only significant with a one-tailed test). It is important to note that harm ratings were not correlated with self-reported affect in response to targets' misfortunes.

In a third study, we attempted to attenuate participants' schadenfreude to high-status, competitive targets' misfortunes by providing counter-stereotypic information about an exemplar from the target's group (Cikara and Fiske, 2012). If high status and competitiveness are sufficient to predict schadenfreude in response to misfortune, then increasing cooperation or decreasing status should reduce it, demonstrating that stereotype content, and not specific relationships to individual targets themselves, predicts pleasure at their misfortunes. The third study examined whether decreasing an envied target's status or increasing the target's cooperativeness would make people respond to envied targets' negative experiences more like the way they respond to disgust, pity, or pride targets' experiences.

We predicted that priming participants with stories about investment bankers who had lower status, were cooperative, or both would make participants feel relatively worse when negative events happen to other targets, who resemble investment bankers (mimicking findings associated with pride, pity, and disgust targets); in contrast, reading about stereotypic investment bankers, whose situation was status quo [high status, competitive], would make participants feel relatively less bad when similar targets experience negative events). Note that we expected participants to feel bad about negative events when they happen specifically to targets that resembled investment bankers because the manipulation focused on that particular group within the envy quadrant. As we predicted, providing counter-stereotypic status and competition information about an investment banker changed participants' subsequent ratings of negative events happening to novel envy targets; moreover, the effect was specific to those targets who resembled investment bankers. Thus, downstream effects of envious prejudice (i.e., schadenfreude) can be attenuated for specific group members when perceivers are primed with situations in which the target group has lower status or is cooperative.

Thus far, our self-reported affect measure did not correlate with other measurements of interest (e.g., ZM response, harm), which we attributed to the influence of social desirability. To address this limitation, we decided to loosen social desirability constraints by assessing intergroup schadenfreude in a context in which pleasure at others' misfortunes is allowed, if not encouraged. Specifically, in Study 4, we measured the affective reactions and neural responses of die-hard Yankees and Red Sox fans – fans of two American baseball teams embroiled in a historic rivalry – as they viewed baseball plays involving favored, rival, and other teams (Cikara, Botvinick, and Fiske, 2011). We predicted that participants would experience pleasure in response to favored-team success and rival-team failure (even against a third party; all subjectively positive outcomes), but that they would feel pain and anger in response to favored-team failure and rival-team success (subjectively negative outcomes). We also predicted that the pleasure and pain associated with viewing these outcomes would engage brain regions associated with processing primary rewards and punishments. Previous research has shown that neural structures such as the ventral striatum (VS) and the anterior cingulate cortex (ACC) are engaged when participants personally receive rewards (Berridge, Robinson, and Aldridge, 2009; O'Doherty, 2004) and punishments (Botvinick et al., 2005; Decety and Ickes, 2009), respectively. These effects, however, are moderated by competition: participants exhibit the opposite neural responses when they witness an individual competitor's rewards and punishments (De Bruijn et al., 2009; Singer et al., 2006; Takahashi et al., 2009). Most importantly, we tested for the first time whether these affective and neural responses were related to a desire to aggress against rival team fans.

Though participants had more than stereotype content to rely on in the context of this study, we predicted that warmth and competence ratings, as well as feelings of envy, should validate SCM predictions. Indeed, both Red Sox and Yankees fans reported that their own team was most warm and most competent, that the Orioles (a relatively less competitive team in the same league) was moderately warm and moderately competent, and, most importantly, that their rival was clearly more competent than the Orioles, but also less warm. Participants also reported that they felt more envy for their rival as compared to the Orioles.

Not surprisingly, participants rated their favored team's success, rival team's failure against the favored team, and the rival's failure against the Orioles (i.e., the pure schadenfreude condition) as significantly more pleasurable than the subjectively negative plays and the plays in the control condition (the Orioles failing and succeeding against a fourth team, the Blue Jays). Participants also rated their favored team's failure and the rival team's success against the favored team as significantly more angering and painful than the plays in the subjectively positive and control conditions. Most importantly, in a follow-up web-survey designed to assess harm, participants reported that they were significantly more likely to heckle, insult, threaten, and hit a rival fan as compared to an Orioles fan.

As we predicted, brain regions associated with the registration of primary rewards and punishments (Berns et al., 2001; Decety, 2011; O'Doherty, 2004) also encoded *groups*' outcomes, the subjective values of which are inherently defined by the perceiver's fanship. More important, pleasure-associated neural activity in response to viewing competitive rival failures was correlated with the self-reported likelihood of harming rival team fans. Finally, the VS response to rival failure was more closely linked to harm than was self-reported pleasure. Though these data are correlational, the current findings suggest that further investigation of neural responses to threatening out-groups' misfortunes and tendencies toward out-group harm is warranted.

Conclusion

In this chapter, we reviewed studies that extend the existing literature by demonstrating that perceived status and competition can determine when and which targets are most likely to evoke schadenfreude. In addition, we illustrated that one can disrupt the deleterious consequences of envious prejudice by manipulating perceptions of status and competition. Finally, these studies highlighted the importance of using a variety of methods to assess the relationships among stereotype content, envy, and schadenfreude. Using indirect measures such as facial EMG to complement explicit self-report helps to circumvent some of the hurdles associated with measuring socially undesirable responses.

People often fail to empathize and may even feel pleasure in response to out-group targets' misfortunes. However, not all out-groups are equivalent: high-status, competitive groups are more likely than other out-groups to be targets of schadenfreude, as well as active harm (Cuddy, Fiske, and Glick, 2007). Knowing that perceptions of warmth and competence drive these responses allows us to predict which groups are at greatest risk in times of social instability. Furthermore, knowing that these perceptions are malleable makes it possible to ameliorate pernicious affective and behavioral responses when out-groups are targets of misfortune or overt harm.

References

Algoe, S. B. and Haidt, J. (2009). Witnessing excellence in action: the "other-praising" emotions of elevation, gratitude, and admiration. *Journal of Positive Psychology* 4: 105–27.

Bavelas, J. B., Black, A., Lemery, C. R., and Mullett, J. (1986). "I show how you feel": Motor mimicry as a communicative act. *Journal of Personality and Social Psychology* 50: 322–9.

Beckman, S. R., Formby, J. P., Smith, W. J., and Zheng, B. H. (2002). Envy, malice and Pareto efficiency: an experimental examination. *Social Choice and Welfare* 19: 349–67.

Berns, G. S., McClure, S. M., Pagnoni, G., and Montague, P. R. (2001). Predictability modulates human brain response to reward. *Journal of Neuroscience* 21: 2793–8.

Berridge, K. C., Robinson, T. E., and Aldridge, J. W. (2009). Dissecting components of reward: "liking," "wanting," and learning. *Current Opinions in Pharmacology* 9: 65–73.

Botvinick, M., Jha, A. P., Bylsma, L. M., Fabian, S. A., Solomon, P. E., and Prkachin, K. M. (2005). Viewing facial expressions of pain engages cortical areas involved in the direct experience of pain. *Neuroimage* 25: 312–19.

Brewer, M. B. and Weber, J. G. (1994). Self-evaluation effects of interpersonal versus intergroup social comparison. *Journal of Personality and Social Psychology* 66: 268–75.

Brickman, P. and Bulman, R. (1977). Pleasure and pain in social comparison. In J. Suls and R. L. Miller (eds.), *Social Comparison Processes: Theoretical and Empirical Perspectives*. New York: Hemisphere, pp. 149–86.

Brigham, N. L., Kelso, K. A., Jackson, M. A., and Smith, R. H. (1997). The roles of invidious comparisons and deservingness in sympathy and schadenfreude. *Basic and Applied Social Psychology* 19: 363–80.

Brosnan, S. F. and De Waal, F. B. M. (2003). Monkeys reject unequal pay. *Nature* 425: 297–9.

Brown, S. L. and Schwartz, G. E. (1980). Relationships between facial electromyography and subjective experience during affective imagery. *Biological Psychology* 11: 49–62.

Cikara, M., Botvinick, M. M., and Fiske, S. T. (2011). Us versus them: social identity shapes neural responses to intergroup competition and harm. *Psychological Science* 22: 306–13.

Cikara, M., Bruneau, E. G., and Saxe, R. (2011). Us and them: intergroup failures of empathy. *Current Directions in Psychological Science* 20: 149–53.

Cikara, M., Farnsworth, R. A., Harris, L. T., and Fiske, S. T. (2010). On the wrong side of the trolley track: neural correlates of relative social valuation. *Social Cognitive and Affective Neuroscience* 5: 404–13.

Cikara, M. and Fiske, S. T. (2011). Bounded empathy: neural responses to out-groups' (mis)fortunes. *Journal of Cognitive Neuroscience* 23: 3791–803.

(2012). Stereotypes and schadenfreude: affective and physiological markers of pleasure at out-groups' misfortunes. *Social Psychological and Personality Science* 3: 63–71.

Combs, D. J. Y., Powell, C. A. J., Schurtz, D. R., and Smith, R. H. (2009). Politics, schadenfreude, and ingroup identification: the sometimes happy thing about a poor economy and death. *Journal of Experimental Social Psychology* 45: 635–46.

Cuddy, A. J. C., Fiske, S. T., and Glick, P. (2007). The BIAS map: behaviours from intergroup affect and stereotypes. *Journal of Personality and Social Psychology* 92: 631–48.

De Bruijn, E. R., de Lange, F. P., von Cramon, D. Y., and Ullsperger, M. (2009). When errors are rewarding. *Journal of Neuroscience* 29: 12183–6.

Decety, J. (2011). Dissecting the neural mechanisms mediating empathy and sympathy. *Emotion Review* 3: 92–108.

Decety, J. and Ickes, W. J. (2009). *The Social Neuroscience of Empathy*. Cambridge, MA: MIT Press.

Dunning, D. and Hayes, A. F. (1996). Evidence of egocentric comparison in social judgment. *Journal of Personality and Social Psychology* 71: 213–29.

Ellemers, N., Spears, R., and Doosje, B. (1999). *Social Identity: Context, Commitment, Content*. Oxford: Blackwell.

Epstein, J. (2003). *Envy*. New York: Oxford University Press.

Feather, N. T. (1999). *Values, Achievement, and Justice: Studies in the Psychology of Deservingness*. New York: Kluwer Academic/Plenum Press.

(2006). Deservingness and emotions: applying the structural model of deservingness to the analysis of affective reactions to outcomes. *European Review of Social Psychology* 17: 38–73.

Feather, N. T. and Nairn, K. (2005). Resentment, envy, schadenfreude, and sympathy: effects of own and other's deserved or undeserved status. *Australian Journal of Psychology* 57: 87–102.

Feather, N. T. and Sherman, R. (2002). Envy, resentment, schadenfreude, and sympathy: reactions to deserved and undeserved achievement and subsequent failure. *Personality and Social Psychology Bulletin* 28: 953–61.

Fehr, E. and Fischbacher, U. (2005). The economics of strong reciprocity. In H. Gintis, S. Bowles, R. Boyd, and E. Fehr (eds.), *Moral Sentiments and Material Interests: The Foundations of Cooperation in Economic Life*. Cambridge, MA: MIT Press, pp. 151–93.

Festinger, L. (1954). A theory of social comparison processes. *Human Relations* 7: 117–40.

Fiske, S. T. (2011). *Envy Up, Scorn Down: How Status Divides Us*. New York: Russell Sage.

Fiske, S. T., Cuddy, A. J. C., and Glick, P. (2007). First judge warmth, then competence: fundamental social dimensions. *Trends in Cognitive Sciences* 11: 77–83.

Fiske, S. T., Cuddy, A. J. C., Glick, P., and Xu, J. (2002). A model of (often mixed) stereotype content: competence and warmth respectively follow from perceived status and competition. *Journal of Personality and Social Psychology* 82: 878–902.

Fiske, S. T. and Ruscher, J. B. (1993). Negative interdependence and prejudice: whence the affect? In D. M. Mackie and D. L. Hamilton (eds.), *Affect, Cognition, and Stereotyping: Interactive Processes in Group Perception*. San Diego, CA: Academic Press, pp. 239–68.

Foster, G. M. (1972). The anatomy of envy: a study in symbolic behaviour. *Current Anthropology* 13: 165–202.

Frank, R. H. (1985). *Choosing the Right Pond: Human Behaviour and the Quest for Status*. Oxford University Press.

Gibbons, F. X. and Gerrard, M. (1991). Downward comparison and coping with threat. In J. Suls and T. A. Wills (eds.), *Social Comparison: Contemporary Theory and Research*. Hillsdale, NJ: Erlbaum, pp. 317–46.

Gilbert, D. T., Giesler, R. B., and Morris, K. A. (1995). When comparisons arise. *Journal of Personality and Social Psychology* 69: 227–36.

Gilbert, D. T. and Malone, P. S. (1995). The correspondence bias. *Psychological Bulletin* 117: 21–38.

Glick, P. (2002). Sacrificial lambs in wolves clothing: envious prejudice, ideology, and scapegoating of Jews. In L. S. Newman and R. Erber (eds.), *What Social Psychology Can Tell Us About the Holocaust*. Oxford University Press, pp. 113–42.

Guth, W. and Tietz, R. (1986). Auctioning ultimatum bargaining positions. In R. W. Scholz (ed.), *Issues in West German Decision Research*. Frankfurt: Lang, pp. 60–73.

Hareli, S. and Weiner, B. (2002). Dislike and envy as antecedents of pleasure at another's misfortune. *Motivation and Emotion* 26: 257–77.

Harris, L. T., Cikara, M., and Fiske, S. T. (2008). Envy as predicted by the stereotype content model: volatile ambivalence. In R. H. Smith (ed.), *Envy: Theory and Research*. Oxford University Press, pp. 133–47.

Hart, S. and Carrington, H. (2002). Jealousy in 6 month old infants. *Infancy* 3: 395–402.

Heider, F. (1958). *The Psychology of Interpersonal Relations*. New York: Wiley.

Holyoak, K. J. and Gordon, P. C. (1983). Social reference points. *Journal of Personality and Social Psychology* 44: 881–7.

Karylowski, J. J. (1990). Social reference points and accessibility of trait-related information in self–other similarity judgments. *Journal of Personality and Social Psychology* 58: 975–83.

Kervyn, N., Fiske, S. T., and V. Yzerbyt, V. (under review). Why is the primary dimension of social cognition so hard to predict? Symbolic and realistic threats together predict warmth in the stereotype content model.

Kirchsteiger, G. (1994). The role of envy in ultimatum games. *Journal of Economic Behaviour and Organization* 25: 373–89.

Leach, C. W. and Spears, R. (2008). "A vengefulness of the impotent": the pain of in-group inferiority and schadenfreude toward successful out-groups. *Journal of Personality and Social Psychology* 95: 1383–96.

(2009). Dejection at in-group defeat and schadenfreude toward second- and third-party out-groups. *Emotion* 9: 659–65.

Leach, C. W., Spears, R., Branscombe, N. R., and Doosje, B. (2003). Malicious pleasure: schadenfreude at the suffering of another group. *Journal of Personality and Social Psychology* 84: 932–43.

Lerner, M. J. and Miller, D. T. (1978). Just world research and the attribution process: looking back and ahead. *Psychological Bulletin* 85: 1030–51.

Morse, S. and Gergen, K. J. (1970). Social comparison, self-consistency, and the concept of self. *Journal of Personality and Social Psychology* 40: 624–34.

Mussweiler, T. and Bodenhausen, G. V. (2002). I know you are, but what am I? Self-evaluative consequences of judging in-group and out-group members. *Journal of Personality and Social Psychology* 82: 19–32.

O'Doherty, J. P. (2004). Reward representations and reward-related learning in the human brain: insights from neuroimaging. *Current Opinion in Neurobiology* 14: 769–76.

Olson, J. M., Herman, C. P., and Zanna, M. P. (1986). *Relative Deprivation and Social Comparison*. Hillsdale, NJ: Erlbaum.

Ortony, A., Clore, G. L., and Collins, A. (1988). *The Cognitive Structure of Emotions*. Cambridge University Press.

Parrott, W. G. and Smith, R. H. (1993). Distinguishing the experiences of envy and jealousy. *Journal of Personality and Social Psychology* 64: 906–20.

Pelham, B. W. and Wachsmuth, J. O. (1995). The waxing and waning of the social self: assimilation and contrast in social comparison. *Journal of Personality and Social Psychology* 69: 825–38.

Range, F., Horna, L., Viranyi, Z., and Hubera, L. (2009). The absence of reward induces inequity aversion in dogs. *PNAS* 106: 340–5.

Ridgeway, C. L. and Berger, J. (1986). Expectations, legitimation, and dominance behaviour in task groups. *American Sociological Review* 51: 603–17.

Rudman, L. A. and Fairchild, K. (2004). Reactions to counterstereotypic behaviour: the role of backlash in cultural stereotype maintenance. *Journal of Personality and Social Psychology* 87: 157–76.

Salovey, P. and Rodin, J. (1984). Some antecedents and consequences of social comparison jealousy. *Journal of Personality and Social Psychology* 47: 780–92.

Scheff, T. (1994). Emotions and identity: a theory of ethnic nationalism. In C. Calhoun (ed.), *Social Theory and the Politics of Identity*. Oxford: Blackwell.

Schoeck, H. (1969). *Envy: A Theory of Social Behavior*. New York: Harcourt, Brace and World.

Sherif, M. and Hovland, C. I. (1961). *Social Judgment*. New Haven, CT: Yale University Press.

Silver, M. and Sabini, J. (1978). The perception of envy. *Social Psychology Quarterly* 41: 105–17.

Singer, T., Seymour, B., O'Doherty, J. P., Stephan, K. E., Dolan, R. J., and Frith, C. D. (2006). Empathic neural responses are modulated by the perceived fairness of others. *Nature* 439: 466–9.

Smith, E. R. (1993). Social identity and social emotions: toward a new conceptualization of prejudice. In D. M. Mackie and D. L. Hamilton (eds.), *Affect, Cognition, and Stereotyping*. San Diego, CA: Academic Press, pp. 297–315.

Smith, H. J. and Kessler, T. (2004). Group-based emotions and intergroup behavior: the case of relative deprivation. In L. Z. Tiedens and C. W. Leach (eds.), *The Social Life of Emotions*. Cambridge University Press, pp. 292–313.

Smith, R. H. (1991). Envy and the sense of injustice. In P. Salovey (ed.), *The Psychology of Jealousy and Envy*. New York: Guilford Press, pp. 79–99.

(2000) Assimilative and contrastive emotional reactions to upward and downward social comparisons. In J. Suls and L. Wheeler (eds.), *Handbook of Social Comparison: Theory and Research*. Dordrecht: Kluwer, pp. 173–200.

Smith, R. H., Eyre, H. L., Powell, C. A., and Kim, S. H. (2006). Relativistic origins of emotional reactions to events happening to others and to ourselves. *British Journal of Social Psychology* 45: 357–71.

Smith, R. H. and Kim, S. H. (2007). Comprehending envy. *Psychological Bulletin* 133: 46–64.

Smith, R. H. Parrott, W. G., Ozer, D., and Moniz, A. (1994). Subjective injustice and inferiority as predictors of hostile and depressive feelings in envy. *Personality and Social Psychology Bulletin* 20: 705–11.

Smith, R. H., Powell, C. A., Combs, D. J. Y., and Schurtz, R. D. (2009). Exploring the when and why of *Schadenfreude*. *Social and Personality Psychology Compass* 3: 530–46.

Smith, R. H., Turner, T. J., Garonzik, R., Leach, C. W., Urch-Druskat, V., and Weston, C. M. (1996). Envy and schadenfreude. *Personality and Social Psychology Bulletin* 25: 158–68.

Srull, T. K. and Gaelick, L. (1983). General principles and individual differences in the self as a habitual reference point: an examination of self-other judgments of similarity. *Social Cognition* 2: 108–21.

Staub, E. (1989). *The Roots of Evil: The Origins of Genocide and Other Group Violence*. New York: Cambridge University Press.

Suls, J. and Wheeler, L. (2000). *Handbook of Social Comparison: Theory and Research*. New York: Kluwer Academic/Plenum Publishers.

Tajfel, H. and Turner, J. C. (1979). An integrative theory of intergroup conflict. In W. G. Austin and S. Worchel (eds.), *The Social Psychology of Intergroup Relations*. Monterey, CA: Brooks-Cole, pp. 94–109.

Takahashi, H., Kato, M., Matsuura, M., Mobbs, D., Suhara, T., and Okubo, Y. (2009). When your gain is my pain and your pain is my gain: neural correlates of envy and schadenfreude. *Science* 323: 937–9.

Tangney, J. P., Wagner, P. E., Fletcher, C., and Gramzow, R. (1992). Shamed into anger? The relation of shame and guilt to anger and self-reported aggression. *Journal of Personality and Social Psychology* 62: 669–75.

Taylor, S. E. and Lobel, M. (1989). Social comparison activity under threat: downward evaluation and upward contacts. *Psychological Review* 96: 569–75.

Tesser, A. (1991). Emotion in social comparison and reflection processes. In J. Suls and T. A. Wills (eds.), *Social Comparison: Contemporary Theory and Research*. Hillsdale, NJ: Erlbaum, pp. 115–45.

Tesser, A., Millar, M., and Moore, J. (1988). Some affective consequences of social comparison and reflection processes: the pain and pleasure of being close. *Journal of Personality and Social Psychology* 54: 49–61.

Tiedens, L. Z. and Leach, C. W. (2004). *The Social Life of Emotions*. Cambridge University Press.

Van Dijk, W. W., Ouwerkerk, J. W., Goslinga, S., and Nieweg, M. (2005). Deservingness and schadenfreude. *Cognition and Emotion* 19: 933–9.

Van Dijk, W. W., Ouwerkerk, J. W., Goslinga, S., Nieweg, M., and Gallucci, M. (2006). When people fall from grace: reconsidering the role of envy in schadenfreude. *Emotion* 6: 156–60.

Van Dijk, W. W., Ouwerkerk, J. W., Wesseling, Y. M., and Van Koningsbruggen, G. M. (2011). Towards understanding pleasure at the misfortunes of others: the impact of self-evaluation threat on schadenfreude. *Cognition and Emotion* 25: 360–8.

Walker, I. and Smith, H. J. (2002). *Relative Deprivation: Specification, Development, and Integration*. New York: Cambridge University Press.

Wedell, D. H. (1994). Contextual contrast in evaluative judgments: a test of pre-versus postintegration models of contrast. *Journal of Personality and Social Psychology* 66: 1007–19.

Wert, S. R. and Salovey, P. (2004). A social comparison account of gossip. *Review of General Psychology* 8: 122–37.
Wills, T. A. (1981). Downward comparison principles in social psychology. *Psychological Bulletin* 90: 245–71.
Zizzo, D. J. (2003). Money burning and rank egalitarianism with random dictators. *Economics Letters* 81: 263–6.
Zizzo, D. J. and Oswald, A. J. (2001). Are people willing to pay to reduce others incomes? *Annales d'Economie et de Statistique* 63–64: 39–62.

11 Schadenfreude in sports and politics: a social identity perspective

D. Ryan Schurtz, David Combs, Charles Hoogland, and Richard H. Smith

After news broke that Osama bin Laden had been found and killed, many Americans erupted in joy and celebration. Some congregated in front of the White House and other public places to wave American flags and cry out "USA, USA, USA!" One of the reasons for this open display of schadenfreude, which seemed unaltered by the fact that someone's brutal death was being celebrated, was that bin Laden fully deserved his fate (see Feather, Chapter 3 in this volume). As President Obama captured the general consensus: "I think that anyone who would question that the perpetrator of mass murder on American soil didn't deserve what he got needs to have their head examined" (MacArthur, 2011). But underlying much of the joy seemed to be the tug of patriotic sentiments. This was the USA finally triumphing over an adversary who had not only been a physical threat but a cultural antagonist as well. Osama bin Laden's death made many Americans feel good about themselves, mediated through a boost to the nation's image.

The social identity perspective

It was a Navy Seal team, not the average American citizen, who accomplished this complex and dangerous mission. But as research guided by a social identity perspective has shown, our self-esteem is affected by the successes and failures of the groups to which we belong as well as our individual ups and downs (e.g., Abrams and Hogg, 1999; Brown, 2000; Hogg, Terry, and White, 1995; Rubin and Hewstone, 1998; Tajfel, 1978; Tajfel and Turner, 1979, 1986). We have a natural tendency to categorize ourselves and others into in-groups or out-groups, and to the extent that the groups to which we belong have admirable characteristics, at least relative to other groups, we can gain by the association and bask in this reflected glory (e.g., Cialdini et al., 1976; Hirt and Zillmann, 1992; Lee, 1985). Even if the groups to which we belong are not superior to other groups in obvious ways, categorization itself can sometimes provide a means to this end, as most of us straight away conclude that our own group is superior to out-groups (e.g., Gaertner et al., 2006; Kahn and Ryan, 1972; Tajfel, 1970; Tajfel and Turner, 1979, 1986; Turner, 1978). Also, knowing the categories to which we belong seems to offer a comforting clarity to the self-concept (Hamilton, 1981; Hogg, 2007; Hogg, Terry, and White, 1995; Knowles and Gardner, 2008). We understand better who "we" are by noting our differences (and superiority) to "them" (e.g., Hogg and Abrams, 1993; Tajfel and Turner, 1979).

From a social identity perspective, the misfortunes of out-group members should have the potential to bring some form of pleasure, even though this pleasure is likely to be mixed with natural feelings of sympathy as well. This perspective, like many theories of human nature (e.g., Baumeister and Bushman, 2008), assumes that most people are motivated to feel good about themselves. Based on social comparison processes, it is further assumed that group categorization and the resulting in-group favoritism and out-group discrimination allow people to infer superiority and to enjoy the enhanced "social" aspect of their overall self-esteem. If people tend to reflexively assume that their own group is superior to an out-group, then any information that further confirms this operating assumption should be welcomed – and enhance self-esteem all the more (see Ben-Ze'ev, Chapter 5 in this volume). It is only natural to feel pleased if one's self-esteem is given a boost, and misfortunes happening to others can serve this purpose (see Van Dijk and Ouwerkerk, Chapter 9 in this volume) insofar as they enhance a sense of superiority in one's own group. And, again, this is not to claim the absence of other countering feelings such as sympathy (e.g., Combs et al., 2009). The social comparison perspective highlights the potential gains to the self from an out-group member's misfortune and the pleasure that such gains can entail.

Competition

In many everyday circumstances, out-groups are more than just passive entities. Often, their collective actions have direct bearing on our individual and group-related outcomes. The terrorist organization led by bin Laden was waging an all-out war on the USA and on Western culture. A considerable portion of human interactions are overlaid with elements of competition between individuals and groups for the acquiring of resources and of various indicators of prestige (e.g., Sherif, 1966; Struch and Schwartz, 1989). Moreover, social identity processes, to the extent that they are undergirded by social comparisons, entail an implicit sense of competition between groups. But direct competition accentuates comparative ways of thinking that may not only further cause people to form "us" versus “them” categories, but may also highlight the substantive consequences (and associated implications for self-esteem and emotions related to self-esteem) resulting from who wins and loses (e.g., Hirt and Zillmann, 1992; Riketta and Sacramento, 2008; Scheepers et al., 2008). Competition accentuates and magnifies the in-group gain following the misfortunes of out-groups and therefore should boost the pleasure in the outcome.

Intergroup biases

There are further reasons why an out-group’s misfortune should tend to be pleasing. Various biasing processes seem to flourish when people regard out-groups. Members of out-groups are more easily stereotyped than in-group members and in a way that underscores negative traits more than positive traits (e.g., Howard and Rothbart, 1980; Linville, Fischer, and Salovey, 1989). Research shows that if participants were randomly assigned to groups and then given a balanced mix of positive and negative information about their own group and another group, they quickly developed more negative expectations about the other group and more positive expectations about their own group – even though they had no interactions with members of either group. Research also shows that people tend to see in-group members as being similar on positive traits compared to their impressions of out-group members, thus favoring positive perceptions of in-group members (Brewer and Kramer, 1985; Hamilton and Trolier, 1986). Even so, out-group members tend to be seen as more similar overall than in-group members, in the sense that they can seem more interchangeable, less individuated, and more homogeneous (e.g., Judd and Park, 1988). And these kinds of laboratory-produced effects can follow simply from a rudimentary categorization into in-groups and out-groups, suggesting that actual groups who have experienced other reasons to favor and cherish their group identities will be even more likely to show such biases. These perceptual biases, together with the catalyzing condition of competition and rivalry (Kilduff, Elfenbein, and Staw, 2010), should work to legitimatize and justify assumptions of in-group superiority, and to enhance schadenfreude and to lessen sympathy if out-group members suffer.

Group motives appear less self-serving

Another reason that a misfortune suffered by out-group members should be pleasing is that emotional reactions that might seem self-serving at the individual level, because personal gain seems to be their source, can seem more noble when the group is benefiting. Listing the virtues of one's group is less likely to come across as boasting compared to doing the same for one's personal strengths and virtues. For instance, an award-winning athlete praising his team as a "dynasty" is more acceptable than his pointing out his statistical superiority to other players. Also, seeking benefits on behalf of the group can seem unselfish (e.g., an athlete representing a players' union trying to negotiate higher salaries for all players), whereas doing the same for the self (e.g., an athlete holding out for a higher paying contract) is likely to seem greedy. It is no surprise that studies show that groups are more competitive than individuals in part because the motive of greed can more easily operate among groups than among individuals (Wildschut et al., 2003). Thus, admitting schadenfreude when an out-group suffers from the expressed vantage point of the in-group perspective is less unlikely to redound to one's disfavor than a similar view expressed from a more individual or personal perspective.

The arbitrary nature of group categorization

It is remarkable how arbitrary our group associations can be and yet still produce the sense of tight group membership and the multitude of biasing effects that can ensue (e.g., Tajfel and Turner, 1979). One can see this in the initial studies on group categorization carried out by Henri Tajfel using British schoolboys at the University of Bristol (Tajfel, 1970). After the boys made estimates of the number of dots flashed on a screen, they were then placed into groups of either "underestimators" or "overestimators." Although this placement was actually random and there was no logical reason to think that either category was intrinsically superior to the other, these boys took advantage of opportunities to discriminate against the "out-group" in distributing rewards and to favor their "in-group." These findings are easy to replicate using even more arbitrary categorization procedures, such as assigning participants to merely group "A" or group "B" using a manifestly random coin flip and in which no prior or future interaction with either in-group or out-group members occurs (see Pinter and Greenwald, 2011 for a review of the categorization procedures). It is no wonder that this basic phenomenon was given the label of the "minimal group paradigm" and is now one of the most celebrated, seminal findings of social psychology.

Schadenfreude in sports

Fan behavior is one domain in which the effects predicted by a social identity perspective seem to operate strongly and often out in the open.

Perhaps there is no more fitting domain in which one can see both the arbitrariness of group categorization and the strong emotions that seem connected with such categorization. We become fans of home teams because of where we have the good fortune (or bad fortune as the case may be) of living. New Yorkers become fans of the Yankees. Baltimoreans become fans of the Orioles. If a New Yorker had, in some alternate universe, been born and raised in Baltimore and not New York, it is likely the pinstriped jerseys of the Yankees in his closet would be replaced with the solid black and orange of the Baltimore Orioles. The *New York Times* writer Warren St. John, in his memoir about his attempts to fathom his intense allegiance to Alabama football, gives a particularly good example of how arbitrary team connections can be (St. John, 2004). St. John was an Alabama fan because his father went to Alabama. However, his father's first preference for college had been for Georgia Tech, until his parents' divorce caused him to attend Alabama, which was closer to home. The breakup was due to St. John's grandfather's drinking problem. And so, why was St. John an Alabama fan? Because his grandfather was an alcoholic!

The happenstantial origins of most fan allegiances do not produce correspondingly mild emotional reactions to winning and losing, nor do these origins make us unmoved by the wins and losses of rival teams. It is extraordinary that the essential randomness of our team associations does not seem to detract from the power that the associations have on us. Most sports fans are acutely aware that the wins and losses of their favourite teams affect them powerfully, despite appreciating, at least implicitly, that they are not directly contributing to the team outcomes. Certainly, any informal study of fan behavior suggests that fans show all the biases that may evolve from group categorization in competitive contexts. The "us" versus "them" perspective is all-encompassing, as are out-group homogeneity effects (all Yankees fans are alike), general intergroup favoritism and out-group discrimination (my team commits fewer fouls than our rival), and a tendency to link oneself with one's own team, especially if it is doing well (wearing team jerseys, etc.). Furthermore, the many pleasures (and agonies) of sports are endemic. No emotion seems more rife in sports than schadenfreude.

Consider the familiar situation is which one's own team beats a rival team. This actually provides at least two sources of pleasure: the pleasure of the win and being able to bask in its reflected glory (Cialdini et al., 1976; Hirt and Zillmann, 1992; Lee, 1985), and the pleasure in the rival losing. The latter element may well be categorized as schadenfreude. Any sports fan will admit that winning over a rival is highly satisfying and it is likely that the mix of pleasures gives it is special, memorable quality. Of course, any loss suffered by a rival is pleasing, and will do in a pinch.

Empirical evidence for sport-related schadenfreude

A study by Leach et al. (2003) provides some empirical evidence in everyday experience. Dutch participants gave their reactions to an article describing the loss of the German national team, the Dutch team's main rival. Indeed, these fans reported schadenfreude over the loss. As one would expect based on a social identity perspective, participants who showed greater interest in soccer (and so should be more highly identified with their team) expressed greater schadenfreude over the loss, presumably because they had the most to gain emotionally from the rival's loss. Also, some participants were primed to think about losses that the Dutch team had suffered in the past, just before giving their reactions to Germany's loss; this heightened the Dutch fans' schadenfreude even more. Thus, the loss of a rival in sports is pleasing, especially for people who gain most from it psychologically – those who have strong interest in their team and those who need a psychological boost because their team's inadequacy is more salient.

A more recent study by Schurtz et al. (2011) provided more precise confirming evidence for the role of social identity in such reactions. College student participants at the University of Kentucky completed a scale measuring how much they identified with their basketball team and later reacted to an article describing the loss of a rival basketball team (Duke University) to a neutral team. Participants reported schadenfreude over this loss, but only if they had indicated being strongly identified with their team. Presumably, only these participants gained in terms of their social identity from learning about the loss because they viewed the team as part of their in-group, whereas the participants who did not identify themselves as fans of the team did not.

Are these effects hardwired?

Clearly, for fans (who are highly identified with their teams by definition), the wins of their own team and the losses of rival "out-group" teams hit home. Cikara, Botvinick, and Fiske (2011; see also Cikara and Fiske, Chapter 10 in this volume) suggest that such reactions are "wired in," in the sense that finding pleasure in both own-team wins and rival losses may have adaptive benefits. They found support for this claim in a study in which brain scans were obtained from Boston Red Sox or New York Yankees fans (notorious rivals) as they watched baseball plays of their own team playing a rival team, a neutral team, or a control condition in which two neutral teams were playing against each other. After each play, the participants reported their pleasure, anger, and pain. Own-team winning, beating the rival, and seeing the rival fail against a neutral team all produced more reports of pleasure than seeing two neutral teams compete against each other. Losing to any team and seeing the rival succeed produced more anger and pain. Activation of brain regions associated with pleasure (the ventral striatum – putamen, nucleus accumbens) was also linked with baseball plays where participants reported being pleased. Activation associated with physical and emotional pain (the anterior cingulate cortex and insula) correlated with plays where participants indicated feeling pain. These findings suggest that reward and pain systems are linked to group identity and thus to information about how one's own group is performing compared to rival out-groups. One's own group doing well is a pleasing experience, but so is a rival's failure, regardless of how this failure comes about. Thus, evolutionarily old brain systems may have adapted to integrate information about both positive and negative events relating to intergroup competition.

What are the limits to sports-related schadenfreude?

Sometimes fans even openly rejoice over an injury to a rival player. The Internet serves up its share of evidence. For example, the Facebook community "Haloti Ngata breaking Ben Roethlisberger's nose" has over 14,000 "likes" and six other Facebook communities relating to the injury also exist. Roethlisberger may be liked in Pittsburgh, where he is quarterback for the Pittsburgh Steelers football team, but the many fans of rival teams seemed to find his nose injury pleasing. When Tom Brady, the New England Patriots' quarterback, tore his anterior cruciate ligament (ACL) at the beginning of the 2008 season, some New York Jets fans were scolded for expressing pleasure on Internet forums, but here is the response of a blogger from Philadelphia:

> From the perspective of a native Philadelphian, this controversy over Jets fans celebrating *Tom Brady*'s injury has to be the most ridiculous story of the young season. Your archrival's quarterback goes down and you're supposed to be respectful? This is the NFL. Of course you celebrate. It would be a sign of disrespect not to ... The average Eagles fan would take a bat to *Tony Romo*'s knees in a heartbeat if they thought they could get away with it. (www.fannation.com/si_blogs)

Are these sentiments atypical? It is hard to say. But research by Wann and others indicates that people may be capable of being inwardly pleased over injuries to opposing players. In one study (Wann et al., 1999), participants were asked to what extent they would be willing to trip up or break an opposing player's leg before an important game if they knew for sure that it would be completely anonymous. Thirty-two percent of participants indicated some willingness to do this, and 48 percent indicated some willingness to trip an opposing player. This pattern was especially pronounced for participants who were highly identified with their own team and so were more invested in their own team's winning and the opposing team's losing. In another study (Wann et al., 2003), it was found that these tendencies were even more apparent if participants believed their team had just lost a prior game. As in the Dutch and Kentucky studies on schadenfreude, factors that would enhance the psychological gain associated with a winning outcome produced a greater likelihood of being willing to harm the opposing player.

Although these studies did not examine actual behavior, it is revealing that so many participants admitted their willingness to perform such actions. Given the viciousness of these actions, one might expect a much lower rate of endorsement. In any event, these results clearly support the idea that misfortunes befalling rivals should be a source of schadenfreude, especially for people highly identified with their team and who have recently suffered a setback – so much so that harm occurring to an opposing player is sometimes an acceptable means to obtaining this pleasure. If a moderate percentage of people express a willingness to *cause* a serious injury, the percentage who would simply feel some pleasure over an injury caused by chance must be higher.

Another study by Schurtz et al. (2011) supports this claim. Participants from the University of Kentucky, who identified themselves as strong fans of the basketball team, reported experiencing pleasure when they read about a member of the Duke basketball team (a intense rival of the Kentucky team) sustaining a concussion. Students who were not strong fans of the basketball team did not report experiencing pleasure, as a social identity perspective would predict.

Schadenfreude in politics

Another arena where social identity plays a strong role in emotions is politics; in fact, some observers may see little difference between sports and politics. Like misfortunes befalling rival sports teams, misfortunes befalling opposing party candidates, ranging from sexual scandals to verbal gaffes, enhance the chances of one's own candidate or party winning an election. In the context of political campaigns, especially during election season, all events for people identified with their political party become appreciated by their implications for victory or defeat. That the event might represent, for example, the exposure of an embarrassing secret may be exactly why the event can create so much schadenfreude for many observers.

Like sports affiliations, political affiliations are probably more arbitrary than most people would like to believe. For example, just as New Yorkers are likely to become Yankees fans, the situations we find ourselves in may have a substantial impact on our politics. Newcomb's (1943) classic Bennington College study bears this out. Newcomb measured the (predominantly conservative) political beliefs of the well-to-do 1935 Bennington College Freshman class and monitored how they changed each year until the class graduated in 1939. Most participants' beliefs changed dramatically, from very conservative to very liberal. Newcomb concluded that these changes were largely due to the exposure the students had to the highly liberal environment of the college. Like Yankees fans who love the pinstripes simply because they live in New York, might the participants in the Bennington study have ultimately identified themselves as liberals as much through passive association as through a careful consideration of the relevant arguments?

This is not to say that political beliefs are only a function of a fairly arbitrary categorization process. In the Bennington Study, strong conformity pressures were also present. Also, some recent research indicates that political beliefs may have a genetic component. Alford, Funk, and Hibbing (2005; see also Alford, Funk, and Hibbing, 2008) demonstrated that identical twins share political beliefs far more than fraternal twins. Similarly, fMRI research by Kaplan, Freedman, and Iacoboni (2007) demonstrated that Republican and Democrat participants tended to process politically related stimuli with different areas of the brain, suggesting that some differences between Republicans and Democrats may well be built in. Thus, the nature and origins of political in-group identification and political beliefs is complex, yet they are at least in some ways less a matter of thoughtful choice than people might suppose.

As with sports, the partly happenstantial origins of political beliefs do not lead to mild emotional reactions to political events. Of course, in-group/out-group biases that produce emotional reactions to sporting events are present in a political context. One can observe the same "us" versus "them" thinking suggested by the out-group homogeneity effect (those Republicans are ignorant), general intergroup favoritism (my party is made of up of true patriots), and out-group discrimination (the Democrats lost and so they don't deserve to have as much representation on important committees). In part because of such biases, politics, as any casual observer will note, produces all manner of emotional responses, and schadenfreude seems a prevalent feature of the emotional mosaic.

Empirical evidence for schadenfreude in politics

A study by Combs et al. (2009) provided empirical support for schadenfreude in politics. In the months before the 2004 presidential election between the Republican incumbent President George W. Bush and the Democratic challenger Senator John Kerry, participants completed a measure assessing their political party and the degree to which they identified with their party. A couple of months later, they reacted to two articles in which Bush or Kerry behaved in an embarrassing way. One article described President Bush crashing his bicycle. It did not seriously harm the President, but it did result in him being photographed with bruises and bandages on his face. The other article described Senator Kerry touring NASA facilities and included a picture of the Senator in a ridiculous-looking suit. Consistent with a social identity perspective, Democrats experienced greater schadenfreude when reading about President Bush's bicycle accident than Republicans, while Republicans experienced greater schadenfreude than Democrats when reading about Senator Kerry's NASA tour. It was striking how differently these events were received depending on the political vantage point. Essentially, it came down to whose ox was being gored. An out-group member's embarrassment was funny; an in-group member's embarrassment was not.

One common feature of these misfortunes happening to Bush and Kerry was that they were mild in nature. Although laughing at these minor embarrassments might be a little unkind, doing so does not risk much social censure, even though personal gain (from political party benefit) might seem to drive the reaction. However, oftentimes political blunders, even though they may lead to the opposing party's gain, can have devastating effects on innocent bystanders. Schadenfreude would seem less likely in such cases and certainly less justified. In 2006, as America prepared for the midterm congressional elections, Combs and colleagues conducted a follow-up study to their 2004 work. In preparation for the election, the public and press were examining a number of important political decisions that were negatively impacting all Americans. One major issue being examined was the continued war in Iraq and the steady news of increasing troop casualties. This issue was selected by the researchers because it clearly negatively affected all Americans regardless of political identification (i.e., it was "objectively negative") and therefore should not have produced schadenfreude. However, as the Republicans were in power, it was expected that Democrats would report more schadenfreude over learning of these casualties than would Republicans, especially to the extent that they identified strongly with their party – which was what happened. Because the pleasure increased as identification increased, it is likely that this pleasure was linked to political gain resulting from these misfortunes. It is important to note that the schadenfreude which Democrats reported was at a very low level and was mixed with a great deal of concern as well. They appeared to feel happy about the political benefits that might result from the unfortunate events in Iraq, but also felt bad about the negative consequences.

The 2006 election was a particularly contentious time in American history. There was a great deal of distrust of the people in charge of the country and many people (particularly Democrats) were angry and hungry for change.[1] It is difficult to determine with certainty why people experienced pleasure at the deaths of members of their own military. However, in the political sphere, mistakes in policy that cost people their lives and jobs and can be blamed on the choices of political rivals can be catalysts for changes in political leadership. In light of this, it is possible that Democrats interpreted these negative events as serving a "greater good" by removing politicians who were inept or deceitful and putting in place those who could better serve the nation.

One of the limitations of Combs and colleagues' study during the 2006 election cycle was that the political climate was such that almost any negative event could be placed at the feet of the Republican Party. However, there is no reason to conclude that schadenfreude is exclusive to Democrats. In response to this limitation, Combs et al. (2009) conducted another study in 2008 before the presidential election, using a constructed article in which an objectively negative event appeared to be the result of either presidential candidate Barack Obama (a Democrat) or John McCain (a Republican). The article was presented as a real article from the *New York Times* and described either Obama or McCain opposing a law that would have limited adjustable-rate mortgages (which were described as the main force behind the housing foreclosure crisis). Similar to the studies of objectively negative events, Democrats experienced schadenfreude when they believed that a Republican was responsible and Republicans experienced schadenfreude when they believed a Democrat was responsible (see Figure 11.1).

Thus, as one would expect, schadenfreude in politics does not appear to be an emotional reaction specific to Democrats. Furthermore (like the results of the sports studies described previously), this pattern of results

[1] The 2006 election did result in changes in political leadership of the House and Senate.

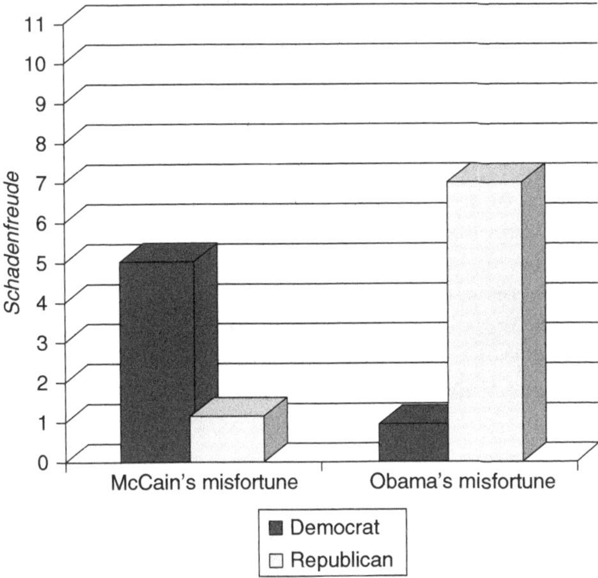

Figure 11.1 Schadenfreude felt by Democrats and Republicans (Combs et al., 2009)

was enhanced by the degree to which the person identified with their political party. Strongly affiliated individuals experienced the most schadenfreude when they read that the opposing political candidate was responsible for the mistake.

Intergroup emotions theory

Smith and Mackie (e.g., Mackie, Silver, and Smith, 2004), in their formulation of Intergroup Emotions Theory (IET), suggest that identification with one's in-group is an especially key predictor of how and when intergroup emotions occur. When individuals are experiencing high social identification, Smith and colleagues theorized that "appraisals are intergroup, rather than personally concerned. Emotions are experienced on the behalf of the group" (Mackie, Silver, and Smith, 2004, p. 229) rather than the individual. Furthermore, these emotions "reflect the relative well-being of the group independent of [one's] personal involvement in the event" (2004, p. 227). In-group identification is key to the occurrence of intergroup emotions because when individuals strongly identify with their group, they become a part of the group, and the group becomes a part of the self: consequently, events that affect the group, for good or for ill, become triggers of emotions. A number of studies have tested Smith and Mackie's framework and have generally (e.g. Garcia et al., 2005; Mackie, Devos, and Smith, 2000), but not always (Gordijn et al., 2006; Iyer and Leach, 2008) been supportive. The research findings by Combs et al. (2009) support the IET approach. With regard to the arena of politics, IET theory would suggest that the more strongly an individual identifies with his or her party, the more he or she would feel pleasure over any event that benefits the party, regardless of whether they might be generally harmful to innocent others *or even to the individual himself or herself.* In other words, gain for the political party – the in-group to which the individual strongly identifies – engulfs both concerns for the welfare of society in general and "personal" concerns. Winning the election is the event that matters; thus, "misfortunes" can be good news indeed.

Conclusion

If we think of the many ways that misfortunes happening to others can actually benefit us either directly or indirectly, it is no surprise that schadenfreude is a common feature of everyday life. In this chapter we have suggested that such benefits are common and powerful at the intergroup level, and have presented evidence from the domains of sports and politics. Human beings are competitive by nature and many intergroup relations seem especially likely to accentuate and enhance this competitive aspect of human nature. What this means is that misfortunes happening to out-group members often give us a comparative advantage in terms of our social identity, and to this extent it is quite natural for us to feel good. The range and scope of such effects are broader than we probably realize. In both politics and sports, a number of other factors not emphasized in this review may well augment the experience of schadenfreude (such as dislike, deservingness, and hypocrisy). In any event, to the extent that we are identified with groups, the failures of out-groups with which we compete should bring us pleasure. Sports and politics are perhaps the best examples of this sort of thing.

References

Abrams, D. and Hogg, M. (1999). *Social Identity and Social Cognition.* Oxford: Blackwell.

Alford, J. R., Funk, C. L., and Hibbing, J. R. (2005). Are political orientations genetically transmitted? *American Political Science Review* 99: 153–67.

(2008). Beyond liberals and conservatives to political genotypes and phenotypes. *Perspectives on Politics* 6: 321–8.

Baumeister, R. F. and Bushman, B. J. (2008). *Social Psychology and Human Nature*, 1st edn. Belmont, CA: Thomson Wadsworth.

Brewer, M. B. and Kramer, R. M. (1985). The psychology of intergroup attitudes and behavior. *Annual Review of Psychology* 36: 219–43.

Brown, R. (2000). Social identity theory: past achievements, current problems and future challenges. *European Journal of Social Psychology* 30: 745–78.

Cialdini, R. B., Borden, R. J., Thorne, A., Walker, M. R., Freeman, S., and Sloan, L. R. (1976). Basking in reflected glory: three (football) field studies. *Journal of Personality and Social Psychology* 34: 366–75.

Cikara, M., Botvinick, M. M., and Fiske, S. T. (2011). Us versus them: social identity shapes neural responses to intergroup competition and harm. *Psychological Science* 22: 306–13.

Combs, D. J. Y., Powell, C. A. J., Schurtz, D. R., and Smith, R. H. (2009). Politics, schadenfreude, and ingroup identification: the sometimes happy thing about a poor economy and death. *Journal of Experimental Social Psychology* 45: 635–46.

Gaertner, L., Iuzzini, J., Witt, M. G., and Orina, M. M. (2006). Us without them: evidence for an intragroup origin of positive in-group regard. *Journal of Personality and Social Psychology* 90: 426–39.

Garcia, S. M., Tor, A., Bazerman, M. H., and Miller, D. T. (2005). Profit maximization versus disadvantageous inequality: the impact of self-categorization. *Journal of Behavioral Decision Making* 18: 187–98.

Gordijn, E. H., Yzerbyt, V., Wigboldus, D. and Dumont, M. (2006). Emotional reactions to harmful intergroup behavior. *European Journal of Social Psychology* 36: 15–30.

Hamilton, D. L. (1981). *Cognitive Processes in Stereotyping and Intergroup Behavior*. Hillsdale, NJ: Erlbaum.

Hamilton, D. L. and Troiler, T. K. (1986). Stereotypes and stereotyping: an overview of the cognitive approach. In J. E. Dovidio and S. L. Gaertner (eds.), *Prejudice, Discrimination, and Racism*. Orlando, FL: Academic Press, pp. 127–63.

Hirt, E. R. and Zillmann, D. (1992). Costs and benefits of allegiance: changes in fans' self-ascribed competencies after team victory versus defeat. *Journal of Personality and Social Psychology* 63: 724–38.

Hogg, M. A. (2007). Uncertainty-identity theory. In M. P. Zanna (ed.), *Advances in Experimental Social Psychology*, Vol. 39. San Diego, CA: Elsevier Academic Press, pp. 69–126.

Hogg, M. and Abrams, D. (1993). Towards a single process uncertainty reduction model of social motivation in groups. In M. A. Hogg and D. Abrams (eds.), *Group Motivation: Social Psychology Perspectives*. London: Harvester Wheatsheaf, pp. 173–90.

Hogg, M. A., Terry, D. J., and White, K. M. (1995). A tale of two theories: a critical comparison of identity theory with social identity theory. *Social Psychology Quarterly* 58: 255–69.

Howard, J. M. and Rothbart, M. (1980). Social categorization and memory for in-group and out-group behavior. *Journal of Personality and Social Psychology* 38: 301–10.

Iyer, A. and Leach, C. W. (2008). Emotion in inter-group relations. *European Review of Social Psychology* 19: 86–125.

Judd, C. M. and Park, B. (1988). Out-group homogeneity: judgments of variability at the individual and group levels. *Journal of Personality and Social Psychology* 54: 778–88.

Kahn, A. and Ryan, A. H. (1972). Factors influencing the bias towards one's own group. *International Journal of Group Tensions* 2: 33–50.

Kaplan, J. T., Freedman, J., and Iacoboni, M. (2007). Us vs. them: political attitudes and party affiliation influence neural response to faces of presidential candidates. *Neuropsychologia* 45: 55–64.

Kilduff, G. J., Elfenbein, H. A. and Staw, B. M. (2010). The psychology of rivalry: a relationally dependent analysis of competition. *Academy of Management Journal* 5: 943–69.

Knowles, M. L. and Gardner, W. L. (2008). Benefits of membership: the activation and amplification of group identities in response to social rejections. *Personality and Social Psychology Bulletin* 34: 1200–13.

Leach, C. W., Spears, R., Branscombe, N. R., and Doosje, B. (2003). Malicious pleasure: schadenfreude at the suffering of another group. *Journal of Personality and Social Psychology* 84: 932–43.

Lee, M. J. (1985). Self-esteem and social identity in basketball fans: a closer look at basking in reflected glory. *Journal of Sport Behavior* 8: 210–24.

Linville, P. W., Fischer, G. W., and Salovey, P. (1989). Perceived distributions of the characteristics of in-group and out-group members: empirical evidence and a computer simulation. *Journal of Personality and Social Psychology* 57: 165–88.

MacArthur, J. R. (2011). Head-examining after Osama bin Laden killing. Available at: www.harpers.org/archive/2011/05/hbc-90008102.

Mackie, D. M., Devos, T., and Smith, E. R. (2000). Intergroup emotion: explaining offensive action tendencies in an intergroup context. *Journal of Personality and Social Psychology* 79: 602–16.

Mackie, D. M., Silver, L., and Smith, E. R. (2004). Intergroup emotions: emotion as an intergroup phenomenon. In L. Z. Tiedens and C. W. Leach (eds.), *The Social Life of Emotions*. Cambridge University Press, pp. 227–45.

Newcomb, T. (1943). *Personality and Social Change: Attitude Formation in a Student Community*. New York: Dryden.

Pinter, B. and Greenwald, A. G. (2011). A comparison of minimal group induction procedures. *Group Processes and Intergroup Relations* 14: 81–98.

Riketta, M. and Sacramento, C. A. (2008). Perceived distributions of the characteristics of in-group and out-group members: empirical evidence and a computer simulation. *Group Processes & Intergroup Relations* 11: 115–31.

Rubin, M. and Hewstone, M. (1998). Social identity theory's self-esteem hypothesis: a review and some suggestions for clarification. *Personality and Social Psychology Review* 2: 40–62.

St. John, W. (2004). *Rammer Jammer Yellow Hammer: A Journey in the Heart of Fan Mania*. New York: Crown.

Scheepers, D., Spears, R., Doosje, B., and Manstead, A. S. R. (2008). Diversity in in-group bias: structural factors, situational features, and social functions. *Journal of Personality and Social Psychology* 90: 944–60.

Schurtz, D. R., Combs, D. J. Y., Powell, C., and Smith, R. H. (2011). Schadenfreude in sports. Unpublished data.

Sherif, M. (1966) *In Common Predicament: Social Psychology of Intergroup Conflict and Cooperation*. Boston, MA: Houghton-Mifflin.

Struch, N. and Schwartz, S. H. (1989). Intergroup aggression: its predictors and distinctness from in-group bias. *Journal of Personality and Social Psychology* 56: 364–73.

Tajfel, H. (1970). Experiments in intergroup discrimination. *Scientific American* 223: 96–102.

(ed.) (1978). *Differentiation between Social Groups: Studies in the Social Psychology of Intergroup Relations*. London: Academic Press.

Tajfel, H. and Turner, J. C. (1979). An integrative theory of intergroup conflict. In W. G. Austin and S. Worchel (eds.), *The Social Psychology of Intergroup Relations*. Monterey, CA: Brooks-Cole, pp. 94–109.

(1986). The social identity theory of inter-group behavior. In S. Worchel and L. W. Austin (eds.), *Psychology of Intergroup Relations*. Chicago: Nelson-Hall, pp. 2–24.

Turner, J. C. (1978). Social comparison, similarity and ingroup favoritism. In H. Tajfel (ed.), *Differentiation between Social Groups: Studies in the Social Psychology of Intergroup Relations*. London: Academic Press, pp. 74–85.

Wann, D. L., Haynes, G., McLean, B., and Pullen, P. (2003). Sport team identification and willingness to consider anonymous acts of hostile aggression. *Aggressive Behavior* 29: 406–13.

Wann, D. L., Peterson R. R., Cothran C., and Dykes, M. (1999). Sport fan aggression and anonymity: the importance of team identification. *Social Behavior and Personality* 27: 597–602.

Wildschut, T., Pinter, B., Vevea, J. L., Insko, C. A., and Schopler, J. (2003). Beyond the group mind: a quantitative review of the interindividual-intergroup discontinuity effect. *Psychological Bulletin* 129: 698–722.

12 Intergroup rivalry and schadenfreude

Jaap W. Ouwerkerk and Wilco W. van Dijk

Don't mention the war! I mentioned it once, but I think I got away with it all right. (Basil Fawlty in the "The Germans" episode of *Fawlty Towers*)

The Dutch authors of this chapter are both passionate fans of the sport of football. That is, the sport in which all participants actually use their feet to play the ball, referred to as "soccer" by North Americans to distinguish it from their own version of football, which paradoxically involves players throwing and catching the ball with their hands most of the time. As season-ticket holders with adjoining seats, they attend all home games of their local club Ajax in Amsterdam and watch other important football matches on television, including tournaments that involve the Dutch national team. The FIFA 2010 World Cup in South Africa was no exception. Not only did we follow all matches of our own national team live on television, but also many games involving teams from other nations. We watched most of these matches on the Dutch public broadcasting network (NOS), although we could also switch to English or German television channels when we felt like it (the BBC or ARD, respectively). And on some occasions we did. For some reason, we like to hear our national team being praised by foreign commentators, so when the Dutch scored the winning goal in the match against Brazil, one of the tournament favorites, we switched to the BBC to bask in the team's reflected glory. However, we also engaged in somewhat more disturbing viewing behavior when watching games that involved teams from other nations. During the semi-final between Spain and Germany (a long-standing rival of the Netherlands), we switched to the German television channel ARD immediately after Puyol scored what turned out to be the winning goal for Spain in the twenty-seventh minute of the second half. Why? We have to admit that we wanted to hear the German commentators suffer when describing the imminent defeat of their national team. It seemed that by doing so, we actually increased our enjoyment or schadenfreude regarding the defeat of the Germans.

We were by no means unique in our viewing behavior. During the semi-final between Spain and Germany, the number of Dutch viewers watching the match on the German television channel ARD was monitored. During the first half and the beginning of the second half, on average 80,000 Dutch viewers (0.5 percent of all Dutch television viewers) watched the game on the German television channel ARD, presumably to avoid commercials on the Dutch channel before the match and during half-time. More than 100,000 additional Dutch viewers switched to the German channel immediately after Puyol scored his goal for Spain against Germany in the twenty-seventh minute of the second half, just as we did. Moreover, the number of Dutch viewers watching the German channel peaked at a staggering 352,000 (2.3 percent of all Dutch television viewers) just before the end of the match, when it was clear that the German defeat was imminent. An analyst of the Dutch public broadcasting network had no other words than "schadenfreude-density" to describe this phenomenon.

The example described above illustrates that schadenfreude is readily evoked in an intergroup context that is characterized by rivalry and competition (see Schurtz et al., Chapter 11 in this volume), thereby providing researchers with an opportunity to investigate the determinants of this emotional reaction to a misfortune suffered by another group. Indeed, the Dutch–German football rivalry was used to study the effects of domain interest and threat of in-group inferiority on schadenfreude experienced by the Dutch following the defeat of Germany by Croatia in the quarter-final of the FIFA 1998 World Cup and the elimination of Germany by England in the 2000 UEFA European Championship (Leach et al., 2003). Consistent with a social identity perspective (see Schurtz et al., Chapter 11 in this volume), schadenfreude experienced by the Dutch regarding both German losses was increased by domain interest (i.e., interest in football) and threats of status inferiority (i.e., reminders of the relative inferiority of the Dutch national team in international competition).

In the present chapter we will argue that intergroup relations are generally more competitive, and less cooperative, than interpersonal interactions. As a consequence, intergroup relations may provide a special breeding ground for schadenfreude. We first discuss evidence from a laboratory experiment with a public good dilemma, showing that intergroup relations are indeed more competitive than individual relations and are therefore more likely to elicit schadenfreude. Next, we present research in the context of Dutch–German relations, demonstrating that increased salience of rivalry and competition results in more intergroup schadenfreude because it strengthens affective identification with one's own nation, while at the same time decreasing affective identification with the other nation. Finally, we present two field studies showing that domain interest and people's strength of in-group identification interactively predict intergroup schadenfreude in a political and consumer context: one focusing on reactions of voters for opposition parties to the downfall of the Dutch coalition government and the other directed at the reactions of BlackBerry users following negative news reports about Apple's iPhone.

Interpersonal and intergroup schadenfreude: the interindividual-intergroup discontinuity effect

A central assumption in appraisal theories of emotion is that specific emotions are elicited by cognitions or interpretations of whether an event benefits or harms an individual's goals or concerns (for an overview of appraisal theories, see Roseman and Smith, 2001). Negative emotions are evoked by events that are perceived to harm or threaten an individual's concerns, whereas positive emotions are elicited by events that satisfy an individual's concerns (e.g., Frijda, 1988). Accordingly, it has been argued that interpersonal schadenfreude may derive from the appraisal that another's misfortune is deserved, thereby serving an individual's goal for justice (see Ben-Ze'ev, Chapter 5 in this volume; Feather, Chapter 3 in this volume). Moreover, we have argued that people can be pleased about another's misfortune because such an event may be evaluated or appraised as an opportunity to protect, maintain, or enhance a positive view of the individual self (see Van Dijk and Ouwerkerk, Chapter 9 in this volume).

However, based on social identity theory (Tajfel, 1978; Tajfel and Turner, 1979), it has been proposed that concerns and appraisals may also influence specific emotions in an intergroup context. According to intergroup emotions theory (see also Schurtz et al., Chapter 11 in this volume), appraisals of whether an event may benefit or harm concerns *of one's group* may elicit specific emotions when one's *social* rather than personal identity is salient. In other words, when a group becomes part of the self (i.e., one's *collective* self), one may experience affect and emotions on behalf of that group (Mackie, Devos, and Smith, 2000; Mackie, Silver, and Smith, 2004). For example, a misfortune or failure of an out-group may evoke *intergroup* schadenfreude when this event is evaluated as being beneficial for people's striving for a positive social identity, despite the fact that this event does not necessarily satisfy any goal for the personal self or may even harm personal interests (see Schurtz et al., Chapter 11 in this volume).

Although interpersonal and intergroup schadenfreude may be evoked in a similar way by appraisals of misfortunes of others as satisfying individual or group goals, respectively, we suggest that intergroup relations may provide a special breeding ground for schadenfreude. There is no reason to assume that groups *in isolation* possess qualities that make them especially competitive, hostile, or aggressive. However, a vast amount of research on cooperation in mixed-motive situations suggests that *interactions* between groups are more competitive than interactions between individuals (see Wildschut et al., 2003 for an overview). At least four explanations have been offered for this so-called interindividual-intergroup discontinuity effect. The social support explanation suggests that group members can provide mutual social support for displaying competitive behavior that violates norms of fairness and reciprocity (i.e., "greedy" behavior), whereas this support is lacking for individuals in interaction (Insko et al., 1990). Another explanation, also focusing on differences in "greed," proposes that groups may provide safety in numbers or anonymity, thereby making it difficult for others to assign personal responsibility for norm-violating behavior (Schopler et al., 1995). Alternatively, the schema-based distrust explanation argues that an out-group schema is activated when groups interact. This fear-based schema consists of expectations and learned beliefs that intergroup interactions are aggressive and competitive (Pemberton, Insko, and Schopler, 1996). Finally, in line with social identity theory (Tajfel, 1978; Tajfel and Turner, 1979), it has been suggested that the interindividual-intergroup discontinuity effect can be explained by a dominant in-group-favoring norm operating in intergroup relations, compelling group members to protect the interests of the in-group before considering the interests of others (Wildschut, Insko, and Gaertner, 2002).

In a laboratory experiment Ouwerkerk et al. (under review) obtained evidence showing that intergroup relations are indeed more competitive than interpersonal relations, and may therefore evoke schadenfreude more readily. More specifically, they investigated whether in a mixed-motive situation, the same manipulation of deservingness of a misfortune would affect schadenfreude differently in an intergroup setting compared to an interpersonal setting. In the interpersonal condition, participants were individually seated in a cubicle behind a computer terminal and were provided with an opportunity to earn money by making decisions about contributions (i.e., their level of cooperation) in a public good dilemma involving three other individuals, which were in fact pre-programmed strategies displaying low cooperation (i.e., a "bad apple"), moderate cooperation and high cooperation (see Kerr et al., 2009, Experiment 2 for a detailed description of the paradigm and the pre-programmed strategies). After twenty trials, participants were informed that one individual had to be excluded from further interaction and that this individual would be selected randomly by the computer. It was emphasized that this would be unfortunate for the selected individual because he or she could not earn anything in the remaining trials. Next, participants were informed that either the "bad apple" (high deservingness) or the individual showing high levels of cooperation (low deservingness) was excluded from further interaction. Subsequently, schadenfreude regarding the exclusion of the selected individual was measured using a highly reliable five-item scale that we also used in other studies (e.g., Van Dijk, et al., 2005; Van Dijk et al., 2006; Van Dijk et al., 2011a; Van Dijk et al., 2011b; Van Dijk et al., 2012). In the intergroup condition the procedure was identical, with the exception that two participants were seated in a cubicle who together made decisions about contributions in a public good dilemma supposedly involving three other pairs of participants. Moreover, following the random exclusion of one of these pairs, together they provided answers to the schadenfreude scale.

The results of this laboratory experiment yielded a replication of the basic interindividual-intergroup discontinuity effect. The mean level of cooperation on the twenty trials was significantly lower in the intergroup than in the interpersonal condition, indicating that intergroup relations are indeed more competitive than interpersonal relations. Moreover, the manipulation of deservingness had a profound main effect on schadenfreude, showing levels that were above the scale mean and higher when an uncooperative individual or group was excluded (high deservingness) rather than when a cooperative individual or group was excluded (low deservingness), thereby providing corroborating evidence for the importance of deservingness in evoking schadenfreude (see Ben-Ze'ev, Chapter 5 in this volume; Feather, Chapter 3 in this volume). More relevant for our present discussion, an interaction effect was obtained demonstrating that this effect of deservingness was stronger in the intergroup than in the interpersonal condition. More specifically, groups reported higher levels of schadenfreude when an uncooperative group was excluded compared to individuals when an uncooperative other was excluded. No such difference was obtained in the low deservingness condition. Moreover, schadenfreude was significantly correlated with the level of cooperation in the high deservingness condition, indicating that differences in competiveness may indeed be the underlying reason why schadenfreude is evoked more readily in intergroup rather than interpersonal relations. However, some caution about this conclusion should be noted, because it is based on a single experiment. Indeed, factors other than differences in competiveness may also have played a role. For example, whereas an individual may be somewhat reluctant to express schadenfreude because he or she is afraid that this could be perceived as socially undesirable, knowing that someone else in your group shares your enjoyment may remove this fear. Indeed, such validation may even strengthen the experience of schadenfreude by itself, just as it might have done when two Dutch guys enjoyed watching a rival football team being eliminated from the FIFA 2010 World Cup on television.

The salience of intergroup competition and schadenfreude: don't mention the war

The study described in the previous section suggests that, *ceteris paribus*, intergroup relations are more competitive than interpersonal relations and that schadenfreude may therefore be evoked more readily in an intergroup context. However, it is important to note that the extent to which specific social groups are perceived to be cooperative or competitive (i.e., their perceived "warmth") may vary systematically and that social groups may therefore differ in their level of automatic activation of emotions or feelings that subsequently facilitate schadenfreude (see Cikara and Fiske, Chapter 10 in this volume). Moreover, the extent to which the *same* social group is perceived to be cooperative or competitive may differ depending on the social context. When competition rather than cooperation between groups is salient, people more easily categorize themselves and others based on group membership (Tajfel, 1982), which may result in stronger affective identification with one's own group and more negative attitudes toward the out-group, including lower affective identification with that out-group. These changes in relative in-group identification may subsequently lead to more schadenfreude following a failure or misfortune suffered by the out-group. Indeed, research shows that social identification is an important determinant of schadenfreude in an intergroup setting (Combs et al., 2009; see also Schurtz et al., Chapter 11 in this volume).

We tested these hypotheses in the context of Dutch–German relations (Ouwerkerk and Van Dijk, 2008). We focused on the intergroup relation between these two neighbouring countries because it contains characteristics of both cooperation and competition. Competitive characteristics include the aforementioned football rivalry and references to the Second World War period, when the Germans occupied the Netherlands. However, Dutch–German relations are also characterized by intensive cooperation as trading nations and founding members of the European Union (EU). An experimental survey was distributed among students from universities of both countries (the VU University Amsterdam in the Netherlands and the University of Bochum in Germany). In the introduction we stated that the goal of the survey was to investigate Dutch–German relations. This was followed by a simple manipulation consisting of two sentences to make either cooperation or competition salient. In one condition participants read that "the relationship between the Dutch and the Germans is characterized mainly by cooperation. In different areas the Dutch an the Germans often work very well together," whereas in the other condition participants read that "the relationship between the Dutch and the Germans is characterized mainly by rivalry. In different areas the Dutch and the Germans often compete with each other." This manipulation was followed by measurements of affective identification with both the Germans and the Dutch using the solidarity subscale of Leach et al. (2008). Next, participants read a short article about the results of a study supposedly conducted by the University of Michigan, investigating the creativity and resourcefulness of workers from different nations in the EU in order to select suitable candidates for American companies abroad. Participants learned that the out-group (either the Dutch or the Germans) ranked only twenty-third out of twenty-five European countries on these desirable attributes. Subsequently, schadenfreude regarding the poor ranking of the out-group was measured using the same highly reliable five-item scale as in the study described earlier.[1]

Consistent with our hypothesis, the results of the survey showed that relative affective identification with the in-group was indeed higher when competition rather than cooperation was made salient. People also experienced more schadenfreude regarding the low ranking of the out-group when competition rather than cooperation was made salient. Thus, in a similar fashion to Basil Fawlty, we mentioned "competition" once, but we certainly did not get away with it. Moreover, as predicted, relative in-group identification was significantly correlated with schadenfreude and mediated the effect of our manipulation of salience of competition or cooperation on intergroup schadenfreude. It should be noted that these effects were obtained for both Dutch and German participants,[2] and were not found on other social emotions (e.g., sympathy). Taken together, these findings suggest that salience of competition is indeed an important determinant of schadenfreude in intergroup relations. One additional finding of this survey is worth mentioning. We also asked the Dutch and German participants how often they visited the other country and had contact with members of the other nation. This frequency of intergroup contact correlated positively with affective

[1] It should be noted that in both the German and the Dutch versions of the scale, one of the five items makes explicit reference to schadenfreude, using the German word *Schadenfreude* and its direct translation in Dutch *Leedvermaak*, respectively.

[2] However, we did obtain interaction effects involving gender showing that the effects of our manipulation on both relative in-group identification and schadenfreude were substantially stronger for male than for female participants.

out-group identification and negatively with schadenfreude, suggesting that intergroup contact may be effective in reducing negative attitudes and hostility toward an out-group.

Domain interest and in-group identification as determinants of intergroup schadenfreude

Having established that competitive intergroup relations provide a special breeding ground for intergroup schadenfreude, we now turn our attention to research investigating determinants of schadenfreude in an intergroup setting. More specifically, we will focus on the combined impact of domain interest and people's strength of affective identification with an in-group on schadenfreude evoked by an out-group misfortune. Leach et al. (2003) have argued that greater interest in a domain increases the self-relevance of others' performance within that domain, thereby making it more likely that a misfortune suffered by an out-group evokes schadenfreude. As mentioned earlier, they accordingly showed that domain interest (i.e., interest in soccer) is indeed an important determinant of intergroup schadenfreude in the context of the Dutch–German football rivalry. They further argued that domain interest "is a better, more context-specific measure of the rival's loss to the self than identification" (Leach et al., 2003, p. 935). The latter argument seems somewhat at odds with the intergroup emotions theory described previously, which proposes that people's strength of social identification with an in-group is an important determinant of intergroup emotions because it makes intergroup comparisons more relevant to the (collective) self (Mackie, Devos, and Smith, 2000; Mackie, Silver, and Smith, 2004; see also Schurtz et al., Chapter 11 in this volume). Indeed, the study described in the previous section, as well as other studies (e.g., Combs et al., 2009), have demonstrated that people's strength of in-group identification can be a strong predictor of intergroup schadenfreude.

However, rather than starting a debate about the relative importance of domain interest and in-group identification, we suggest that both factors are important in determining intergroup schadenfreude. In other words, we propose that they may interactively predict intergroup schadenfreude. More specifically, we suggest that stronger affective identification with an in-group will increase schadenfreude regarding an out-group misfortune only when this misfortune occurs in a domain of interest. Going back to our example of the Dutch–German football rivalry, when a Dutch person has no interest in football, there is no reason to assume that stronger affective identification with the Dutch will increase his or her level of schadenfreude when the German football team loses. Even if he or she identifies strongly with the Dutch, he or she will simply not care about the outcome of a football match. By contrast, affective in-group identification with the Dutch should increase schadenfreude when football is considered an important domain for the self. We tested this hypothesis in two field studies investigating intergroup relations in a political and consumer context: one focusing on reactions of voters for opposition parties to the downfall of the Dutch coalition government and the other directed at the reactions of BlackBerry users following negative news reports about Apple's iPhone.

Determinants of intergroup schadenfreude in a political context: when a government falls

Research in a political context shows that affective dispositions toward a political in-group are important determinants of the level of schadenfreude people experience regarding a misfortune of a political out-group. For example, Zillmann and Knobloch (2001) found that more favorable affective dispositions towards Republicans increased enjoyment of news revelations about a political setback for Democrats in the US. More recently, Combs et al. (2009) demonstrated that party affiliation and strength of party identification in the US strongly predicts schadenfreude regarding events that are presumed to be harmful for the political out-group, even if these events negatively affect society more broadly regardless of political party affiliation (see Schurtz et al., Chapter 11 in this volume). However, as argued in the previous section, we expect that stronger in-group identification will increase schadenfreude regarding an out-group's misfortune only when this misfortune occurs in a domain of interest.

Support for this hypothesis was first provided by a study investigating determinants of schadenfreude following the fall of the Dutch government led by Prime Minister Jan Peter Balkenende on October 16, 2002 (Ouwerkerk et al., under review). The Dutch have a multi-party system and governments are always formed by a coalition of two or more parties. The right-wing coalition government led by Balkenende included his own party, the centre-right Christian Democrat Party (CDA), a conservative party (the VVD), and a brand new populist party founded by the controversial politician Pim Fortuyn (the LPF), who himself was murdered nine days before the elections. The LPF and its new leadership had tremendous trouble keeping the party together without the unifying strength of its founder, resulting in a government running from one conflict to another, and its ultimate downfall after ruling for just 87 days. The day after the fall of the government, a survey was distributed at seven Dutch universities among students from a wide range of disciplines. In this survey, political affiliation was measured by asking students whether they had voted for a party from the (fallen) coalition government in the previous elections or a party in the opposition. Affective in-group identification with this party was assessed with a scale consisting of items that are also included in the solidarity subscale of Leach et al. (2008). Moreover, domain interest (i.e., interest in politics) was assessed by scoring answers of open-ended political knowledge questions as suggested by Zaller (1990). Finally, schadenfreude regarding the fall of the government was measured by both the highly reliable five-item scale used in the research described previously and a less explicit measure assessing the extent to which participants thought a fake "obituary" mocking the event was funny.

The results of this survey showed a main effect of party affiliation on both our schadenfreude measures. People who voted for an opposition party (i.e., when the misfortune was suffered by the out-group) reported schadenfreude levels that were above the scale mean and higher than those who voted for a coalition party (i.e., when the misfortune was suffered by the in-group). More relevant to our present discussion, for people who voted for an opposition party, political interest and affective in-group identification interactively predicted their level of schadenfreude on both measures. More specifically, consistent with the hypothesis outlined in the previous section, stronger affective identification with the in-group increased schadenfreude regarding the out-group misfortune when interest in politics was high, whereas no such effect of identification on schadenfreude was obtained when interest in politics was low. Moreover, this interaction effect was not obtained when the fall of the government constituted an in-group misfortune. In other words, the interaction effect between political interest and affective in-group identification on both schadenfreude measures was attenuated for people who had voted for a coalition party in the previous elections. Further evidence for the interactive influence of domain interest and affective in-group identification on schadenfreude toward an out-group was obtained in a field study discussed below, investigating intergroup relations in a consumer context.

Determinants of intergroup schadenfreude in a consumer context: fruit fight

Research shows that people may experience schadenfreude about the downfall of an individual's prestige product. Moreover, this emotional reaction is predictive of subsequent "trash talk" or negative word-of-mouth, thereby making the study of schadenfreude directly relevant for consumer behavior (Sundie et al., 2009; see also Sundie, Chapter 8 in this volume). A study among rival brand communities (PC versus Apple users) reveals that schadenfreude in a consumer context can also be evoked at the intergroup level. Hickman and Ward (2007) found that stronger social identification with one's brand community resulted in more schadenfreude after reading a scenario in the form a news article describing a serious virus afflicting the rival brand of computers. However, as argued in the previous sections, we expect that stronger in-group identification will increase schadenfreude regarding an out-group's misfortune only when this misfortune occurs in a domain of interest. In order to test this hypothesis in a consumer context, Ouwerkerk et al. (under review) investigated the impact of domain interest and affective in-group identification on schadenfreude experienced by young BlackBerry users after reading negative news about Apple's iPhone.

Reports in the popular media suggested that intense rivalry had emerged between young members of the two consumer groups in the Amsterdam area. A survey was therefore distributed among young adults seen using a BlackBerry on schoolyards or university campuses in Amsterdam. In this survey, domain interest (i.e., relevance of smartphones) was measured using a three-item scale (e.g., "Having a smartphone is important to me") and affective in-group identification with other BlackBerry users with the solidarity subscale of Leach et al. (2008). In addition, other scales were included assessing brand cognitions, positive and negative affect regarding both brands, and hostile feelings toward iPhone users. In the second part of the survey the misfortune suffered by the rival consumer group was introduced in the form of a short fictitious news article from a consumer organization with the heading "Problems for iPhone users are piling up." In this article, several problems that iPhone users experienced with their smartphone were described (e.g., slow network, warranty problems, dangerous levels of radiation). Subsequently, the highly reliable five-item scale used in previous research assessed schadenfreude regarding the misfortunes suffered by iPhone users. In addition, we measured the intention of BlackBerry users to share the news about the problems for iPhone users with others (i.e., to engage in negative word-of-mouth).

The results of the survey revealed that domain interest and affective in-group identification interactively predicted schadenfreude following the negative news report about Apple's iPhone. More specifically, and remarkably consistent with the research in a political context reported in the previous section, stronger affective identification with other

BlackBerry users increased schadenfreude regarding the out-group misfortune only when interest in smartphones was high. Importantly, this interaction effect was obtained even when controlling for brand cognitions, positive and negative affect regarding both brands, and hostile feelings toward iPhone users. In addition, the results show that both hostile feelings toward iPhone users and schadenfreude were strongly correlated with intentions to engage in negative word-of-mouth. Moreover, additional analyses revealed that the effect of hostile feelings toward iPhone users on negative word-of-mouth was mediated by schadenfreude, thereby replicating findings of Sundie et al. (2009) at the individual level (see Sundie, Chapter 8 in this volume).

Conclusion

Taken together, the results of the studies described in this chapter suggest that schadenfreude can be readily evoked in intergroup relations that are characterized by rivalry and competition. Although enjoying the defeat of a long-standing rival out-group when watching a football match on television can to some extent be perceived as harmless fun, this may be less innocent than meets the eye. For example, in the context of the sports rivalry between the Red Sox and Yankees baseball teams, Cikara, Botvinick, and Fiske (2011) demonstrated that valuation-related neural responses of avid fans to a rival team's loss against a third party (i.e., reactions associated with subjective pleasure) correlate with the self-reported likelihood of aggressing against a fan of that rival team (see Cikara and Fiske, Chapter 10 in this volume). Moreover, in the arena of (international) politics, even the death of thousands of people may evoke schadenfreude. Wang and Roberts (2006) analyzed texts from postings on the Beijing University bulletin board and observed that many Chinese citizens expressed schadenfreude over the suffering inflicted on Americans with the 9/11 attacks on the World Trade Center and the Pentagon. Combs et al. (2009) showed that Democrats were more likely to express schadenfreude than Republicans when reading about the increase in US troop deaths during the Bush administration (see Schurtz et al., Chapter 11 in this volume). Indeed, Spears and Leach (2004) have argued that opportunistic schadenfreude may very well be the first step toward direct aggression against out-group members, thereby turning intergroup relations into something more hostile (see Leach, Spears, and Manstead, Chapter 13 in this volume). Future research should therefore continue to focus on understanding expressions of intergroup schadenfreude and its implications for intergroup relations.

References

Cikara, M., Botvinick, M. M., and Fiske, S. T. (2011). Us versus them: social identity shapes neural responses to intergroup competition and harm. *Psychological Science* 22: 306–13.

Combs, D. J. Y., Powell, C. A. J., Schurtz, D. R., and Smith, R. H. (2009). Politics, schadenfreude, and ingroup identification: the sometimes happy thing about a poor economy and death. *Journal of Experimental Social Psychology* 45: 635–46.

Frijda, N. H. (1988). The laws of emotion. *American Psychologist* 43: 349–58.

Hickman, T. and Ward, J. (2007). The dark side of brand community: inter-group stereotyping, trash talk, and schadenfreude. *Advances in Consumer Research* 34: 314–19.

Insko, C. A., Schopler, J., Hoyle, R. H., Dardis, G. J., and Graetz, K. A. (1990). Individual–group discontinuity as a function of fear and greed. *Journal of Personality and Social Psychology* 58: 68–79.

Kerr, N. L., Rumble, A. C., Park, E. S., Ouwerkerk, J. W., Parks, C. D., Gallucci, M., and Van Lange, P. A. M. (2009). "How many bad apples does it take to spoil the whole barrel?": social exclusion and tolerance for bad apples. *Journal of Experimental Social Psychology* 45: 603–13.

Leach, C. W., Spears, R., Branscombe, N. R., and Doosje, B. (2003). Malicious pleasure: schadenfreude at the suffering of another group. *Journal of Personality and Social Psychology* 84: 932–43.

Leach, C. W., Van Zomeren, M., Zebel, S., Vliek, M. L. W., Pennekamp, S. F., Doosje, B., Ouwerkerk, J. W., and Spears, R. (2008). Group-level self-definition and self-investment: a hierarchical (multi-component) model of in-group identification. *Journal of Personality and Social Psychology* 95: 144–65.

Mackie, D. M., Devos, T., and Smith, E. R. (2000). Intergroup emotion: explaining offensive action tendencies in an intergroup context. *Journal of Personality and Social Psychology* 79: 602–16.

Mackie, D. M., Silver, L., and Smith, E. R. (2004). Intergroup emotions: emotion as an intergroup phenomenon. In L. Z. Tiedens and C. W. Leach (eds.), *The Social Life of Emotions*. Cambridge University Press, pp. 227–45.

Ouwerkerk, J. W. and Van Dijk, W. W. (2008). "Don't mention the war": social identification and salience of rivalry as determinants of intergroup schadenfreude. Paper presented at the XVth General Meeting of the European Association for Experimental Social Psychology, Opatija, Croatia.

Ouwerkerk, J. W., Van Dijk, W. W., Pennekamp, S. F., and Spears, R. (manuscript under review). Forbidden fruit and forbidden pleasures: individual versus intragroup schadenfreude following the exclusion of bad apples.

Ouwerkerk, J. W., Van Dijk, W. W., Vonkeman, C., and Spears, R. (manuscript under review). When we enjoy bad news about other groups: a social identity approach to out-group schadenfreude.

Pemberton, M. R., Insko, C. A., and Schopler, J. (1996). Memory for and experience of differential competitive behavior of individuals and groups. *Journal of Personality and Social Psychology* 71: 953–66.

Roseman, I. J. and Smith, C. A. (2001). Appraisal theory, overview, assumptions, varieties, controversies. In K. S. Scherer, A. Schorr, and T. Johnstone (eds.),

Appraisal Processes in Emotion: Theory, Methods, Research. Oxford University Press, pp. 3–19.

Schopler, J., Insko, C. A., Drigotas, S., Wieselquist, J., Pemberton, M., and Cox, C. (1995). The role of identifiability in the reduction of interindividual-intergroup discontinuity. *Journal of Experimental Social Psychology* 31: 553–74.

Spears, R. and Leach, C. W. (2004). Intergroup schadenfreude: conditions and consequences. In L. Z. Tiedens and C. W. Leach (eds.). *The Social Life of Emotions*. Cambridge University Press, pp. 336–55.

Sundie, J. M., Ward, J., Beal, D. J., Chin, W. W., and Oneto, S. (2009). Schadenfreude as a consumption-related emotion: feeling happiness about the downfall of another's product. *Journal of Consumer Psychology* 19: 356–73.

Tajfel, H. (1978). Social categorization, social identity and social comparison. In H. Tajfel (ed.), *Differentiation between Social Groups: Studies in the Social Psychology of Intergroup Relations*. London: Academic Press, pp. 61–76.

(1982). Social psychology of intergroup relations. *Annual Review of Psychology* 33: 1–39.

Tajfel, H. and Turner, J. C. (1979). An integrative theory of intergroup conflict. In W. G. Austin and S. Worchel (eds.), *The Social Psychology of Intergroup Relations*. Monterey, CA: Brooks/Cole.

Van Dijk, W. W., Ouwerkerk, J. W., Goslinga, S., and Nieweg, M. (2005). Deservingness and schadenfreude. *Cognition and Emotion* 19: 933–9.

Van Dijk, W. W., Ouwerkerk, J. W., Goslinga, S., Nieweg, M., and Gallucci, M. (2006). When people fall from grace: reconsidering the role of envy in schadenfreude. *Emotion* 6: 156–60.

Van Dijk, W. W., Ouwerkerk, J. W., Van Koningsbruggen, G. M., and Wesseling, Y. M. (2012). "So you wanna be a pop star?": schadenfreude following another's misfortune on TV. *Basic and Applied Social Psychology* 34: 168–74.

Van Dijk, W. W., Ouwerkerk, J. W., Wesseling, Y. M., and Van Koningsbruggen, G. M. (2011a). Towards understanding pleasure at the misfortunes of others: the impact of self-evaluation threat on schadenfreude. *Cognition and Emotion* 25: 360–8.

Van Dijk, W. W., Van Koningsbruggen, G. M., Ouwerkerk, J. W., and Wesseling, Y. M. (2011b). Self-esteem, self-affirmation, and schadenfreude. *Emotion* 11: 1445–9.

Wang, Y. and Roberts, C. W. (2006). Schadenfreude: a case study of emotion as situated discursive display. *Comparative Sociology* 5: 45–63.

Wildschut, T., Insko, C. A., and Gaertner, L. (2002). Intragroup social influence and intergroup competition. *Journal of Personality and Social Psychology* 82: 975–92.

Wildschut, T., Pinter, B., Vevea, J. L., Insko, C. A., and Schopler, J. (2003). Beyond the group mind: a quantitative review of the interindividual-intergroup discontinuity effect. *Psychological Bulletin* 129: 698–722.

Zaller, J. (1990). Political awareness, elite opinion leadership, and the mass survey response. *Social Cognition* 8: 125–53.

Zillmann, D. and Knobloch, S. (2001). Emotional reactions to narratives about the fortunes of personae in the news theatre. *Poetics* 29: 189–206.

13 Situating schadenfreude in social relations

Colin Wayne Leach, Russell Spears, and Antony S. R. Manstead

Two somewhat distinct trends seem to have put schadenfreude on the scholarly and the popular agenda: (1) the academic (re)turn to emotion as a concept; and (2) the popular interest in seeing others suffer in the media. Recent media coverage has used the term "schadenfreude" to describe pleasure at the precipitous fall of celebrities; public rejoicing at the destruction of the World Trade Center on September 11, 2001; and laughter at the public embarrassment of poor singers and misguided lovers on "reality TV" shows (see Kristjánsson, 2006; Lee, 2008). As shown in this volume, a good deal of the scholarly research of schadenfreude also focuses on pleasure at the fall of high achievers and the adversity suffered by the arrogant, the unfair, or others who seem to deserve adversity.

Although we have no doubt that things like material gain, envy, and perceived injustice can increase the pleasure that people take in others' adversity, we focus on more minimal and mundane instances of schadenfreude. We think that these more minimal and mundane instances of schadenfreude offer a particularly clear picture of the emotion. In our view, the more minimal and mundane instances of schadenfreude also come closer to the pragmatic meaning of *Schadenfreude* in German. In everyday usage, Germans use the term *Schadenfreude* to refer to a moderate, modest pleasure felt in response to others' minor falls and foibles. In other words, schadenfreude is pleasure about others' misfortunes. Unlike other sorts of adversity, a misfortune is an adversity caused by happenstance (*Oxford English Dictionary*, 1989; see Leach and Spears, 2008, 2009). Thus, schadenfreude is pleasure about an adversity caused by bad luck or by the vagaries of competition. More forthright and fulsome

We thank Tina Campt, Kai Epstude, Nicole Harth, and Thomas Kessler for discussing the use and meaning of schadenfreude among German speakers. We thank Brian Koenig for his comments on our definition and conceptualization of schadenfreude. This chapter reports research that was supported by the UK Economic and Social Research Council (grant RES-000–23-0915).

pleasures are defined in other terms in German. For example, pleasure at seeing justice done is defined as *Genugtuung.*

Because of our focus on the more minimal and mundane instances of schadenfreude, we conceptualize schadenfreude as situated within social relations that render this particular pleasure passive, indirect, and opportunistic (see Leach et al., 2003; Spears and Leach, 2004). We conceptualize schadenfreude as a passive, indirect, and opportunistic pleasure because it is *about another's misfortune* – an adversity caused by happenstance. In addition, our conceptualization of schadenfreude is based in Nietzsche's (1887/1967) argument that schadenfreude is a pleasure taken by those too weak to more actively cause other's misfortunes themselves through direct competition (see Leach et al., 2003). In schadenfreude, the other's misfortune is not caused by the *schadenfroh* (i.e., the person experiencing schadenfreude). As such, schadenfreude can be distinguished from pleasure about outdoing a rival in direct competition, which we define as *gloating* (Leach, Snider, and Iyer, 2002; Leach et al., 2003; see also Ortony, Clore, and Collins, 1988). Unlike schadenfreude, we argue that gloating is active, direct, and self-caused (see Table 13.1). Because the pleasure of gloating is "earned" through the achievement of directly defeating a rival, it should be more intensely experienced and expressed. In this chapter, we discuss several recent studies designed to highlight the distinctions between schadenfreude and active, direct, and self-caused gloating.

Although most of our research has examined schadenfreude in intergroup relations, our conceptualization is general and should therefore apply across levels of analysis, and thus also to interpersonal relations. Two recent studies that support this claim are discussed below. Across levels of analysis, contexts, and methods, we aim to illustrate that schadenfreude is situated in particular social relations that give this pleasure its passive, indirect, and opportunistic qualities. It is these qualities, and the social relations that produce them, that make schadenfreude a particular kind of pleasure, different from less modest and moderate pleasures like pride, joy, or gloating.

Table 13.1 *Distinctions between schadenfreude and gloating*

	Active/ passive	Direct/ indirect	Comparative/ absolute	Gain
Schadenfreude	Passive	Indirect	Absolute (misfortune)	Psychological
Gloating	Active	Direct	Comparative	Psychological and material

Situating schadenfreude

As evaluations of ongoing person–environment interactions, all emotions are situated in social relations (Lazarus, 1991; Parkinson, Fischer, and Manstead, 2005; Tiedens and Leach, 2004). However, the socially situated nature of schadenfreude may be more obvious than that of other emotions because it is an emotion about the adversity of another (see Heider, 1958; Spears and Leach, 2004). Unlike joy on one's birthday or pride in one's home, schadenfreude is about an (adverse) event that befalls another party rather than oneself. Beyond this obvious way in which schadenfreude is more socially situated than other pleasures, we believe that schadenfreude has a particular quality of experience and expression because observing another's misfortune situates the *schadenfroh* in a particularly passive, indirect, and opportunistic social relation to the sufferer and their misfortune. For example, the passive observation of a misfortune caused by happenstance rather than oneself situates the self in a different social relation to the other than does causing the other's adversity by defeating them in direct competition. As such, the pleasure of gloating is based in a different social relation from the more moderate and modest pleasure of schadenfreude.

Consistent with appraisal theories of emotion (see Lazarus, 1991), the distinct experience and expression of schadenfreude should be tied to a unique set of appraisals that establish the meaning that people give to the social relation in which they are situated. Together, these appraisals of the other's misfortune combine to create a signature unique to schadenfreude. We believe that the three defining appraisals of the other's misfortune are of the external agency of the misfortune, the indirect control of the misfortune and thus the pleasure of schadenfreude, and the unexpected nature of the misfortune. Together, these three appraisals make schadenfreude a passive, indirect, and opportunistic pleasure.

Most important is the appraisal that someone other than the self is the agent of the other's misfortune (see also Ben-Ze'ev, 2000 and Chapter 5 in this volume; Portmann, Chapter 2 in this volume; Seip et al., Chapter 15 in this volume; Van Dijk and Ouwerkerk, Chapter 1 in this volume). That the misfortune is appraised as caused by happenstance is what makes schadenfreude a passive emotion. In contrast, gloating and pride are more active states of self-agency. In addition, people should appraise themselves as having little perceived control over events in schadenfreude. This is what makes schadenfreude indirectly gained, rather than the more directly gained pleasures of pride and gloating. As an opportunistic pleasure, schadenfreude should be characterized by an appraisal that the misfortune is unexpected. The passive and indirect nature of schadenfreude means that one must wait for the misfortune (or be pleasantly surprised by its occurrence) rather than bring it about oneself.

Because we view schadenfreude as a passive, indirect, and opportunistic pleasure about another's misfortune, we have empirically examined schadenfreude in ways consistent with this conceptualization. Thus, we have tended to examine feelings about the (ambiguously caused) failure and other misfortunes of parties not engaged in direct competition with the self. We have mainly examined schadenfreude in the context of individuals witnessing an equal-status rival fail against another party due to the vagaries of competition. We think that the absence of direct competition between the *schadenfroh* and the target, and the resultant preclusion of material gain, provides the purest context for schadenfreude. Again, these more minimal and mundane instances of schadenfreude seem to come closer to the German usage of the term to describe pleasure at other's minor falls and foibles.

Given our definition of schadenfreude, we do not examine pleasure at clearly deserved failures or pleasure at the punishment or other adversity of obvious wrongdoers. In our view, seeing justice done is likely to lead to a less moderate or modest pleasure than schadenfreude. We also worry that pleasure about seeing justice done may not be the same sort of pleasure as that about seeing someone suffer a misfortune caused by happenstance (see also Koenig, 2009; Kristjánsson, 2006; however, see also Portmann, 2000). For similar reasons, we do not examine pleasure at serious misfortunes or those that are likely to be seen as highly undeserved or unfair. In fact, we believe that there is good reason to expect that highly undeserved misfortunes will not encourage much schadenfreude (e.g., Leach et al., 2003; for discussions, see Feather, 2006; Spears and Leach, 2004). Taking pleasure in the serious and undeserved adversity of others may come closer to sadism than to schadenfreude. Thus, we think schadenfreude is best examined in social relations that are not marked by obvious or extreme justice or injustice, because in such instances any pleasure is likely to be more about the (in)justice than about the misfortune.

Unlike much other research on schadenfreude, the targets of schadenfreude that we examine tend to be of equal status to the *schadenfroh* rather than vastly superior. When we do establish targets of schadenfreude as successful in the domain of their eventual failure, this success is typically established independently of the *schadenfroh*'s performance (Leach et al., 2003, Studies 1 and 2; Leach and Spears, 2008, Studies 1 and 2). We have also tended to independently establish the *schadenfroh* as unsuccessful in the domain of the target's failure. With these aspects of our approach in mind, we can now turn to our specific examinations of schadenfreude and the social relations in which they are situated.

Schadenfreude is opportunistic – open to many targets

As a result of the emphasis on envy and undeserved success as causes of schadenfreude, most empirical work has examined schadenfreude toward highly successful targets who suffer a deserved failure or other adversity. However, our conceptualization of schadenfreude suggests that pleasure can be felt about the misfortunes of many targets. The target need not be more successful than the self. If the target is more successful, the success need not be undeserved, and thus the adversity need not be deserved. We have documented schadenfreude in many such cases.

One approach has been to examine schadenfreude at the failure of third parties who are relevant rivals, but who are not engaged in direct competition with the self. For example, we examined Dutch participants' pleasure at the loss of the German football team in an important world competition in 1998. The Germans were seen as near-equal in status. Their failure eliminated them from the competition at an earlier stage than the Dutch. Thus, the Germans were neither more successful nor unfairly so. In addition, their failure was not particularly deserved. Indeed, it was viewed as mildly undeserved (because Germany lost to lower-ranked Croatia). Nevertheless, the Dutch expressed moderate schadenfreude at Germany's loss. Leach et al. (2003, Study 2) found the Dutch to express near-moderate schadenfreude at a similar German loss in a European competition in 2000.

In two further studies, we dealt with some of the difficulties of studying schadenfreude in a real competition by leading students to believe that their university was involved in a competition (Leach and Spears, 2008). This allowed us to control the performance of the in-group and their cross-town rival. To establish in-group and rival performance independently, we had each group compete against a different set of opponents. Thus, consistent with our conceptualization of schadenfreude, the in-group and the out-group rival were never involved in direct competition. This means that the rival's eventual failure could provide no material benefit to the in-group (a factor that can also contribute to pleasure at a rival's failure: see Spears and Leach, 2004). Our paradigm also established participants as passive observers of their rival's eventual failure in the final stage of competition.

To align with most previous work on schadenfreude, we established the rival out-group as independently successful in their section of the competition. In one experimental condition (Leach and Spears, 2008, Study 1), participants only knew about the rival's general success before being told of the rival's eventual failure. In the absence of material benefit, participants tended to express a little schadenfreude at their rival's loss.

Those who perceived the rival's previous success as undeserved did not feel much more schadenfreude. In Study 2, we manipulated the deservingness of the rival's success. Here again, deservingness played little role. This is likely because the rival's loss in the competition was not a punishment, was not self-caused, and was not deserved. The rival simply lost against a closely matched opponent due to the vagaries of competition. This had little to do with justice, and thus pleasure at this misfortune had little to do with justice. Feeling a little pleasure at a rival's failure is the simple satisfaction of schadenfreude. When the stakes are fairly low, the pleasure is fairly modest (Iyer and Leach, 2008; Lazarus, 1991). However, the low stakes here are characteristic of everyday schadenfreude. Where there is material gain for the self, unjust success, or deserved adversity for the other, the pleasure in response is likely to be greater.

We have not always examined schadenfreude toward third parties not in direct competition with the self. In Leach et al. (2003, Study 2), we found that Dutch participants expressed moderate schadenfreude toward the Italian team's loss in the 2000 European competition. What is interesting about this is that Italy defeated the Dutch in this competition. We revisited this competition with a view to providing a better account of schadenfreude towards second and third parties. We found that greater schadenfreude was expressed toward (third party) Germany than toward (third party) Italy. This occurred despite the fact that Italy defeated the in-group and was seen as slightly better than the in-group in the domain of competition. More importantly, participants' feelings of dejection at their loss to Italy predicted schadenfreude toward Germany slightly better than it predicted schadenfreude toward Italy. In addition, dislike of Italy was a stronger predictor of schadenfreude toward Germany than toward Italy. Thus, being defeated by Italy, feeling dejected at this defeat, and disliking Italy all fed schadenfreude toward Germany – an uninvolved third party. In other studies, too (Leach et al., 2003, Study 1; Leach and Spears, 2008, Studies 1 and 2), performing poorly in a competition fed schadenfreude toward third parties who did not compete against the self.

Taken together, the five studies discussed above demonstrate that people can feel pleasure at a rival's failure in normal competition. In none of the cases examined did the rival clearly deserve to lose; rivals lost against closely matched adversaries as a result of the vagaries of competition. It did not seem to matter much whether the rivals were more or less successful than the self or roughly equal in performance. Neither did it matter whether the rival's prior performance was deserved or undeserved. In every case we examined, the (in-group) self could not gain materially from the rival's failure. People simply took pleasure in seeing an equal-status rival fail in a domain of some importance to them. Thus, the pleasure of schadenfreude can follow from the misfortune of nearly any relevant party whom the *schadenfroh* is fortunate enough to observe. However, where the rival is not undeservedly successful and where the rival's adversity is not seen as a punishment or otherwise deserved, the pleasure taken at their adversity is likely to be modest. In the minimal and mundane circumstances of an everyday misfortune caused by happenstance, schadenfreude is only a moderate and a modest pleasure.

Schadenfreude is passive and indirect

Recently, we conducted two studies to examine the pattern of appraisal that we expect to distinguish schadenfreude from other forms of pleasure (Leach, Spears, and Manstead, 2013). These studies differ from our previous work in at least two important ways. First, we combined our previous focus on intergroup competition with attention to interpersonal competition. In this way, we could assess how well our approach works across levels of analysis. Second, we diversified our methodological approach. In Study 1, we examined people's narratives of actual events in order to compare schadenfreude events to those of gloating, pride, and joy. In Study 2, we asked people to imagine themselves in a particular schadenfreude (or gloating) event of our own design. As discussed above, passive, indirect, and opportunistic schadenfreude should be distinct from active, direct, and self-caused gloating. Because of these differences in what the emotions are about, and the corresponding appraisals, schadenfreude should be less intensely experienced and expressed than gloating. Of course, schadenfreude should also be distinguishable from active and direct pride about achievement and the more general pleasure of joy about unanticipated events.

Emotion narratives

In Study 1 of Leach, Spears, and Manstead (2013), we asked 121 students to recall an instance of pleasure about an event described in ways that match schadenfreude, gloating, pride, or joy. In addition, we specified the event at either the individual or the group level. This study used emotion-recall methodology to examine the social appraisals, phenomenology, and action tendencies characteristic of schadenfreude (compared to those of gloating, pride, and joy). As far as we are aware, this is the first time that emotion-recall methodology has been used to examine schadenfreude. In the schadenfreude condition, we asked British participants to recall a time when they had "a *positive feeling* resulting from someone else [or a group to which you did *not* belong] suffering a defeat, failure, or other negative outcome ... even though you [or your group] *played no role* in causing this outcome." This is consistent with our conceptualization of schadenfreude as passive and indirect. Using this minimalist prompt also served to focus participants on what the particular pleasure of schadenfreude is about, rather than on their semantic knowledge or implicit emotion theories.

Although our emotion prompt made it clear that we were interested in pleasure about a passively observed adversity, our minimalist prompt did not specify that the adversity was a misfortune caused by happenstance, nor did our prompt specify that the participant could not benefit materially from the other's adversity. As a result, participants could report events that did not meet our definition of schadenfreude. For this reason, we assigned extra participants to the schadenfreude condition of the study. This allowed us to isolate participants who reported clear gloating or pride events.

Two independent coders examined all 80 (individual and group) narratives in the schadenfreude conditions to gauge whether participants reported a genuine case of schadenfreude. The coders agreed in 90 percent (i.e., thirty-six) of the forty cases. Disagreements were settled by discussion. In the end, the coders found twelve participants who did not produce an individual or group event where the pleasure was passive, indirect, opportunistic, and without material gain. The majority of these twelve participants wrote about succeeding in a competition where a rival failed. The vast majority of these narratives involved direct competition between rivals and, in most cases, the other's adversity provided some material benefit to the self. For example, when asked to report an example of individual schadenfreude, a participant reported: "I was competing at a big synchronized swimming competition and won gold two years in a row against the same people. I was really shocked when they announced I had won as I thought that the other girls were better than me." When asked for an example of group schadenfreude, this participant reported: "At another competition ... we won a very unexpected Bronze medal. [The other team] was visibly devastated, but we were extatic [sic]." She described her feeling about both events as "happiness," but the individual event was coded as an example of pride and the group event was coded as gloating.

Another of these twelve participants reported on a competition for an internship: "I went on an industrial placement year last year as part of my degree. I found the interview process very daunting and was very surprised when I was offered the job. I was also delighted. However, my friend who applied for the same job didn't get it, as I had been chosen. Obviously, I felt pleased that she hadn't got the job because it would have meant that I didn't [get the job] if she had." This person reported "pride" when asked to sum up her feelings, but her emotion was coded as gloating because she felt good about outdoing a rival in the absence of any obvious material benefit. The narrative she provided for the group schadenfreude condition was a case where she "had to take part in a team summer event, involving 'it's a knockout' style competitions. My team won, meaning the other teams lost. We won wine and money which I was very happy with. We won because we were the best on the day so I felt very good about myself." She described her feeling about this event as "happiness," but it was coded as pride given her emphasis of deserved achievement.

A more obvious example of a narrative coded as gloating was provided in an individual-level narrative involving an "intelligent" classmate whose parents "would always try to brag about her and compare her to me." The participant reported that the two girls got "almost identical" grades in their subjects, except for Spanish. She went on to say: "Her father was blaming poor teaching for his daughter's 'C' grade, and that the whole class did poorly. It was a great feeling to reveal [that] I gained an A+ grade, despite being in the same class. It was the first time I'd ever heard him go silent. It was satisfying that I had done better than her, and that she couldn't imply I was inferior to her. It was petty, but I enjoyed it." She summarized her feeling as "satisfaction/smugness."

Our elimination of the twelve participants who produced narratives that did not meet our definition of schadenfreude improved the quality of our data. However, it did not guarantee that the twenty-eight remaining participants produced "pure" cases of schadenfreude. In fact, 29 percent of the narratives these twenty-eight participants produced involved outdoing a rival in ways similar to the excluded narratives. Nevertheless, to maximize the comparability of the schadenfreude condition to the other three, we retained all twenty-eight participants to maintain near-equal numbers of participants in each condition. This makes our design a conservative test of our hypotheses.

To contrast schadenfreude to gloating, pride, and joy, we asked participants about events that fit our (minimal) definition of each emotion. Thus, in the gloating condition, we asked about "*positive feelings* resulting from (a group to which you belonged) *triumphing over*, or defeating, another person (group)." In the pride condition, we asked about "strong *positive feelings* (as a member of a group) resulting from an individual (group) achievement." And, in the joy condition, we asked about a "sudden and intense *positive feeling* (as a group member) resulting from something pleasurable happening."

A second pair of coders coded all of the narratives, blind to experimental condition. After extensive training on a pilot set of narratives, their average level of agreement was above 80 percent. Thus, the coders could evaluate whether the particular appraisals and features of the event were present with a good degree of accuracy. Perhaps most important for our purposes is the appraisal of agency in the narratives. When given the joy, pride, and gloating prompts, 85–96 percent of the narratives contained an appraisal that the (individual or group) self was the agent "responsible" for the event described. In the condition that asked participants to report an instance of schadenfreude, less than half appraised the self as the agent responsible for the event. This is not surprising given that the prompt asked participants to report pleasure at an event that they did not cause. More telling is the fact that just over a quarter of the participants reported appraising a party other than the rival or the self as the agent that caused the undesirable event that befell the rival. In no other condition was this appraisal of other-agency present even once. In just over 10 percent of cases, participants appraised the other's adversity as due to "luck" or happenstance. This was at least twice the frequency observed in any other condition. Thus, even without focusing on pure cases of schadenfreude, it is clear that the pleasure not clearly caused by the self is more often attributed to uninvolved parties or luck.

Despite the fact that a non-trivial number of the narratives in the schadenfreude condition are better characterized as gloating, numerous features of the schadenfreude narratives distinguished them from the gloating narratives. For instance, two-thirds of the gloating narratives were coded as involving direct competition between the self and a second party. Only about a quarter of the schadenfreude narratives were coded as such. More than half of the gloating narratives involved direct material benefit to the self from the other's adversity. Just under a quarter of the schadenfreude narratives involved direct material benefit to the self.

Considered as a whole, the coding of participants' emotion narratives showed the minimal prompts we provided to yield very different events. In each of the four experimental conditions, the pleasure was about something quite different. Consistent with our conceptualization, recalled instances of schadenfreude were appraised as events that tended not to be caused by the self. Instead, the rival, a third party, or luck caused these undesirable events. In addition, schadenfreude (as well as pride and joy) involved much less direct competition and material benefit than gloating.

In another part of Study 1, we asked participants to make a number of closed-ended ratings of their appraisals of the reported event and to answer closed-ended questions about its features. These questions allowed us to analyze the full design of the study. Thus, we could examine whether the four emotions differed from each other as well as across the individual and group levels of analysis. There were only two, very small, effects of level of analysis. Thus, across the numerous appraisals and event features assessed, the four emotions did not tend to differ as a function of whether they were individual or group events. Although we can imagine circumstances under which group emotions, like schadenfreude, might be more intense than individual-level emotions (see Ouwerkerk and Van Dijk, Chapter 12 in this volume), there is no reason why this should generally occur (for reviews, see Iyer and Leach, 2008; Parkinson, Fischer, and Manstead, 2005; Tiedens and Leach, 2004).

Importantly, the four emotion conditions did not differ from each other on appraisals that do not map onto the conceptual distinctions between schadenfreude and the other types of pleasure. Thus, the schadenfreude condition was no different from the others in terms of how changeable the situation was appraised to be. Neither did the four emotion conditions differ in the appraisals that the event was "unfair" or "illegitimate." Indeed, none of the events (pride, joy, gloating, or schadenfreude) was appraised as particularly unjust. In addition, schadenfreude was not associated with lower perceived status than gloating, pride, and joy. Participants tend to appraise themselves to be "in a good position" and "better than" the other.

Other appraisals showed schadenfreude to have the distinctive pattern that we expected. In corroboration of our coding of participants' narratives, closed-ended responses showed participants to appraise the schadenfreude events as not caused by the self. In contrast, gloating, pride, and joy were all equally appraised as caused by the self. In addition, those reporting on schadenfreude events appraised themselves as a passive observer rather than an active agent. Both of these differences were large and highly statistically significant. Those reporting an instance of schadenfreude were also distinct in appraising themselves as somewhat lacking in power and resources. This is consistent with participants' appraisal of themselves as only moderately successful in the schadenfreude condition. Those reporting gloating, pride, and joy appraised themselves as highly successful. Thus, schadenfreude does indeed appear to be a passive pleasure caused by external events rather than by an active, powerful, and successful self. As expected, whether the pleasure examined was individual or group in nature made little difference to the reported appraisals.

Participants' reported behavior in response to the emotion-eliciting event was consistent with our view of schadenfreude as a less intense, more muted pleasure. Although those who reported a schadenfreude episode reported a great deal of smiling (i.e., nearly seven on a nine-point scale), they reported less smiling than those who reported an episode of gloating, pride, or joy. Participants in the schadenfreude condition reported moderate celebrating at the time of the event. Those reporting on episodes of gloating, pride, and joy reported celebrating more. The experience of schadenfreude was also characterized by less free expression of glee and less "flaunting" of the pleasure. As with the appraisals, whether the pleasure examined was individual or group in nature made little difference to the actions that participants reported.

It is somewhat difficult to ask people about their experiences of schadenfreude, given that many languages lack a commonly known word for this emotion (see also Ben-Ze'ev, Chapter 5 in this volume; Van Dijk and Ouwerkerk, Chapter 1 in this volume). In this study, we turned this difficulty into an opportunity by asking people to recall and report on a positive feeling about someone else's adversity. Thus, we avoided the ambiguity, the idiosyncratic meaning, and the implicit emotion theories likely generated when people are asked to report their experience of an emotion term. Our minimalist event-based description of schadenfreude and the pleasures of gloating, pride, and joy did not fully specify the appraisals and actions that we expected to characterize these emotions. Despite our minimalist emotion prompts, schadenfreude was quite distinct from gloating, pride, and joy. Most importantly, participants reported being a passive, less powerful observer of events rather than an active, powerful cause of events. Consistent with this, the pleasure of schadenfreude was more moderate and more moderately expressed. Schadenfreude appeared to be a quiet pleasure, characterized more by smiling than by gleeful celebration. This stands in stark contrast to gloating and to joy, which are pleasures characterized by the free expression of an intense pleasure.

Vignette study

Although there are many advantages to emotion-recall studies, we wished to corroborate the above findings with a more controlled experimental method. Thus, in Study 2 of Leach et al., we developed carefully scripted vignettes of schadenfreude and gloating at the individual and the group levels. Thus, the study was a 2x2 design, with participants randomly assigned a vignette about either schadenfreude or gloating, at either the individual or the group level. A total of 125 UK psychology students participated.

We wished to make this study comparable to our previous studies of intergroup schadenfreude. Thus, we asked participants to imagine being very interested in sport and being involved in the university field hockey team. We focused on field hockey because participants' general lack of knowledge about the sport allowed us to more freely manipulate the features of the competition. Specifically, in the individual condition, participants imagined competing against a rival for a position on the university team. In the group condition, participants imagined being part of a university team that competed against rival universities from around the UK. In both conditions, participants were led to believe that they and their rivals were about equal in status based on past performances.

Our schadenfreude scripts were based on our conceptualization of schadenfreude, our previous studies of (intergroup) schadenfreude, and the features of the real episodes of the emotion that participants described in Study 1. Thus, in both the individual and group conditions, participants passively observed the eventual failure of a rival because they were excluded from the competition at an earlier stage. In neither condition did the rival's previous success or eventual failure suggest that deservedness or justice was at issue; the rival's failure was a simple result of the vagaries of close competition. For instance, in the group schadenfreude condition, it was stated that: "A very close game meant that the outcome was decided in the last few moments, when the Plymouth attack put the ball in the back of the net, taking the final score to 7–6. Plymouth went on to the national finals, but Bath [i.e., the schadenfreude target] were out of the running!" In the individual and group gloating vignettes, participants imagined beating their rival in a close competition between equals. For example, in the individual gloating condition, participants were told: "The match was very close, but in the end you were selected for the team and [your rival] was not selected. So [his or her] hopes of representing Cardiff University at hockey had come to an end."

Importantly, participants rated the four vignettes as equivalent in ways unimportant to the manipulated distinctions between them. Thus, participants reported feeling moderate rivalry and little hostility toward the other party in all four conditions. Participants reported equivalent interest in sport and in field hockey across conditions. However, the schadenfreude and gloating vignettes produced very different emotional experiences. Schadenfreude led to a near-moderate level of general pleasure, whereas gloating led to very high general pleasure (e.g., satisfied, happy). In addition, the schadenfreude vignettes led to lower levels of triumphant (e.g., triumphant, victorious) and emboldened (i.e., bold, fearless) feelings than the gloating vignettes. Consistent with this, the schadenfreude vignettes led to low levels of the elevated phenomenology we expected to be more characteristic of gloating. In contrast, the gloating vignettes led to moderate levels of feeling "ten feet tall" and "on top of the world." As with the emotion-recall method of Study 1, the schadenfreude and gloating vignettes of this study produced very different emotional expressions. Although schadenfreude led to moderate smiling, gloating led to an even greater level of smiling. Those who imagined themselves in the schadenfreude situations also reported that they would celebrate the event, flaunt their pleasure, and boast much less than those who imagined gloating. As in Study 1, the individual or group nature of the events had no notable effect on people's expected experience or expression of the emotions.

When considered together, these two studies offer firm support for our conceptualization of schadenfreude and the distinctions we drew between this passive and indirect pleasure about a misfortune and other pleasures, such as gloating. In these studies, we contrasted passive, indirect, and opportunistic schadenfreude with more active, direct, and self-caused pleasures to highlight the distinctive features of schadenfreude. Unlike schadenfreude, gloating is afforded by the view that one's group has prestige and thus presumably has a right to openly celebrate its triumph over a rival group. In contrast, the passive pleasure of schadenfreude is more furtive and of lower intensity and behavioral consequence. Thus, these two studies show that schadenfreude is characterized by a distinct relational context as well as a distinct pattern of appraisal, phenomenology, and expression. In addition, these studies demonstrate that the characteristics of schadenfreude are quite similar across the individual and group levels of the emotion.

Conclusion

Thankfully, people do not appear to regularly or easily take pleasure in the serious adversities suffered by other people. Except when serious adversity is seen as deserved, it leads to little pleasure. Indeed, floods, fires, and grave failures precipitating human harm seem to lead most people to feel sympathy for victims. Although it is still malicious and malevolent in nature, schadenfreude at the minor adversity that happenstance causes another party is a fairly moderate and modest pleasure. Because the misfortune observed is caused by bad luck or the vagaries of competition, the social situation in which schadenfreude is situated renders the experience passive, indirect, and opportunistic. For us, these qualities are what distinguish schadenfreude as a particular sort of pleasure that warrants its own emotion concept. Consistent with this view, we reviewed evidence that schadenfreude can be directed at many different targets, as long as they suffer a misfortune that is sufficiently relevant to the self. The targets of schadenfreude need not be superior to the self, undeservedly successful, or particularly deserving of their misfortune. Neither does the target of schadenfreude need to be in direct competition with the self and nor does their misfortune need to provide the self with any material gain. Our examinations of the minimal and mundane circumstances of schadenfreude serve to highlight the essential elements of the social relation in which this particular pleasure is situated. In fact, serious adversity, clear superiority, or undeserving victims are likely to limit people's pleasure. Schadenfreude is closer to slapstick than sadism.

In addition to showing that schadenfreude is observed in the more minimal and mundane social relations that we examined, we also showed that schadenfreude can be distinguished from other pleasures like joy, pride, and gloating. Distinguishing schadenfreude from gloating is important because these two pleasures share some similarities (and thus might be confused). Despite this, schadenfreude and gloating are quite opposite in a number of important ways. Whereas schadenfreude is the passive, indirect, and opportunistic observation of adversity caused by some agent other than the self, gloating is the active, direct, and purposive pleasure at defeating another party oneself. This is why, as Nietzsche suggested some time ago, gloating is a less moderate and less modest pleasure than schadenfreude. Taking pleasure in defeating a rival appears to entitle victors to boast openly and to thereby elevate themselves above the vanquished. After all, "to the victor go the spoils."

Although schadenfreude is more moderate in experience and more modest in expression than gloating, its furtive nature should not fool us into thinking that it does little harm to social relations. As a good feeling about a bad event that befalls another, schadenfreude is inherently malevolent (Heider, 1958). Because it is typically based on some degree of dislike for the sufferer of a misfortune, schadenfreude is also inherently malicious (Leach and Spears, 2008; Leach et al., 2003; Smith et al., 1996). As a result of its inherent malevolence and malice, schadenfreude appears to bring further damage to already-compromised social relations. Indeed, we showed that experiencing schadenfreude at a third party rival's failure was associated with greater negativity toward the third party. Such "displaced" schadenfreude did not make people feel better about the self, however. Thus, schadenfreude took social relations from bad to worse. As we have discussed elsewhere (Spears and Leach, 2004), the passive, indirect, and opportunistic pleasure of schadenfreude may be an initial step down the slippery slope to more active, direct, and purposeful acts of malice when circumstances allow. Because of the clear antagonism in taking pleasure in another's adversity, schadenfreude is one particularly disturbing way in which feeling good can be bad. Future work would do well to extend our focus on the social relations in which schadenfreude is situated to better understand the ways in which social relations are further damaged by schadenfreude.

References

Ben-Ze'ev, A. (2000). *The Subtlety of Emotions*. Cambridge, MA: MIT Press.

Feather, N. T. (2006). Deservingness and emotions: applying the structural model of deservingness to the analysis of affective reactions to outcomes. *European Review of Social Psychology* 17: 38–73.

Heider, F. (1958). *The Psychology of Interpersonal Relations*. New York: Wiley.

Iyer, A. and Leach, C. W. (2008). Emotion in inter-group relations. *European Review of Social Psychology* 19: 86–125.

Koenig, B. L. (2009). Using schadenfreude-like emotions to test an assumption of the motivation-satisfaction model of emotions: are motivating emotions and satisfying emotions two distinct kinds of emotions? PhD dissertation, New Mexico State University.

Kristjánsson, K. (2006). *Justice and Desert-Based Emotions*. Aldershot: Ashgate.

Lazarus, R. S. (1991). *Emotion and Adaption*. New York: Oxford University Press.

Leach, C. W., Snider, N., and Iyer, A. (2002). Spoiling the consciences of the fortunate: the experience of relative advantage and support for social equality. In I. Walker and H. J. Smith (eds.), *Relative Deprivation: Specification, Development, and Integration*. New York: Cambridge University Press, pp. 136–63.

Leach, C. W. and Spears, R. (2008). "A vengefulness of the impotent": the pain of in-group inferiority and schadenfreude toward successful out-groups. *Journal of Personality and Social Psychology* 95: 1383–96.

(2009). Dejection at in-group defeat and schadenfreude toward second- and third-party out-groups. *Emotion* 9: 659–65.

Leach, C. W., Spears, R., Branscombe, N. R., and Doosje, B. (2003). Malicious pleasure: schadenfreude at the suffering of another group. *Journal of Personality and Social Psychology* 84: 932–43.

Leach, C. W., Spears, R., and Manstead, A. S. R. (2013). Parsing (malicious) pleasures: schadenfreude and gloating at others' adversity. Unpublished manuscript.

Lee, L. (2008). *Schadenfreude, Baby: A Delicious Look at the Misfortunes of Others (and the Pleasure it Brings Us)*. Guilford, CT: Globe Pequot Press.

Nietzsche, F. (1967 [1887]). *On the Genealogy of Morals* (translated by W. Kaufmann and R. J. Hollingdale). New York: Random House.

Ortony, A., Clore, G. L., and Collins, A. (1988). *The Cognitive Structure of Emotions*. Cambridge University Press.

Oxford English Dictionary (1989). Oxford University Press.

Parkinson, B., Fischer, A. H., and Manstead, A. S. R. (2005). *Emotion in Social Relations: Cultural, Group, and Interpersonal Processes*. New York: Psychology Press.

Portmann, J. (2000). *When Bad Things Happen to Other People*. New York: Routledge.

Smith, R. H., Turner, T. J., Garonzik, R., Leach, C. W., Urch-Druskat, V., and Weston, C. M. (1996). Envy and schadenfreude. *Personality and Social Psychology Bulletin* 25: 158–68.

Spears, R. and Leach, C. W. (2004). Intergroup schadenfreude: conditions and consequences. In L. Z. Tiedens and C. W. Leach (eds.). *The Social Life of Emotions.* Cambridge University Press, pp. 336–55.

Tiedens, L. Z., and Leach, C. W. (2004) (eds.). *The Social Life of Emotions.* Cambridge University Press.

Part IV

Schadenfreude and related phenomena

14 Schadenfreude and laughter

F. H. Buckley

We are apt to think of schadenfreude, the pleasure we take in the discomfiture of others, as the dark side of laughter, a peripheral and unwholesome perversion of a warmly human and welcome emotion. Our laughter expresses and strengthens bonds of affection, which schadenfreude maliciously weakens. Others might take pleasure in another person's reverses, but we are too noble, too lofty of soul to do so.

I see it differently. Schadenfreude is not some nasty outlier, but more like the epitome of laughter. When we laugh, we do take pleasure in the butt of the joke's discomfiture. We just don't want to admit it.

Laughter as superiority

There is no laughter without a victim, and no victim without a message about a risible inferiority. Laughter signals our recognition of a comic vice in another person – the butt. We do not share in the vice, for we could not laugh if we did. Through laughter, the butt is made to feel inferior, and those who laugh reveal their sense of superiority over him.

This is not a new idea. It even has a label – the superiority thesis (see Buckley, 2005; Feather's idea of "deservingness" in Chapter 3 of this volume is also an expression of the superiority thesis). Plato first proposed it, and indeed thought that schadenfreude was at the root of all laughter. In the *Philebus*, he argued that the pleasure derived from comedy was based on malice and our enjoyment of others' misfortune. Aristotle also proposed a superiority explanation, defining the risible as a mistake or deficiency. So too, in Descartes' dualist account of the passions, laughter is produced by either a bodily impulse or a mental process, but in either case reveals one's sense of superiority to a butt.

Notwithstanding the forerunners, the superiority thesis is most closely identified with Thomas Hobbes. In *The Leviathan*, Hobbes thought that we were motivated solely by a desire for power, the power to procure our good. Possessing power over others is glory, and the sudden realization of that power produces laughter. It is a "sudden glory," a cry of triumph that signals our discovery of superiority to a butt, "and is caused either by some sudden act of their own, that pleaseth them; or by the apprehension of some deformed thing in another, by comparison whereof they suddenly applaud themselves" (Tuck, 1991, p. 43).

When we laugh, we always express a sense of superiority to the butt; and the butt will always sense this. Relative to the wit, the butt is degraded; relative to the butt, the wit moves up a notch. The butt knows this, of course, and that is why he resents the joke. Speaking for butts everywhere, Hazlitt (1818/1907, p. 7) said that our humiliation is their triumph.

The leading modern statement of the superiority thesis is Henri Bergson's *Le rire* (1900/1940). Bergson defined the risible as a rigidity (*raideur*) of body or character. For the anglophone, this might at first seem a quirky, Gallic *hommage* to Jerry Lewis. By rigidity, however, Bergson meant something more than a physical clumsiness. Instead, rigidity served as a metaphor for a want of suppleness in any aspect of life.

Consider the simplest of butts, the man who clumsily slips on the ice. He falls because he sought to walk after his grip gave way. A more agile man might have kept his balance by standing still, but the butt lacks the alertness to change gears quickly. So down he goes, to our great amusement; and in him Bergson saw the very type and model of all our laughter. The butt who cannot navigate the obstacles erected by social customs is like the man who cannot navigate a patch of ice. Both are comically inadequate to the dexterity society requires of us. They are marionettes whose actions are circumscribed and mechanical. Like machines, their actions follow a determined program. They keep on walking when their feet have left the ice, and that is why we find them comic.

By following a single program, said Bergson, the comic butt is a machine-man. Our actions are risible to the exact extent that they remind us of a mechanical thing, and the most amusing people are those whose actions are least human and most mechanical. They have betrayed their nature, and for their *gran rifiuto* merit our deepest scorn.

The machine-man is inadequate to life's complexities. He trusts in his rules and ignores the more reliable guide of experience, like the man in Molière's *Critique de L'École des femmes* who likes the sauce but wants to check it against the cookbook recipe. He takes a single principle and absurdly extends it beyond its reasonable scope; where erudition turns into pedantry, polish into slickness and solidity into dullness. He is the miser who takes frugality to the point of vice; the gourmand who becomes a glutton; and the health Nazi. (In Germany, the Fascists goose-step, notes John O'Sullivan; in America, they jog.)

Bergson's machine-man is an amusing butt. Nevertheless, there is something a little devilish in laughter. There will be joy in Heaven, but will there be laughter? No, said Baudelaire (1855/1976), for laughter reveals our impurity. It is man's way of biting, said the *poète maudit*, and those who laugh at others can never be innocent themselves. Innocents would not enjoy asserting their superiority over others, and therefore would not laugh. "Neither laughter nor tears may be seen in the paradise of all delights; both are the children of suffering" (1855/1976, pp. 525–8).

And what's wrong with that?

We might resist the idea that, in laughing, we express our sense of superiority. We want to think of ourselves as non-judgmental and accepting of the foibles or vices of others. And yet we do laugh, and would indeed be ashamed if others thought us humorless. The superiority thesis will therefore seem troubling – unless one finds the self-deception of pious butts amusing.

Let me therefore say something about the utility of laughter's signal of superiority. Bergson sought to explain why we laugh by identifying a feature common to all butts, but at the same time he argued that rigidity *ought* to be risible and that the butt deserved to be ridiculed. Our laughter teaches him valuable lessons about life. Laughter always sanctions a butt's comic vice and reveals a correlative comic virtue that immunizes us from laughter.

Laughter's ability to correct our morals – *castigare ridendo mores* – has long been employed as a literary device by satirists (Buckley, 2005). In the Preface to *Absalom and Achitophel*, Dryden announced that: "The true end of Satyre is the amendment of Vices by correction. And he who writes Honestly, is no more an Enemy to the Offendour, than the Physician to the Patient, when he prescribes harsh remedies to an inveterate Disease." Later, in his famous rules for satire, Dryden said "The Poet is bound, and that *ex Officio*, to give his Reader some one precept of moral virtue; and to caution him against some one particular vice or folly" (1693/1961). And delivering his own eulogy, Swift (1939–74; *Life and Character of Dr. Swift*) said: "Tis plain, his writings were design'd / To *please*, and to *reform* Mankind." All of this is consistent with the superiority thesis, for there is no satire without a butt who is satirized, no butt without a signal of inferiority, and no signal of inferiority without a normative message.

Laughter assumes an informational asymmetry between wit and butt. The butt is unaware of his comic vice, said Plato, and the ridiculous might be described as the opposite of the inscription at Delphi: know not thyself. After the more alert wit points out the defect, the butt might correct it, but until then he is risible. In this sense, laughter performs what economists call a signaling function, communicating information from one party to another.

While the butt must be unaware of his comic vice, the wit must be in the know. A wit cannot tell a joke without meaning to do so. At Trafalgar, Nelson's dying words to his captain were "Kiss me, Hardy." As that was a little *de trop* for the naval hagiographer, however, the tradition arose that Nelson's last thoughts were on fate and not love, and that what he had said was "Kismet, Hardy." One thing is certain: he did not mean both, for if he had, he would have died with a pun on his lips. Absent the specific intent, he did not jest. Nor did George IV, who misunderstood a courtier and thought Queen Caroline was dead. Alas, it was only Napoleon.

> "It is my duty to inform Your Majesty that your greatest enemy is dead."
> "Is she, by God." (Longford, 1972, p. 77)

The comic defect must be correctable, since the signal would otherwise be pointless. We do not laugh when the blind or lame stumble, but only when laughter might make a difference. What Swift (1939–74; *Verses on the Death of Dr. Swift*) said of his satire is generally true of most laughter:

> His Satyr points at no Defect,
> But what all Mortals may correct; . . .
> He spar'd a Hump or crooked Nose,
> Whose Owners set not up for Beaux
> True genuine Dulness mov'd his Pity
> Unless it offer'd to be witty.

There is a vulgar laughter that mocks the dwarf and cripple. But for most of us, a natural defect awakens our sympathy, and only correctable comic vices provoke our laughter.

Sociability

Let me now turn to two (of the several) objections to the superiority thesis. The first of these is our sense that laughter has a sociable side, that we do in fact feel closer to other people in laughing. For example, we have a natural desire to share a joke with others, and our laughter at a butt is heightened if a third person is around to enjoy it.

One can better understand how a sense of superiority may coexist with feelings of sociability by recognizing that three persons may be found in most laughter: wit, listener, and butt. The wit tells a joke to a listener at the expense of a butt. By laughing along with the wit, the listener cements a relationship of trust – a *lien de rire* – between himself and the wit, and both signal their superiority to the butt.

What is remarkable about laughter is how difficult it is to camouflage. Sudden genuine laughter is written on our faces, by muscles over which we lack full self-control. The counterfeit laugh, produced for purely strategic purposes, is a pale imitation. Imagine being told an unfunny joke by a boorish superior, where it is politic to affect a laugh. One might bare one's teeth and emit the sound of laughter, but this can ordinarily be distinguished from companionable, uproarious laughter. The subordinate's pretended laugh might usefully communicate subservience to a domineering superior, but does not signal a shared mirth and friendship.

In 1862, the French anatomist Duchenne de Boulonge (1862/1990) took a series of photographs to illustrate the difference between true and false smiles. In one picture the man was in his normal state; in the second he was naturally smiling; but in the third the smile was false. The lips curled up, but the signs of hilarity were absent, suggesting a masked threat. When Darwin (1892/1998) tested the photos on a small group of subjects, everyone could tell the genuine from the false smile.

The difference between the two kinds of smiles is physiological. In the false smile, the corrugator muscle is more contracted, causing a frown. In the true smile, the eyelid muscles are more contracted and the upper lip is drawn up more. The corners of the mouth are retracted and the cheeks are drawn upwards. In older people, wrinkles are formed under the eyes. The eyes are bright and sparkling, as they are when one is in love. And all of this happens in a flash, without conscious effort.

Because it is unconscious, we might fail to recognize how complicated a thing it is to smile. If the smile or laugh is insincere, there are simply too many muscles to move, and no one is fooled. On command, we might move one facial muscle, mechanically, as we might lift an arm, but we cannot will *all* of the right muscles to move in the required way. When the smile passes into a laugh, the facial movements intensify. We move fifteen facial muscles in a coordinated manner and alter our breathing patterns. For virtually everyone, the false smile or laugh is simply too hard to counterfeit. We must imagine ourselves laughing to produce the false laugh. We must fool ourselves. And even when we try, false smiles and laughter are usually detected. We learn to see through the politician's bonhomie and the car salesman's coprophagous grin.

This explains why laughter is a more reliable indicator of beliefs than emotionally neutral expressions of opinion. When political dissent is suppressed by criminal sanctions (as in the former Soviet Union), people will learn to camouflage their true opinions. However, it is a harder thing to suppress one's emotions, and joke telling against the regime became one of the most reliable expressions of public opinion before the fall of communism. One could fake political speech much more easily than laughter.

Laughter therefore permits us to show loyalty, or reveals our disloyalty, to friends. We signal loyalty when we demonstrate our happiness for a friend's good fortune or where we take delight and share in his high-spirited laughter.

Telling a joke reveals a vulnerability to the listener, who might betray the wit in a variety of ways. The listener might repeat the joke to the butt or to third parties as an example of the wit's indiscretion or political incorrectness. Or the listener might simply fail to laugh, to signal the jester's want of wit. Suppose instead that the listener does laugh. Not feigned laughter either, but honest, heart-easing mirth. By doing so, he signals that he accepts the special bond that the wit has proposed between them. The listener has agreed to take the wit's side against the butt.

Joke telling is a means of sniffing out friends. Sincere friends laugh together in a special way that false friends cannot duplicate. The laughter is open, unreserved, and joyful. When Carlyle (1833–4/1987) said "the man who cannot laugh is only fit for treasons, stratagems and spoils," this was what he had in mind. The weaker the tie, the more strained the laughter. Where the listener has recently betrayed the wit, the laughter often has a lupine quality: the cheeks are pulled back and the teeth are barred; the listener's gaze rests on the wit and the general expression is ironic. The emotional cost of hiding the enmity is simply too great for most false listeners, and the appropriate inference will be made. If you cannot laugh with me, how can I trust you? You say you like me and share my interests? Then come into my bar and laugh at my jokes. Only then will I trust you. And the more risqué the joke, the stronger the signal of friendship.

Innocent laughter

Darwin (1872/1998) suggested that laughter is primarily an expression of mere joy or happiness, like that of a child. If so, this is a critique of the superiority thesis, since an infant's laughter does not make comparisons with a butt. But is an adult's laughter like that of a child? Darwin thought that adult laughter begins with a smile that graduates into laughter through sheer exuberance. The muscles employed in a gentle laugh and a broad smile are very nearly the same, with no abrupt line of demarcation between faint smiles and violent laughter.

Adult laughter is different, however. It is more conscious of sin and thus less innocent than infantile laughter. Some forms of adult humor may indeed retain their innocence, but only at the expense of their mirth. Mere nonsense is never risible, but may amuse where it surreptitiously mocks some target. Thus, Lewis Carroll's nonsense verse might seem droll as a parody of Middle English verse ("Twas brillig, and the slithy toves") and the court scene in *Alice in Wonderland* amuses as a satire of unfair judicial procedure. But in less skilled hands, nonsense humor is cloying and tiresome, like the adult who thinks it cute to speak in baby talk. Such humor appeals to a retarded personality, in which the proprieties are accorded too great a weight and the comic sense cannot mature. This was how the nursery humor of the Victorians found its audience in the nineteenth century. Satire was too adult a taste for such people, but they could laugh at *David Copperfield*'s Mr Dick and at those who acted insane in a childish way.

For most adults, the most innocent kind of laughter occurs at the conclusion of comedies of integration. Here the theme is the transformation and regeneration of society, in which obstacles to the fulfillment of normal, healthy desires are confronted and removed. Typically, two lovers seek to marry, but are opposed by established authorities (the father in Plautus' *Pot of Gold*) or societal conventions (Lady Bracknell in *The Importance of Being Earnest*). The young rebel against an elder – the *senex* – and we always take the former's side. However, the tension between constraint and regeneration is necessary, for we cannot do without either. The impediment usefully restrains chaotic impulses, yet a society without a principle of rebirth has lost the power of transmission to future generations. At the end of the play, the opposition is removed, often through a wedding in which the generations are reconciled.

Comedies of this kind emphasize the element of sociability in laughter, in the bond between wit and listener, or between playwright and audience. The playwright takes us into his confidence and invites us to laugh at the butts on stage. "Good gentlemen," Harpgon whispers to us, "my thief, is he hidden in the pit amongst you?" The resolution of the comedy seems to come from the side of the audience. *Plaudite, comedia finita est* ("Applaud, the comedy is over") was the invocation at the end of the Roman comedy, as though the integration was incomplete unless the audience applauded the rebirth of civil society. *Plaudite, spectatores, et valete*.

But even here, in Arcadia, there is also a butt, in the comic *senex*. Comedy celebrates the transfer of authority from one generation to another, from the tyrannical and comic *senex* to the young lovers. What makes the play a comedy is not the change in power relations, but the reintegration of the defeated parent into the new society. Otherwise, we would have the tragedy of *King Lear*.

Conclusion

A sense of superiority may therefore be found in all adult laughter. Is this necessarily malicious, as schadenfreude is by definition? I believe so, if malice is defined as nothing more than the pleasure taken in another's discomfiture. There is, however, a stronger kind of hate-filled malice, dripping in contempt, which excludes any kind of enjoyment, and this, I think, would exclude the possibility of laughter. Laughter is necessarily playful, and while we can play with a butt's inferiority, there comes a point where the sense of play is lost, and darker emotions eliminate the enjoyment that comes from laughter. That apart, we can and do laugh in good conscience.

References

Baudelaire, C. (1976 [1855]). "De l'essence du rire," in *Œuvres complètes, II.* Paris: Pléiade.

Bergson, H. (1940 [1900]). *Le rire.* Paris: Presses Universitaires de France.

Buckley, F. H. (2005). *The Morality of Laughter.* Ann Arbor: University of Michigan Press.

Carlyle, T. (1987 [1833–4]). *Sartor Resartus.* Oxford University Press.

Darwin, C. (1998 [1872]). *The Expression of the Emotions in Man and Animals.* Oxford University Press.

Dryden, J. (1961 [1693]). Original and progress of satire. In W. P. Kerr (ed.), *Essays of John Dryden,* Vol. 2. New York: Russell & Russell, pp. 15–104.

Duchenne, B. (1990 [1862]). *The Mechanism of Human Facial Expression or an Electro-physiological Analysis of the Expression of the Emotions* (translated by A. Cuthbertson). Cambridge University Press.

Hazlitt, W. (1907 [1818]). *Lectures on the English Comic Writers.* Oxford University Press.

Longford, E. (1972). *Wellington: Pillar of State.* New York: Harper & Row.

Swift, J. (1939–74). *Prose Works.* Oxford: Blackwell.

Tuck, R. (ed.) (1991). *Hobbes: Leviathan.* Cambridge University Press.

15 Schadenfreude and the desire for vengeance

Elise C. Seip, Mark Rotteveel, Lotte F. van Dillen, and Wilco W. van Dijk

Revenge is probably as old as humankind itself. Take, for example, the Greek myth of Medea. When her husband Jason leaves her for Glauce, daughter of Creon, King of Corinth, Medea kills her two sons to avenge her husband's betrayal and says: "It is the supreme way to hurt my husband." Revenge's propensity to debouch into drama has made it an excellent theme for literature (e.g., Homer's *Odyssey*, William Shakespeare's *Hamlet*, and Herman Melville's *Moby Dick*) and cinematography (e.g., Sergio Leone's *Once Upon a Time in the West*, Mike Hodges' *Get Carter*, and Quentin Tarantino's *Kill Bill Volumes 1 and 2*). But revenge is not only prevalent in fiction, it is also very real, and forms the basis of many sequences of tragic events. The world's historical and current affairs teach us that revenge often leads to a violent and escalatory spiral of revenge and counter-revenge, which continues as long as the different parties involved are convinced that they have justice on their side (Asadi, 2011). One recent example is Al-Qaeda's attack on the World Trade Center on September 11, 2001, which killed thousands of people and was intended as revenge on the USA for insulting Islam and for its presence in Saudi Arabia. This attack was avenged within a month by the US bombing of Afghanistan and ten years later (May 1, 2011) by the killing of Al-Qaeda's founder and leader Osama bin Laden. This latter event was followed eleven days later by a deadly suicide bombing of the Pakistani Taliban, whose spokesman stated: "We have done this to avenge the Abbottabad incident," referring to the killing of Osama bin Laden (Khan, 2011). These events show that the desire for vengeance is perhaps one of the most potent human emotions, which is deeply rooted in human nature and is both a cause and a consequence of intense grief and suffering in the world.

In this chapter we compare the desire for vengeance with schadenfreude (pleasure at the misfortunes of others), the emotion that is the focus of this book. Although several studies have addressed the causes and consequences of taking revenge (e.g., Aquino, Tripp, and Bies, 2001, 2006; Carlsmith, Wilson, and Gilbert, 2008; Crombag, Rassin, and Horselenberg, 2003; Gollwitzer and Denzler, 2009; Gollwitzer, Meder, and Schmitt, 2011), few major psychological studies have focused on the desire for vengeance. Exceptions are the works of Susan Jacoby (1983), Thomas Scheff (1994), Robert Solomon (1990), and Nico Frijda (2007). Since revenge can have a profound impact on people's lives, it is important to gain additional insight into the desire for vengeance. Therefore, we recently started a line of empirical research to systematically investigate this desire, and together with Frijda's (2007) theorizing, we will use the findings of this research as the basis for our current chapter. We will first discuss the emotional experience of the desire for vengeance and will then address its most important differences and similarities with schadenfreude. We conclude our chapter by addressing how research on the desire for revenge may provide avenues for future research on schadenfreude.

The desire for vengeance

Revenge is defined as "The action of hurting, harming, or otherwise obtaining satisfaction from someone in return for an injury or wrong suffered at his or her hands; satisfaction obtained by repaying an injury or wrong" (*Oxford English Dictionary*, 2012). Whereas revenge refers to actual behavior, the desire for vengeance is an emotion that motivates revenge, but does not necessarily lead to actually taking revenge. In other words, revenge is always preceded by the desire for vengeance, but taking revenge does not necessarily follow the desire for it. In his book *The Laws of Emotion*, Nico Frijda describes the desire for vengeance as "one of the most potent human passions" (2007, p. 259) and defines it as "a state of impulse, of involuntary action readiness, generated by an appraisal, often accompanied by bodily excitement, and with every aspect of control precedence: preoccupation, single-minded goal pursuit, neglect of unwelcome information, and interference with other activities" (2007, p. 260). The action readiness and pervasiveness of the desire for vengeance is clearly captured by the monologue of the main character in the opening scenes of Quentin Tarantino's first volume of *Kill Bill*:

> Looked dead, didn't I? Well I wasn't, but it wasn't for the lack of trying, I can tell you that. Actually Bill's last bullet put me in a coma. A coma I was to lie in for five years. When I woke up . . . I went on what the movie advertisements refer to as a roaring rampage of revenge. I roared and I rampaged and I got bloody satisfaction. In all, I've killed 33 people to get to this point right now. I have only one more. The last one. The one I'm driving to right now. The only one left. And when I arrive at my destination . . . I'm gonna kill Bill.

In line with Frijda (2007), we regard the desire for vengeance as an emotion that is elicited (or at least associated) with a specific pattern of appraisals, action tendencies, and motivational goals. In a recent study we used this conceptualization as a starting point to investigate the emotional experience of the desire for revenge (Seip et al., 2014a). We asked our respondents to recall an event from their lives in which they experienced a desire for vengeance and we assessed how they subjectively evaluated this situation (appraisals), what they wanted to do in this situation (action tendencies), and what they wanted to achieve with their actions (motivational goals). Results showed that the desire for vengeance was associated with appraising the situation as damage to one's dignity and a hindrance in achieving one's goals. This damage or goal blockage was perceived as being intentionally caused by the offender's actions and these actions were perceived as morally wrong. Furthermore, our findings showed that once the desire for vengeance was evoked, the action tendencies of the vengeful individuals were twofold. On the one hand, the desire for revenge was related to confrontational action tendencies: the stronger one's desire for vengeance, the stronger one's tendency to humiliate the offender and to make him or her suffer. On the other hand, the desire for vengeance was related to avoidant action tendencies: the stronger one's desire for vengeance, the stronger one's tendency to avoid the offender and to end the relationship with the offender. Moreover, the motivational goals of vengeful individuals were also twofold, that is, they were directed both at the offender and oneself. Vengeful individuals wanted to teach the offender a lesson and make him or her feel guilty about the offense. But, on the other hand, vengeful individuals wanted to defend their own honor, protect their positive self-views, and prevent the offense from happening to them again. The finding that the desire for vengeance is associated with a specific pattern of appraisals, action tendencies, and motivational goals corroborates the notion further that the desire for vengeance is indeed an emotion and has all the usual features of one (see also Frijda, 2007).

In addition to the act of revenge, vengeance has been defined as "an attempt, at some cost or risk to oneself, to impose suffering upon those who have made us suffer" (Elster, 1990, p. 155). The main aim or tendency of vengeance is thus to make those who wronged us suffer. Since taking revenge follows one's suffering and cannot stop, prevent, or undo the damage done, both taking revenge and the desire for it appear "irrational" and "useless" (Frijda, 2007; Stuckless and Goranson, 1992). The apparent uselessness of (the desire for) vengeance is also highlighted by the fact that revenge may also be harmful for the vengeful individual. For example, empirical research has shown that the desire for vengeance can fuel such violent behaviors as arson (O'Sullivan and Kelleher, 1987), rape (Scully and Marolla, 1985), and domestic murder (Milroy, 1995). These behaviors are not only damaging for the avenged offender, but potentially also for the avenger, who risks prosecution and (severe) sentences for these unlawful actions. Thus, is the desire for vengeance a form of "madness" or "blind fury," or does it provide a vengeful individual with benefits that might outweigh the potential costs?

In *The Laws of Emotion*, Frijda discusses five possible gains of vengeance. He argues that emotions "are considered to be functionally appropriate in dealing with the emotion-arousing situation. Every kind of emotion has some functional role, in seeking to establish or modify a person-environment relationship." Emotions thus are "geared to some sort of gain" (2007, p. 261). So what are the possible gains of vengeance? First, vengeance can deter the offender from repeating the offense and thus protects the avenger's interests. Second, vengeance might restore balance in suffering – by taking revenge, one attempts to even the scores of comparative suffering. Third, as a willful wrongdoing causes an imbalance of power between the offender and the offended, vengeance might diminish or annul this imbalance. Fourth, vengeance can be a way to escape from shame and restore pride. Fifth and finally, vengeance can help to escape the pain of the wrongdoing. Several of these goals of vengeance also showed up in our own earlier described study. In other words, our vengeful respondents indeed indicated that teaching the other a lesson, preventing the offense from happening again, humiliating the offender and making him or her suffer, and defending one's honor and protecting a positive self-view were important goals for them when they experienced desire for vengeance. Thus, although at first sight vengeance might seem an irrational and useless act motivated by a blind and disorganized passion, a closer view indicates that it can serve important functions for the vengeful individual. Some of these gains of vengeance also seem relevant in schadenfreude. In the next section we will look at the similarities and differences between the desire for vengeance and schadenfreude.

Comparing the desire for vengeance and schadenfreude

The desire for vengeance and schadenfreude both involve pleasure and satisfaction toward the suffering of other persons. This might also be the reason why both emotions are regarded with a certain degree of ambivalence. When asked for an immediate moral judgment, many people may condemn these "outcast" emotions, yet they may also admit to having some sympathy or at least understanding for an avenger or a *schadenfroh* person. Although the desire for vengeance and schadenfreude are both emotional reactions toward the suffering of others, they differ in their causal role and intentionality. Whereas a vengeful person derives (anticipated) pleasure from actively and intentionally hurting or harming another person in return for a perceived wrongdoing by this person, a *schadenfroh* person passively derives pleasure from merely witnessing the other suffer and did not play a causal role in the suffering (see also Ben-Ze'ev, Chapter 5 in this volume; Leach, Spears, and Manstead, Chapter 13 in this volume; Portmann, Chapter 2 in this volume; Van Dijk and Ouwerkerk, Chapter 1 in this volume).

The desire for vengeance and schadenfreude both encapsulate pleasure at the suffering of others; in other words, they both feel good. The pleasure of both emotions is also illustrated in our language. For example, "Revenge is sweet" is an adage that is probably familiar by most readers. Perhaps less known is the adage used in the Japanese language: "Others' misfortunes taste like honey." Although these adages may merely reflect lay theories about the pleasantness of these emotions, recent neuroimaging studies corroborate the pleasure elicited from revenge and schadenfreude. For example, in one study an economic game was used in which participants had the opportunity to punish the unfair behavior of their interaction partner by reducing the total amount of money this partner earned in the study. The findings of this study showed that punishing an unfair other increased activity in the (dorsal) striatum, a brain area associated with reward processing and feelings of satisfaction and enjoyment (De Quervain et al., 2004). It is interesting to note that no increased activity in the reward network of the brain was found when a punishment was merely symbolic (i.e., when it did not affect the offender's earnings), suggesting that revenge is most satisfying when it really hurts the offender. Other neuroimaging studies showed that schadenfreude is also associated with the reward network of the brain. For example, Tania Singer and her colleagues had participants play an economic game in which their interaction partners (actually confederates of the researchers) treated them either fairly or unfairly. Subsequently, in a second part of the study these participants observed the interaction partners receiving pain (mild electric shocks), while their brain activity was measured. One of the findings of this study was that male participants showed increased activation in reward-related areas (e.g., ventral striatum) when they observed an unfair interaction partner receiving pain (Singer et al., 2006). Moreover, other studies have corroborated these findings by showing that reading about the misfortune of an envied other or watching the failure of a rival team increased activation in the ventral striatum, part of the reward network of the brain (Cikara, Botvinick, and Fiske, 2011; Takahashi et al., 2009; see also Cikara and Fiske, Chapter 10 in this volume). Thus, revenge and schadenfreude activate similar brain areas indicative for reward processing and feelings of satisfaction and joy.

Although research indicates that both revenge and schadenfreude are pleasurable emotions and corroborate the notion of both being "sweet," some studies indicate that they might be different flavors of sweetness. Whereas schadenfreude "taste[s] like honey," (the desire for) vengeance seems to be a more bittersweet experience, as illustrated by a phrase from *Jane Eyre* by Charlotte Brontë: "Something of vengeance I had tasted for the first time; as aromatic as wine it seemed, on swallowing, warm and racy; its after-flavour, metallic and corroding, gave me a sensation as if I had been poisoned" (1847/2006, p. 40). One reason why (the desire for) vengeance also yields negative emotions is that being the agent of revenge includes being responsible for the harm inflicted on the other. The "bitter-sweet" character of revenge is supported by a study of Carlsmith, Wilson, and Gilbert (2008), which showed that avengers tend to continue to ruminate about the offender (which increased their negative emotions). Being the agent of revenge includes being responsible for the harm inflicted upon the other. The victim, in that sense, also becomes an offender and this may conflict with one's self-view of being a good person who does not inflict harm upon others and elicits negative emotions (cf. Carlsmith, Wilson, and Gilbert, 2008). Interestingly, this study also showed that people felt more positive when they merely witnessed an offender being punished than when they carried out the punishment themselves. This raises the question why people still desire and instigate vengeance themselves? According to Frijda (2007), revenge can truly be instrumental in restoring self-respect. In taking revenge, one has regained the initiative in the relationship with the offender who had damaged their self-respect. Vengeance thus offers distinct proof of effectance. Whether one's own revenge is more satisfactory than the offender's punishment by a third party might depend upon the intensity of the perceived wrong-doing of the offender. The more severe the offense, the more the offended has a need for restoring self-respect by perpetrating the revenge oneself. In a recent study we investigated this possibility (Seip et al., 2014b). In this study we put participants in a series of situations in which they were confronted with the behaviors of others, which ranged from fair to extremely unfair. Subsequently, the wrongdoers could be punished by either the participants themselves (direct revenge) or by another person (third party punishment) and we measured their satisfaction with the administered punishment. Results showed that in moderately unfair situations, participants derived more satisfaction from a third party punishment than from their own direct revenge. However, when the other's behavior was extremely unfair, participants derived more satisfaction from their own direct revenge than from third party punishment. These findings suggest that when people appraise a wrongdoing by another as very unfair and immoral, they seem to derive the most pleasure of being the one who enacts the revenge and probably are more willing to incur (any) costs that may go with this vengeance. Thus, in both (the desire for) vengeance and schadenfreude, people derive pleasure from the suffering of others. Appraisal theories posit that events that satisfy an individual's goals, motives, or concerns (or promise to do so) evoke positive emotions (for an overview, see Roseman and Smith, 2001). Thus, within this conceptualization of emotions, to elicit joy and pleasure at the suffering of another person should then be appraised by vengeful and *schadenfroh* people as a situation that satisfies an important personal concern (see also Van Dijk and Ouwerkerk, Chapter 9 in this volume). Earlier we described five possible gains of the desire for vengeance. From these gains, two important concerns can be extracted that may underlie both the desire for vengeance and schadenfreude: first, a concern for justice (deterrence, imbalances in suffering and power); and, second, a concern for a positive self-evaluation (escape shame and pain, and restore pride). In the next two sections we will elaborate upon these two concerns and how they underlie both the desire for vengeance and schadenfreude.

The desire for vengeance, schadenfreude, and a concern for justice

One of the concerns in the desire for vengeance is restoring equity in suffering. Offenders should pay for what they obtained in offending the victim and for the sufferings caused to the victim. In other words, there should be a balance in costs and benefits between offender and victim. This comes close to an elementary sense of justice (Frijda, 2007). A perception of injustice results from another person acting in a manner that is inconsistent with one's personal values and expectations (Bies and Tripp, 1996; Sitkin and Roth, 1993). Most people care about justice and react with positive emotions toward just and deserved outcomes, and with negative emotions toward unjust and undeserved ones (see also Feather, Chapter 3 in this volume; Van Dijk and Ouwerkerk, Chapter 1 in this volume). For example, being confronted with a perceived unfair and unjust outcome or interaction can evoke feelings of anger and outrage. These strong negative emotions can give rise to a motivation to get even and take revenge for a perceived wrongdoing (e.g., Fehr and Gächter, 2002; Seip, Van Dijk, and Rotteveel, 2009). Our own research provided empirical support for this notion. In a series of studies we confronted our participants with an unfair interaction partner who betrayed their trust by not sharing monetary gains in an economic interaction. Our findings showed that these situations were perceived as unjust and fueled participants' anger toward their interaction partner. This anger subsequently motivated participants to give up some of their own money to destroy the financial benefits of their offending partner (Seip, Van Dijk, and Rotteveel, 2014c). This retaliation is a way of getting even with the offender and an effort to restore equity and justice. As most people care about just situations, vengeance might thus evoke positive emotions in the avenger. The restoration of justice also seems to be an important motive for acts of revenge in the world's current affairs. For example, following the 9/11 attack on the World Trade Center in New York, Al-Qaeda's founder and leader Osama bin Laden literally stated: "Terrorism against America deserves to be praised because it was a response to injustice." Unjust situations thus seem an important elicitor of the desire for vengeance and reflect the need to protect one's personal concern for justice.

The concern for justice also underlies many experiences of schadenfreude. Feather (Chapter 3 in this volume) argues that schadenfreude is likely to occur when another person's suffering is deserved and he or she gets his or her just deserts. This is in line with several philosophical analyses of schadenfreude (Ben-Ze'ev, Chapter 5 in this volume; Portmann, Chapter 2 in this volume). Ample empirical evidence corroborates the notion that schadenfreude is evoked when another person gets his or her deserved comeuppance (see Feather, Chapter 3 in this volume; Powell, Chapter 4 in this volume; Van Dijk, Goslinga, and Ouwerkerk, 2008; Van Dijk, Ouwerkerk, and Goslinga, 2009; Van Dijk et al., 2005). For example, Van Dijk et al. (2005) showed that individuals who were seen to be responsible for their own misfortune evoked more schadenfreude and less sympathy than individuals who were not held responsible for their misfortunes, and that these effects were mediated by the perceived deservingness of the misfortune (i.e., misfortunes for which a target was held responsible were seen as more deserved and in turn elicited more schadenfreude and less sympathy). Moreover, Van Dijk, Ouwerkerk, and Goslinga (2009) showed that people experienced more schadenfreude and less sympathy toward high achievers with undeserved achievements who suffered misfortunes as opposed to those with deserved achievements. Again, these effects were mediated by the perceived deservingness of the misfortunes (i.e., misfortunes befalling high achievers with undeserved achievements were seen as more deserved and in turn elicited more schadenfreude and less sympathy). Together these findings indicate that a concern for justice might be an important motivator for the experience of schadenfreude.

Thus, revenge and schadenfreude both elicit pleasurable feelings because for both emotions, the suffering of others is appraised as deserved and satisfies people's concern for just and deserved outcomes. In his book *When Bad Things Happen to Other People*, the contemporary philosopher

John Portmann writes: "It is not the suffering of others that brings us joy, but rather the evidence of justice triumphing before our eyes" (2000, p. xiii).

The desire for vengeance, schadenfreude and a concern for a positive self-evaluation

A second concern that revenge and schadenfreude share is a concern for a positive self-evaluation. Many psychologists consider people's motivation to feel good about themselves as an important human concern (e.g., Taylor and Brown, 1988; Tesser, 1988). Events that threaten people's self-evaluation, for example, being wronged by others or being confronted with a successful other, might evoke strong negative emotions, such as anger, humiliation, shame, and envy. These negative emotions in turn might provoke a strong motivation to defend or restore a damaged self-worth. One such motivation is the desire for revenge directed toward the person who caused your damaged self-worth. Indeed, feelings of revenge that seem designed to thwart downward revision of the self are associated with damage to one's self-worth. By avenging, the victim proves that he or she does not fear the offender (Nietzsche, 1887/1994, p. 139) and is again in control (Frijda, 1994), which might help in restoring a threatened or damaged self-worth. This notion is supported by research showing that damage to one's self-worth is associated with aggression and (a desire for) revenge (Baumeister, Bushman, and Campbell, 2000; Baumeister, Smart, and Boden, 1996; Bies and Tripp, 1996; Bushman and Baumeister, 1998). Individuals with damaged or threatened self-worth have a strong need to restore or protect a positive self-evaluation, and the desire for revenge might reflect their efforts to satisfy this need.

In a similar way, schadenfreude can be enjoyable because the misfortunes of others provide people with an opportunity for self-enhancement (see Van Dijk and Ouwerkerk, Chapter 9 in this volume). Several studies support this view. For example, in a series of studies, Van Dijk and colleagues have shown that people with a strong motivation for protecting or enhancing their self-worth derive more pleasure from the misfortunes of others (Van Dijk et al., 2011a; Van Dijk et al., 2011b; Van Dijk and Ouwerkerk, Chapter 9 in this volume). Arguably, individuals with a strong motivation for self-enhancement often engage in downward comparison processes (Aspinwall and Taylor, 1993; Wills, 1981). The more intense schadenfreude experienced by these individuals then reflects their heightened concern for a positive self-evaluation, as the misfortunes of threatening others may provide them with social comparison benefits that may help to enhance or restore their self-evaluation. This line of reasoning is also supported by another study that showed that providing low self-esteem people with an alternative means to restore their self-evaluation reduced their schadenfreude toward the misfortunes of others (Van Dijk et al., 2011b). Thus, both a desire for vengeance and schadenfreude can be enjoyable because they can restore a damaged self-worth.

Future avenues for research on schadenfreude

In the previous sections we have addressed the desire for vengeance and compared it to schadenfreude. Both emotions are concerned with the pleasure derived from the suffering of others. Whereas vengeance involves deriving satisfaction and pleasure from actively and intentionally hurting or harming another, in schadenfreude the satisfaction and pleasure arises from merely passively witnessing another's misfortune. In his book *On the Genealogy of Morality* (1887/1994), Nietzsche already emphasized the relation between vengeance and schadenfreude as he described schadenfreude as a form of "imaginary revenge" and as "a vengefulness of the impotent" (for empirical support for Nietzsche's ideas about schadenfreude, see Leach and Spears, 2008; Leach et al., 2003). Despite some important differences between (the desire for) vengeance and schadenfreude, there are also striking similarities between these emotions and this overlap may provide a fruitful start for future research on schadenfreude. In the final section of our chapter we will therefore suggest some possible avenues for future studies on schadenfreude.

One possible avenue for future research concerns the mixed emotions associated with a desire for vengeance. As noted before, vengeance and schadenfreude both involve pleasurable feelings toward the suffering of others. Although the adage suggests that revenge is sweet, vengeance seems to be a mixed blessing. It is not only associated with (anticipated) satisfaction and pleasure, but also with a mix of negative emotions. Until now, little is known about the experienced emotions that co-occur or blend in with the experience of schadenfreude. For example, do *schadenfroh* people also experience shame or guilt after they have witnessed and laughed about someone else's misfortune? Is schadenfreude as sweet as the Japanese adage "the misfortunes of others taste like honey" suggests or is the experience of schadenfreude more a bittersweet feeling akin to revenge?

A second related avenue for future research concerns people's affective forecasts of schadenfreude. A study by Carlsmith, Wilson, and Gilbert (2008) showed that people expected to feel better than they actually did after taking revenge on an offender. Does this impact bias also occur for schadenfreude? One could argue that this will indeed be the case, because the impact bias (people's tendency to forecast stronger emotional reaction than they actually experience) seems to be a robust phenomenon (e.g., Gilbert et al., 1998; Van Dijk et al., 2012) and why would schadenfreude be different from other emotions? Although one could argue that people might overestimate their pleasure in merely observing someone else's misfortune, this bias is probably smaller than for revenge. As Carlsmith, Wilson, and Gilbert's results indicated, the misprediction of pleasure from revenge was mainly due to the fact that vengeful individuals underestimated the extent to which they ruminated about the offender after taking revenge. In revenge the avenger actually hurts the offender and this causal role in inflicting suffering upon another person might instigate rumination and, subsequently, increase negative emotions, while decreasing positive ones. With respect to schadenfreude, the *schadenfroh* did not cause the harm, but was merely an observer of another person's suffering. This passive role in the suffering of others is less likely to increase rumination and subsequent negative emotions. This might make schadenfreude sweeter than revenge.

A third direction for future research relates to the concern for justice that underlies both (the desire for) vengeance and schadenfreude. An interesting question is whether schadenfreude can satisfy the concern for getting even in one's desire for vengeance. In other words, when someone has wronged us and evoked a strong desire for vengeance, does merely witnessing this offender getting hurt (due to a third party or to circumstances) attenuate our desire to take revenge ourselves? Our own research, as we described earlier, indicates that people derive more pleasure from a third party punishment than from their own punishment in moderately unfair situations, but they derive more pleasure from their own revenge when an offense was perceived as extremely unfair. This suggests that schadenfreude might serve as a good substitute for actively taking revenge for mild unfair situations, but not for severe unfair situations. In these situations our concern for justice might not fully be satisfied when we have not avenged the suffering ourselves; consequently, we will continue to have a desire for vengeance.

A fourth and last direction for future research we discuss in this chapter concerns the role of social norms. Future studies could address the influence of these norms in the experience and expression of both (the desire for) vengeance and schadenfreude. In a recent study of our own, we found that participants who were in a first (allegedly unrelated) study confronted with a social norm that approved taking revenge (as compared with participants who were confronted with a social norm that disapproved of taking revenge) actually took more revenge on another participant (i.e., destroying this participant's earnings in the study) that treated them unfairly during a second study. Moreover, in a survey study on the desire for revenge we compared the respondents who took revenge (avengers) with the respondents who did not take revenge (non-avengers).

Although there were no significant differences in the appraisals, emotions, and action tendencies between both groups of respondents, avengers differed from non-avengers in that they had a social environment that was supportive of actually taking revenge. These results indicate that when it is more acceptable – or even expected – to take revenge, people might be more likely to actually take revenge. Although schadenfreude is often a private emotion, when it is generally accepted to experience pleasure over another's misfortune, it could be that schadenfreude is more openly expressed. This might be an interesting line of research, along with the other avenues of future research we suggested, to pursue in the near future and to gain more insight into two intriguing emotions: the desire for vengeance and schadenfreude.

Conclusion

In this chapter we compared the desire for vengeance with schadenfreude and looked at the underlying concerns that motivate these emotions. Both emotions are elicited in response to a perceived wrong and involve pleasure and satisfaction toward the suffering of the person who caused the wrong. Two important concerns that seem to underlie both the desire for vengeance and schadenfreude are a concern for justice and a concern for positive self-evaluation. Schadenfreude and (the desire for) vengeance both elicit pleasurable feelings because for both emotions, the suffering of others is appraised as deserved and satisfies people's concern for just and deserved outcomes. Moreover, both emotions are enjoyable because they can restore a damaged self-worth. They do, however, differ in their causal role and intentionality. Whereas a vengeful person derives (anticipated) pleasure from actively and intentionally hurting or harming another person in return for a perceived wrongdoing by this person, a *schadenfroh* person passively derives pleasure from merely witnessing the other suffer. Therefore, the desire for vengeance may be sweet, but schadenfreude might perhaps even be sweeter. By gaining insight into the concerns underlying the desire for vengeance and schadenfreude, we can come to a better understanding of why these "outcast" emotions still exist today. The concerns are real and perhaps reflect a natural strive for justice and self-worth.

References

Aquino, K., Tripp, T. M., and Bies, R. J. (2001). How employees respond to personal offense: the effects of blame attribution, victim status, and offender status on revenge and reconciliation in the workplace. *Journal of Applied Social Psychology* 86: 52–9.

(2006). Getting even or moving on? Power, procedural justice, and types of offense as predictors of revenge, forgiveness, reconciliation, and avoidance in organizations. *Journal of Applied Psychology* 91: 653–68.

Asadi, S. (2011). A study on revenge. Unpublished manuscript. Department of Psychology, Leiden University, the Netherlands.

Aspinwall, L. G. and Taylor, S. E. (1993). The effects of social comparison direction, threat, and self-esteem on affect, self-evaluation, and expected success. *Journal of Personality and Social Psychology* 64: 708–72.

Baumeister, R. F., Bushman, B. J., and Campbell, W. K. (2000). Self-esteem, narcissism, and aggression: does violence result from low self-esteem or from threatened egotism? *Current Directions in Psychological Science* 9: 26–9.

Baumeister, R. F., Smart, L., and Boden, J. M. (1996). Relation of threatened egotism to violence and aggression: the dark side of high self-esteem. *Psychological Review* 103: 5–33.

Bies, R. J. and Tripp, T. M. (1996). Beyond distrust: "getting even" and the need for revenge. In R. M. Kramer and T. R. Tyler (eds.). *Trust in Organizations. Frontiers of Theory and Research.* Thousand Oaks, CA: Sage Publications, Inc., pp. 246–60.

Brontë, C. (2006 [1847]). *Jane Eyre* (edited by P. Moliken, L. M. Miller, and L. Stewart). Clayton, DE: Prestwick House.

Bushman, B. J. and Baumeister, R. F. (1998). Threatened egotism, narcissism, self-esteem, and direct and displaced aggression: does self-love or self-hate lead to violence? *Journal of Personality and Social Psychology* 75: 219–29.

Carlsmith, K. M., Wilson, T. D., and Gilbert, D. T. (2008). The paradoxical consequences of revenge. *Journal of Personality and Social Psychology* 95: 1316–24.

Cikara, M., Botvinick, M. M., and Fiske, S. T. (2011). Us versus them: social identity shapes neural responses to intergroup competition and harm. *Psychological Science* 22: 306–13.

Crombag, H., Rassin, E., and Horselenberg, R. (2003). On vengeance. *Psychology, Crime & Law* 9: 333–44.

De Quervain, D. J. F., Fischbacher, U., Treyer, V., Schellhammer, M., Schnyder, U., Buck, A., and Fehr, E. (2004). The neural basis of altruistic punishment. *Science* 305: 1254–8.

Elster, M. (1990). Norms of revenge. *Ethics* 100: 862–85.

Fehr, E. and Gächter, S. (2002). Altruistic punishment in humans. *Nature* 415: 137–40.

Frijda, N. H. (1994). The lex talionis. On vengeance. In S. H. M. van Goozen, N. E. van de Poll, and J. A. Sergeant (eds.), *Emotions: Essays on Emotion Theory.* Hillsdale, NJ: Erlbaum, pp. 263–90.

(2007). *The Laws of Emotion.* Mahwah, NJ: Erlbaum.

Gilbert, D. T., Pinel, E. C., Wilson, T. D., Blumberg, S. J., and Wheatley, T. P. (1998). Immune neglect: a source of durability bias in affective forecasting. *Journal of Personality and Social Psychology* 75: 617–38.

Gollwitzer, M. and Denzeler, M. (2009). What makes revenge sweet: seeing the offender suffer or delivering a message? *Journal of Experimental Social Psychology* 45: 840–4.

Gollwitzer, M., Meder, M., and Schmitt, M. (2011). What gives victims satisfaction when they seek revenge? *European Journal of Social Psychology* 41: 364–74.

Jacoby, S. (1983). *Wild Justice: The Evolution of Revenge*. New York: Harper & Row.

Khan, R. (2011). Pakistani Taliban claim responsibility for deadly suicide bombing. *Associated Press*. Available at: www.huffingtonpost.com/2011/05/13/pakistani-taliban-suicide-bombing_n_861436.html.

Leach, C. W. and Spears, R. (2008). "A vengefulness of the impotent": the pain of ingroup inferiority and schadenfreude toward a successful outgroup. *Journal of Personality and Social Psychology* 95: 1383–96.

Leach, C. W., Spears, R., Branscombe, N., and Doosje, B. (2003). Malicious pleasure: schadenfreude at the suffering of another group. *Journal of Personality and Social Psychology* 84: 932–43.

Milroy, C. M. (1995). Reasons for homicide and suicide in episodes by dyadic death in Yorkshire and Humberside. *Medicine, Science, and the Law* 35: 213–17.

Nietzsche, F. (1994 [1887]). *On the Genealogy of Morality* (edited by K. Ansell Pearson and translated by C. Diethe). Cambridge University Press.

O'Sullivan, G. and Kelleher, M. (1987). A study of firesetters in the south-west of Ireland. *British Journal of Psychiatry* 151: 818–23.

Portmann, J. (2000). *When Bad Things Happen to Other People*. New York: Routledge.

Roseman, I. J. and Smith, C. A. (2001). Appraisal theory: overview, assumptions, varieties, controversies. In K. Scherer, A. Schorr, and T. Johnstone (eds.), *Appraisal Processes in Emotion: Theory, Methods, Research*. Oxford University Press, pp. 3–19.

Scheff, T. J. (1994). *Bloody Revenge: Emotions, Nationalism, and War*. Boulder, CO: Westview Press.

Scully, D. and Marolla, J. (1985). "Riding the bull at Gilley's": convicted rapists describe the rewards of rape. *Social Problems* 32: 251–63.

Seip, E. C., Rotteveel, M., Harris, L., Van Dijk, W. W., and Fischer, A. H. (2014b). More satisfaction after enacting punishment or observing punishment? Manuscript in preparation.

Seip, E. C., Van Dijk, W. W., and Rotteveel, M. (2009). On hotheads and Dirty Harries: the primacy of anger in altruistic punishment. *Annals of the New York Academy of Sciences* 1167: 190–6.

(2014c). Anger motivates costly punishment. *Motivation and Emotion* (forthcoming).

Seip, E. C., Van Dijk, W. W., Rotteveel, M., Van Dillen, L. F., and Fischer, A. H. (2014a). The experiential content of desire for vengeance: : appraisals, action tendencies and motivational goals. Manuscript in preparation.

Singer, R., Seymour, B., O'Doherty, J., Kaube, H., Dolan, R. J., and Frith, C. D. (2004). Empathy for pain involves the affective but not sensory components of pain. *Science* 303: 1157–62.

Sitkin, S. B. and Roth, N. L. (1993). Explaining the limited effectiveness of legalistic "remedies" for trust/distrust. *Organization Science* 4: 367–92.

Solomon, R. (1990). *A Passion for Justice: Emotions and the Origins of the Social Contract*. Reading, MA: Addison-Wesley.

Stuckless, N. and Goranson, R. (1992). The vengeance scale: development of a measure of attitudes toward revenge. *Journal of Social Behavior and Personality* 7: 25–42.

Takahashi, H., Kato, M., Matsuura, M., Mobbs, D., Suhura, T., and Okubo, Y. (2009). When your gain is my pain and your pain is my gain: neural correlates of envy and schadenfreude. *Science* 323: 937–9.

Taylor, S. E. and Brown, J. D. (1988). Illusion and well-being: a social psychological perspective on mental health. *Psychological Bulletin* 103: 193–210.

Tesser, A. (1988). Toward a self-evaluation maintenance model of social behavior. In L. Berkowitz (ed.), *Advances in Experimental Social Psychology*, Vol. 21. New York: Academic Press, pp. 181–227.

Van Dijk, W. W., Goslinga, S., and Ouwerkerk, J. W. (2008). The impact of responsibility for a misfortune on schadenfreude and sympathy: further evidence. *Journal of Social Psychology* 148: 631–6.

Van Dijk, W. W., Ouwerkerk, J. W., and Goslinga, S. (2009). The impact of deservingness on schadenfreude and sympathy: further evidence. *Journal of Social Psychology* 149: 290–2.

Van Dijk, W. W., Ouwerkerk, J. W., Goslinga, S., and Nieweg, M. (2005). Deservingness and schadenfreude. *Cognition & Emotion* 19: 933–9.

Van Dijk, W. W., Ouwerkerk, J. W., Wessling, Y. M., and Van Koningsbruggen, G. M. (2011a). Towards understanding pleasure at the misfortunes of others: the impact of self-evaluation threat on schadenfreude. *Cognition & Emotion* 25: 360–8.

Van Dijk, W. W., Van Dillen, L. F., Seip, E. C., and Rotteveel, M. (2012). Emotional time travel: emotion regulation and the overestimation of future anger and sadness. *European Journal of Social Psychology* 42: 308–13.

Van Dijk, W. W., Van Koningsbruggen, G. M., Ouwerkerk, J. W., and Wesseling, Y. M. (2011b). Self-esteem, self-affirmation, and schadenfreude. *Emotion* 11: 1445–9.

Wills, T. A. (1981). Downward comparison principles in social psychology. *Psychological Bulletin* 90: 245–71.

16 Schadenfreude and pouting

John Portmann

Pouting deepens understanding of schadenfreude by highlighting consequences of interpreting suffering. Pouting can arise from at least two distinct sources, both of which concern justice. In the first instance, we pout because others have rejoiced in our misfortune and we do not think we deserved to suffer. In the second instance, we feel ourselves the victim of some injustice and resent others for not helping us, for not rectifying the injustice. My aim in analyzing pouting is both to point to likely candidates for schadenfreude and to mine Nietzsche's invaluable contribution to the philosophy of the emotions. Pouting is a form of *ressentiment*, which Nietzsche considered a widespread emotional state, one sometimes referred to as "upward contempt."

Although we rarely learn of the schadenfreude others feel toward us, we may sometimes hear second-hand reports of it. Because we may pout after hearing that others smiled because our chips were down, I will dissect pouting in the context of, and as a corollary to, schadenfreude. We will see that neither schadenfreude nor pouting threatens the social order. At the same time, few of us, when pondering the kind of person we would ideally become, will choose to associate either schadenfreude or pouting with our best-case scenario. That is not to suggest that either schadenfreude or pouting is immoral, only that an individual may reasonably decide against emotional indulgence of these sorts.

Pouting

Mark Twain once observed that it takes two to wound us to the heart: one person to utter something awful about us and then a "friend" to let us know what the other said. Although schadenfreude usually passes undetected (either because others don't want us to know that our misfortune has made them happy or because others fear that their personal reputations will suffer as a result of admitting to schadenfreude), we do sometimes suspect or learn of joy at our expense. We may disguise our disappointment; and perhaps wait for revenge; or nobly shrug off our disappointment, or we may choose to pout.

I deliberately bypass the sexual connotations of pouting (think of a "pouty lip") and flirting. In John Webster's Jacobean tragedy *The Duchess of Malfi* (1623), the Duchess laments: "The misery of us that are born great! We are forc'd to woo, because none dare woo us." She is pouting and flirting, feeling just a little sad for herself, because she would prefer that her beloved Antonio court her instead (he cannot because of the class barrier between them). Sexual pouting may pertain to missed opportunities of the sort I analyze in this chapter, but I do not have the space to pursue an analogy.

Pouting is not masochism: the two differ in kind, not in degree. Masochists deliberately harm themselves and then feel satisfaction. Pouters suffer from a misfortune they do not believe they have designed. Pouters do not enjoy their own suffering, but they may well enjoy using it as a bargaining chip.

We often believe that self-serving, passive people – pouters – deserve to suffer, and so we may feel schadenfreude in watching them fail, seeing them fall short of receiving the sympathy or victory they crave. A pouter believes he is right and you are wrong; he waits for the moment that he is proven right in order to triumph over you. Sometimes English speakers will say "I'll wait for you at the bend" in order to indicate the belief that someone else who refuses to heed a warning will drive off the road, metaphorically speaking. When we learn that our friends do not support our goals or believe us capable of achieving them, we may pout.

Scholars were slow to turn to the fascinating, prevalent, and complex emotion schadenfreude. Scholars have also largely neglected pouting. That English has a word for it might suggest it poses less of a social threat than schadenfreude. In French, one says *bouder* or *faire la tête*; in German, one says *schmollen* or *einen Schmollmund machend*. In English, virtually everyone – especially small children – understands *pouting*. Nietzsche effectively subsumed it under the category of *ressentiment*, having intentionally chosen the French word in order to emphasize a difference between this emotion and resentment (see Portmann, 2000, pp. 34–5).

Although *pouting* the word may be much more familiar to English speakers than schadenfreude, the concept may surprise us with its complex core. We may characterize pouting by inadequacy, dependence, injustice, and pettiness. These feelings often inhibit settling a score in a mature fashion and instead become a mild reproach designed to obtain or preserve sympathy from another. Pouting indicates that another person or group has disappointed us; we had pointedly hoped for more. The psychologist Richard Lazarus has stipulated that pouting reveals us to be in an inferior position with respect to the person who has disappointed us, but we cannot afford to attack in order to enhance our wounded integrity (Lazarus, 1991).[1] Pouting may ultimately lead to some form of overt retaliation, but empirical research would be needed to indicate any frequency.

Pouting expresses not only wounded vanity but also neediness, which is why it is commonly seen as childish. Pouting differs from sarcasm, which can be an uninhibited, spicy, or witty verbal expression of anger, almost but not quite akin to contempt. Pouting is a coping strategy in which a person consciously decides not to attack out of fear of further alienating the person whose approbation and concern are still needed. From the standpoint of its developmental origins and formulated within a psychoanalytic perspective, the aim of pouting is an attempt, recapitulating childhood, to force one's mother (lover, offspring, etc.) to pay attention (see Adatto, 1957). As an example we might think of Richard Nixon's public *cri de coeur* after losing the 1960 presidential election in the USA: "You won't have me to kick around anymore!" When we suffer and then suspect others of enjoying our suffering, we may realize more keenly than ever our dependence on others. We may pout as a way not only to stop the schadenfreude of others but also to earn a victory over those who felt it: "They should be ashamed of themselves for having failed to honor me," we affirm silently. We cast ourselves in the role of victim and then try to arouse some sympathy.

The diagnosis of pouting stands on a judgment of what suffering we will be credited for. In the early twentieth century, an American legal scholar coined the term "laughing heir" to denote someone "who is so loosely linked to his ancestor as to suffer no sense of bereavement at his loss" (Cavers, 1935). On this interpretation, laughing heirs didn't really suffer, and so they didn't really deserve sympathy. Of course, it is possible that a young person might in fact suffer when learning about the death of someone she hardly knew – not so much because she might have received a considerable fortune from that person, but perhaps for reasons involving racial or religious identification. When others accuse us of pouting, they first guess at how much a reasonable person could claim to suffer in similar circumstances. Their guess could be wrong.

Suffering, which underlies both schadenfreude and pouting, often confers a sense of moral superiority. "Because I have suffered more than you, I deserve more respect than you," the thinking goes. Donning this

[1] I follow Lazarus closely in the following few paragraphs.

mantle of superiority amounts to a form of aggression. The downtrodden imaginatively cast themselves in the role of unsung heroes, unacknowledged martyrs (this mental strategy resembles the one embedded in *ressentiment*).

Thinking of pouting in terms of suffering is quite useful. I stipulate that pouting is a value judgment that refuses to acknowledge: (1) that another suffers in an important way; or (2) in an undeserved way. Accordingly, some low-wage labourers will deny that kings or queens can suffer (see Portmann, Chapter 2 in this volume); the affluent tend to exaggerate minor problems, the thinking goes, and simply pout about nothing. By the same token, some conservatives sneer at the complaints about racism occasionally made by students of color at elite American universities; such students were only admitted through affirmative action programs, the thinking goes, and don't really deserve to be there in the first place (see Feather, Chapter 3 in this volume). The pouting of students of color can appear a form of aggression, a means of asserting the superiority of their particular suffering.

Nietzsche (1887/1986) pondered the use of suffering as a way of manipulating sympathy in order to get what we want; he also associated this stratagem with children. In *Human, All Too Human*, he wrote: "Observe how children weep and cry, so that they will be pitied, how they wait for the moment when their condition will be noticed; the thirst for pity is a thirst for self- enjoyment, and at the expense of one's fellow men" (1887/1986, p. 38). Waiting for others to recognize our superiority, compelling them to recognize it, is a form of pouting. Enjoying our own suffering is a more subtle and more interesting form of schadenfreude than, say, slapstick comedy or cheering at the imprisonment of a tax fraud (which both involve the suffering of another person). This enjoyment of our own suffering (as in sentimentality) differs importantly from identifying with the aggressor, a neurosis identified by Anna Freud, or the kind of virtuous Christian self-debasement famously articulated by Augustine in the *Confessions* and then later developed in *The Rule of Saint Benedict*.

I define pouting as an insistence that others recognize the extent and importance of our suffering, an insistence that others pooh-pooh as trivial. Pouting pivots on the distance between how others see us and how we see ourselves. Others may not view our suffering as significant or even rational, and we lament their intransigence or ignorance. Pouting may include self-righteousness, insofar as our suffering elevates us over others who cannot see or understand it. Their inability isolates us from them.

Kant once expressed confidence that we will all agree when the guilty should suffer. In the *Critique of Practical Reason* he maintained:

> When, however, someone who delights in annoying and vexing peace-loving folk receives at last a right good beating, it is certainly an ill, but everyone approves of it and considers it as good in itself even if nothing further results from it; nay, even he who gets the beating must acknowledge, in his reason, that justice has been done to him, because he sees the proportion between welfare and well-doing, which reason inevitably holds before him, here put into practice. (1788/1956, p. 63)

Kant expresses undue confidence about the conscience of a guilty person; for him, pouting makes no sense. Against Kant, we should readily see that a person humbled through punishment or social circumstances may in fact strongly disagree with the appropriateness of his plight – Richard Nixon is a case in point here. Humiliated and angry, Nixon protested his suffering as unjust. Nixon pouted. He had lost the election to a man he considered plainly less qualified – though more wealthy and better connected socially – than himself.

Sometimes suffering afflicts an entire group. In the 1970s, civil rights activist Jesse Jackson built a career out of raising the social status of African Americans. Certainly, individual African Americans had suffered discrimination in discrete instances. At the same time, and this was Jackson's point in part, the whole subgroup of African Americans suffered discrimination. The media either largely ignored African Americans or portrayed them disparagingly and unfairly. At the same time, a smaller group of Americans, Jews, seemed to receive more media attention, almost all of it positive. Jackson allegedly complained to the *New York Times* in 1979: "I'm sick and tired of hearing about the Holocaust" (quoted in Finkelstein, 2003, p. 31). He lamented the unfairness of one group continuing to profit from the suffering of its forebears, while African Americans did not.

Like Nixon, Jackson wanted sympathy. Each might have said he wanted justice – Nixon for himself and Jackson for his race – and this putative link to justice establishes an instructive parallel between schadenfreude and pouting. In *ressentiment*, one deliberately and consciously alters the very meaning of terms such as good and bad, winner and loser, in order to promote oneself; in pouting, one decries an injustice which shows no sign of stopping. Indignation, sometimes referred to as righteous anger, also prompts wounded parties to demand justice. Pouting combines indignation and resignation.

Of course, riots or violent attacks can erupt from the frustration of *ressentiment*. Like schadenfreude, though, pouting is a minor emotion. Pouting indicates the absence of a violent agent; pouting bespeaks inability or incapacity. Consider the dissatisfaction of obese, athletically unskilled men who watch sports on television and ridicule players for having let down their team and their fans. The wails of these sedentary men rest on a pretence of athletic and intellectual superiority to the players on television. These dissatisfied men pout; their pouting is a complaint gloved in powerlessness to do anything about it. Pouting is a temporary, episodic form of what the psychologist Martin Seligman theorized as "learned helplessness."

Pouting is a word of potential interest to Germans, as the German language lacks an equivalent to the English word *frustration* (usually translated as *Versagung*; Freud discussed this distinction in the 1912 essay "Types of Onset of Neurosis"). Quite apart from the sexual connotations with which Freud imbued it, frustration and pouting overlap to a significant degree, pouting being a specific manifestation of frustration.

As a favorable contrast to pouting, we might think of resolving to overcome an obstacle through hard work (as in studying harder in order to earn higher grades or to achieve a higher score on a standardized test); going out on strike; entering therapy; or inviting those whom we resent to discuss a grievance openly and candidly. Of course, certain social policies will disappoint or even enrage people (think of smoking bans or affirmative action). Those who oppose social policies, which pass a popular vote or gain the support of a legislative body, may pout out of a sense that there is nothing else to be done.

According to Lazarus, we can distinguish pouting from something like schadenfreude by focusing on what a person stands to lose upon being discovered with the emotion. What sets pouting apart from other forms of anger is the threat (and its anxiety) of what an uninhibited expression of anger is thought to produce – namely, retaliation and loss of succour. Pouting no doubt plays an important role in what schoolteachers and guidance counselors refer to as "bad attitude" or what some parents refer to simply as "attitude."

Personality traits involving helplessness or self-confidence should contribute to the appraisals underlying schadenfreude and pouting. In the same vein, some people are not given much to aggression anxiety, whereas others are made quite anxious by their own anger. In addition, some encounters are more conducive to schadenfreude, as when a victim of misfortune appears, for the moment at least, powerful and safe, and other encounters are more conducive to pouting, as when the person toward whom we might feel angry is too powerful to attack – for example, the police or someone whose approbation and affection are greatly valued and desired. Although a boss with control over our job or salary may also be threatening, we are not likely to pout when we are denied patronage, because this would make us look childish in a competitive workplace where we would prefer to look masterful. No doubt much of the depression men feel comes down to or involves repression in such a context; this is not the place to probe male depression, though.

Before moving on, I want to note that pouting is something we may not even be fully conscious of doing. And pouting is rarely how we ourselves would describe what we are doing or feeling. Pouting is a description foisted upon us by others; it is their interpretation of how we are coping with an unpleasant circumstance. The same is true in schadenfreude: others may imagine that we may take pleasure in the actual suffering of another human being, but in fact we may be taking pleasure in seeing justice done or in the restoration of some sort of equality. This difference will become important when I examine racism later on.

Other psychologists have tried to rank the relative effectiveness of various coping strategies. George Vaillant's work in *The Wisdom of the Ego* (1993) and later *Aging Well* (2002) suggests that pouting is not something we need associate with violence or social unrest. Vaillant's central concerns are psychoanalytic adaptations or unconscious responses to pain, conflict, or uncertainty. Borrowing in part from the insights of Anna Freud, Vaillant theorizes adaptations as unconscious thoughts and behaviors, which mold a personality. For Vaillant, the pettiness of pouting (to which he does not refer by name) contrasts with the more serious, "neurotic" defences of ordinary people (such as intellectualization, dissociation, and repression) and the most serious, indeed quite worrisome, adaptations (such as paranoia, hallucination, and megalomania). "Immature" adaptations include: acting out; passive aggression; hypochondria; projection; and fantasy. Pouting would fit well into Vaillant's category of immature adaptations; those who pout may one day advance to the "mature" adaptations, such as humor, altruism, anticipation (looking ahead and planning for future discomfort), or suppression (a conscious decision to postpone attention to a conflict until a later time).

So much for a brief overview of pouting, a cousin of schadenfreude. I will now try to shed light on victimization, which often leads to pouting. We will see that an analysis of pouting splits liberals and conservatives: liberals tend to see genuine victims of misfortune where conservatives see pouters. The American psychologist Jon Haidt (2012) has argued that well-meaning people on both the right and the left will often view suffering quite differently, and an analysis of pouting would seem to confirm Haidt's conclusions.

Pouting and social movements

When do social movements end? How can we tell that they have run their course? At what point should a civil rights struggle close up shop, having achieved its goals? What incentive, if any, does a movement have for stopping? A quest for social justice is also an appeal for sympathy from the masses. Continuing to complain after a social condition has improved is a form of pouting. Offering examples of group pouting often involves adjudicating sometimes obstreperous political battles. Allegations of pouting underscore the social dimension of emotions, specifically with regard to what emotions others feel we are entitled to, as well as the amount of sympathy others choose to send our way.

Disenfranchised persons or groups may have a legitimate claim when they protest that they have been unfairly treated or perhaps excluded. We might expect such persons or groups to possess a clear idea of what they want and of when they will cease their protest. The question of whether people are satisfied with what they achieve or receive matters to the public perception of greed. Beyond that, public opinion counts for a lot in determining how much compassion is due to an aggrieved person or group. Also at stake is the pride an individual may take in identifying with a group; if the group is perceived to behave badly or follow pouting leaders, it will likely suffer internal defections.

In the late twentieth century, many gay Catholics in the USA lobbied their religious leaders to soften institutional opposition to homosexuality. The literary critic and social commentator Camille Paglia wrote in the early 1990s:

> As a lapsed Catholic of wavering sexual orientation, I have never understood the pressure for ordination of gay clergy or even the creation of gay Catholic groups. They seem to me to indicate a need for parental approval, an inability to take personal responsibility for one's own identity. (1992, p. 36)[2]

Paglia essentially accused organized gay Catholics of pouting. A decade later, controversy over gay marriage swept through the USA; despite widespread success in gaining the right to a civil union, gay people nonetheless continued to fight on for "marriage equality," perhaps prompting many bystanders to conclude that gay activists were pouting. Gays and lesbians in the USA had profited considerably from the controversial 2003 Supreme Court ruling in *Lawrence v. Texas*, which decriminalized sodomy. Some conservatives thought gay activists should be grateful for that victory and should stop whining about social prejudice.

Of course, gay activists would not have seen themselves as pouting. Again, pouting is a conclusion reached by the "them" in an "us" versus "them" skirmish. Let's consider a few other examples; we will see that

[2] Paglia made the same point in a Canadian interview conducted in 2009: www.towleroad.com/2009/06/camille-paglia-gay-activists-childish-for-demanding-rights.html#more.

victimization is the common thread running through them and that even powerful people can claim to be victims.

Anti-Catholicism: Pope Benedict XVI in 2009

The international media pilloried Pope Benedict XVI for honoring a British bishop who had trivialized the Holocaust. Pope Benedict had honored Richard Williamson in an attempt to woo back to the fold the conservative followers of a splinter group of Catholics in the Society of St. Pius X. Williamson and his followers had been excommunicated for disobeying Pope John Paul II a couple of decades earlier, and Benedict wanted them back.

In response to the uproar, Benedict wrote a letter (a "word of clarification") in March 2009 to the bishops of the world.[3] The pontiff acknowledged that he had regrets:

> An unforeseen mishap for me was the fact that the Williamson case came on top of the remission of the excommunication . . . Another mistake, which I deeply regret, is the fact that the extent and limits of the provision of 21 January 2009 were not clearly and adequately explained at the moment of its publication.

Richard Williamson's excommunication had been lifted in January 2009, when Benedict did not know that Williamson was a Holocaust denier. He conceded that a simple Internet search could have made him aware of Bishop Williamson's remarks. An interesting aspect of the letter is Benedict's sense of betrayal by a wide spectrum of Catholics who had criticized his move. It was as if Benedict had caught his own mother rooting for a rival in a swimming competition.

Benedict's response separated Catholics from Jews, praising Jews for having shown him more respect:

> I was saddened by the fact that even Catholics who, after all, might have had a better knowledge of the situation, thought they had to attack me with open hostility. Precisely for this reason I thank all the more our Jewish friends, who quickly helped to clear up the misunderstanding and to restore the atmosphere of friendship and trust which – as in the days of Pope John Paul II – has also existed throughout my pontificate and, thank God, continues to exist.

Here a powerful man asked for sympathy. Whereas the pontiff could easily have chosen not to acknowledge the grumbling among Catholics who criticized his admittedly bad decision to lift the excommunication against Bishop Williamson, Benedict chose to address it. In the letter, he couched his reproach in a reference to biblical squabbling:

[3] Benedict XVI, 2009.

But sad to say, this "biting and devouring" [Gal. 5:15] also exists in the Church today, as expression of a poorly understood freedom. Should we be surprised that we too are no better than the Galatians? That at the very least we are threatened by the same temptations? That we must always learn anew the proper use of freedom? And that we must always learn anew the supreme priority, which is love?

Rhetorically, this move showed some boldness. Instead of just saying "You're right, I made a mistake," Benedict contextualized squabbling in a way that may have distracted attention from his mistake. He found his critics guilty of a shortage of love. What merits emphasis here is that much of the Catholic laity had felt disappointed by him at first. It was already rare for a pontiff to apologize for having made a mistake; to express his hurt feelings at having been criticized for the mistake humanized a powerful institutional leader and exposed his curious need for love and support. Although Benedict never said it explicitly, he wanted people who consider themselves Catholic to deflect the blame for his mistake. The pope pouted.

Racism: using the past as a way to win arguments

Some political commentators proclaimed the 2008 election of Barack Obama as the end of what could be called black pouting in the USA. One influential journalist wrote that some black civil rights leaders had made a career out of manipulating "white guilt," out of portraying African Americans as victims (Dowd, 2008; see also Steele, 2008; for a discussion on "white guilt" generally, see Steele, 2006). In the example of African Americans, we can see that the question of who is pouting may come down to pigeon-holing an observer as conservative or liberal. Pouting lies in the eyes of the beholder, perhaps, but if the goal of a person or group is to gain sympathy and power, then convincing those in power that one is not pouting but rather pushing for social justice becomes crucial.

Much has been written about the politics of victimization in the USA, and complaints of African Americans "playing the race card" had already become commonplace before the presidential election of 2008. It is worth noting that the risk of being labeled a racist carried significant consequences for white Americans, perhaps significant enough to inhibit frank discussion of the civil rights struggle of black Americans. Bill Cosby, a well-known entertainer and himself a black man, stirred up controversy in 2004 when he exhorted economically disadvantaged African Americans to stop pleading victimization.[4] The movement would fail to arouse

[4] For a critique of Cosby's speeches criticizing lower-income blacks, see Dyson, 2005. Juan Williams (2006) passionately defended Cosby. For more on the idea that blacks pout instead of work toward bettering their economic circumstances, see Daniels, 2007.

popular sympathy if African Americans were suspected of greed or pouting.

No one denies the profound difficulties black people have faced in the USA: what scholars and social commentators sometimes question is whether some accusations of racism are in fact pouting – sanctimonious sulking which distracts us from serious incidents involving hatred. No matter how many concessions the white community may make, individual blacks may cry for more sympathy or power. Or so some conservative thinking goes.

Racism and responses to it require nuanced distinctions. That said, I will proceed through a few examples of black Americans who criticized the black community. Debra Dickerson claimed that blackness was collapsing under the weight of its own contradictions, much as overt racism had earlier done. Like Cosby, Dickerson[5] objected to self-victimization; she accused many blacks of pouting:

> If blacks celebrated the vastness of their vision and experience, they'd have to share the world's regard, not to mention its pity, with others. Just like whites, they want the glory, even of their victimization, all to themselves. They are no more empathetic of others' problems than whites are of blacks. They are bored, annoyed even, at the gall of the Chinese in trying to include themselves as victims in slavery's holy hell, at some Japanese girl deflecting attention from martyred Malcolm. (2004, pp. 152, 282)

Criticizing political approaches to race on both the right and the left, Dickerson faulted black politicians for defining black identity in terms of inadequacy and failure. She insisted:

> Surely we can acknowledge that overt racism has indeed been officially vanquished by the movement even as we recognize that practical racism remains lodged in many people's hearts, however subconscious, clandestine, and cloaked in seemingly color-blind rhetoric. We can also acknowledge that although some black political tactics, customs, and worldviews are not constructive, in no way are blacks' shortcomings biological or even cultural except as a rational, if regrettable, response to external stimuli (such as police brutality, structural inequality, and substandard education).

Dickerson, like Shelby Steele before her, tried to draw attention to the economic advancement of the black middle class in the 1980s and 1990s. She stressed the importance of focusing the black community on self-betterment as opposed to fixating on claims of victimization. True freedom for African Americans, she contended, would be liberation from

[5] Dickerson can profitably be read alongside the sociologist Orlando Patterson and the historian Elisabeth Lasch-Quinn, who analyze more or less these same social struggles.

inherited notions of blackness. She wanted African Americans to stop pouting.

Anyone who believed black Americans were pouting might have felt some schadenfreude when affirmative action was voted down, state by state. In every American state in which affirmative action had been put to a vote, the majority rejected it. African Americans may view this result as a manifestation of racism, injustice. Voters who oppose affirmative action would presumably describe their decision at the ballot box in another way. True, some who felt happiness at the rejection of affirmative action in a particular state might well have felt schadenfreude at the imagined suffering of African Americans. It would be irresponsible to over-generalize here: just as opposition to affirmative action need not signify latent racism, secret schadenfreude need not signify buried resentment of African-American leaders. It could be that Americans who voted against affirmative action saw it purely as a step toward social justice. (Chief Justice John Roberts declared in 2007: "The way to stop discrimination on the basis of race is to stop discriminating on the basis of race.") It could be that such voters also reacted against what they perceived to be pouting, much in the same way that Bill Cosby has articulated.

I turn now to Earl Ofari Hutchinson, my final example of a writer who protested pouting in the black community. In *The Latino Challenge to Black America*, he asserted that many blacks minimize the suffering and plight of poor Mexican immigrants and that newer immigrants accuse blacks of demanding expensive and wasteful government programs rather than emphasizing self-help and personal initiative to lift themselves out of economic difficulties. "The reality that blacks will lose even more ground in the numbers comparison to Latinos as fresh waves of immigrants come to America will likely stir more complaints from many blacks," Hutchinson predicted. An African American himself, he acknowledged "the dread many blacks have of being bypassed in the eternal battle against poverty and discrimination is not totally groundless" (2007, p. 11). He took seriously a public boast made on March 15, 2005 by Mexican President Vincente Fox that Mexicans are willing to work at menial jobs blacks refuse to do. This remark angered a number of African Americans, for reasons having to do with confusing fake suffering (that is, pouting) with real suffering.

This brief discussion of racism and pouting culminates in the shaming of an American writer who not only accused blacks of pouting generally but also of the entrenched institutionalization – perhaps professionalization – of pouting. By the twenty-first century, a significant number of American universities included black studies as a major field of study. When the American critic Naomi Schaefer Riley (2012) publicly questioned the academic legitimacy of this field, she was attacked in print. She had gone so far as to characterize the discipline as "a collection of left-wing victimization claptrap." Students and professors in the discipline, along with non-specialist sympathizers, collected 6,500 signatures to an online petition demanding that she be fired. She accused the black establishment of abusing its newfound power, of pouting in order to gain even more power.

Of course, social struggles erupt in other countries, where accusations of pouting will also fly. Dutch right-wing politician Geert Wilders (b. 1963) popularized the term "*Huillie Huillie*" (referring to a crying baby) to undermine the indignation of left-wing politicians over spending cuts on what Wilders had called "left-wing hobbies" (such as culture).[6] Wilders formed his own political party, the "Party for Freedom," which became quite successful. Frightened of the "Islamicization of the Netherlands," he advocated for a ban on immigration from Muslim countries and on the construction of any new mosques. A conservative, he viewed his opponents and critics as crybabies, pouters.

By invoking victimization, I aimed to illustrate the contested link to social justice of both schadenfreude and pouting. It is all too easy to accuse any disliked minority of pouting; it is more difficult to see the very real suffering behind the attitude and behavior, which appears to be pouting. If every action causes an equal and opposite reaction, appropriate social criticism may stir resentment from those at whom the criticism was aimed. The guilty may feel schadenfreude when their opponents suffer an eventual setback; until the setback happens, the guilty may pout.

Sympathy for the vulnerable

Schadenfreude is related to pouting through justice: in schadenfreude we celebrate that justice has been done and in pouting we resent that it has not yet. When others accuse us of pouting, we may well feel they misunderstand: we are protesting, not pouting. Anyone falsely accused or unjustly treated may choose to pout (among other options discussed here).

Pouting is an act of weakness, of weakness striking out. Pouting delights in success, in bringing down someone higher to a level of equality. Pouting anticipates this joy. Schadenfreude usually has little to do with anticipation, but rather ignites after a sudden discovery of misfortune.

Neuroscientists can contribute much to our understanding of pouting. It could be that we pout because of an excess of cortisol in our bodies: if that were the case, then medicine could prevent some pouting. Cambridge

6 I thank Wilco van Dijk and Jaap Ouwerkerk for this reference.

University neuroscientist John Coates (2012) has elucidated the effects of two steroid hormones – cortisol and testosterone – on human behavior, particularly stock trading. Young men tend to have more testosterone than women and older men. After winning at any sort of competition, animals will experience a rush of testosterone. This rush spurs them on to compete yet again, to take more risks (referred to as the "winner effect"). Prolonged stress, on the other hand, prompts the body to release cortisol, which inhibits risk-taking. Competitive failures and personal problems may trigger a bodily response akin to pouting: neuroscientists may one day show us that social factors (such as being trapped by more powerful people) are no more instrumental in triggering pouting than an accumulation of cortisol in the body.

Studying the emotions can make us more sensitive people and more responsive leaders. Schadenfreude, pouting, and envy each reveal the potentially painful and politically volatile gap between our interpretation of the social world and another's. The challenge of analyzing these three interrelated emotions lurks in this gap. No one considers pouting a vice – it is at worst an irritating character flaw. It could be argued that schadenfreude is a virtue because of its positive tie to justice. No one would ever claim pouting as a virtue: the relevant virtue here would be hope.

This chapter has highlighted the social and political aspects of schadenfreude and pouting. Some Americans may feel schadenfreude when the black community suffers political losses not because such Americans are racists, but rather because they believe the black community has already received too much or inappropriate protection from the government (or perhaps that the black community has failed to show sufficient gratitude for civil rights victories). A similar problem surrounds protests by those demanding gender equality, marriage equality, or related social movements.

It is all too easy to wave off the weakness of pouters and to spit on the schadenfreude of life's minor players. It would be noble to respond with sympathy, bearing in mind the countless difficulties any one person may bear on any given day. This was the attitude of Nietzsche, who understood well both schadenfreude and pouting: "To this day, I still have the same affability for everyone; I even treat with special respect those who are lowliest" (*Ecce Homo* I, 6).

References

Adatto, C.P. (1957). On pouting. *Journal of the American Psychoanalytic Association* 5: 245–9.

Benedict XVI (2009). Letter of His Holiness Pope Benedict XVI to the bishops of the Catholic Church concerning the remission of the excommunication of the four bishops consecrated by Archbishop Lefebvre. Available on the Vatican's website www.vatican.va.

Cavers, D. F. (1935). Change in the American family and the "laughing heir." *Iowa Law Review* 20: 203–15.

Coates, J. (2012). *The Hour between Dog and Wolf: Risk-Taking, Gut Feelings and the Biology of Boom and Bust*. New York: Penguin.

Daniels, C. (2007). *Ghettonation: A Journey into the Land of Bling and the Home of the Shameless*. New York: Doubleday.

Dickerson, D. J. (2004). *The End of Blackness: Returning the Souls of Black Folk to their Rightful Owners*. New York: Pantheon.

Dowd, M. (2008) McCain's green-eyed monster. *New York Times*, August 5.

Dyson, E. M. (2005). *Is Bill Cosby Right? Or Has the Black Middle Class Lost its Mind?* New York: Basic Civitas.

Finkelstein, N. (2003). *The Holocaust Industry*, 2nd edn. New York: Verso.

Haidt, J. (2012). *The Righteous Mind: Why Good People are Divided by Religion and Politics*. New York: Pantheon.

Hutchinson, E. O. (2007). *The Latino Challenge to Black America: Towards a Conversation between African-Americans and Hispanics*. Los Angeles: Middle Passage Press.

Kant, I. (1956 [1788]). *Critique of Practical Reason* (translated by L. W. Beck). Indianapolis: Bobbs-Merrill.

Lazarus, R. S. (1991). *Emotion and Adaptation*. New York: Oxford University Press.

Nietzsche, F. (1986 [1887]). *Human, All Too Human* (translated by R. J. Hollingdale). Cambridge University Press.

Paglia, C. (1992). *Sex, Art, and American Culture*. New York: Pantheon.

Portmann, J. (2000). *When Bad Things Happen to Other People*. New York: Routledge.

Riley, N. S. (2012). The academic mob rules. *Wall Street Journal*, May 9.

Steele, S. (2006). *White Guilt: How Whites and Blacks Together Destroyed the Promise of the Civil Rights Era*. New York: HarperCollins.

(2008). Why Jesse Jackson hates Obama. *Los Angeles Times*, July 22.

Vaillant, G. (1993). *The Wisdom of the Ego*. Cambridge, MA: Harvard University Press.

(2002). *Aging Well: Surprising Guideposts to a Happier Life from the Landmark Harvard Study of Adult Development*. New York: Little, Brown & Co.

Williams, J. (2006). *Enough: The Phony Leaders, Dead-End Movement, and Culture of Failure that are Undermining Black America – and What We Can Do about it*. New York: Crown Publishers.

Part V

Schadenfreude in society, language, and literature

17 Schadenfreude and social life: a comparative perspective on the expression and regulation of mirth at the expense of others

Giselinde Kuipers

Schadenfreude is interwoven into the fabric of human life. It is centrally connected with the moral order. This order exists, at least partly, thanks to the possibility of the immoral suffering as a result of their immorality – to the enjoyment of the morally righteous. Schadenfreude is also linked with competition: your loss may be my gain, hence my pleasure. Finally, schadenfreude is the natural counterpart of human struggle and strife: we love to see our enemies fall.

There are many reasons to enjoy the suffering of others. Such enjoyment is considered dubious and is surrounded by social restrictions and taboos. But in all societies, we find schadenfreude, expressed in everyday interactions or embedded in culturally codified rituals and genres (Apte, 1985; Proyer et al., 2009). While modern Western societies have removed schadenfreude from formalized institutions like law and education, there are still places where schadenfreude can be expressed, for instance, in sports, in the tabloid press, and – increasingly – in politics and political media (cf. Ouwerkerk and Van Dijk, Chapter 12 in this volume; Schurtz et al., Chapter 11 in this volume). New genres in popular culture, from reality TV to candid camera, zoom in on other people's suffering for the amusement of their audiences. Schadenfreude clearly is not so tabooed as to be completely hidden from public life. Instead, each culture has its own ways of channeling, shaping and regulating schadenfreude.

This chapter investigates the emotion of schadenfreude from a sociological perspective: how is this emotion socially shaped and embedded? What is its role in social life? Do expressions and meanings of schadenfreude vary across time and space? Such cross-cultural comparison allows us to better understand the social workings and functions of schadenfreude.

Because of a dearth of research and empirical findings, this chapter is explorative in nature, piecing together observations from sociological, historical, psychological, and journalistic sources. I look mainly at institutionalized forms of schadenfreude, as these are better documented and more easily observable. I supplement this with findings from my own research on humour. Humour obviously is not the same as schadenfreude – but often it borders onto it.

There is remarkably little sociological research or theorizing on schadenfreude. This chapter therefore begins with an attempt to conceptualize schadenfreude as a social and cultural phenomenon, drawing on insights from the sociology of emotions. Then, I discuss how schadenfreude is connected with society. First, I explore how social life shapes schadenfreude: how is this emotion regulated and socially constructed? How do its meanings vary across cultural contexts? Then, I look at the inverse relation, exploring how schadenfreude shapes social life. What does schadenfreude contribute to social relations? How is it embedded in social rituals and institutions?

Sociology and schadenfreude

Recently, there has been a growing sociological interest in emotions. However, in the standard works by Turner and Stets (2005; Stets and Turner, 2007) schadenfreude is only mentioned in passing, in a discussion on envy. Generally, when sociologists mention schadenfreude, they point out that this word exists in German, but not in many other languages (cf. Ignatow, 2009). Besides leading to snide remarks on the German-speaking peoples, this often results in rather far-reaching (and unconvincing) conclusions about the culture-specificity of emotions or the relation between language and reality.

Sociologists study emotions from various perspectives. Turner and Stets (2005, p. 23) distinguish no less than seven clusters of theories. All these approaches stipulate that emotions, while having a biological basis, are socially shaped and subject to social regulation. Moreover, emotions both reflect and shape social relations. An influential group of sociologists of emotion, mainly working in the Durkheimian paradigm, argues that emotions are central to the social and moral order (cf. Alexander, 2006; Collins, 2004; Durkheim, 1912/1995; Goffman, 1967; Hochschild, 1979). To these sociologists, all emotions are moral: they contribute to group boundaries and group cohesion, defining whom or what is 'out of order'.

To understand schadenfreude, I find it particularly helpful to understand it as fundamentally concerned with social and moral order. Recent research in social psychology corroborates the moral nature of schadenfreude, showing that people feel more joy at the misfortune of others when they feel those people deserve it, when it befalls people with higher social status, and when they envy those people. Moreover, schadenfreude is strongly related to group boundaries, with typically more schadenfreude experienced and expressed at the expense of out-group members (Leach and Spears, 2008; Ouwerkerk and Van Dijk, Chapter 12 in this volume; Smith et al., 2009; Vandello, Goldschmied and Richards, 2007; Van Dijk, Ouwerkerk and Goslinga, 2009; Van Dijk et al., 2006). Hence, rather than being randomly amoral or even immoral, schadenfreude follows a clear moral logic. We rejoice when the deserving, the envied and the mighty suffer, and are much less amused when it concerns our friends, the undeserving and the underdogs (see Ben-Ze'ev, Chapter 5 in this volume; Feather, Chapter 3 in this volume).

Here, I combine insights from the sociology of emotions with the basic methodology of comparative sociology: finding patterns of behaviour existing in one time and place, but not in others. Such patterns are best observed in institutionalized schadenfreude: recurring social interactions, following particular conventions, where the enjoyment of the suffering of others is central. In an unexplored research field, such institutions function as beacons for the sociologist: apparently, some forms of schadenfreude 'work' in some places, but not so well in others.

Rather than one specific emotion, schadenfreude refers to a gamut of experiences. The umbrella term of *Freude* – 'enjoyment' – includes pleasant emotions from humorous amusement and moral gratification to the vindication of seeing an enemy suffer. Gratification and vindication are generally caused by a specific occurrence in real life: the downfall of a disliked person, the humiliation of the arrogant. Fiction may evoke the same emotions – an insight gratefully applied in vignette studies.

Humorous amusement requires a specific stimulus like a joke or a witticism. Such humorous stimuli may be entertaining in themselves – some jokes are just very good. Hence, people sometimes find themselves laughing at the misfortune of people about whom they had no particular feelings before. Many comedians have this knack of producing schadenfreude more or less out of thin air. Thus, humorous schadenfreude does not require previous (negative) feelings about the 'laughee'. However, negative emotions vis-à-vis the butt of a joke increase enjoyment of a joke, while sympathy often diminishes it (Ferguson and Ford, 2008).

Moreover, the nature and character of 'other' in 'enjoyment of the misfortune of another' varies greatly: real and imagined persons, known and unknown, groups and individuals, in-group and out-group, persons to whom one does or does not bear ill will, people who deserve or do not deserve their misfortune. Therefore, it is misleading to describe schadenfreude, as was done in the recent *Handbook of Social Psychology*, as 'the malicious pleasure that derives from seeing a privileged other meet with some misfortune' (Yzerbyt and Dumoulin, 2010, p. 1050). Similarly, it is too easy to dismiss it as 'repugnant' (Smith et al., 2009) or 'morally objectionable' (McNamee, 2003).

Schadenfreude – as commonly understood in German – does not have one single specific intent, and certainly not 'malice'. Nor is it limited to particular relationships. Instead, it occurs with different emotional or social 'backdrops' – from soccer matches to collegial envy, from comedy clubs to the political arena. While in modern Western societies it is rarely considered an attractive emotion, it is not universally loathed or even discouraged. Moreover, it may be quite functional.

Social life shapes schadenfreude

Regulating schadenfreude

How does society shape schadenfreude? Most obviously, this happens via social regulation. All societies have rules about when, where and how certain emotions may be expressed. Consequently, in all cultures and epochs, some emotions are allowed to bloom, while others are discouraged and tabooed (Elias, 1939/2012; Wouters, 2007). We can witness a certain 'conjunctural fluctuation' in laughter in Western European countries: encouraged in the early modern era, increasingly restricted and suppressed after the mid-1700s, praised and admired again today – that is, as long as it is not 'at the expense of others' (Kuipers, 2006, pp. 21–39). Modern-day laughter must be 'positive' and stay away from schadenfreude (Lewis, 2006).

In Europe and North America, schadenfreude has become increasingly restricted. Today, it is ideally not too visibly enjoyed, being relegated to the 'backstage' of social life. Children are taught not to express it. The gradual shift in societal regulation of the enjoyment of other people's suffering has become the starting point for several academic treatises: Foucault's *Discipline and Punish* (1977) opens with a description of public enthusiasm at a rather gruesome execution in 1757. Robert Darnton, in *The Great Cat Massacre* (1984), wonders 'why are these people laughing' at the torturing and hanging of cats in 1730s Paris. Both authors point to the enjoyment of the onlookers as something impossible a century later. In *On the Process of Civilisation* (1939/2012), Elias described the medieval love of fighting and killing one's enemies. Nowhere does the distance between the Middle Ages and modernity become as vivid as in the contrast between our sensitivity to other people's suffering and the laughter of earlier ages.

The coming of modernity came with the gradual emergence of a new emotional regime of intensifying emotional control and 'psychologization': growing identification with others and more insight into and awareness of other people's experiences and emotions (Elias, 1939/2012; Wouters, 2007). This resulted in growing sensitivity to the suffering of others and in the expansion of the notion of 'the other' – from only close circles and social equals to one's fellow nationals, to all humanity and finally to animals. As Darnton noted, people today find the notion of laughing at the suffering of cats immoral – they, too, are included in our definition of 'other'.

Consequently, schadenfreude vanished from many social institutions. In the legal system, any emotions previously associated with the meting-out of justice – schadenfreude, vengefulness and disdain – were increasingly suppressed (Spierenburg, 1984). Much care is taken to remove the 'fun' from legal punishment. Orchestrated forms of violence, previously often considered entertaining spectacles, were banned and suppressed in many domains. Public caning and whipping disappeared from pedagogical contexts. In the field of entertainment we see the decline and suppression of blood sports, games involving the torture of humans and animals, and the public display of deformed people. To modern Western audiences, such entertainments seem pointlessly cruel and inhumane.

This brief historical sketch shows how schadenfreude is not 'naturally' or 'necessarily' tabooed in the manner common in the twenty-first-century Western world. Instead, sensitivity to others' misfortunes is learned, socially shaped and involves considerable regulation and suppression. Books of manners from the early modern times until today reflect growing pressure not to ridicule or insult others, not to publicly express aggression and not to laugh at others' mishaps (Wouters, 2007). Children, especially, have to be taught not to laugh at others and to show empathy even to strangers and enemies. The next frontier in this expanding regime of empathy and suppression of malice appears to be the treatment of animals.

Constructing schadenfreude

Emotions are socially regulated – suppressed or encouraged according to cultural mores – but also socially shaped: their expression and the meanings attached to them vary across cultures. As Hochschild (1979) argued, different groups have different 'feeling rules' and 'framing rules' to make sense of emotions. Moreover, different cultures and groups classify and separate emotions differently (Wang and Roberts, 2006). *Schadenfreude* is an interesting case in point. In German, *Freude* appears to refer to a variety of pleasurable emotions (mirth, glee, triumph, satisfaction, vindication, humorous amusement). What this word does, then, is to take a wide selection of positive emotions, uniting them on the basis of stimulus or target: the misfortune of others.

As a consequence of different 'feeling rules', 'framing rules' and classifications and delineations of emotions, different cultures have their own, rather distinct emotional landscapes. Such differences are not always as radical as the wide gap separating today from the Middle Ages. Comparative studies have found many smaller, subtler cross-cultural differences.

To my knowledge, there is no systematic comparative research on schadenfreude and, indeed, little systematic comparative sociological work on emotions. However, I have done comparative research in a related field: humour. Using interview and survey data, I compared what respondents in the Netherlands and the USA consider a 'good sense of humor' (Kuipers, 2006). While schadenfreude is not always humorous amusement and not all humour has to do with the suffering of others, there is sufficient overlap to highlight some significant cultural patterns.

In the Netherlands, humour is overwhelmingly associated with transgression. For Dutch people of all ages and classes, 'hard humour' is a positive qualification: a certain shock value, in professional comedy as in everyday humour, is believed to signal openness, authenticity and informal egalitarianism. While this preference for 'hard humour' plays out differently across social strata, it often favours humour offensive or aversive to others. Hence, Dutch humour is strongly linked with in-group exclusion and the drawing of social boundaries. In this Dutch understanding of humour, humour regarding the suffering of others is contested, but not uncommon. In effect, the large bonus on humour dealing with taboo subjects makes attempts to regulate humour rather self-defeating. For instance, the fact that joking about illnesses and the disabled is considered tasteless made it attractive to many comedians always on the lookout for the next boundary to cross. As a consequence, the local definition of 'humour' – its mapping in a semantic space – is not that far removed from schadenfreude: something to make you laugh, that is fun, yet taboo-ridden, offensive, sharp, preferably not too friendly or too 'soft'.

The culture-specificity of this understanding of humour becomes obvious when compared with the USA. Americans place 'a good sense of humour' in a rather different semantic space. First, my American respondents saw a different part of the wide field of 'things that make you laugh' as the essence of humour: for them, humour had primarily to do with self-mockery, exuberance, playfulness, openness and a positive outlook. Second, Americans' understanding of humour was more diverse, allowing for more variations, weaker group boundaries and less exclusivity. Hence, humour was neither associated strongly with transgression nor with the drawing of group boundaries. All humour at the expense of others, and particularly enjoyment of others' misfortunes, in this logic entails a deviation from 'a good sense of humour'. Incidentally, this cultural pattern may also explain the overwhelmingly negative definitions, often including 'malicious', in American-dominated scholarship on schadenfreude.

Recently, these cross-cultural differences were partly corroborated by the work of Swiss psychologist Proyer and colleagues on 'gelotophobia': the fear of being laughed at. In a comparative study they found that gelotophobia occurred in all sample countries, but carried different associations (Proyer et al., 2009). The USA and the Netherlands were diametrically opposed in this respect: Americans were generally more suspicious of others' laughter and more insecure when laughed at by others, whereas Dutch were less suspicious of others' laugher and responded to being laughed at with avoidance rather than insecurity. The Netherlands was closest to Israel and Italy, whereas the USA, more unexpectedly, resembled Hong Kong and Indonesia. One could conclude from this that the Dutch, on average, are less worried about being laughed at than the Americans.[1]

Neither of these studies expressly dealt with schadenfreude, so any conclusions about schadenfreude are tentative at best. However, both my own research and the study by Proyer et al. underline how similar emotional experiences – laughing at others and the fear of being laughed at – are framed differently cross-culturally. Laughter and the possibility of being hurt by it are classified differently and carry different connotations. Presumably, this leads to culture-specific forms of habituation: what the Dutch consider relatively good-natured banter may seem shockingly malicious mockery to Americans. Consequently, the Dutch may be more 'hardened' and hence less hurt or embarrassed by enjoyment of people's misfortunes than the Americans.

A testable hypothesis one could derive from this is that schadenfreude in the Netherlands is less feared, less problematic and more freely expressed than in the USA. Cultural definitions of emotions affect their regulation. When something is considered more inappropriate, more attempts will be made to suppress it. Hence, a second hypothesis would be that in the USA, we expect sharper demarcations of specific situations or rituals where 'forbidden emotions', such as enjoyment of and laughter at other's misfortunes, may be expressed.

[1] Recently, the same researchers have explored katagelasticism – the enjoyment of laughing at others – which comes close to the notion of schadenfreude. However, so far there is no comparative research on this particular topic (Proyer and Ruch, 2010).

However, both American and Dutch views on schadenfreude are rooted in the more general late-modern humour regime, which stipulates that, even under the pretext of 'just a joke' or someone 'has deserved it', deriving pleasure from another's misfortune is dubious. However, all such cultural shapings and regulations do not preclude people from sometimes enjoying the sufferings of others. There are many reasons why the suffering of others would be pleasing – some of them, in fact, quite moral. Yet, schadenfreude has become an ambiguous pleasure, and even more so in some places than in others: it has to be restricted, relegated to specific domains and cannot be expressed too openly.

Schadenfreude shapes social life

Schadenfreude and social solidarity

Society not only shapes emotions – emotions also shape social life. Sociologists of emotions have argued that emotions *do* things to the world: they mould identities and selves, build solidarity and hierarchy, bound and unite groups – both in small-scale interactions and larger societal contexts. To produce large-scale emotional effects, collective rituals are especially important: they unite large groups of people in orchestrated emotions.

Here, I explore how schadenfreude shapes social life, using Collins' work on the shaping of large-scale social patterns through 'interaction ritual chains' (Collins, 2004). In this groundbreaking work, Collins argues that the sharing of 'emotional energy' in face-to-face interactions forms the basis of macro-social structures. People seek to repeat successful encounters, characterized by successful emotional exchange and growing solidarity, while avoiding situations generating less 'emotional energy'. This leads to increasingly fixed social patterns, rituals and institutions, characterized by the sharing of emotions. Because of this repeated nature of such interactions, Collins, following Goffman, calls them 'rituals'. The media play an increasingly important role in such collective rousing and experiencing of emotions (Alexander, 2006).

In an interesting case study of emotional interaction, Wang and Roberts (2006) explore Chinese schadenfreude in response to the attacks of September 11, 2001. In an analysis of online discussions among students, they found unadulterated expressions of glee and amusement, along with admiration for the perpetrators. Americans were presented as bullies and the attacks as deserved – the standard conditions for schadenfreude. Interestingly, the authors analyse the collective 'discursive construction' of this emotion. For them, the shared enjoyment reflects existing feelings, but specifically entails the collective *creation* of these emotions. The sharing of schadenfreude reinforces and even *produces* affect: pride, group solidarity and identity, as well as processes of identification and disidentification.

Tellingly, in this case such processes were both provoked by a mediated event and discussed and constructed via online interactions. The co-construction of schadenfreude and the resulting social processes happened via virtual interaction. Although the authors do not note this, this distancing likely made it easier to express and experience schadenfreude. Moreover, while the article notes that in China, too, the expression of schadenfreude is considered taboo, the participants in the discussion clearly seek to share their feelings – underlining Collins' point about the need to share emotions to build lasting social patterns.

The Chinese schadenfreude after 9/11, as well as better-known instances of Muslim and Arab joy, are paradigmatic cases of 'righteous' schadenfreude: the downfall of a powerful and arrogant actor, easily constructed as bully or enemy, which can be collectively celebrated. The sharing of such enjoyment is a time-tested way to produce group solidarity and a sense of superiority, both in small groups and in larger societies. Many collective rituals and celebrations, for instance, in the context of war or the production of nationalist sentiments, follow this logic (Alexander, 2006; Collins, 2004). In our pacified day and age, such emotions, while not considered tasteful, are not particularly tabooed. In 1982, the British tabloid *The Sun* produced the famously schadenfroh headline 'Gotcha!' after the bombing of an Argentine warship.[2] In 2011, cheering Americans took to the streets to celebrate the killing of Osama bin Laden.[3] In such cases, schadenfreude shapes collective (often national) pride and demarcates social boundaries.[4]

Sportive competitions follow a similar logic, often with comparable emotional expressions. Triumph in sports is often marked by glee,

[2] See www.bl.uk/onlinegallery/features/frontpage/gotcha.html.

[3] See also Schurtz et al., Chapter 11 in this volume. This provokes an interesting ethical discussion. See www.washingtonpost.com/opinions/theres-nothing-to-cheer-about-in-bin-ladens-death/2011/05/06/AFJx47BG_story.html and http://yourlife.usatoday.com/mind-soul/spirituality/story/2011/05/Is-it-OK-to-cheer-Osama-bin-Ladens-death/46759110/1.

[4] Another form of enjoyment of misfortunes of others (sometimes self) is sick humour. While similar to schadenfreude in some respects, the main component of sick humour seems to be distancing and trivializing of the suffering rather than glee or amusement. Consequently, sick humour is not related to a specific feeling vis-à-vis the person(s) affected by the suffering. In the context of 9/11, sick humour emerged most specifically in contexts where observers were distant but sympathetic: first in other Western countries, later in the USA. Sick humour often works as a coping mechanism. In the case of modern media disasters, it also serves as a disengaging mechanism for the constant confrontation with suffering strangers and the resulting emotional ambivalence (Kuipers, 2011).

denigrating behaviour vis-à-vis the losing party and remarkably undisguised expressions of schadenfreude. While sometimes denounced as incompatible with the ethic of sportsmanship (McNamee, 2003), the joy of winning cannot really be separated from the joy of seeing another lose.

This form of competitive schadenfreude also appears unproblematic. Indeed, sportive competition has become central to the formation of collective identities: of schools and universities, of cities and – specifically – of nations. Their repetitive nature, and the careful delineation of insiders and outsiders, makes this a particularly effective social ritual.

Sport stands out from the regime of sensitivity to the misfortune of others because of its careful 'framing' (Goffman, Lenert and Branahan, 1997): a domain of its own, delineated by rules and regulations, with carefully balanced competitors. In this separate, autonomous domain, one can safely enjoy the downfall of one's 'enemy' because the enmity is not 'really' real. This is ritualized, demarcated – and increasingly mediated – schadenfreude.

The special status of sport as a 'reservation' for schadenfreude and the ensuing solidarity rituals becomes particularly clear when contrasted with other forms of competition. When schadenfreude reaches across social boundaries and is directed at relative outsiders, it may form the basis of solidarity rituals – an example would by the misfortunes of competitors in another organization. However, within social groups, schadenfreude leads to more hierarchy and exclusion that we can bear today. In work and organizations, friendships, love and families, schadenfreude is typically enjoyed, if at all, in private or in small groups, often in the 'backstage' context of gossip. Such forms of schadenfreude squarely fall into the regime described above and cannot be easily institutionalized. Consequently, they may build solidarity in small groups, but their effect in larger constellations is harder to gauge.

Schadenfreude and morality

In the contexts of strife and competition, schadenfreude generates group solidarity and produces vertical realignment. This works best, and is least problematic, when people are separated by clear opposing interests and clear social boundaries, like national boundaries or the boundaries of a soccer team. Here, disidentification comes relatively easy. Conspicuous framing, as in sports, may make facilitate distancing and thus enjoyment.

When schadenfreude manifests itself *within* a group, not only is this a breach of etiquette, it also produces a social rift. In a regime where all persons are significant others whose feelings must be respected, schadenfreude threatens social solidarity and moral order. In such situations, schadenfreude is most shameful and suppressed. However, this is also where enjoyment of other's misfortunes emerges as most directly linked with morality. In hostile and competitive situations with clear social boundaries, morality is relatively straightforward: us against them. Within social groups, it becomes us versus us. Solutions are limited: hide the schadenfreude. Or redraw social boundaries, temporarily or permanently: either the *schadenfroh* or their 'victim' must be reformed or expelled.

This redrawing of social boundaries is the most significant way in which schadenfreude affects the moral order. When schadenfreude is experienced as legitimate, this implies a moral denunciation of the suffering other: they deserve what they get. Sympathy is withheld. When this happens within a social group, this is a form of exclusion tantamount to social punishment. This was sharply observed by Erving Goffman, pioneer of micro-sociology and the main inspiration for Collins' theory on interaction rituals. For Goffman, social interaction was centrally concerned with the upkeep of the social and moral order (Goffman, 1963; Goffman, Lenert and Branahan, 1997).

Goffman observes how schadenfreude occurs when another's self is compromised – their social identity crumbles. Especially when this 'social death' is considered legitimate, various social mechanisms and rituals are employed to hamper the victim's restoration of self:

> there are barbarous ceremonies in our society, such as criminal trials and the drumming-out ritual employed in court-martial procedures, that are expressly designed to prevent the mark from saving his face. And even those cases where the cooler makes an effort to make things easier for the person he is getting rid of, we often find that there are bystanders who have no such scruples. Onlookers who are close enough to observe the blow-off but who are not obliged to assist in the dirty work often enjoy the scene, taking pleasure in the discomfiture of the cooler and in the destruction of the mark. What is trouble for some is Schadenfreude for others. (Goffman, Lenert and Branahan, 1997, p. 18)

In this passage, schadenfreude emerges as morally motivated: it delineates and isolates those who fall outside of the social order, simultaneously uniting those within the order in their collective enjoyment. Loss of face may lead to schadenfreude and to social rituals of retaliation and exclusion. This fosters prevention of rehabilitation: a permanent redrawing of boundaries. Most significantly, for Goffman, moral schadenfreude is particularly associated with *onlookers* – it is an outsider's enjoyment. Hence, like the schadenfreude of Chinese students in response to 9/11, it involves 'distancing'.

For Goffman, as for Collins, the emotional component of social processes is crucial: this is what endows the rituals and symbols of the moral order with special significance. In this reasoning, shared enjoyment, as expressed through laughter, for instance, is central to the shaping of social bonds and symbols. Moral pleasure, then, is not a byproduct of moral judgment, but is at the heart of it. In this perspective, one can never fully remove schadenfreude from morality or justice. Even when relegated to the backstage of social life – gossip, fleeting jokes or snide remarks – this is where morality is made and social boundaries are drawn.

Etiquette and morality today appear to suggest that the *schadenfroh* be expelled rather than their targets: schadenfreude itself has become a moral mis-step in most contexts. However, as with competitive schadenfreude, 'reservations' have been created to enjoy this forbidden fruit. Comedy is one field where schadenfreude, often in highly moral forms (cf. Friedman and Kuipers, 2013), can be safely exploited – more openly in some countries than in others. Moreover, the past decades have witnessed the emergence of entertainment genres strongly based on schadenfreude.

Candid camera and blooper TV are the oldest forms of televised schadenfreude (Clissold, 2004). Several strategies neutralize the potential offensiveness of this genre. One solution is 'distancing': framing the trick played on unwitting victims as funny and 'unreal' by adding humorous sound or visual effects, or by showing the victim laughing heartily afterwards. But most strategies are moral: targetting the rich and famous (hence tapping into envy); presenting people with temptations and punishing them only when they cave in; or stressing their stupidity and hence their deservingness. Television adds another layer of distance and thus schadenfreude becomes a legitimate moral pleasure (cf. Kuipers, 2006).

In contrast with candid camera and blooper TV, reality TV rarely uses comedy or other distancing measures. Instead, this new genre draws on moral framings to make other's misfortunes enjoyable. Most reality TV formats revolve around misfortunes and embarrassments of others: starving on desert islands, bored to death locked up in a house filled with cameras, competing for the attentions of a millionaire, humiliated in front of ruthless juries, forced to watch one's lover cheat. These shows are often spectacularly moral in tone: the typical voting system of reality shows privileges the nice and the agreeable, punishing the selfish and the unpleasant. Moreover, this competitive element makes pointless suffering into a meaningful 'sportive' test of self. The voluntary character of participation, framed easily as stupid, greedy or vain by onlookers, makes all suffering deserved. Finally, montage, voiceover and other constructions of narrative are generally deeply moralistic in tone (Krijnen and Tan, 2009).

Reality shows are Goffman's 'barbarous ceremonies' in twenty-first-century form: they reinforce moral boundaries, punish the wrongdoers and generate a plethora of moral and immoral pleasures – all at a safe, televised distance. While the moral functions of schadenfreude in everyday life have become so suppressed as to be almost inaccessible to researchers, mediated forms take over. Reality TV provides the onlooker's delights of schadenfreude, with the moral benefits but without the moral risks.

Interestingly, while reality show *formats* travel very well, the shows themselves are generally remade for each national audience, even when a version in the national language is available (e.g., the UK and the USA, and the Netherlands and Belgium have separate versions of most reality shows). In my view, this is not related to the particularities of language and culture, but instead with the in-group identifications needed for moral enjoyment. In contrast with competitive schadenfreude, moral schadenfreude requires belonging. Moral schadenfreude is an in-group delight.

Conclusion: schadenfreude as moral emotion

This chapter explored the emotion of schadenfreude from a sociological perspective. It asked, first, how social life shapes schadenfreude and, second, how schadenfreude shapes social life. Drawing on insights from the sociology of emotions and comparing research findings and results from various disciplines, sources, cultures and periods, I have tried to chart how schadenfreude functions in society.

Although there were frustratingly few research findings and theories to draw upon, this has resulted in a number of tentative conclusions and hypotheses regarding the role of schadenfreude in different modern societies. This may lead to interesting new avenues for sociological (and psychological) research. What cross-cultural difference can we discern in the enjoyment, interpretation and regulation of schadenfreude? Do they result in varying degrees of 'framing' of ritualized enjoyment of other people's misfortunes? How, when and why do people or societies attempt to remove schadenfreude from moral rituals? What strategies do people use to neutralize schadenfreude, for instance, in media entertainment? Is the mediatized 'moral' schadenfreude of reality TV harder to export than mediated 'competitive' schadenfreude, for instance, in sports, because of their different relation with in-group identifications? In effect, this chapter may have raised more questions than it has answered.

From this analysis, schadenfreude emerged as a paradoxical emotion. It is widely considered immoral: it breaches decorum, breaks up groups and creates social rifts. At the same time, it is a deeply moral emotion, deeply interwoven into the social and moral order. This morality is rooted in group boundaries and the withholding of identification and sympathy to outsiders and undeserving. Admittedly, this is not highest-level Kohlberg morality, but moral it is.

This paradox raises the question, then, why schadenfreude has become so suppressed and contested. Both the historical analysis and the comparison of the USA and the Netherlands showed that enjoyment of the misfortune of others is not always, everywhere and necessarily considered wrong. Even today, in the context of war, sports and media entertainment, schadenfreude can be made attractive and morally palatable.

In my view, the moral danger of schadenfreude is caused by two things. One is probably universal: its capacity to undermine social solidarity. As mentioned above, schadenfreude entails social exclusion. This is alright when someone is an out-group member, but can be quite disruptive within a group. Today's mores even seem to suggest that the *schadenfroh* rather than their victim should be punished.

The other reason why schadenfreude is considered immoral is historical and has to do with the definition of 'the other' whose misfortunes are enjoyed. As the historical overview shows, this definition of 'other' has expanded immensely in the past centuries, coming to include more or less everyone. The humanistic sentiment underlying this emotional regime requires considerable pedagogical investment, as well as regular reminders. The effect of this is that virtually everyone is now a 'significant other' to be respected and not laughed at – including strangers, cats and quite a few people whom we may feel deserve some ridicule. As a result, schadenfreude has now become a fundamentally ambiguous emotion. Even when it feels morally right – and it regularly does – it always feels morally reprehensible too.

References

Alexander, J. C. (2006). *The Civil Sphere*. New York: Oxford University Press.

Apte, M. L. (1985). *Humor and Laughter: An Anthropological Approach*. Ithaca, NY: Cornell University Press.

Clissold, B. (2004). Candid Camera and the origins of reality TV: contextualising a historical precedent. In S. Holmes and D. Jermyn (eds.). *Understanding Reality Relevision*. London: Routledge, pp. 33–53.

Collins, R. (2004). *Interaction Ritual Chains*. Princeton University Press.

Darnton, R. (1984). *The Great Cat Massacre and Other Episodes in French History*. New York: Basic Books.

Durkheim, E. (1995 [1912]). *The Elementary Forms of the Religious Life* (translated by K. E. Fields). New York: Free Press.

Elias, N. (2012 [1939]). *On the Process of Civilisation* (translated by E. Jephcott). Collected works of Norbert Elias, Vol. 3. University College Dublin Press.

Ferguson, M. and Ford, T. (2008). Disparagement humor: a theoretical and empirical review of psychoanalytic, superiority, and social identity theories. *HUMOR* 21: 283–312.

Foucault, M. (1977). *Discipline and Punish. The Birth of the Prison*. New York: Random House.

Friedman, S. and Kuipers, G. (2013). The divisive power of humour: comedy, taste and symbolic boundaries. *Cultural Sociology* 7(2): 179–95.

Goffman, E. (1963). *Stigma: Notes on the Management of Spoilt Identity*. New York: Prentice Hall.

(1967). *Interaction Ritual: Essay in Face-to-Face Behavior*. New York: Anchor Books.

Goffman, E., Lemert, C. and Branahan, A. (1997) (eds.). *The Goffman Reader*. London: Wiley-Blackwell.

Hochschild, A. (1979). Emotion work, feeling rules and social structure. *American Journal of Sociology* 85: 551–75.

Ignatow, G. (2009). Why the sociology of morality needs Bourdieu's habitus. *Sociological Inquiry* 79: 98–114.

Krijnen, T. and Tan, E. (2009). Reality TV as a moral laboratory: a dramaturgical analysis of The Golden Cage. *Communications* 34: 449–72.

Kuipers, G. (2011). 'Where was King Kong when we needed him?' Public discourse, digital disaster jokes, and the functions of laughter after 9/11. In T. Gournelos and V. Greene (eds.), *A Decade of Dark Humor: How Comedy, Irony and Satire Shaped Post-9/11 America*. Jackson, MS: University Press of Mississippi, pp. 20–46.

(2006). *Good Humor, Bad Taste: A Sociology of the Joke*. Berlin: Mouton de Gruyter.

Leach, C. W. and Spears, R. (2008). 'A vengefulness of the impotent': the pain of in-group inferiority and schadenfreude toward successful out-groups. *Journal of Personality and Social Psychology* 95: 1383–96.

Lewis, P. (2006). *Cracking Up: American Humor in a Time of Conflict*. University of Chicago Press.

McNamee, M. (2003). *Schadenfreude* in sport: envy, justice, and self-esteem. *Journal of the Philosophy of Sport* 30: 1–16.

Proyer, R. and Ruch, W. (2010). Dispositions towards ridicule and being laughed at: current research on gelotophobia, gelotophilia, and katagelasticism. *Psychological Test and Assessment Monitoring* 52: 49–59.

Proyer, R. et al. (2009). Breaking ground in cross-cultural research on the fear of being laughed at (gelotophobia): a multinational study involving 73 countries. *HUMOR* 22: 253–79.

Smith, R. H., Powell, C. A. J., Combs, D. J. Y. and Schurtz, D. R. (2009). Exploring the when and why of schadenfreude. *Social and Personality Psychology Compass* 3: 530–46.

Spierenburg, P. (1984). *The Spectacle of Suffering: Executions and the Evolution of Repression: From a Preindustrial Metropolis to the European Experience*. Cambridge University Press.

Stets, J. and Turner, J. (2007) (eds.). *Handbook of the Sociology of Emotions*. New York: Springer.

Turner, J. (2007). Moral emotions. In J. Stets and J. Turner (eds.), *Handbook of the Sociology of Emotions*. New York: Springer, pp. 544–66.

Turner, J. and Stets, J. (2005). *The Sociology of Emotions*. Cambridge University Press.

Vandello, J., Goldschmied, N. and Richards, D. (2007) The appeal of the underdog. *Personality and Social Psychology Bulletin* 33: 1603–16.

Van Dijk, W. W., Ouwerkerk, J. W. and Goslinga, S. (2009). The impact of deservingness on schadenfreude and sympathy: further evidence. *Journal of Social Psychology* 149: 290–2.

Van Dijk, W. W., Ouwerkerk, J. W., Goslinga, S., Nieweg, M. and Gallucci, M. (2006). When people fall from grace: reconsidering the role of envy in schadenfreude. *Emotion* 6: 156–60.

Wang, Y. and Roberts, C. W. (2006). Schadenfreude: a case study of emotion as situated discursive display. *Comparative Sociology* 5: 45–63.

Wouters, C. (2007). *Informalization. Manners and Emotions since 1890*. London: Sage.

Yzerbyt, V. and Dumoulin, S. (2010). Intergroup relations. In S. T. Fiske, D. T. Gilbert and G. Lindzey (eds.), *Handbook of Social Psychology*, Vol. II. Hoboken, NJ: John Wiley & Sons, pp. 1024–83.

18 Tracing down schadenfreude in spontaneous interaction: evidence from corpus linguistics

Kurt Feyaerts and Bert Oben

Introduction

The concept of schadenfreude has a long and impressive history of negative characterizations. Schopenhauer bluntly categorized it as "the worst emotion of which humans are capable" (quoted in Smith et al., 2009, p. 543) and about a century later, in his book *The Psychology of Interpersonal Relations* (1958), the famous person perception psychologist Fritz Heider estimated schadenfreude to be harmful to social relations (quoted in Van Dijk, Goslinga, and Ouwerkerk, 2008, p. 631; see also Leach et al., 2003).

Even in modern science, where the 1990s witnessed a renewed and empirically founded interest in the role of schadenfreude among psychologists, sociologists, and scholars in (business) communication, the concept of schadenfreude still suffers its negative reputation. Nowadays, the concept of schadenfreude is commonly described as a negative emotion, which is "socially undesirable" (Smith et al., 2009, p. 530) as this "malicious joy" (Van Dijk, Ouwerkerk, and Goslinga, 2009) derives pleasure from someone else's misfortune or suffering (see also Feather and Nairn, 2005; Hickman and Ward, 2007, among others).

In line with these characterizations as a socially marked and non-desirable emotion, current studies about schadenfreude mainly focus on identifying the conditions that seem favorable for its activation (see, among others, Van Dijk, Goslinga, and Ouwerkerk, 2008). In their recent overview of the empirical studies of schadenfreude, Smith et al. (2009) do not refer to any study in which the concept receives any other meaning(s) than the negative ones already mentioned. In the present volume, however, some contributions with different scientific backgrounds provide a more differentiated view on this phenomenon. Van Dijk and Ouwerkerk (Chapter 9 in this volume) discuss schadenfreude in terms of a positive evaluation of the self, whereas Kuipers (Chapter 17 in this volume) refers to the ways in which schadenfreude shapes our social life.

Despite these inspiring insights, it seems that in the current scientific literature the global conceptual structure of schadenfreude is still a fairly straightforward and undisputed one.[1] In this contribution, we do not want to further explore the conditions that favor the occurrence of this prototypical concept of schadenfreude. Our aim, instead, is to present on empirical linguistic grounds an entirely different aspect of schadenfreude which hitherto has not been notified as such. On the basis of observations gathered from a new data corpus of spontaneous conversations among peers, we will demonstrate more specifically that the experience and expression of schadenfreude can serve a positive and socially desirable goal of strengthening existing in-group relations among peers. From our observations, we derive the more fundamental claim that schadenfreude serves multiple social purposes of both negative and positive polarity. Hence, our major theoretical claim will be that an adequate description of the meaning or functionality of schadenfreude requires a careful and empirically validated consideration of both situational and contextual circumstances, under which the experience of schadenfreude takes place.

This chapter is structured as follows. First, in the next section, we will introduce some key concepts such as "common ground" and "intersubjectivity," "layered meaning" and – related to irony – "mental spaces," which play a central role in current socio-cognitive paradigms of linguistic analysis and which are highly relevant for our present purposes. Next, we present the major characteristics of the Corinth-datacorpus, which served as the empirical basis for our observations. Subsequently, we investigate to what extent and under what conditions the concept of schadenfreude is expressed in the Corinth-data. We will first briefly touch upon the methodological issue of quantitative observations for sequences of schadenfreude in our corpus. In this section, we will analyze schadenfreude in different contexts. From there, we will derive our conclusions about the semantic and pragmatic features of the concept of schadenfreude for which we then identify interesting topics for further (linguistic) research.

Aspects of a socio-cognitive model of meaning

In this chapter, we adopt a socio-cognitive model of linguistic analysis, according to which the essence of meaning, as opposed to the claims of traditional cognitive accounts of meaning, does not reside in the active

[1] Kuipers (Chapter 17 in this volume), however, discusses the complex interplay between schadenfreude and social life from a sociological perspective.

cognitive involvement of a single participant (the speaker *or* the hearer) in the process of conceptualization. We claim, instead, that an adequate description of meaning also involves analyzing the constant process of meaning coordination among *interlocutors* as members of the ground[2] (see Brône, 2010; Zima and Feyaerts, 2010). With this view, we advocate the primacy of dialogue as the most basic form of language use. Speakers who engage in interaction do not produce their utterances in a social-interactional vacuum, but design them for an addressee. This is obvious in face-to-face conversation, but equally holds for less directly interactional activities where the interlocutors must be imagined, such as composing a song, writing a newspaper article, or releasing an advertisement.

Common ground and intersubjectivity

This socio-cognitive view on meaning heavily borrows from Clark's (1996) *joint action hypothesis*, according to which language use is basically and inherently an interactive process, in which interlocutors coordinate their production and interpretation. In Clark's view, it is essentially a joint activity, very much like dancing a tango. Dancers like interlocutors need to be able to react or adjust to their dance or communication partners as much as they need to be able to anticipate their partners' movements or utterances. For its impact on the semantic construction of an interaction, this process of mutual coordination among discourse participants depends on the extent to which interlocutors share a (mutual belief of) *common ground* (Clark, 1996) that is made up of individually or socially established structures of shared knowledge, experiences, beliefs, attitudes, emotions, etc.

Although this socio-cognitive view on language may seem rather uncontroversial to cognitive-functional paradigms of linguistic analysis, the social dimension of interaction is traditionally relegated to the periphery in cognitive research (Barlow and Kemmer, 2000). Only recently, a number of studies in cognitive and interactional linguistics have started to explore both the cognitive structure and the interpersonal dynamics of interactional discourse, commonly referring to it in terms of intersubjective aspects of meaning (see Langacker, 2001; Verhagen, 2005, 2008, among others).

Our account of *intersubjectivity* does not concern the interactive process of explicit meaning negotiation as it occurs among interlocutors and in

[2] As the central element of the context of speech, the *ground* consists of the speech event itself, the interlocutors (traditionally: "speaker" and "hearer" or several "speakers"), their interaction and the specific circumstances (time and place) of the utterance (Langacker, 2008, p. 259).

which different opinions about a commonly focused topic are discussed. Instead, we define it as our cognitive ability to take other people's perspective and to model the mental states of our interlocutors. This view is very much in line with – and supported by – the *theory of mind* (Givón, 2005; Whiten, 1991), which evolves around our ability to identify and differentiate the mental from the physical world and, more specifically, the ability to conceptualize thoughts, ideas, emotions, attitudes, beliefs, etc. in other people's mind (Brône, 2010, pp. 91–2). During interaction, both at the stage of interpretation and production, interlocutors imagine what they assume to be in the minds of their conversational partners and align their construal with it. Accordingly, conversation can be characterized as a process that requires constant alignment and negotiation among *intersubjective* viewpoints:

> Linguistic expressions are cues for making inferences, and understanding thus not primarily consists in decoding the precise content of the expression, but in making inferences that lead to adequate next (cognitive, conversational, behavioral) moves. (Verhagen, 2005, p. 22)

Layered meaning

With regard to the impact of these perspectival aspects of intersubjective meaning coordination on everyday language use, Clark (1996) identifies the notion of *layered meaning* as a key concept of his theory of language use as a joint activity. He points out that in many so-called *staged communicative acts* (1996, p. 368) like sarcasm, irony, lying, teasing, and others, participants do not necessarily act and communicate in line with the expectations and norms of that specific situation. He links this observation with the crucial insight that the experience of common ground does not have the status of an independent or inherent value in communication. Instead, "when [we] act on the basis of our common ground, we are in fact acting on our individual beliefs or assumptions about what is in our common ground" (1996, p. 96). Indeed, interlocutors may always come in handy and exploit or manipulate the individual status of common ground for humorous, ironic, or other communicative purposes. Clark describes the meaning in staged communicative acts in terms of different meaning layers,[3] where the primary or basic layer corresponds to the concrete situation of the communication between speaker(s) and

[3] With this distinction, Clark relates his model to the work of Russian linguist Mikhail Bakhtin, but also to relevance theory (Sperber, 1984, 2000), several discourse models (Ducrot, 1984; Roulet, 1996), and more cognitively oriented paradigms (Brône, 2008, 2010; Coulson, 2005; Dancygier and Vandelanotte, 2009).

hearer(s) (the "ground" as Langacker calls it). On top of this primary layer, interlocutors may decide to create and elaborate another, secondary layer of meaning, which can only operate relative to and is hence dependent on the primary layer of interpretation.

In their analysis of adversarial humor, Veale, Feyaerts, and Brône (2006), Brône (2008, 2010), and Brône and Oben (2013) identify prominent patterns of layered meaning through which interlocutors achieve a *trump* over their opponents by pretending and then elaborating a misunderstanding in which (parts of) the expressions used by the interlocutor before them are recycled and successfully turned against their original users, as illustrated in (1) below:

(1) (our translation) Spectator shouting at Dutch politician H. Wiegel: *Son of a bitch!*
H. Wiegel: *How nice of you to introduce yourself; my name is Hans Wiegel.*

In this construal, the second interlocutor creates a secondary layer of interpretation, involving a pretended misunderstanding, in which he activates an unanticipated alternative meaning, allowing him to achieve both verbal and social superiority over his opponent. On the basis of common ground, both speakers know (of each other) that the first speaker intended his utterance to be understood as an insult. Also on the basis of common ground, both speakers must conclude that the meaning construal in the reply of the second speaker will be generally be regarded as superior compared to the initial insult by the first speaker.

Irony

We further illustrate our point about the construction of layered meaning by having a closer look at irony, which plays an important role in our account of schadenfreude. Within linguistics, there exists a vast and vivid literature about irony involving different accounts and views, which we cannot possibly present or even summarize in the course of this contribution (for a recent and accurate overview, see Brône, 2012). Our intention, however, is to demonstrate a semantic account of irony, in the processing of which different layers of meaning are activated. Clark views irony as a (joint) pretence (Clark, 1996; Clark and Gerrig, 1984), which involves "a speaker setting up a pretence layer in discourse, in which the pretend speaker addresses the pretend hearer (who may or may not have a counterpart in the actual communicative situation)" (quoted from Brône 2012, p. 492). Compare the short exchange in (2):

(2) a) Teacher returning a bad paper to a student: *This is a brilliant piece of writing, Mr Jones!*
b1) Mr Jones: *Thank you indeed, sir!*
b2) Mr Jones: *I am sorry about that, sir.*

In returning a disastrous paper to a student, this teacher feels safe enough to decide to be ironic. He is convinced that both Mr Jones and he know perfectly well that the paper was of poor quality. So, in other words, if the teacher 'knows' that Mr Jones knows this, he may decide not to reply in the way in which this assumed common ground between speaker and hearer would expect him to reply. He decides, instead, to react in an entirely different or even opposite way,[4] and sets up a counterfactual pretence layer of praising of which the teacher expects that Mr Jones will see through.

Clark points out that these secondary layers of interpretation can only operate relative to and are hence dependent on the primary layer of interpretation, and as such these staged communicative acts represent a more indirect way of communication. Indeed, the ironic remark about Mr Jones' paper can only be interpreted as such through the perspective of the primary layer where both Mr Jones and his teacher know (of each other) that the quality of the paper is not good.

In line with Clark's view, Coulson (2005) gives an illuminating account of irony in terms of the conceptual integration of elements from two distinct *mental spaces*. One space corresponds to "the actual (communicative) situation and the corresponding verbal behaviour (the so-called *expected reaction space*)," whereas the other represents a "counterfactual space that is set up for the purpose of the ironical utterance (*counterfactual trigger space*)" (Brône, 2012, p. 493). A positive utterance like the one in (2a), which refers to a negative achievement, essentially points at a desired state of affairs (students hand in well-prepared, carefully written papers) and therefore, in this rather negative situation, it activates a counterfactual scenario. It is safe to conclude, then, that irony "essentially involves the integration of an expression from the counterfactual trigger space with contextual information from the expected reaction space" (Brône, 2012, p. 493).

As far as the hearer, Mr Jones in our example, is concerned, he may decide to play along with the teacher and elaborate the pretence by answering in an ironic way (as in 2b1), or, conversely, to ignore the

[4] We do not claim that irony should be defined in the traditional way as "saying the opposite from what is meant." For an overview, see Brône (2010) as well as Brône (2012).

pretence and remain on the primary layer of the exchange between teacher and student as in (2b2). As Brône (2012, p. 492) rightly observes, the ironist's purpose of setting up a pretence layer is to express a critical attitude toward what the pretend speaker is saying: "the speaker intends the addressee of the irony to discover the pretence and thereby see his or her attitude toward the speaker, the audience and the utterance" (Clark and Gerrig, 1984, p. 12). This semantic aspect of appealing to the addressee to reflect about the utterance as such but also, most importantly, about the social relationship between speaker and hearer will play a major role in our analysis of schadenfreude as a staged communicative act in spontaneous conversations among friends.

The Corinth-corpus

Before we turn to the empirical part of this chapter, we first give a brief characterization of the database – or "corpus" in linguistic terminology – from which all the examples of schadenfreude in this chapter have been drawn. The examples are taken from the Corinth-corpus, which stands for Corpus Interactional Humour. It was designed, built, and is still being enlarged and maintained at the Department of Linguistics at the University of Leuven (Feyaerts et al., in press). The corpus is an open corpus of spontaneous conversations among friends, relatives, fellow-students, etc. and is made up of sequences that all contain some element of humorous or creative interaction.[5] Most of the material is gathered by students of the third bachelor course "Humour and Creativity in Language" in the "Linguistics and Literature" program at KU Leuven.

For the Dutch-speaking community, Corinth represents a unique corpus in two respects. First, it fills (the Flemish part of) a methodological and empirical gap in the existing corpora of Dutch language, as it gathers and provides access to phonetic, syntactic, lexical, and discursive aspects of genuinely spontaneous conversation in Dutch. In bigger corpora, such as the CGN ("Corpus Gesproken Nederlands"), the subcorpora for "spontaneous speech" turn out to contain data which appear not to be spontaneous enough to capture staged communicative acts like irony, sarcasm, staged schadenfreude, or any other form of interactional humor. Second, Corinth is also a unique corpus because of its focus on creative and humorous patterns in interaction.

[5] Currently, the corpus only contains Flemish (Dutch) dialogues, but in the future, other languages may be added.

The Corinth-corpus contains four types of data on four different levels. Apart from the audio files of the digital recordings (a), the corpus contains the transcriptions of these recordings (b), as well as a layer with part-of-speech-tags (c), and, finally, a layer with humor-analytical annotation codes. The corpus currently contains 4.5 hours of compiled sequences from 97 recordings, which are fully annotated on each of these four dimensions.

Schadenfreude in spontaneous conversations among peers/friends

Since the aim of the present chapter is to identify and describe expressions of schadenfreude in spontaneous interaction among peers, we used the Corinth-corpus as the empirical base for our investigation. As the data in the corpus are not annotated for the concept of "schadenfreude," we searched the database for the value "teasing," expecting that interaction sequences that qualify for this type of adversarial humor provide good candidates for the additional expression of schadenfreude. Yet, since the material in the corpus consists of recordings made among friends – taken in the most general sense – we were curious about the qualitative nature of the expressions of schadenfreude, if it were to be found at all in this type of data. Our query resulted in 566 sequences of teasing, 28 cases of which (about five percent) expressed an aspect of schadenfreude. We will, however, not further elaborate on the quantitative aspect of our results since doing so would require a more thorough empirical investigation, for example, by using a larger corpus and including more annotations than just "teasing" in the initial query. We will thus restrict our focus in this chapter to the qualitative aspect of the concept schadenfreude. This means that on the basis of empirical corpus methodology, we will lay out an analysis of the major conceptual structures that make up a multifaceted picture of the concept of schadenfreude.

In our data, we came across only very few sequences, if any, in which schadenfreude was expressed in its prototypical, negative sense of taking pleasure from someone else's misfortune.[6] The example in (3) below shows an interaction in which participants laugh about the way redheads were treated in high school ("they were bullied out of school"):[7]

[6] We are well aware of the fact that both our search strategy (a query on "teasing") and the specific nature of the conversations in the Corinth-corpus do not favor the occurrence of this type of schadenfreude.

[7] We do not present the sequences in their original Dutch corpus transcription, but use an English translation instead. Capitals indicate syllables being stressed.

(3)	Sam	in your in your high eh in in your high school how many redheads were there
	John	<laughter>
	Hank	really zero
	John	two
	Martijn	well certainly one
	Group	<laughter>
	Harry	never
	Harry	zero
	Hank	in our school, they were bullied out of school
	All	<laughter>

In this sequence it is not very clear whether the expressed schadenfreude is staged or not as it is directed at a generically defined "third person" (an external target), who is obviously not present in the conversation. When we look at the broader circumstances under which this sequence takes place, it becomes clear(er) that the prominent meaning of this utterance is not negatively colored. Since one of the participants in this conversation (Sam) is a redhead himself, this remark about bullying redheads out of school is clearly meant as a provocative act of teasing directed at Sam, with probably no ground of reality in it. Most of our findings exhibit schadenfreude in a strictly deictic context, in which direct reference is made (*I, you*) to the interlocutors participating in the conversation. Although it seems interesting and necessary to further explore conceptual differences for the concept of schadenfreude along the lines of these different types of interactional contexts, we will focus our attention in the remaining part of this section on interactional contexts with explicit and direct reference to (one of) the interlocutors.

Staged schadenfreude with explicit reference among interlocutors

In the Corinth-corpus, most of the sequences with traces of schadenfreude are found in strictly deictic contexts, meaning that interlocutors explicitly address each other, as in the following examples. In sequence (4), three female students are sharing their fears for the official driving license test, which appears to be rather difficult to pass. Melanie reports about her failure ("I have hit all the posts"), which then is commented on by her friends with sarcasm and laughter:

(4)	Stacy	yeah and now you really have to do this on the street right
	Melanie	on the street you must do it yes park your car and stuff

Annabel	exciting
Melanie	and I had almost hit every post in parking the car
Annabel	well congratulations
Melanie	oops
Stacy	well done melanie <laughter>
Group	<laughter>

Similarly, in example (5) Neville reports about his misfortune in the past, namely that he fainted on important occasions. At first, Sam thinks that this had happened during Neville's job interview, which he finds quite hilarious. Neville specifies that he had once fainted during a biology class in high school, something which Hank then appears to remember, and makes him laugh:

(5)	Neville	i really did faint at that time ...
	Sam	did <laughter> you faint <laughter> on your job interview
	Hank	<laughter>
	Neville	no i fainted before that during biology class ...
	Sam	ah yes
	Hank	ah biology <laughter> as well <laughter> that's <laughter> true
	Hank	<laughter>

Unlike the sequences in (4) and (5), where the victim's misfortune is reported as part of an anecdote, the two following examples describe an interaction in which one of the addressees suffers physical misfortune as well as a subsequent reaction of schadenfreude as the interaction unfolds. In (6), members of a student club gather for their weekly meeting, which is opened by the chairman (Hank) by ritually hitting the table with a particular stone. At the beginning of the meeting, all participants are well aware that their friend AG suffers a terrible headache, and yet John decides to hit the table with the stone very hard. As a result, AG complains about the noise and all the others start laughing:

(6)	Action	<Hank knocks with a stone on the table>...
	PL	do not knock too hard because ehm
	Group	<laughter>
	Action	<John knocks hard with the stone on the table>
	FE	<laughter> ...
	AG	no really do not knock too hard because i have got such a terrible headache

	FE	what
	Hank	oh yes
	Group	<laughter>

In the exchange in (7), a reaction of schadenfreude unfolds as Neville is suddenly hit on his fingers with a small bat by Sam:

(7)	Hank	yes that is allowed
	Action	<Sam hits Neville with a small bat>
	Hank	woohoo <laughter>
	Neville	that was a nice hit
	Hank	<laughter>
	Sam	<laughter> it did not even hurt
	Neville	yes it did

Although we have identified a contextual difference between the last two examples and the two preceding them in terms of a manifest (as in [6]–[7]) versus reported misfortune (as in [4]–[5]), all four examples in this section have an important aspect of meaning in common as far as the expression of schadenfreude is concerned. What these sequences share, essentially, is the expression of schadenfreude without any negative polarity being involved. As such, these examples run counter to the outspoken and negative characterization of schadenfreude in the psychological studies mentioned in the introduction to this chapter.

It appears that in sequences (4)–(7), schadenfreude is conceptualized as a staged communicative act, in the interpretation of which two layers of meaning collide, thus rendering positive, often ironic effects of playfulness and friendly teasing. On the one hand, speakers express their misfortune they experience(d) (a failed exam, fainting, bruised fingers, a headache) on the basic level of direct communication between speakers or, in terms of mental spaces, in the "expected reaction space." The victim's interlocutors, on the other hand, do not react on the same, basic meaning layer, but open up a second, staged layer of pretence on which they express unexpected attitudes and emotions like laughter, joy, admiration, etc. Analogous to what we have described for irony, this integration of both layers within a single communicative sequence is rooted in an intersubjective process of establishing common ground among the members of these small communities of friends, housemates, etc. On that basis, this staged communicative act triggers a fundamentally positive meaning, which does not qualify as a "moral emotion" (Kuipers, Chapter 17 in this volume). What emerges in these examples, then, is a concept of schadenfreude that is essentially positive in nature as it is operated among friends to (re)confirm or even strengthen in-group schadenfreude as a "passive" emotional concept, which lacks feelings of friendship and mutual understanding and respect. This observation runs counter to the view of any active personal involvement by the agent (Ben-Ze'ev, Chapter 5 in this volume). The positive conceptualization of schadenfreude as identified in our observations does not depend on the variable of deservingness with regard to someone else's misfortune, as investigated by Feather (Chapter 3 in this volume), nor does it relate to the concept of envy (Smith, Thielke, and Powell, Chapter 6 in this volume). It appears, instead, to express or maybe even shape a genuinely positive social relationship among friends.

Staged misfortune and schadenfreude

To close off the empirical part of this contribution, we focus our attention on one last conceptual aspect that characterizes many of the schadenfreude sequences in our corpus. In the examples discussed so far, we have analyzed schadenfreude as a staged communicative act in which all participants know that everyone else in their circle knows that the schadenfreude is a pretend reaction. The concept of misfortune, however, in examples (4)–(7) is located on the basic level of direct communication among speakers. What we hear, then, are the real misfortunes of the speakers involved. Also, on the basis of existing studies that define schadenfreude in terms of "pleasure taken from the misfortune of others," one might believe that this concept is inherently grounded in real-life events and actions that count as misfortunes. Yet, it would be erroneous to assume that any such grounding link between the concept and reality would be a categorical feature of the concept of schadenfreude.

Consider the following examples taken from the Corinth-corpus, in which the experience of schadenfreude hinges on no "real" misfortune at all. Instead, group members laugh at the misfortunes they themselves construe at the expense of the victim of their teasing and fantasy. In example (8) Sarah, Annabel, and Ron discuss aspects of women's intimate hygiene, one of which concerns the use of a specific washing emulsion. In this sequence, Sarah construes a conditional counterfactual space – which is not targeting anyone specific – in which she imagines and partially expresses what might happen if one should forget to wash away the emulsion with clean water. As a reaction, all participants start laughing and hence experience and express schadenfreude about a staged, generically described misfortune. In their experience of schadenfreude, the other speakers maintain and elaborate the layer of pretend (counterfactual) meaning set up by Sarah:

(8) Sarah it helps to keep the natural balance of the vagina
Annabel there you go
Sarah the soapfree washing emulsion
Ron washing emulsion <laughter> what a word just say soapfree soap . . .
Annabel yeah
Sarah but you have to wash it out with water afterwards right because otherwise <laughter>
Group <laughter>

Similarly, in (9) Hank spills some beer on the table and then licks his hand, which leads to John's claim that he already knows who is going to suffer from diarrhea the day after. Again, one speaker moves the ongoing conversation onto a playful layer of counterfactual reasoning as he conceptualizes a staged misfortune, which is temporal-causally linked with what has happened on the basic level of direct, real interaction. As a consequence, the reaction of schadenfreude following this staged misfortune and expressed through laughter occurs on the pretence layer as well, as it further elaborates John's imagined scene of someone being sick:

(9) Hank oh crap <spills beer and licks his hand>
John I already know who is going to suffer from diarrhea tomorrow
Group <laughter>

Our last example shows that a misfortune can be staged through a metaphorical conceptualization as well. In (10) the participants are discussing the stereotype of redheads and wonder what percentage of the Belgian population are redheads. This leads Martijn and John to imagine red-colored hair as an extremely rare phenomenon, which then leads to the fantasy of keeping these "creatures" safely in a special cage. This idea quickly evolves into the conceptualization of redheads as monkeys:

(10) Sam I estimate about one [percent]
Hank one
Martijn I mean it is not like wo::w a readhead or so, right
Group <laughter>
Martijn we put him behind glass or so
Action <John imitates movements of a Monkey>
John here is a banana and act like this ow ow <imitates sound of monkey>

There is no doubt that in staged communicative acts like these, many more conceptual relationships can be identified as operating between the different layers of meaning. For our present purposes, the last three examples may suffice to demonstrate the power of conceptualization. A misfortune – and the reaction of schadenfreude with it – exists when we conceptualize it, no matter on what layer or in which mental space that may be: reality or our mutually shared imagination. Just like the previous examples, the sequences in (8)–(10) express schadenfreude in a socially constructive way through which in-group values and knowledge are being (re-)established and enriched as an important element of the group's common ground.

Conclusions

On the basis of empirical data and through the use of a corpus-linguistic research method, this contribution offers new insights into both the conceptual structure and the actual expression of schadenfreude. Although these findings may primarily raise interest among (cognitive) linguists or interactional linguists, other disciplines may benefit from them as well.

In our study, we have observed, first, that a conceptual definition of schadenfreude should not be narrowed down to the negatively stigmatized social characteristic of a malicious joy, which derives pleasure from other people's misfortune. On the basis of our data from the Corinth-corpus, we have shown that just like any other concept, schadenfreude can also be construed as a staged communicative act through which it operates as a positive expression of coherence and identification within a community. In line with this observation, second, we have clarified that the experience of schadenfreude does not require any link with "reality" whatsoever. Schadenfreude exists through the conceptualization of interlocutors in interaction, regardless of the layer(s) that are involved in this process. Speakers may even decide to construe both the concept of schadenfreude and experienced misfortune on a secondary layer of a pretended meaning.

More on a methodological level, third, we have demonstrated the crucial role of including specifics of concrete usage events in the analysis of an utterance or the characterization of a concept. Accordingly, an adequate conceptual description of schadenfreude in authentic speech must take such aspects as context, situation, setting, and genre into account. In our database, we only came across interactional contexts involving explicit reference to the interlocutors involved and characterized by staged expressions of schadenfreude.

From a linguistic point of view, this study of schadenfreude still leaves many questions unanswered, some of which directly relate to the topics raised in this contribution. To close this chapter, we give a brief overview of the most important issues which are still at hand.

In the light of our observations with the Corinth-data, it would be interesting to broaden the empirical scope and collect similar spontaneous data involving other types of communities in order to get a more accurate picture of the pragmatic circumstances under which schadenfreude is expressed. Related to the previous question, one may want to know in what contexts people feel confident enough to express their experience of schadenfreude at all. Our data show that on the solid base of a broad common ground knowledge among friends, schadenfreude is commonly expressed as a staged communicative act, which is operated as a positive strategy of social strengthening among in-group members of a community. It would be interesting to investigate along which conversational patterns schadenfreude is expressed among the members of other communities. Most challenging, especially, seems the question whether we can collect authentic conversational data in which the negatively profiled concept of schadenfreude is expressed. This does not seem obvious since non-staged schadenfreude is severely sanctioned in society, where it is categorized as a negatively marked and hence socially undesirable verbal behavior. From this observation we derive the hypothesis that among friends, staged schadenfreude is produced and processed so easily because on the background of these social and moral norms and expectations, the mere formal expression of schadenfreude functions by itself as some sort of *marker* for the immediate interpretation of schadenfreude as a staged communicative act.

It is safe to say that from a linguistic point of view, the concept of schadenfreude appears in many different shapes and values, most of which still await first or further investigation. This observation relates to the innovative sociological view on schadenfreude as adopted by Kuipers (Chapter 17 in this volume). Kuipers also points to the need of a more differentiated, systematic analysis of this complex phenomenon, in which attention should be paid, among other issues, to a clarification of the link between schadenfreude and humor. Through the present analysis of empirical conversational data, we have offered a differentiated view on the concept of schadenfreude, and we hope to have demonstrated that any adequate description of this concept – regardless from which discipline – requires a careful consideration of all the dimensions that make up a concept's concrete usage event.

References

Barlow, M. and Kemmer, S. (2000). *Usage-Based Models of Language*. Stanford, CA: CSLI Publications.

Brône, G. (2008). Hyper- and misunderstanding in interactional humor. *Journal of Pragmatics* 12: 2027–61.

(2010). *Bedeutungskonstitution in verbalem Humor: ein kognitivlinguistischer und diskurssemantischer Ansatz*. Frankfurt am Main: Lang.

(2012). Humour and irony in cognitive pragmatics. In H. J. Schmid (ed.), *Cognitive Pragmatics*. Berlin: Mouton de Gruyter, pp. 463–504.

Brône, G. and Oben, B. (2013). Resonating humour: a corpus-based approach to creative parallelism in discourse. In T. Veale, K. Feyaerts, and C. Forceville (eds.), *Creativity and the Agile Mind: A Multidisciplinary Approach to a Multifaceted Phenomenon*. Berlin: Mouton de Gruyter, pp. 181–204.

Clark, H. (1996). *Using Language*. Cambridge University Press.

Clark, H. and Gerrig, R. (1984). On the pretense theory of irony. *Journal of Experimental Psychology: General* 113: 121–6.

Coulson, S. (2005). Sarcasm and the space structuring model. In S. Coulson and B. Lewandowska-Tomaszczyk (eds.), *The Literal and the Nonliteral in Language and Thought*. Berlin: Peter Lang, pp. 129–44.

Dancygier, B. and Vandelanotte, L. (2009). Judging distances: mental spaces, distance and viewpoint in literary discourse. In G. Brône and J. Vandaele (eds.), *Cognitive Poetics. Goals, Gains and Gaps*. Berlin: Mouton de Gruyter, pp. 319–70.

Ducrot, O. (1984). *Le dire et le dit*. Paris: Editions de minuit.

Feather, N. T. and Nairn, K. (2005). Resentment, envy, schadenfreude, and sympathy: effects of own and other's deserved or undeserved status. *Australian Journal of Psychology* 57: 87–102.

Feyaerts, K., Oben, B., Brône, G., and Speelman, D. (in press). Corinth. The corpus interactional humour. In Leuven Working Papers in Linguistics. KU Leuven.

Givón, T. (2005). *Context as Other Minds. The Pragmatics of Sociality, Cognition and Communication*. Amsterdam/Philadelphia: John Benjamins.

Heider, F. (1958). *The Psychology of Interpersonal Relations*. New York: John Wiley.

Hickman, T. and Ward, J. (2007). The dark side of brand community: inter-group stereotyping, trash talk, and schadenfreude. *Advances in Consumer Research* 34: 314–19.

Langacker, R. W. (2001). Discourse in cognitive grammar. *Cognitive Linguistics* 12: 143–88.

(2008). *Cognitive Grammar. A Basic Introduction*. Oxford University Press.

Leach, C. W., Spears, R., Branscombe, N. R., and Doosje, B. (2003). Malicious pleasure: schadenfreude at the suffering of another group. *Journal of Personality and Social Psychology* 84: 932–43.

Roulet, E. (1996). Polyphony. In J. Verschueren, J.-O. Östman, J. Blommaert, and C. Bulcaen (eds.), *Handbook of Pragmatics*. Amsterdam/Philadelphia: John Benjamins, pp. 1–18.

Smith, R. H., Powell, C. A. J., Combs, D. J. Y., and Schurtz, D. R. (2009). Exploring the when and why of schadenfreude. *Social and Personality Psychology Compass* 3: 530–46.

Sperber, D. (1984) Verbal irony: pretense or echoic mention. *Journal of Experimental Psychology: General* 113: 130–6.

(2000). *Metarepresentations. A Multidisciplinary Perspective*. Oxford University Press.

Van Dijk, W. W., Goslinga, S., and Ouwerkerk, J. W. (2008). Responsibility, schadenfreude, and sympathy: further evidence. *Journal of Social Psychology* 148: 631–6.

Van Dijk, W. W., Ouwerkerk, J. W., and Goslinga, S. (2009). The impact of deservingness on schadenfreude and sympathy: further evidence. *Journal of Social Psychology* 149: 290–2.

Veale, T., Feyaerts, K., and Brône, G. (2006). The cognitive mechanisms of adversarial humor. *Humor: The International Journal of Humor Research* 19: 305–38.

Verhagen, A. (2005). *Constructions of Intersubjectivity: Discourse, Syntax and Cognition*. Oxford University Press.

(2008). Intersubjectivity and the architecture of the language system. In J. Zlatev, T. P. Racine, C. Sinha, and E. Itkonen (eds.), *The shared Mind: Perspectives on Intersubjectivity*. Amsterdam: John Benjamins, pp. 307–31.

Whiten, A. (1991). *Natural Theories of Mind: Evolution, Development and Simulation of Everyday Mindreading*. Oxford: Blackwell.

Zima, E. and Feyaerts, K. (2010). *Heckles in Austrian parliamentary debates. Subjectivity and intersubjectivity in interaction*. T2PP Workshop (From Text to Political Positions), April 9–10, 2010, Amsterdam, www2.let.vu.nl/oz/cltl/t2pp/docs/ws2010/papers/P7-Zima.

19 "Smile not, however, I venture to repeat": schadenfreude in nineteenth-century American literature

Diederik Oostdijk

The impulse to derive pleasure from the misfortune of others is universally acknowledged by literary authors. Aristotle already discerned it in Greek drama, and writers have continued to explore forms of schadenfreude in Western literature ever since. Social scientists regularly use examples from literary texts to illustrate what schadenfreude is, as John Portmann does in *When Bad Things Happen to Other People* (2000), and literary historians occasionally mention the term when analyzing fictional characters and describing possible responses of readers. Yet so far schadenfreude has largely been ignored or neglected by literary historians and literary theoreticians. There are various reasons that may explain this oversight. The unfamiliarity of the word and concept to Anglo-American audiences and the dominance of those cultures in academia may have contributed to its lack of scholarly attention. Yet this is also the case for the social sciences where schadenfreude has caught on much more. It is likely that the disregard of schadenfreude in literary studies is related to ambivalent reactions to the study of emotions within literary studies.

Literary criticism and emotion

If there is one golden rule of literary scholarship that is imprinted on the minds of all students of literature, it is not to develop a personal and emotional attachment to literary characters and literary works. This collective antipathy against focusing on emotions evoked by literature is a relic from the New Criticism with its "strong antipsychological bent," as Blakey Vermeule has argued (2010, p. x). "Most of our criticism in literature and the arts," wrote René Wellek in 1941, "is still purely emotive: it judges works of art in terms of their emotional effect" (quoted in Wimsatt and Beardsley, 1954, p. 51). Other New Critics concurred. W. K. Wimsatt and Monroe Beardsley called evaluating a literary work by describing the emotions it aroused in its readers "The Affective Fallacy" (1954, p. 21). The critic engaged in that kind of analysis confused the literary work "and its *results* (what it *is* and what it *does*)" (1954, p. 21, emphasis in original). The fact that a literary work induces in readers "vivid images, intense feelings, or heightened consciousness, is neither anything which can be refuted nor anything which it is possible for the objective critic to take into account" (1954, p. 32). This verdict and that of like-minded New Critics put the lid on emotional approaches to literature for decades to come.

From the 1970s onwards, the discussion about emotions aroused by literature was no longer a taboo, and the issue generally divided literary scholars. Was it even possible to study the emotional reactions of readers? It appears that literary critics were initially inclined to think that emotions evoked by literature were so personal, irrational, inconsistent, and incoherent that it was impossible to study them systematically. A number of critics, for instance Bijoy H. Boruah (1988), argued that since literature represents what the reader knows to be fictional, the feelings that are aroused by it cannot be considered to be real feelings. Yet articles and books gradually started to appear that investigated the influence of literature on the reader's emotions more precisely, detailing which reactions could be measured and which not. Alex Neill (1993), for example, suggested that readers can feel real empathy and pity for characters, but that once they analyze them on the level of the plot, readers lose this emotional attachment.

Yet insights from other (scientific) discourses also impinged on literary scholarship, making the study of emotions more popular. Critical theorists, such as Giles Deleuze and Félix Guattari (1994), adopted the concept of affect from psychology, which seriously impacted a generation of more theoretically inclined scholars. Willie Van Peer and Henk Pander Maat (1996) are representative for scholars who investigated empirically, for instance, how point of view may impact readers' emotions. Does a first-person narrative give the reader a more direct sense of identification to a character than a third-person narrative? Articles and books on emotions and literature were gradually becoming more commonplace, and it is not far-fetched to suggest that literary scholarship is going through an emotional turn. There are, however, so many unsolved problems and unverified speculations about emotions and literature that we are really at the beginning of understanding this field.

Suzanne Keen's (2007) study on *Empathy and the Novel* is a good example of where literary scholarship on emotions in situated at this moment. She is well informed about neurological and psychological experiments, but ready to admit that there are many clichés about fiction and emotions that are accepted without investigating them. Keen has suggested that more empirical research needs to be done to understand an ostensibly simple concept such as character identification (2007, p. 93). Among teachers of literature and the general public, there is a tacit understanding that reading literature teaches readers to be empathetic and subsequently to become better citizens. This may be the reason why empathy is the most popular of all the emotions out there. Keen argues that evoking the reader's empathy is a strategy of many contemporary – especially female – novelists, and that readers often react accordingly by being more empathetic than they would otherwise be. Novels thus act as social scripts, and readers know how they should behave when confronted with the emotions represented what is socially accepted behavior. Other emotions are less prominently studied, least of all schadenfreude it seems. Yet since schadenfreude is intrinsically connected to the concept of empathy, it should be possible to study how it features in literary texts and whether readers experience it when reading.

Schadenfreude and nineteenth-century American literature

This chapter is an exploratory attempt to suggest a method for studying schadenfreude in some classic, nineteenth-century American texts. What are possible ways to understand or discuss the subject of schadenfreude in literature? How can we isolate it in literary texts? Is there a method that can be used productively to study the effect of schadenfreude on readers? When compared to more recent texts, the nineteenth century seems to have produced more texts that mostly indirectly comment on what schadenfreude is. This may be due to the fact that nineteenth-century American writers seem to have felt the need to educate their readers morally, which included emotional edification. Following Giselinde Kuipers' argument (Chapter 17 in this volume) that emotions are shaped by society and vice versa, we could say that the nineteenth-century American novel was a medium through which emotions could be shaped and socially regulated.

Ralph Waldo Emerson, Herman Melville, Mark Twain, Walt Whitman, and others were aware of and commented on schadenfreude in their work. They all implicitly accepted the notion that reading literature evokes readers' empathy for imaginary, make-belief people, thereby educating their readers to be more altruistic. The methods of reflecting on schadenfreude differ in these authors' works, however. Whitman appeals directly to his reader's sense of compassion in "Song of Myself" and other parts of *Leaves of Grass* (see Whitman, 1982). Take, for instance, this passage from section 15 of "Song of Myself":

The opium-eater reclines with rigid head and just-open'd lips,
The prostitute draggles her shawl, her bonnet bobs on her
tipsy and
pimpled neck,
The crowd laugh at her blackguard oaths, the men jeer
and wink to
each other,
(Miserable! I do not laugh at your oaths nor jeer you;)
The President holding a cabinet council is surrounded by
the great
Secretaries . . . (1982, p. 41)

Following his democratic principles, Whitman treats an "opium-eater" and a "prostitute" on the same level as the "President," also linguistically through the alliteration of the letter "p." Parenthetically, he indicates that he does not take part in the urge to feel superior or to ridicule anybody for their low status in society.

Such instances in poetry are rare, however, and the novel seems a more apt form to investigate schadenfreude in literature. Nineteenth-century novelists also differ in the way in which they introduce schadenfreude. Twain (1884/1999) highlights the cruelty of the mob in *The Adventures of Huckleberry Finn*, but tells his narrative from young Huck's perspective; thereby Twain refrains himself from commenting directly. When the Duke and the King who have wronged Huck and Jim are literally tarred and feathered by an equally cheated mob, Twain's main character does not feel an impulse to mock or laugh at them:

We see we was too late – couldn't do no good. We asked some stragglers about it, and they said everybody went to the show looking very innocent; and laid low and kept dark till the poor old king was in the middle of his cavortings on the stage; then somebody give a signal, and the house rose up and went for them. So we poked along back home, and I warn't feeling so brash as I was before, but kind of ornery, and humble, and to blame, somehow – though *I* hadn't done nothing. But that's always the way; it don't make no difference whether you do right or wrong, a person's conscience ain't got no sense, and just goes for him *anyway*. If I had a yaller dog that didn't know no more than a person's conscience does I would pison him. It takes up more room than all the rest of a person's insides, and yet ain't no good, nohow. (1884/1999, p. 209)

What is particularly striking about Huck's vernacular musings is his confusion about how he feels or ought to feel. Before the Duke and the King were being punished, he felt revengeful which he describes here as feeling "brash." Now that they have been humiliated, he feels pity ("poor old king"), irritation ("ornery"), and guilt ("to blame"). Trying to account for these conflicted emotions, Huck concludes that a person's conscience "ain't got no sense." Readers will not all react similarly to these passages, but they do provide the guidelines about appropriate social behavior. The intelligent reader should be able to get the message in terms of which emotions are socially acceptable and which are not. Conversely, Whitman's speaker sets a moral and egalitarian example for the reader in one line: "(Miserable! I do not laugh at your oaths nor jeer you;)." It follows that readers will follow this piece of advice and realize that it is morally better not to laugh at people who are less fortunate than others as all have a specific role to play that is valuable and honorable. However, both these authors are socially regulating their readers' emotions, as Giselinde Kuipers explains (Chapter 17 in this volume), even though they do not entirely spell out these rules for the reader. It is unclear, for instance, whether the adjective plus exclamation mark "Miserable!" refers to the unhappy state of the prostitute or to the behavior of the people taunting her, so it remains ambiguous how we ought to interpret this text.

The same can be said about Herman Melville's novella *Billy Budd, Sailor* (1924/1985) to which Richard Smith, Stephen Thielke, and Caitlin Powell refer (Chapter 6 in this volume). There is a clear example of schadenfreude when shipmates start laughing when Claggart mentions "'Handsomely done, my lad! And handsome is as handsome did it, too!" after Billy Budd spills soup (1924/1985, p. 350). Billy interprets the comment in a good-natured way, but other characters are unsure whether they see a "grimace" on Claggart's face or an "involuntary smile" (1924/1985, p. 350). Smith, Thielke, and Powell suggest that Claggart's envy is caused by "a sickly, painful malady lodged at the center of Claggart's being," but how can we know for sure that this is accurate? To complicate matters further, Melville's narrator and various critics have also suggested that a covert sexual desire may be the cause of Claggart's obsession with Billy Budd. The irresolvable ambiguity that resides in the text makes it impossible to say with any certainty what the characters' motivations are, thus also partly mystifying which emotions are supposed to come to the fore.

Like in *Billy Budd, Sailor*, the reference to schadenfreude in the passage from *The Adventures of Huckleberry Finn* is hidden in a confusing mix of emotions that Huck is experiencing after the Duke and the King have been shamed after their fraudulent behavior. Yet even though young Huck may not be able to understand his own emotions, the reader might be able to make sense of them. Huck's initial feeling of revenge after being wronged makes way for a sense of justification that the Duke and the King are being punished. When he subsequently finds out that they are being humiliated, he feels offended at the mob's behavior and he feels guilty about wanting them punished in the first place. Since *The Adventures of Huckleberry Finn* is an exploration of Huck's "sound heart" colliding with society's "deformed conscience," as Twain himself described his novel, the message is the same as in Whitman's poem: it is understandable but ultimately wrong to have feelings of schadenfreude. Nevertheless, these short passages from "Song of Myself," *Billy Budd, Sailor*, and *The Adventures of Huckleberry Finn* show how complex it is to isolate schadenfreude and keep it apart from other emotions that are at play in the texts.

Schadenfreude in Henry James' *The Portrait of a Lady*

In the remainder of this chapter, I will focus on Henry James's *The Portrait of a Lady* (1881/1987) as the key sample text, since James was even more interested in analyzing the psychology of human emotions than Whitman and Twain. *The Portrait of a Lady* is one of James' best and most well-known early novels, an instant critical and popular success and still widely read today. James is firmly established in the canon of American literature and is part of what F. R. Leavis once hailed as "The Great Tradition," a selection of prime nineteenth- and twentieth-century novelists who perfected the psychological and realistic novel. In more recent times, James is still studied widely from a variety of different perspectives, for instance, in terms of sexuality and gender. *The Portrait of a Lady* is also a typical text for James as it traces the rise and fall of an American girl "affronting her destiny" in Europe, as James later called the travails of his heroine, Isabel Archer. The remainder of this chapter has a three-pronged approach. First, I want to analyze the role of the narrator in evoking but also warning readers against schadenfreude. Second, I will focus on what James himself called a "reflector," a character who is part of the narrative but also reflects on the actions of the principal character. Third, I will discuss how both the narrator and reflector may impact feelings of schadenfreude in readers and how they are supposed to deal with these.

Novels can be told by any variety of narrators. The narrator can be part of the story (diegetic) as in *The Adventures of Huckleberry Finn* or an outside source telling the story (extradiegetic). *The Portrait of a Lady* is told by what is called an omniscient narrator. He, she, or it is not a character in the narrative, but a linguistic instrument invented by the author to guide readers through the novel. I will refer to the omniscient narrator as "him" or "he," although it is important to see him as a narrative tool rather than a 'real' person or character. The narrator in *The Portrait of a Lady* is "omniscient" in the sense that he can see into the future and report about what happens in the minds of the characters – something ordinary people cannot do. It is tempting to see the narrator as somehow related to the author himself, but it is best not to equate the two even if their views, opinions, and dispositions may significantly overlap. The omniscient narrator in *The Portrait of a Lady* is essentially an instrument that James has at his disposal to tell the story, to provide and to conceal information as he sees fit. I would argue that it is the omniscient narrator who principally regulates the schadenfreude in the novel.

The story of *The Portrait of a Lady* is fairly simple. Set in the second half of the nineteenth century, Isabel Archer is a young American woman who moves to England after her father dies. She stays with her wealthy aunt, uncle, and cousin who provide for her. When her uncle dies, he leaves a considerable amount of money in her name. Although she is pursued by several eligible bachelors, including a young American industrialist (Caspar Goodwood) and an English lord (Warburton), she falls for the obscure figure of Gilbert Osmond, in part thanks to the encouragement of the equally mysterious Madame Merle, who befriends her. Gradually it dawns on the reader that Osmond has married her for her money and that Madame Merle and he have a daughter (Pansy) together. Isabel is unaware of these facts until the very end of the novel, and when she finds out she is devastated and then resolves to reconfigure her own life and her future. The narrator plays a key role in determining what information readers receive and when they receive it. To a large extent he also controls how they think about Isabel Archer and the other principal characters.

Sometimes he does this indirectly. Early on in his novel, James' narrator, for instance, describes Isabel Archer's childhood in Albany, New York. He establishes that Isabel has had a sheltered upbringing and was considered cleverer than her peers. This has made her a bit fanciful, but also somewhat stubborn and self-righteous as the narrator lets on:

> Isabel Archer was a young person of many theories; her imagination was remarkably active. It had been her fortune to possess a finer mind than most of the persons among whom her lot was cast; to have a larger perception of surrounding facts and to care for knowledge that was tinged with the unfamiliar. It is true that among her contemporaries she passed for a young woman of extraordinary profundity; for these excellent people never withheld their admiration from a reach of intellect of which they themselves were not conscious, and spoke of Isabel as a prodigy of learning, a creature reported to have read the classic authors – in translations. (James, 1881/1987, p. 103)

The narrator does not simply report objectively what kind of character Isabel Archer has. There is also a clear hint of irony in these lines. Isabel and the people around her are convinced of her superiority, but the narrator and (through him) the reader know that it is a bookish and studious sort of intelligence. The narrator pokes fun at her pretension, but by letting the reader in on that knowledge, he gives readers a sense of superiority over her. Readers can delight in her peccadilloes, even though we also realize that these are no major flaws.

At other times James' narrator will tell readers more directly how they ought to think about Isabel. The most remarkable instance of this occurs when Isabel receives a marriage proposal from Lord Warburton. Dashing, elegant, and intellectually superior, this English lord is more than Isabel's equal, but Isabel declines because Lord Warburton is too perfect for her. She is too adventurous to settle for the comfortable life he has in store for her. Anticipating the amusement or irritation readers may feel at her unexpected reluctance and subsequent refusal to marry Lord Warburton, James' narrator interrupts his narrative to address the reader directly:

> Smile not, however, I venture to repeat, at this simple young lady from Albany, who debated whether she should accept an English peer before he had offered himself, and who was disposed to believe that on the whole she could do better. She was a person of great good faith, and if there was a great deal of folly in her wisdom, those who judge her severely may have the satisfaction of finding that, later, she became consistently wise only at the cost of an amount of folly which will constitute almost a direct appeal to charity. (James, 1881/1987, p. 155)

This is one of the most relevant and complex passages of *The Portrait of a Lady* in terms of how the reader feels about and judges the principal character, and the role the narrator plays in that sense of judgment. First, it is an example of narrative (or even authorial) intrusion. James' narrator stops the flow of the story to inform the reader that we should not judge Isabel too harshly for her superiority and for not realizing the error of her ways. Ironically, however, it was he who also poked fun at Isabel's arrogant disposition and encouraged readers to laugh at that part of her character, as we saw in the previous passage. Now he urges readers not to "smile." It suggests – as the novel does elsewhere too – that the narrator is not to be entirely trusted. Besides the dialogue, he is the reader's only source of information, but he clearly manipulates the reader's feelings about Isabel and thus proves to be what is called an unreliable narrator. This untrustworthiness of the narrator is a second reason that makes this passage intricate and noteworthy.

The third reason why this excerpt is extraordinary is that it reflects how dramatic irony works emotionally. Dramatic irony is a literary technique that occurs when the reader's (or viewer's) knowledge of events or individuals surpasses that of the characters (Colebrook, 2004, p. 180). Without specifying what exactly will happen to Isabel, the narrator (or James) intimates in the last sentence of this excerpt something about Isabel's future that she does not yet know herself. We can only guess at what will make her "consistently wise" and what will make us pity her, but we know that it is not good news for Isabel. Usually dramatic irony evokes or increases the reader's sense of superiority over a character as it reflects how much we know and how little someone else knows. Yet since the narrator lets on that Isabel will wise up, but in an unspecified painful way, the reader may at the same time also experience feelings of sympathy for Isabel. James' narrator manipulates his readers in feeling both superior as well as sympathetic to his heroine. James perfectly controls these seemingly conflicting emotions.

The fourth and most important reason why this is an intriguing passage is what it indicates about schadenfreude. It comments more directly on schadenfreude than other passages in James' novel or than Whitman or Twain did in their works. James' narrator is aware that readers who judge Isabel "severely" may experience a kind of "satisfaction" that she will soon encounter hardship. The word "satisfaction" may be taken ironically or even sarcastically, but I would argue that James acknowledges here that some readers who will read about the impending downfall of Isabel Archer may experience a sense of pleasure, contentment, and fulfillment from that. James does not comment on the reason why readers may be experiencing those feelings, but they are most likely caused by the irritation the reader may feel about Isabel's pride and arrogance early on in the novel. As various researchers have shown, people feel inclined to experience more schadenfreude when they feel their targets of this deserved it (Hareli and Weiner, 2002; Van Dijk et al., 2005). Yet, as James' narrator implies, the unspecified punishment that will await Isabel in the future far outweighs the indiscretion she has committed. Since the misfortune that befalls someone should always be commensurate with the fault, as Smith, Thielke, and Powell argue (Chapter 6 in this volume), the reader will quickly abandon his or her feelings of schadenfreude. The reader will trade in his or her lingering schadenfreude for sympathy or even pity.

The reader's wavering position about Isabel, feeling both sympathy for and occasionally aversion to her character, is mirrored by her cousin, Ralph Touchett. He is what James and several James scholars have termed a "reflector." Like the narrator, Ralph mirrors and reflects the author's and narrator's views on Isabel, although never in a direct or uncomplicated way. He loves Isabel. It is ambiguous how we ought to define this love; it may be a brotherly love, but it is possibly also romantic. Since he is her cousin and is additionally sickly because he has contracted tuberculosis, he "loves without hope," as he mentions. From the opening scene of the novel until his death at the end of the book, Ralph watches her, and through him we as readers also observe Isabel. Ralph is similar to the narrator as through his gazing and observations, we gain information about Isabel too. Yet he is also, like the reader, a voyeur constantly prying into her private life, watching her every move. While his illness debilitates him more and more throughout the novel, he increasingly lives vicariously through Isabel's adventures.

Ralph is instrumental in ensuring that Isabel receives part of his father's inheritance. It allows her to live the kind of life she wants, and Ralph believes that will give him pleasure. When Isabel is reluctant about giving details as to why she refuses to marry Lord Warburton, he asks: "What's the use of being ill and disabled and restricted to mere spectatorship at the game of life if I really can't see the show when I've paid so much for my ticket?" This is a crude question, as Isabel does not know that Ralph forfeited part of her inheritance so that she could receive it. Irrespective of Ralph's playful irony, it emphasizes that Ralph expects joy and pleasure as compensation for the money that he has invested, as if he is watching a play or a movie. When Isabel's life develops into a tragedy rather than a comedy after she marries Osmond, Ralph attempts to intervene. He could have known that Isabel would be prey for fortune hunters and he was warned about this risk by his father, but he took the risk in part because he wanted to see the action of Isabel's life up close. Considering that schadenfreude is a passive emotion, the question arises whether Ralph's behavior can be judged as such. I believe Ralph's behavior has elements of schadenfreude, although they are hard to locate textually. His thwarted love for Isabel (different but also similar to Claggart's feelings for Billy Budd) and his own unfortunate fate make him love, envy, and resent Isabel at different points of the novel. How to isolate feelings of schadenfreude from other emotions remains difficult in literary texts as the emotions are often ambiguous and fleeting, and are not described in a detailed fashion.

Conclusion

Surveying these examples from classic American literature proves how hard it is to find a method for studying schadenfreude in literature and for assessing its possible effects on readers. One concrete way to do it may be to look at how people react to the role of the omniscient narrator and how that instrument evokes or assuages feelings of schadenfreude in readers. It should be possible to erase the passage in which the narrator urges them not to smile at this young lady from Albany without changing the main narrative of the particular. Sample groups could read the chapter with the narrator's nuanced words and sample groups could read it without it, and we could find out whether the second group feels more feelings of schadenfreude. The same can be done regarding Whitman's attitude toward prostitutes and Huckleberry Finn's attitude toward the Duke and the King. The testing could be done with surveys or by measuring the schadenfreude readers experience more exactly.

Another line of research to gain a better understanding of how schadenfreude works in literature is to compare and contrast different (national) bodies of literature in terms of schadenfreude, or to compare the role of the novel to that of television or film. Is there a tendency for schadenfreude to be presented as a dark emotion more readily in the latter media and in a more moralizing way in the former? It is remarkable that the nineteenth-century American authors all seem to agree that schadenfreude is a negative emotion that needs to be eradicated. The notion that schadenfreude may also contribute to a positive self-evaluation, as Van Dijk and Ouwerkerk argue (Chapter 9 in this volume), is not readily traceable in these texts, but it is of course possible that they are present in others. Kuipers' conclusion (Chapter 17 in this volume) that the references to schadenfreude in the USA are "overwhelmingly negative" may explain why these nineteenth-century American authors all support this position, but she suggests that this may be different in a country such as the Netherlands, which favors a kind of humor that is "offensive or aversive" to others. It is not unlikely that contemporary American novels have more diverse approaches to schadenfreude than the nineteenth-century texts do.

References

Boruah, B. H. (1988). *Fiction and Emotion: A Study in Aesthetics and the Philosophy of Mind*. Oxford: Clarendon Press.

Colebrook, C. (2004). *Irony*. New York: Routledge.

Deleuze, G. and Guattari F. (1994). *What is Philosophy?* (translated by Hugh Tomlinson and Graham Burchell). New York: Columbia University Press.

Hareli, S. and Weiner, B. (2002). Dislike and envy as antecedents of pleasure at another's misfortune. *Motivation and Emotion* 26: 257–77.

James, H. (1987 [1881]). *The Portrait of a Lady*. New York: Penguin.

Keen, S. (2007). *Empathy and the Novel*. New York: Oxford University Press.

Melville, H. (1985 [1924]). *Billy Budd, Sailor and Other Stories*. New York: Penguin.

Neill, A. (1993). Fiction and the emotions. *American Philosophical Quarterly* 30: 1–13.

Portmann, J. (2000). *When Bad Things Happen to Other People*. New York: Routledge.

Twain, M. (1999 [1884]). *The Adventures of Huckleberry Finn*. Oxford University Press.

Van Dijk, W. W., Ouwerkerk, J. W., Goslinga, S., and Nieweg, M. (2005). Deservingness and schadenfreude. *Cognition & Emotion* 19: 933–9.

Van Peer, W. and Pander Maat, H. (1996). Perspectivation and sympathy: effects of narrative point of view. In R. G. Kreuz and M. S. MacNealy (eds.),

Empirical Approaches to Literature and Aesthetics. Norwoord, NJ: Ablex Publishing, pp. 143–54.

Vermeule, B. (2010). *Why Do We Care about Literary Characters?* Baltimore: Johns Hopkins University Press.

Whitman, W. (1982). *Complete Poetry and Collected Prose*. New York: Library of America.

Wimsatt, W. K. and Beardsley, M. (1954). *The Verbal Icon: Studies in the Meaning of Poetry*. Lexington: University of Kentucky Press.

20 Schadenfreude, concluding notes

Agneta H. Fischer

After reading this book, one cannot escape the conclusion that schadenfreude is an important and ubiquitous phenomenon. Of course, this conclusion can easily be dismissed as an attempt to please the editors, or as a simple result of availability after reading nineteen chapters on this topic, or as a conclusion that could apply to any emotion. Yet, the conclusion is not so self-evident, because the emotion of schadenfreude has for a long time been regarded as peripheral and insignificant. Schadenfreude has never had an edited volume of its own, and has never been the centre of public and scientific attention as many other emotions have been in the past. This lack of interest may have been due to different reasons, such as its presumed infrequent occurrence – compared to so-called basic emotions – or the fact that no single English word is available for schadenfreude (so it cannot be that important!), or because it is so specific compared to emotions like anger, fear or sadness. Big media events during the past decade, however, have brought schadenfreude into the public arena, such as the triumph after the 9/11 attacks in parts of the Arab world, the schadenfreude expressed by European ministers after the downfall of the American economic system, the TV shows like 'Cops', 'Idols' or other 'caught on tape' TV programmes, or the media attention for the sexual or moral transgressions of tall poppies (Feather, Chapter 3 in this volume), such as President Bill Clinton, Dominique Strauss-Kahn or Lance Armstrong.

The editors of this book should therefore be praised for this enterprise to raise the scientific interest in schadenfreude by bringing together different research lines and theoretical perspectives on this emotion. The chapters in this volume provide an excellent overview of this neglected emotion and show when it occurs, how it relates to other emotions, how it forms relationships between individuals and groups, how it serves our selves and manages our relations with others, and how it has always been part of human nature and culture. The interdisciplinary focus sheds new light on the study of emotion more generally and on schadenfreude specifically, and paves the way for new research and further theorizing.

In this concluding chapter, I will summarize the main findings, try to spell out some gaps in our knowledge (if any) and in passing reflect on potential future avenues for research and theorizing.

The antecedents of schadenfreude

Schadenfreude is an emotion term that refers to a specific antecedent, not to a specific appraisal or action. Unlike other emotion labels such as anger (the aim to remove a goal blockage) or fear (trying to escape from threat), the definition of schadenfreude is based on the description of its antecedent, namely the misery of the other person. Not surprisingly, therefore, many chapters are devoted to identifying situations that may elicit schadenfreude. Slipping over a banana peel is often mentioned as the prototypical antecedent of schadenfreude, but most authors also agree that this may not be the best or most interesting example. Clearly schadenfreude comes in many flavours and the banana example is the most salient one because everyone can visualize it. This form of innocent joy about another's mishap is referred to as the minimal and mundane form of schadenfreude (Leach, Spears and Manstead, Chapter 13 in this volume). However, according to various authors, schadenfreude may also take the form of a deeper, darker emotion, reflecting one's envy or the wish to see others fall from grace (Cikara and Fiske, Chapter 10 in this volume; Feather, Chapter 3 in this volume; Smith, Thielke and Powell, Chapter 6 in this volume; Van de Ven, Chapter 7 in this volume; Van Dijk and Ouwerkerk, Chapter 1 in this volume). In other words, schadenfreude may vary from ordinary, short-lived amusement about a small accident of a stranger to genuine and malicious pleasure about the misfortunes of our competitors.

There are a variety of factors eliciting or facilitating schadenfreude. According to Ben-Ze'ev (Chapter 5 in this volume), the main concern of schadenfreude is a personal comparative concern, implying that the other is a relevant comparison figure. If the other also has higher status, moral superiority or belongs to a group with these characteristics (Cikara and Fiske, Chapter 10 in this volume), schadenfreude may become even more likely. The difference between oneself and the other need not be large, however, as is for example evident from research showing that bronze medallists in the Olympic games are happier than silver medallists because for the latter group, the gold is within reach (Ben-Ze'ev, Chapter 5 in this volume). In addition, Van Dijk and colleagues (see Van Dijk and Ouwerkerk, Chapter 9 in this volume) also showed that we feel more schadenfreude the more similar the comparison other is to us.

There are two perspectives when comparing oneself to others. One is to focus on what the other has or befalls, and the other is the perception of one's own status and qualities. Various chapters report research showing that belonging to a low-status group or having low self-esteem is more likely to lead to schadenfreude than belonging to a high-status group and having high self-esteem. These characteristics make social comparison between oneself and the other person or group very salient, and most authors agree that social comparison is at the heart of schadenfreude (Ben-Ze'ev, Chapter 5 in this volume; Schurtz et al., Chapter 11 in this volume; Smith, Theilke and Powell, Chapter 6 in this volume; Van de Ven, Chapter 7 in this volume; Van Dijk and Ouwerkerk, Chapter 9 in this volume).

Whether one feels schadenfreude or another emotion is also related to the way in which the misfortune is explained. Many authors follow some form of appraisal theory and argue that being in a low-status position or having low self-esteem reinforces specific appraisals that elicit schadenfreude. Three types of appraisals are regularly mentioned as typical of schadenfreude. *First* of all, the other's misfortune or bad luck is not caused by oneself, but by circumstances or other persons (Leach, Spears and Manstead, Chapter 13 in this volume; Seip et al., Chapter 15 in this volume; Van Dijk and Ouwerkerk, Chapter 1 in this volume). If we would be involved in the deliberate downfall of a competitor, we would experience gloating and we would be motivated by sadism, which is more evil and extreme than is schadenfreude.

A *second* appraisal is that the other person deserves the misfortune in some way or other (Ben-Ze'ev, Chapter 5 in this volume; Feather, Chapter 3 in this volume; Portmann, Chapter 2 in this volume; Van Dijk and Ouwerkerk, Chapter 1 in this volume). Many studies have shown that the more the misfortune is deserved, the stronger we feel schadenfreude, although the deservingness should be proportional to the mishap (Ben-Ze'ev, Chapter 5 in this volume; Feather, Chapter 3 in this volume). Normally, people would not feel schadenfreude when hearing that someone who exceeded the speed limit, just died in a car accident. Various determinants of deservingness have been examined. One is hypocrisy (Powell, Chapter 4 in this volume). Hypocrisy is embedded in a weak moral belief system of persons who say one thing, but do another, and who are therefore easily seen as moral transgressors who deserve punishment. In line with this finding, Van Dijk and Ouwerkerk (Chapter 9 in this volume) report research showing that when a misfortune is due to someone's own responsibility, it is seen as more deserved and thus schadenfreude is more intense than when this is not the case.

A *third* appraisal is that schadenfreude is a passive experience (see also Ben-Ze'ev, Chapter 5 in this volume; Leach, Spears and Manstead,

Chapter 13 in this volume; Portmann, Chapter 2 this volume; Seip et al., Chapter 15 in this volume; Van Dijk and Ouwerkerk, Chapter 1 in this volume), that is, the event is not the result of one's own active behaviour. The essence of schadenfreude is that one is merely the merry witness of the misfortune caused by others or by unfortunate circumstances. The glee of the medieval masses during public tortures and punishment of criminals (Kuipers, Chapter 17 in this volume) illustrates this very well. The fact that *schadenfroh* persons do not do anything, but still see their wishes come true, is what makes the pleasure of watching others' suffering so sweet.

The expression of schadenfreude

Following from the fact that schadenfreude is defined on the basis of its antecedents rather than its implied actions, it is obvious that less attention has been paid to the question of how we express schadenfreude, in what types of behaviour it results and, for that matter, how we recognize it in others. I think it would be useful to distinguish between the immediate expression of schadenfreude on the one hand and behaviour in the long term that may eventually result from schadenfreude on the other hand. Immediate expressions take the form of smiling or even laughing and cheering when it is expressed in a group setting. Most evidence on *schadenfroh* smiling comes from self-reports ('I could not resist a little smile'), but there is also some evidence from behavioural studies. For example, envious individuals who are exposed to a negative event smile more than when they are exposed to a positive event (Cikara and Fiske, Chapter 10 in this volume), whereas the reverse is true for individuals who feel pride, pity or disgust. As envious individuals who perceive a negative event are likely to experience schadenfreude, this can be regarded as evidence for smiling as an expression of schadenfreude.

It is unclear, however, if we can distinguish smiles of schadenfreude from other types of smiles, and therefore it is also unclear whether we can recognize schadenfreude on the basis of its non-verbal expression. Given that schadenfreude refers to a specific context in which one feels joy, it seems unlikely that we can recognize schadenfreude smiles unless we infer it from the situation in which it occurs. It could be, however, that schadenfreude smiles are different because they reflect more malicious motives, which could be perceived in a combined frown and smile, forming a malicious smile. Another option could be that schadenfreude smiles would be more strongly inhibited and can therefore be recognized by attempts to suppress them.

Another way to examine the direct expressions of schadenfreude is to conceive it as part of a communicative act (Feyaerts and Oben,

Chapter 18 in this volume). In an analysis of spontaneous conversations among peers, it is clear that schadenfreude is never directly mentioned or discussed, but often staged as a positive expression of in-group bonds. In other words, the misfortunes of members of the group, for example, having red hair, are not real, and the victim is teased ('in our school, they [redheads] were bullied out of school') in a staged linguistic expression of belonging. Because we probably often express schadenfreude verbally and because such utterances would be subtle, it would be interesting to examine how spontaneous talk would evolve in situations where schadenfreude really does occur, for example, when someone's favourite sport's team has lost.

Although schadenfreude is often immediate and short-term joy in reaction to an incident, there are also instances in which schadenfreude endures and may have longer-term behavioural consequences, for example, when one sees the downfall of an envied tall poppy. However, because schadenfreude implies a passive stance, such behaviours should be considered as consequences rather than expressions of schadenfreude. One example of such a consequence is the sharing of information with others (Ouwerkerk and Van Dijk, Chapter 12 in this volume) when a product of a rival consumer group fails or breaks down. BlackBerry users who feel hostile towards iPhone users, for example, feel schadenfreude when hearing about problems with iPhones and cannot wait to share this negative information. Other more long-term consequences that have been associated with schadenfreude are retribution (Feather, Chapter 3 in this volume), the tendency to harm (Cikara and Fiske, Chapter 10 in this volume) or to take revenge (Seip et al., Chapter 15 in this volume), although in most studies no explicit relation with schadenfreude has been studied. Cikara and Fiske (Chapter 10 in this volume), for example, found that participants in their study were most likely to harm, that is, give mild shocks to the target they envied most. This was corroborated in a functional magnetic resonance imaging (fMRI) study where brain regions such as the ventral striatum and the anterior cingulate cortex, associated with primary rewards and punishments, were correlated with the tendency to harm out-group rivals (see also Schurtz et al., Chapter 11 in this volume, for similar findings). It should be noted that this neural activity and the self-reported tendency to harm were not correlated with self-reported feelings and thus cannot be seen as an immediate or direct expression of schadenfreude, which supports the assumption that the connection between the feeling and the behaviour is loose and that schadenfreude may be regulated to a great extent.

Indeed, a sociological and historical perspective on humour and laughing at the expense of others (Kuipers, Chapter 17 in this volume) clearly suggests that schadenfreude is regulated in social life. Kuipers shows changes in the social regulation of schadenfreude based on changing norms of modern civilized behaviour. In medieval times, the joy at seeing presumed criminals being publicly punished or hanged was a common spectacle and was not seen as immoral, under the pretext that they deserved their public punishment. In the late modern era, however, schadenfreude lost its innocence and became a dubious emotion. People were explicitly taught to be good citizens and to become sensitive to the needs of others. The collective expression of schadenfreude did not fit into this new regime and laughing at another's misfortune became not only inappropriate, but also immoral. Oostdijk (Chapter 19 in this volume) also very nicely illustrates how these emotional display rules were incorporated in nineteenth-century novels, such as *The Adventures of Huckleberry Finn*, *Billy Budd, Sailor* or *The Portrait of a Lady*, through which readers are educated to fine-tune their senses and to restrain their emotional impulses.

Schadenfreude: good or bad?

The degree to which schadenfreude is seen as morally good or bad has raised some discussion (Van Dijk and Ouwerkerk, Chapter 1 in this volume). There are two ways in which we can discuss the moral nature of schadenfreude. The first is to look at the *motives* for schadenfreude. According to Ben-Ze'ev (Chapter 5 in this volume), feelings of schadenfreude do not reflect a vicious character, contrary to sadism, hate or cruelty, because one has not contributed to the bad events that happened to others. In his view, it is not necessarily the suffering of the other that produces the delight, but rather the relief or advantages for oneself that is at the core of schadenfreude. Indeed, Van Dijk and Ouwerkerk (Chapter 9 in this volume) show that schadenfreude improves feelings about oneself and operates as a way to protect oneself. Following this line of work, schadenfreude is mostly beneficial, because the motives for schadenfreude are self-focused rather than other-focussed and do not originate from a bad character.

However, Sundie (Chapter 8 in this volume), among others, suggests that schadenfreude stems from a more malevolent motive, because especially individuals feel hostile envy (rather than envious admiration) towards others (Feather, Chapter 3 in this volume; Ouwerkerk and Van Dijk, Chapter 12 in this volume; Smith, Theilke and Powell, Chapter 6 in this volume; Van de Ven, Chapter 7 in this volume), experience strong feelings of schadenfreude. Cikara and Fiske (Chapter 10 in this volume), for example, show that exposure to competitive high-status groups automatically elicits envy, pain and anger at this group, even if there is no direct competition with the in-group. Thus, when another group member is envied, schadenfreude replaces pity. This conclusion clearly suggests that schadenfreude is not above suspicion and reflects an envious character, which does not allow others to be better or to have more.

The second way to discuss the moral character of schadenfreude is to examine the social implications of schadenfreude. Is schadenfreude merely a passive emotion, which does no harm to others, or does it actually have detrimental effects on its victims? There is not much research on the direct effects of schadenfreude on its victim. Would it make a difference to see others laugh at your misfortune or to see them empathize with you? I think that it would be interesting to examine the effects of overt expressions of schadenfreude on how the victim feels, and I would expect that such expressions would intensify the bad feelings already caused. Indeed, there is evidence from our own lab (Mann et al., 2014) that an audience that laughs when someone is insulted leads to stronger feelings of humiliation, which is exactly what one would expect when showing schadenfreude. The social implications of schadenfreude could therefore be more damaging than suggested by some authors. Another question is what would be the best reaction of a victim in order to make *schadenfroh* persons change their mind or at least make them aware of the damage they may be causing. One potential reaction that is discussed in the present volume is pouting (Portmann, Chapter 16 in this volume), which implies an expression of disappointment in the other person who felt schadenfreude and wounded vanity in oneself. Whether pouting actually would evoke sympathy in others or is seen as an act of weakness which only enhances schadenfreude is another empirical question that requires further research.

Finally, I assume that the most detrimental effects of schadenfreude can be found in its effect on intergroup relations. The present chapters suggest that intergroup relations are fertile ground for schadenfreude and that identification, hostility and envy play an important role. The collective experience and expression of schadenfreude can have both positive effects on in-group bonds, but at the same time severe negative effects on outsiders. When the focus is on positive bonding, as is mostly the case in fan behaviour, for example, in sports contexts or in politics (see Ouwerkerk and Van Dijk, Chapter 12 in this volume; Schurtz et al., Chapter 11 in this volume), the effects of schadenfreude can generally be positive as it sustains a healthy, competitive relationship between two groups. However, when power relations are more skewed, schadenfreude can have devastating effects on the self-esteem of the victim (group), especially when it is expressed in a public and collective setting. It would be most interesting and important to further investigate in what circumstances the expression of schadenfreude would have such negative effects on its victims rather than positive effects on the *schadenfroh* persons. Schadenfreude not only implies celebration, but also suffering.

References

Mann, M., Feddes, A., Doosje, B. and Fischer, A. H. (2014). When laughing hurts: antecedents of humiliation. Manuscript under review.

Index